The Life Model of Social Work Practice

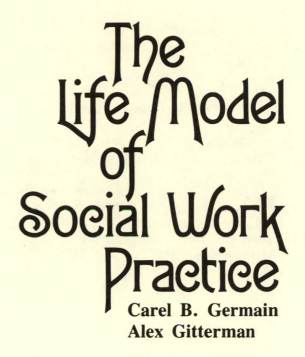

The Life Model of Social Work Practice

Carel B. Germain
Alex Gitterman

Columbia University Press •• New York

Library of Congress Cataloging in Publication Data

Germain, Carel B
The life model of social work practice.

Includes bibliographical references and index.
1. Social case work. 2. Man—Influence of environment. I. Gitterman, Alex, 1938– joint author. II. Title.
HV43.G47 361 79-17816
ISBN 0-231-04152-7

Columbia University Press
New York Guildford, Surrey

Printed in the United States of America
20 19 18 17 16 15 14

Clothbound editions of Columbia University Press books are Smyth-sewn and printed on permanent and durable acid-free paper.

This book is dedicated to our clients, our students, and our practice and faculty colleagues—from whom we have learned to value human potentiality and environmental diversity.

Contents

Preface

FOR THE AUTHORS, this book symbolizes a long and adventurous journey. It began in 1972 at the Columbia University School of Social Work when we and another colleague were asked by the dean to develop a plan for the first semester of a two-year sequence of courses in social work practice. Earlier, the faculty had decided to restructure the total curriculum to take account of emerging knowledge, new human needs brought about by rapid social change in every sector of human life, and developments occurring in practice itself as agencies sought to meet the challenges of our era. The effort to reconceptualize practice and to develop an integrated social work method was but the first step in the School's plan to relinquish its traditional structure based in separate methods and to adopt a two-concentration curriculum.* Ultimately, with other colleagues in the former casework, group work, and community organization sequences, we participated in the design of the second, third, and fourth semester courses in the practice method and the reformulation of content and criteria for its field component and student performance. Out of this joint work on curriculum structure and content came our further collaboration in workshops, consultation, and writing.

Not surprisingly, we found that ecological ideas helped us understand how each of us became a source of learning for the other. Sometimes our different professional traditions, knowledge base, and practice experiences seemed like barriers to mutual understanding, but actually facilitated and enriched the development of our ideas. Similarly, our own transactions were embedded in a larger environment of school, practice community, and the human phenomena with which

* The two concentrations: services to individuals, families, and groups; policy, planning, and organizing, were later joined by a third which combined elements of both.

social work is engaged. This larger environment was sometimes inhibiting and baffling, but always stimulating.

This book represents a beginning attempt to work out the dimensions of an integrated method of practice with individuals, families, groups, organizations, and selected aspects of neighborhoods or communities. It rests on the assumption that there are many common skills in working with people, no matter on what level people are organized. There are also some distinctive skills such as the skills used in forming groups or influencing organizations. These skills are presented within the context of a conceptual framework that offers a dual, simultaneous focus on people and environments. The book also attempts to differentiate the underlying theories and knowledge at each level of human organization—individual, family, group, bureaucratic system, social network, neighborhood, and community, as well as the properties of physical environments, social environments, and their interaction with culture. The authors have attempted to connect the integrated method of the life model, and its associated common and distinctive skills, to the diverse theoretical and knowledge bases.

For some readers, the content on the neighborhood or community as client may seem less abundant than content on individuals, families, and groups as clients in what may appear to be an urban emphasis. We have indeed moved cautiously in both areas. We are continuing to study the pertinence of additional aspects of community or neighborhood practice for incorporation into the model. With many others, we are presently examining similarities and differences in rural and urban practice in order to enhance the model's relevance for both. Nevertheless, we believe rural practitioners can adapt much of the urban-oriented content to their own practice situations. In so doing, they will make important contributions to the further development of the ecological perspective and an integrated method of practice.

We have touched minimally on interdisciplinary practice because we are presently engaged in developing for future publication an ecological perspective on this important and growing aspect of practice. While we have pursued the connections between "private troubles" and "organizational issues," we have not attempted to integrate what some have called "macro" and "micro" forms of practice. We do feel, however, that the connections between client problems or needs and social legislation or policy issues need to be actively pursued, and may represent a future area for collaborative work.

And, finally, the book is intended to be a text for undergraduate and graduate students in social work. We hope it will also be useful to experienced practitioners who are interested in the life model of social work practice.

July 1979

Carel B. Germain
Alex Gitterman

Acknowledgments

THE LIST OF those to whom we are indebted is long. Our students at the baccalaureate, master's, and doctoral levels have kept us informed of the influence of ecological ideas and the life model on their practice and their professional development. Examples of their experiences are included at many points. In addition, we are indebted to practitioners and administrators who graciously gave us the illustrative materials indispensable to a book on practice. Class and field faculty at the Columbia University and the University of Connecticut schools of social work, as well as teachers and practitioners in other parts of this country and Canada, have influenced our work in countless ways.

In particular, Professor Irving Miller provided criticism of a high order that helped shape the early chapters and made the later chapters easier to write. Professor George Brager's contributions to the chapters on organizational influencing were invaluable. Dean Mitchell I. Ginsberg and Associate Dean Sidney Berengarten of the Columbia University School of Social Work provided the structure through which our collaboration in curriculum development could proceed, and their confidence in us was important. We thank John D. Moore, editor in chief of the Columbia University Press, for his unflagging encouragement. Naomi Pines Gitterman contributed stimulating practice ideas and editorial suggestions. We also thank Grace Derrick for her skilled participation in moving the manuscript through its many drafts.

Finally, we would like to acknowledge our families and social networks for continuous caring.

The Life Model of Social Work Practice

1

Introduction to the Life Model

CONTEMPORARY SOCIAL WORK is characterized by two intellectual tendencies. One views human needs and problems as originating within the person; the other views them as generated by the social order. In this book, we introduce what we call an ecological perspective and a life model of practice. The ecological perspective presents our view that human needs and problems are generated by the transactions between people and their environments. We draw upon several bodies of thought for a conceptual framework that affirms the complementarity between person and environment in what we regard as an integrated system. We derive a particular method of practice from the social work profession's social purpose and the ecological perspective, and connect the method to the conceptual framework. All of these together—the social purpose, the ecological perspective, the conceptual framework, and the practice method—comprise what we call the life model of practice.

The social purpose of the profession has been stated in various but similar ways as having to do with service to people experiencing problems in social functioning. We find the definition of social purpose offered by William E. Gordon and by Harriett M. Bartlett to be congenial to our own conception. Both Gordon and Bartlett suggest that the social purpose of the profession is the matching of people's adaptive capacities and environmental properties to produce transactions that will maximize growth and development, and improve environments.[1] The social purpose, so defined, calls for a practice method that will have a dual, simultaneous focus on releasing adaptive capacities of people and improving their environments—whether "environment" refers to a classroom, a housing project, a hospital ward, a work site, or a social agency. Thus, the social purpose calls for a practice method that is designed to engage people's strengths and the forces pushing toward growth, and to influence organizational structures, other social systems, and physical settings so they will be more responsive to people's needs.

We suggest, further, that the social purpose calls for an integrated method of practice that is responsive to client need rather than to worker and agency self-definitions arising from casework or group work origins. Today's environments impose an overwhelming array of adaptive tasks upon people as individuals and within their families and groups. It seems unreasonable to define their need for help with these tasks in terms of a particular practice modality and the restrictive preferences of worker and agency. For us, it is the nature of people's needs or problems, and the associated life tasks involved in their resolution, that determine where boundaries are drawn that "encase" the individual, the family, or the group. Our own experience in social work practice, and in teaching practice, leads us to conclude that a unified or integrated method of social work practice serves people—no matter where that boundary is drawn—and serves them more effectively.

The integrated method of practice that we have derived from the social purpose we call the life model. More accurately, the life model, in toto, refers to the social purpose, the ecological perspective, the conceptual framework, and the practice method. In this chapter, we present the ecological perspective and a brief overview of the practice method and its conceptual framework or theory base. Subsequent chapters present in detail the knowledge and skills of the practice method.

The Ecological Perspective

Philosophic and Scientific Base

Until recently, social work, in common with other professions and with the physical and life sciences, tended to view human beings and their environment as separate entities. It is easy to understand why this was so. Western scientific and religious traditions set the human being apart from the rest of nature, a view that is difficult to relinquish when it is reinforced by systems of education and prevailing vocabularies. Out of an anthropocentric orientation that placed human beings at the center of the universe and at the apex of terrestrial life, Western culture led to the interest in mastering the forces of nature. To gain such control, science searched for ever more accurate knowledge of the laws underlying natural phenomena. In this search, value was placed on the use of logic and reason. From the gradual ascendancy of rational thought came the great achievements of Western science, and the wonders and perils of its technology.

With Newton's discoveries, the universe came to be regarded as a giant machine whose operational laws could be discovered by careful analysis of the various parts. The physical sciences flourished in proportion to the refinements made in the operational and experimental aspects of this rational, analytic method. Taking heed of the spectacular successes of the scientific method, the biological and social sciences modeled themselves after the physical sciences. Nineteenth-century biology analyzed the parts of the human organism in ways that tended to atomize the whole and to overlook the fact that certain properties emerge from the whole that weren't found in any of the parts alone. Nineteenth-century social science viewed the human being as an object apart from his setting. The person was fragmented, and the variability of behavior as the person moved from situation to situation was ignored.[2]

Such imperfect views of person-in-environment reflected the linearity of time, space, and causality characteristic of the scientific method before the twentieth century. The method had been fruitful in the study of physical and biological entities and processes up to a point, but had obscured the wholeness of living organisms and their interdependence with their environments.[3] By way of contrast, it is interesting to note that traditional Eastern thought expressed the oneness of the person with nature, the sense of kinship with other forms of life, and the striving to reach harmony with the relentless forces of the environment. In Eastern religion, art, and life styles, the human being was not viewed as ascendant over nature, but each was part of the other. The human being's relation to environment was one of appreciation, not mastery.[4] In Eastern thought, all events and processes were interwoven, mutually influencing, and endlessly moving in a dynamic flow. Thus, time itself was not linear and one-directional. Instead, time was experienced as cycles of returning events and recurring patterns and relationships.

By the twentieth century, however, profound changes had occurred in Western science, philosophy, and other systems of thought. The impact of Darwin's theory of evolution and its later refinements, the discoveries and speculations of Freud, and the revelations of the physical sciences began to erode the West's world view.[5] In physics, the ideas of Bohr, Einstein, Heisenberg and others undermined the traditional concepts of space, time, and causality. These ideas set in motion a shift away from certainties to probabilities, from dichotomies to complementarities, and from the dualism of subject–object to interactional fields.[6] The biological and social sciences developed an interest in patterns, wholeness, and relationships between and among parts and wholes. The general drift of thought in the behavioral sciences led to the emergence of field theories, gestalt theory, organismic approaches and, ultimately, to general systems constructs. In philosophy, existentialism called attention to the "absurdity" of the human condition that resulted from one's having placed oneself at the center of creation, only to find oneself alone in an uncaring, non-purposive universe.[7]

The second half of the twentieth century has seen a growing disenchantment with the value-free posture of science and the blindness of technology, which has solved human problems by creating still greater problems. The counter-culture of the 1960s created a tissue of anti-intellectualism,[8] while some scientists and humanists worked to integrate science with other elements of the culture.[9] Within this latter stance, the biological discoveries of the interdependence of ecological systems have led to a new view of the human being's place in nature. In the sciences, art, and philosophy, Western thought now appears to be approaching a view of the world that is closer to traditional Eastern thought. Ecology may, so far, be the clearest expression of such a rapprochement.

Ecology as a Practice Metaphor

Ecology seeks to understand the reciprocal relations between organisms and environments: how species maintain themselves by using the environment, shaping it to their needs without destroying it; and how such adaptive processes increase the environment's diversity and enhance its life-supporting properties. Finally, human ecology asks us to consider human beings within "the evolutionary, ecologic, and social 'wholes' of which we are 'parts.' "[10] It is not surprising that in the last two decades, the insights of ecology have exerted a growing influence on all the helping professions—social work, psychiatry, psychology, and teaching.[11] For social work, ecology appears to be a more useful metaphor than the older, medical-disease metaphor that arose out of the linear world view, because social work has always been committed both to helping people and to promoting more humane environments. This commitment has been difficult to implement because the medical-disease metaphor tends to locate people's problems and needs within the person, obscuring social processes in which the person is embedded.[12] Also, until recently, we lacked dynamic theories of the environment and instrumental knowledge about people–environment relations.

The ecological perspective provides an adaptive, evolutionary view of human beings in constant interchange with all elements of their environment.[13] Human beings change their physical and social environments and are changed by them through processes of continuous reciprocal adaptation. When it goes well, reciprocal adaptation supports the growth and development of people and elaborates the life-supporting qualities of the environment. When reciprocal adaptation falters, however, physical and social environments may be polluted. Physical environments become polluted by man's release of non-biodegradable matter produced by his technology. Social environments become polluted by poverty, discrimination, and stigma produced by man's social and cultural pocesses. When human beings use any component of their physical or social environments destructively, the environmental systems are damaged and will tend, reciprocally, to have a negative impact on all who function within them, whether the system is a family, a school, a geriatric facility, or a redwood forest.

Like all living systems, human beings must maintain a goodness-of-fit with the environment. The Darwinian concept of "fit" applies both to organisms and environments: to the fitness of the environment and the fitness of organisms, each with the other, and through which both prosper. If human beings do not secure the appropriate nutriment (input, stimuli, information, energy, resources) from the environment at the appropriate time, their biological, cognitive, emotional, and social development may be retarded and their functioning impaired. Disorganization and even death may ensue. An infant without love fails to thrive. Children who are undernourished may have their growth stunted. Old people in unstimulating institutional environments may lapse into pseudo-senile states. The physical environment may be so harsh, or the social environment so noxious or inadequate that the required nutriments are missing or deficient. Excessive amounts of environmental stimuli may overload people's adaptive capacities. Too much noise in the physical environment, for example, or certain kinds of crowding in the social environment may produce adverse physiological and psychological effects. In other words, if adaptive exchanges of information, energy, and matter do not take place between persons and environments, then either or both are damaged.

Adaptation is an active, dynamic, and often creative process. Put another way, people, like all living organisms, together with their environment, form an ecosystem in which each shapes the other. At times, people change environments to make them conform to physical and psychological needs, and they must then adapt to the changes they have induced. The invention of the automobile not only changed the face of the physical environment but created many changes in the social environment and in the culture, to which people then had to adapt. Vast highway systems, smog, and encroachment on the land brought about by the automobile posed new adaptive tasks. The automobile also brought changes in social mores, including those pertaining to sex, in patterns of family life, and in lifestyles which posed new adaptive tasks.

At other times, people change themselves to conform or adjust to environmental imperatives or to satisfy needs and reach goals. Socialization of the child, for example, proceeds as he gives up freedom for love and approval. Recruits into a profession, including social work, incorporate new norms and attitudes that may represent changes in the self. At still other times, people adapt by seeking new environments, a process represented by a move from one place to another, the design of new social forms such as communes, or the creation of a new religious sect and the experience of conversion.[14]

Human needs and goals, of course, change over time and are variable across cultures and places. But environments also change. They are changed by physical processes of nature such as weathering, volcanic activity, and earthquakes. They are also changed by the biological processes of all forms of life on earth. And they are changed by the social and cultural processes of human beings.

People's Problems in Living

In these complex transactions between people and environments, upsets in the usual adaptive balance or goodness-of-fit often emerge. These upsets create stress.[15] In our conception of the life model, we treat stress as a psycho-social condition generated by discrepancies between needs and capacities, on the one hand, and environmental qualities on the other. It arises in three interrelated areas of living: *life transitions, environmental pressures,* and *interpersonal processes*.[16]

Life transitions impose new demands and require new responses.[17] Such transitions include changes that occur developmentally, as in adolescence; changes that occur in status and role, as in becoming a parent for the first time; and changes brought about by crisis, such as the loss of a loved one. All life transitions require changes in the self-image, ways of looking at the world, the processing of information derived from cognition, perception, and feeling, patterns of relating to others, uses of environmental resources, and goals. All require the restructuring of one's life space. If a life change is gradual, there is time for advance preparation, as in leaving home for college, and the stress is likely to be less than if the change is sudden and unexpected. In the latter instance, there is no time for preparation, and the stress is likely to be greater, as for example, in the unexpected loss of employment.

The environment can support or interfere with life transitions, but more than that, it can itself be a source of stress. The opportunity structures of the society may be closed to particular groups by virtue of race, class, sex, and age. Organizations designed to meet adaptive needs, such as schools, welfare organizations, and hospitals, may instead impose stress through harsh or unresponsive policies and procedures. Relatives, friends, or neighbors may be absent, or present but unresponsive, so that isolation or conflict results. Unsuitable physical settings can lead to stress because of overcrowding, insufficient protection from hazards, lack of amenities, and other conditions.

Primary groups, in dealing with life transitions or unresponsive environments, may experience added stress because of relationship patterns within the group itself. Maladaptive processes such as inconsistent mutual expectations, exploitative relationships, and blocks in communication are sources of stress to individual members and to the family or group itself.

The following case illustrates the impact of multiple stresses.

Mr. and Mrs. Clayton were seen in a family agency after Mrs. C had asked for help in maintaining the marriage for three more years until the youngest son was ready for college. The family consisted of Mr. C, a 45-year-old businessman; Mrs. C, a 40-year-old teacher; and their three children, ages 18, 17, and 15. After a lifetime spent in another region of the country, the family moved to Garden City a year ago; Mr. C's company had changed hands and he had accepted an offer from another company for a position of higher status and greater responsibility. It was his first job change. The family sold their home, Mrs. C gave up her enjoyable teaching position, and they left friends and Mrs. C's mother behind. Also remaining behind was their daughter, who wished to stay on at her college and live on campus. Mrs. C had been unable to work since the move because of a serious bladder condition, which had also kept her from getting out and making new friends. Mr. C was worried and tense about his job, and increasingly put in extra time at night and on the weekends. The boys were in school during the day, and Mrs. C found herself more and more alone. She began to overeat, gained fifty pounds, and became unhappy with her appearance. Mr. C resented her refusal to entertain business and professional contacts, and to give him support in his new endeavor. Several months ago, during a quarrel, Mr. C. struck his wife, refused to apologize, and they hadn't spoken since. One month ago, Mrs. C returned to their former home city for needed surgery. While convalescing at her mother's home, she received a letter from the youngest son, saying he thought he would choose suicide rather than choose which parent to live with. Mrs. C returned home at once, and requested the social worker's help in keeping the marriage together for three more years. She was acutely anxious, almost panicky; Mr. C was controlled, but angry. Neither really wanted a divorce.

This was a family that had successfully passed through earlier life transitions, both as individuals and as a family. Now, however, a number of stressful events and processes have converged, producing multiple demands, and the stress has become excessive. They have experienced a major uprooting from a treasured home and their sense of place, and have faced this challenge without the support of their networks of kin and friends. In addition, Mr. C has had the worries of a transition to a new position, especially difficult in mid-life, with no earlier experience in job changing. Mrs. C was without her accustomed anchor of a satisfying professional position, an important component of her sense of identity. She suffered a debilitating health problem, then underwent surgery, and finally has had to face the problem of a new and apparently distasteful "obese self." Both parents quite likely felt the "loss" of their daughter, the first child to leave home, and are anticipating yet another such "loss" very soon. Both also now face the developmental tasks of middle adulthood, but with greatly diminished environmental supports available for coping with them. In addition, their usual reciprocal need-meeting abilities have been undermined by the lack of communication and intense anger between them.

The two boys, each at a different stage of adolescence, face their own complex developmental tasks. Superimposed on these are the demands of the move, including a new school and new peer groups. They also have had to cope with knowledge of their parents' marital upset, the stress of which culminated in the youngest son's suicide threat. It is not surprising, with the convergence of so many tasks at once and with their usual environmental supports not available, that this family and its members are experiencing an upset in adaptive balance, both among its members and between itself and the environment.

We have located the potential for stress in life transitions, unresponsive environments, and maladaptive interpersonal processes. Whether potentially stressful events or processes lead to actual stress depends upon many personal and environmental variables. In this case, members' perceptions of events and circumstances, the attributed meanings, the adaptations required, individual and collective skills for coping, and the degree of the environment's responsiveness have all affected how the Claytons are dealing with their new life situation. In all probability, the Claytons could have successfully handled any one or several of the stresses, but their cumulative effect has proved overwhelming.

Whether an event or process will be experienced as stressful varies according to age, sex, social class, ethnic membership, life style and culture, state of health, previous experience, attitudes, vulnerability, and other personality features. Not all stress that is experienced is unpleasant or even undesirable. Some stress is necessary. Life without stress would be bland, if not actually antagonistic to life itself. Moreover, particular events or processes are not necessarily experienced by all people in the same way as either negative or positive. To make matters still more complex, even life events that are experienced as positive and desirable may nevertheless carry a burden of stress—physiological and/or emotional. Getting engaged or married, for example, may be a positive and desirable event, yet it could also be excessively stressful for some.[18]

The ecological perspective, with its emphasis on the life processes of adaptation and reciprocal interaction between people and their social and physical environments, seems to us to be well suited as a platform for social work practice. Social work's distinctive function, and the associated roles and tasks, arise from its social purpose: to strengthen the adaptive capacities of people and to influence their environments so that transactions are more adaptive. Professional action is directed toward helping people and their environments overcome obstacles that inhibit growth, development, and adaptive functioning. The social worker places himself in the midst of the person–primary group–environment encounter. The professional function, as it relates to the three areas of problems of living, is represented in figure 1.1.

This conception of function in the life model affects the features of the practice method: problem definition, client and worker roles, phases of the helping process, assessment, and professional action.

Practice Method

Problem Definition

How a need or predicament is defined determines in large measure what will be done about it. If problems experienced by people are

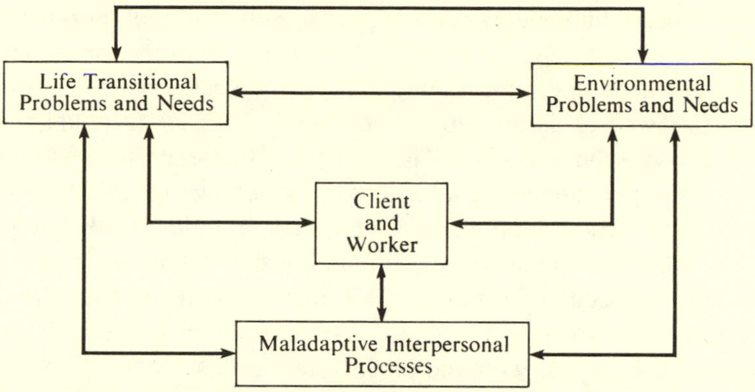

Figure 1.1 Professional Function and People's Problems in Living

located *within the person* and defined as psychopathology, then the professional intervention is likely to be formulated in psychotherapeutic terms, on a clinical model. Goals will refer to internal change. The practice method will depend on the use of psychological techniques to help the client gain awareness of his feelings and attitudes and thus achieve behavioral change. Some attention may be given to environmental manipulation, narrowly conceived as "concrete service."

For example, Ricky, age 8, refuses to go to school, and the school now threatens to transfer him to a special school. The problem is defined as a school phobia. The emphasis on psychopathology leads to a linear, dichotomized view of the child, apart from his life space. He is considered to have an internal disorder requiring psychological "excision." At best, he and his mother may be considered to have similar problems in separating, so mother may be added to the treatment process. Even then, each may be treated separately, and perhaps by different therapists. Help is focused on internal psychological processes, and limited attention is given to school and neighborhood conditions which may be contributing to the problem.

If people's problems and needs are located *within the environment* and defined as social pathology, then the professional intervention is likely to be formulated in social–institutional terms, on a social action model. Goals will refer to external change. The practice method will depend on the use of class- or case-advocacy techniques.

While there is humane concern for the well-being of populations, little attention can be given to individual needs, frailties, or responses to the pain that sometimes accompanies large scale change.

In this way of defining problems, Ricky's problem is defined as an oppressive school system. The worker either mobilizes parents in the community to undertake a legal class-action against the threatened transfer as a school policy, or undertakes individual advocacy on Ricky's behalf. In either event, limited further attention is given to the individual needs of Ricky and his family or to the pain they are experiencing in their life situation. It is even possible that while Ricky's rights may be won and he can stay at this school, he will not have been helped. The problem that kept him from attending school in the first place still remains, and he is unable to return.

If people's needs and problems are located in the interface *between person and environment,* and defined as maladaptive transactions within the life space, then the professional intervention is likely to be formulated in terms of reciprocal adaptive processes, on a life model. Goals will refer to a strengthened adaptive capacity and increased environmental responsiveness. Psychologically-oriented techniques will be directed to progressive forces in the personality with an emphasis on cognition, perception, feeling and action. At the same time, use will be made of supports in the social field and physical setting, and work will be directed to increasing the responsiveness of the organizations on which the client depends, including the worker's own agency.

In Ricky's case, depending upon the salient and relevant factors, several entry points into the life space may be possible for effective help: 1) The problem might be located in the family's internal relationships, so that help might be given on that level. 2) The problem might be located in the transactions between family and school, so help might be directed toward removing barriers to their communication and increasing their reciprocity. 3) The child's realistic fear of walking past the neighborhood junkies or assaultive teenagers on his way to school might be seen as the source of the problem. His parents might then be helped to join with other parents in approaching the school or the police in order to gain patrols or bus service within the school's range. 4) Then too, the social structure and emotional climate of Ricky's classroom could be its cause. Social worker

These aspects may then become part of the client's self-image and of his stereotyped image in the eyes of the worker. Differences in social class, ethnicity, or gender may also affect worker–client interaction by giving rise to incongruent perceptions and expectations.[19] Lower-class and working-class clients may seek advice and direction, while workers may search for psychodynamic meanings. Clients may expect help with current problems, while workers attempt to uncover the underlying cause in order to effect a long-range solution. In other words, clients may desire help with situational issues, while workers may focus on personality issues; such discrepant expectations leave client and worker with feelings of frustration and a sense of failure.[20]

The agency directly influences the client–worker relationship. Eligibility for services, the nature of problem definition and assessment, and the selection of helping modality are all influenced by the agency's formal and informal structures and functions. While clients are often blamed for dropping out, it may be that agency arrangements interfere with their use of services. Complex screening procedures, intake processes that interpose a delay between request and service, inaccessible office locations, or lack of evening hours may cause client dissatisfaction and dropping out.[21] These agency arrangements also serve a covert and possibly unintended function of maintaining for the agency a pool of highly motivated clients whose problems are not so intractable or their environments so harsh that they can't wait for service, and whose job or child care responsibilities don't interfere with daytime appointments. Since these characteristics are more commonly found among lower-middle and middle-class clients than among poor and working-class clients, the agency may also regard the clients in the pool as more introspective and verbal, with more hopeful prognoses, and thus, more "desirable."

In the process of becoming socialized to the profession, social workers, like other professionals, incorporate particular philosophical and theoretical perspectives and value orientations that lead to particular assumptions about the client, and her behavior and situation. These assumptions may or may not be accurate, but in either event they affect worker and client roles and the nature of their relationship.[22] Almost unwittingly, we tend to try to fit people and their situations into our theories. As a result, we select and "hear" only those elements from the client's communications that confirm our

and teacher might then consider classroom meetings, so that teacher and children learn to express their feelings and ideas about their shared experiences. Such an approach would not only help Ricky, but on a preventive level, it would be helpful to all the children and to the teacher. Scapegoating by the children, biased responses or expectations held by the teacher, or other maladaptive transactions within the classroom could be reduced. Most often, the problem will be located in several areas, each requiring professional involvement.

It should now be clear that problem definition is a critical feature of practice. The social worker needs to take into account the client's perception of the problem or need, as well as the interplay of transacting forces. If the worker's definition is different from the client's, or too narrow in scope, the interventions that flow from it will not help.

Foci of Attention

As previously suggested, in the life model, people's needs, problems or predicaments fall into three interrelated areas: 1) life transitions involving developmental changes, status role changes, crisis events; 2) the unresponsiveness of social and physical environments; and 3) communication and relationship difficulties in families and other primary groups. While these foci are interrelated and may be simultaneously addressed by worker and client, each also represents a primary area of concern and suggests differential professional interventions.

Mrs. Tolland, age 62, asked for help from the family agency, as she was feeling depressed. Her husband, age 65, was expecting to retire from his job as salesclerk in two months. Mrs. T had been forced to relinquish her office job several years ago because of severe health problems, and she has been receiving social security. The couple was living in undesirable quarters in a rapidly deteriorating neighborhood. Mrs. T and her husband were not getting along. She felt they had never had a very happy marriage because she had had to make all the decisions, and she was considering a divorce. She also wondered if it wouldn't be better to move, instead, to Florida or even to the east coast where their only child, a bachelor son, age 35, lived and worked.

Mr. Tolland was asked to come with his wife to the second interview. The worker focused on their marital problems, which Mr. Tolland saw as resolvable once they moved to a better apartment. In observing the Tollands' interaction, the worker defined the problem, to herself, as individual psychopathologies reflected in Mrs. T's controlling and castrating attitudes toward Mr. T, and Mr. T's provoking these attitudes by his hostile pattern of passive–aggressiveness. She decided to ask them to return for one more intake interview before offering ongoing service, so that she could determine the degree of their accessibility for personality change.

To begin with, one wonders if Mr. and Mrs. Tolland will even return for the next interview, since their despair is more likely to increase than diminish from such an approach to problem definition. If, however, Mr. and Mrs. Tolland are engaged in a mutual defining of the problem, they might also, like the worker, locate it in each other or in their interaction. If the worker, in exploring the problem with them, discovers they have not considered the impact of retirement, she needs to redirect their attention. Together, clients and worker might examine possible financial, relational, and other implications of the retirement, including what the role loss might mean to Mr. Tolland's self-image. The problem might then be cast as a life transition calling for novel solutions and coping skills by Mr. and Mrs. T individually and as a marital pair. Help with budgeting, help in deciding on various alternatives in the search for the new home, help in moving outward to their environment for activities to restore a sense of competence, help in restructuring the use of time, and help in securing adequate health care are all possibilities—depending on the Tollands' goals and interests and their expectations of themselves and of the worker. With this kind of help, marital interaction is likely to improve. But the worker may go further and help them recognize each other's needs and responses to the crisis of retirement and the tasks of aging, thus restoring reciprocity. Strengths in each partner and in their marriage can be identified and engaged instead of focusing on the regressive forces. Working solely on the personality features, as this worker proposes, or even on the marital interaction, would overlook the critical aspects of the life transition and the associated tasks.

Mr. and Mrs. Tolland, when viewed within their life space, are experiencing problems and needs in all three areas. They are facing a

very difficult life transition involving the developmen
aging, and the change in status and role brought about b
They may also be facing an unresponsive environment,
agency and worker, the health care system, inadequate
rangements, neighborhood, landlord, friends and relative
vironmental factors were, unfortunately, not examined in
interviews, so we can only speculate about them. The
also experiencing difficulties in communicating their
their needs to each other. It is very likely that for cha
worker and clients must be engaged together in all thre
must be in agreement, however, about the particular
attention at any given moment. Otherwise, the clients
focus on one aspect while the worker is focusing o
seems about to happen in the Tolland case.

Client and Worker Roles

In the life model, the client–worker relationship is reg
actional: each brings to the encounter the influence of
forces in his own life space. These forces can affect
congruence worker and client will achieve in their
Their transactions with each other will affect both of t
will shape the other as a result. In this view, client an
shift from those of subordinate recipient and supero
often assumed to be characteristic of a "professional
to roles permitting greater mutuality and reciprocity
tion. This conception of client and worker roles invo
tention to variations required by age, interest and ca
expectations, and life styles.

Distorted communications or maladaptive relatio
sometimes appear in the client–worker interaction,
to the helping process. They are often defined as
when, in fact, they are transactional in origin. There
of transactional difficulties: social definitions of
agency structures and functions, and professional pe

Both worker and client are affected by society
their statuses and its expectations of their roles. Wh
is stigmatized, as in "welfare client" or "menta
worker and client may have incorporated the stig

theoretical, philosophical, or ideological positions, and we may then disregard those that don't fit the positions. In response to the worker's subtle influence, the client may either seek to satisfy the worker's interests and intentions or struggle against them.

Good social work practice has always emphasized the worker's responsibility for developing awareness of her biases and blind spots, increasing her sensitivity to what is going on in the relationship, and being aware of the nature of her impact on the client and on the relationship. The life model of practice also makes this demand of the worker, expanding it to include a more vigilant stance toward socially-induced barriers to communication and the impact of social forces on the relationship, especially those emanating from the agency.

Phases of the Helping Process

Like life itself, the model of practice is phasic. Its processes and operations constitute three phases: the initial, ongoing, and ending phases. They, like other life processes, ebb and flow in response to the interplay of personal and environmental forces. We will separate these phases in order to analyze their elements; they are not always distinct in actual practice.

In the initial phase, the worker prepares herself to enter the client's life space before the actual encounter with the objective and subjective realities of that life space. The worker considers the client's objective reality through thinking about the available data, however minimal at this point, their meaning for life processes, and their potential impact on the initial session. She considers the client's subjective reality by an effort to empathize with the client's likely perceptions and feelings about the problem situation. Through such anticipatory processes, the worker readies herself to be responsive to client concerns and to "hear" both manifest and latent communications. In the first session and throughout, the worker seeks to provide a welcoming climate. She communicates interest and concern, invites the expression of needs and problems, and conveys a realistic sense of hope. She presents the agency's services and her professional function clearly, and elicits the client's responses to the presentation. Together, worker and client attempt to develop a mutual understanding of the next steps to be taken.

In the ongoing phase, the worker helps the client to work on the coping tasks associated with life transitions, environmental issues, and interpersonal processes. Professional skills in meeting a client's needs require the flexible use of individual, group, and family modalities; the engagement of organizations, social networks, and physical settings; and the use of temporal arrangements such as duration, pacing, and frequency of service.

In the ending phase, the worker prepares for and carries out the termination of service. The ending of a helping relationship can be difficult for both client and worker. The worker must anticipate both her or his, and the client's, likely responses to the anticipated loss in order to help the client deal with stages of termination. Depending upon the length of their contact and other factors, these stages may include denial, intense reactions and feelings, and release. In this final stage, discussing the objectives achieved and work yet to be done affords both client and worker an opportunity for mutual evaluation and gives each a sense of closure.

Assessment

As in any systematic approach to practice, interventions in the life model are guided by professional values and knowledge and rooted in continuous processes of assessment. Since professional knowledge is not so much knowledge for its own sake as it is knowledge for use, we will present the pertinent knowledge and theory underlying the life model in the later chapters on the practice method itself. We hope that in this way the critical connections between professional knowledge, values, and skills will be made clear to the reader.

Through processes of assessment, worker and client seek an understanding of objective facts; for example, what happened, how did it happen, when did it happen, etc. Much more exists, however, than objective reality. An understanding of the subjective reality must also be reached. People's views of their inner and outer worlds influence their adaptive and coping responses. Their personal reactions, the meanings attributed to events and processes, and feelings about them, are facts, too.

From the objective and subjective facts, the worker makes tentative inferences and entertains hypotheses to be tested against client feedback, outcomes of worker–client actions, and their mutual interaction. Inferences about the meanings of the facts, and hypotheses about interventive possibilities, are tempered by the worker's continuing openness to new subjective and objective facts. Rooted in the canons of logical thought, processes of assessment reflect concern for evidence, and the connecting of empirical data to knowledge and theory.

To understand another person and his situation fully, the worker must possess the empathy that enables her to enter into the concerns of another, and to understand and feel with that person in his unique situation. This process calls forth the compassionate concern and respect for human experience and individual uniqueness that is the art of practice. Professional assessment, like professional action, requires an integration of the scientific and artistic/humanistic traditions—the rigor of a scientifically based practitioner and the creative artistry of a compassionate participant. Understanding then becomes real and not stereotypic.

In helping a depressed person, for example, the worker considers the person's own perceptions of her situation and the perceptions held by others who are significant in the situation—such as family members, employer, and friends—and the nature of the person's transactions with them. The worker analyzes the functions the depressive behavior serves, both for the person and for these others. He also examines his own reactions to the person and the situation, relating these data to pertinent knowledge about cultural, social, personality, and biological factors. Out of this individualized understanding of the meaning and impact of the relevant and salient forces, worker and client set objectives and plan actions to reach the objectives. Action will be directed to engaging positive forces in the person and environment and reducing negative transactional features.

Assessment as a habit of mind is present from moment to moment as the worker "listens," to make sure his interventions are responsive to client concerns.[23] Assessment occurs at the end of each session as the worker reflects upon the session's themes, and evaluates his effectiveness in the light of session goals. Occasionally, assessment is formalized as the worker conceptualizes the major factors involved in the situation at a particular point in the helping process. Finally, assessment may involve the examination of content themes across sessions.

Assessment in all its forms strives for mutual client and worker understanding of what has produced and maintained the problem; how the need or problem manifests itself at any particular point in the helping process; what has taken place, so far, in relation to the goals and proposed solutions; what has been helpful or not helpful; and what the next steps should be. Client involvement in assessment assures of a shared focus and direction.

Professional Action

In helping people with their problems in living, the social worker needs an extensive repertoire of techniques and skills designed to increase self-esteem, problem-solving, and coping skills; to facilitate primary group functioning; and to engage and influence organizational structures, social networks and physical settings. No technique or skill is really specific to the life model. What may be different is its use—being directed to adaptive capacities and environmental properties, and their interaction. What may also be different is the emphasis on client action, autonomy (self-regulation), and competence.

It is important that people have opportunities to act in their own situations and on their own behalf. Action plays a crucial role in development and learning, both across the life cycle, and in coping and adaptation. When one has an effect upon his environment, takes responsibility for an aspect of his situation, makes decisions in areas that count, one's sense of identity and self-esteem is strengthened, and the skills for further mastery are developed.

Miss Roberts, for example, had been a patient in a state hospital for a number of years. For several months she had refused to take responsibility for changing her clothes, and her behavior was declared to be a "function of the rigidity of her schizophrenia." It occurred to the social worker that Miss Roberts' behavior might be related to the lack of opportunity for selecting her own clothes. She and Miss Roberts went on a shopping trip together, and Miss Roberts gleefully selected clothing items, making all the necessary arrangements with sales clerks and cashiers. From then on, she changed her clothes regularly and proudly.

Through such experiences, social workers not only earn the clients' trust and respect, but clients achieve self-confidence, self-esteem, and increased abilities.[24]

In order to assure successful action, the worker and client must determine the client's readiness and motivation to undertake action, and the availability and responsiveness of support systems. The nature of tasks, activities, and actions must be carefully considered so that they are achievable and appropriate to the client's life style, interests, and capacities, with risks of failure minimized as much as possible.[25]

The life model of practice emphasizes the translation of values, knowledge and self-awareness into professional competence. The disciplined use of values, knowledge and skills is the hallmark of the professional social worker, and is characterized by individuality and creativity. By contrast, a "professionalism" that is expressed by projecting an impression of neutrality and impersonality is not helpful. Social workers who are willing to risk revealing their humanness, their weaknesses, their spontaneity, and humor are viewed by clients as helpful and caring.[26] Successful practitioners are "dependably real," rather than "rigidly consistent."[27]

Each worker integrates skills, techniques, and modes of helping with his own personal style, creativity, and artistry. Such integration is used at every moment in the helping process as the worker risks human responses, uses spontaneous humor, and "pours some self" into the interaction.[28] Where an intervention is awkward or imperfect, the worker's desire to engage and involve the client will nevertheless be experienced positively by the client. The worker's commitment, empathic understanding, and willingness to become involved speak louder than the awkwardness or imperfection. This blend of knowledge and value with the skills of helping, the art and science of social work practice, provides the content in the chapters that follow.

Case Illustration

Mrs. Richards

Mrs. Richards is a 44-year-old white woman who was deserted by her husband twelve years ago, leaving her with a 3-month-old daughter, Debbie. Mrs. R is a college graduate (English major) and she and Debbie have been supported by public assistance. Because of Mrs. R's inability to make child care arrangements for Debbie, and her constant complaints of being bothered by noisy neighbors, the case was referred to a special counseling unit within the department of social services. The worker writes:

> When I arrrived at Mrs. Richards' home for the first visit, she seemed to be under considerable stress, complaining of sleepless nights and an increasing inability to concentrate on anything besides her "noise problem," caused by "vicious upstairs, downstairs, and next-door neighbors." These neighbors all persist in "ganging up" on her by "purposely annoying" her, beginning at 5:00 A.M. and continuing until 1:00 A.M. the following day. They speak loudly, play TV and radios at high volumes, repeatedly drop shoes and "go out of their way" to walk very heavily. Mrs. R also refuses to pick up mail at the post office, fearing a bomb may have been mailed to her. Further proof of the "conspiracy" against her is the notice she just received from the landlord informing her that her lease is to be terminated because neighbors have complained of noise coming from her apartment. Mrs. R has also received a summons from one of her neighbors charging her with harassment. Mrs. R admits she rings her neighbors' bells frequently to ask them to be quiet. She views the termination of the lease as an act by "malicious people who are jealous" of her because she is so quiet.
>
> After my first visit, Mrs. Richards had another agency call the department to verify I have no secret intent to harm her. In the second visit, Mrs. R told me she always did well in school, but all her life she has felt out of place and inferior to those around her. She states her social life consists of Debbie and one friend, whom she rarely sees. Debbie also has only one friend and prides herself on being a "bookworm." Mrs. R also said that for ten years she has lived in various buildings with "noisy, inconsiderate neighbors," whom she has often taken unsuccessfully to court, but the present noise level is the most bothersome of all because she can't rest or even think of anything else.

The worker viewed the problem as poor perceptions of the inside and outside worlds which prevent adaptive interchanges between Mrs. Richards and her environment, and impair her ability to cope with the tasks of adulthood. Mrs. R saw her problem as "vicious people out to get me." The consulting psychiatrist, noting that Mrs. R had been a patient in a state hospital twenty years before, defined the problem as a long-standing psychosis exacerbated by threat of eviction. Despite these varying definitions, worker and client found a common ground and agreed to meet together so Mrs. R would have what she preferred to call "a friend" to talk with her about her "noise problem," since she is alone all the time and has no one with whom to discuss the problem. They set their mutual goal as a solution to Mrs. R's discomfort with her environment. The worker adds, "I feel that Mrs. R's extremely poor self-image projected onto others keeps her from expanding her horizons beyond her two-room apartment and her relationship with her daughter, and the current crisis allows even less energy to be available for the relationships, activities, and interests of adulthood." Excerpts from the work follow:

> 10/24—I asked Mrs. R if she has thought about the possibility that she may have to move. She says she has, and she has begun to look in the papers to see if anything is available in the neighborhood. She stated she had seen what sounded like a beautiful apartment advertised in the paper, and when she called up it was already taken. Mrs. R feels sure the vacancy never existed at all, and that the brokerage firm played a trick on her so that she'd call and inquire about a more expensive apartment. I agreed that might be possible, but wondered if the apartment had sounded so attractive to her that someone else might have thought so, too, and telephoned before her. Mrs. R said that she doubted that—she's pretty sure it was all a "gimmick" to trick her. On further discussion, she remembered she had, in fact, bought the newspaper late in the day, and said, yes, maybe I was right.

10/31—I mentioned that I knew she felt unsure who I was, for Mr. Quill had called us. Mrs. R blew up and said it was none of my business whom she called, she could call whomever she wishes. I said that of course she could, but I mentioned it because I wanted her to know that I was only coming to see if I could be of help to her in some way, and no one meant her any harm. I emphasized that our services were voluntary and if she would like me to stop coming, she could tell me. At this, Mrs. R looked somewhat reassured and said she was glad I said that. Mrs. R then pulled out a picture of Debbie taken at a birthday party given for her by the mothers of Debbie's classmates in the Head Start program some years ago. Mrs. R reflected on the picture a few moments, and then said that people always did nice things for Debbie because they liked her. I said that maybe they did it because they like her, too. Mrs. R smiled and said she never looked at it that way, but maybe what I said was true.

During the next month, the worker accompanied Mrs. Richards to court, at Mrs. R's request, and each time they went to a coffee shop afterward, which pleased Mrs. R. Whenever Mrs. R's anxiety mounted, the worker offered support.

11/11—Mrs. R stated that she was not at all sure why she had asked me to come, since there was nothing that I could do to help her with her case. I said I knew that sitting alone in a courtroom is not the most pleasant thing, and I would not like to wait alone. Mrs. R then turned and thanked me for coming with her today.

When the case was put over a week, Mrs. Richards expressed fear that her attorney might not come.

She seemed very anxious about this, saying she wouldn't know who else to call. I then told Mrs. R that if he

> couldn't make it for the 19th, the date of her next appearance in court, I would try to help her find another lawyer. She said she would appreciate that. She stated again that her noisy neighbors are only "picking on" her. I told Mrs. R that while she may be bothered by some noise, it is something that we must all put up with while living in the city. Mrs. R did not deny this, but expressed fear that she would have to go through moving again. She anxiously stated that she's afraid that she "won't live through" the court case. I reassured her that she will, and that if she has to move I will be there with her to help her clear things through the Department of Welfare. Mrs. R then seemed much calmer and said it was so nice to talk to me, adding that Miss P at the other agency really hadn't understood her, and she would like to have coffee with me again.

At the next court hearing, after a long wait,

> 11/19—Mrs. R seemed to be getting more and more nervous and suddenly, sounding as if she were going to cry, stood up and said "What will happen to me if I get thrown out? I have no family, no one to go to. I'm all alone." I immediately reassured her that whatever happens, she won't be out on the street. If she is evicted, I will make sure that everything is cleared at the welfare center. Mrs. R then worried that she won't get permission to move, because she has not been living in her present apartment for the required two years. I assured her that under the circumstances, the time element will not count, and that I will try to have everything arranged for her quickly. Mrs. R looked at me, smiled, and thanked me for being there with her today.

The case was postponed indefinitely, and afterward, at the coffee shop, Mrs. R asked if the worker would go looking for an apartment with her.

> I pointed out that she may not even have to look for another place to live—she may not be evicted at all. Mrs. R

> then asked if she would be able to move even if she weren't evicted. I said that I had been under the impression that she wanted to stay in her apartment. She said she does, but she can't stand her "vicious neighbors." I reminded her that wherever she would move in the city she'd be faced with neighbors and noise. Mrs. R said I was right, even the lawyer had said the same thing, and she'd been bothered by neighbors for ten years. I reinforced this, and wondered if she would feel less aggravated by trying to get out of the house a little more. Mrs. R nodded and said that maybe that's what she should be doing, and she'll try it. Mrs. R then said she did not want to discuss it today, but asked if on Thursday we might discuss the possibility of her getting a part-time job because she wants to be more independent. As we walked together to the corner, Mrs. R thanked me again many times, and before my leaving, she turned to me and said, "I like you." I said I liked her too.

A month later, Mrs. Richards reported some changes in her situation.

> She said she sometimes still hears her neighbors, but they "seemed to be bothering her" less. She is trying not to pay so much attention to them, she "has her own life." Mrs. R said that all day yesterday she hadn't been home, having gone to the "Y" for swimming, and then to the library. I said that was good, and she might find the more she continues to pay attention to other things, the less bothered she may be by her neighbors. Mrs. R nodded in agreement. She said she knows she is "smart" because she has an IQ of 132, but she has always felt inferior to others. She could never mingle or feel at home with others. She remembers reading that people who are smart are good in everything, and should be able to get along well with others. She said that she's been thinking about it lately, and there's no reason for her to think she's not as good as everyone else. I nodded in support, and she said she's thinking of being more independent, and was think-

> ing of getting some part-time work. She asked if I could find out if this would be possible under the WIN program.

Not only did the worker focus on Mrs. Richards' strengths, but she successfully bypassed the pathology. Instead of treating someone with a psychosis, the worker, operating on the life model, viewed Mrs. Richards' difficulties as lying in the interface between herself and the environment. She sought to interrupt transactional processes that had created and sustained the present problem, and did this successfully by a focus on strengths. In a purposeful way, she sought to increase Mrs. Richards' badly damaged self-esteem, and at the same time to engage her perceptual–sensory capacity by clarifying the distinctions between inner and outer experiences at every opportunity. Together, these two areas of work created a beginning trust in interpersonal relationships.

As Mrs. Richards' anxiety diminished, progressive forces in her personality were released. She began to feel better about herself; her thinking, perceptions, and behavior began to change. The behavioral changes elicited different responses from her environment (neighbors, landlord), thus helping in the restitution process. Within two months, Mrs. Richards began to transact differently with her environment. Instead of spending her days frantically listening for traces of noise to prove people were out to get her, Mrs. Richards began to reestablish adaptive interchanges of energy and information with the environment. She readied herself for taking action that could lead to learning and competence.

Several months later, she had successfully planned for Debbie to attend summer camp, made arrangements for her own vocational counseling at the division of vocational rehabilitation, and was expressing an interest in meeting men. Reestablished adaptive ties with the environment led to growing freedom from autistic processes of projection and self-reference. More accurate processing of perceptions (reality-testing) developed.

Mrs. Richards was willing to relinquish her preoccupation with inner phenomena and to reconstitute connections with the outer world (action) through the support and clarifications provided by the worker. The sense of herself as a worthwhile person was nurtured by the worker's caring, respect, and positive expectations. Successful experiences led to growth, and growth increased the likelihood of further successes, interrupting the previous cycle of frustration and failure in transactions with the environment. Mrs. Richards is beginning to build a sense of trust, to increase her capacity for autonomy (self-regulation), decision making, and initiative, and seems ready to take action for developing competence in the tasks of adulthood.

Summary

Ecology seeks to understand the reciprocal relations between organism and environments. For social work, ecology appears to be a more useful metaphor than the older, medical-disease metaphor that tended to view human being and environment as relatively separate entities and to reflect the linearity of time, space, and causality characteristic of the scientific method before and during the early part of the twentieth century. It appears to be more useful because social work has always been committed both to helping people and to promoting more humane environments. However, the commitment was difficult to implement because the medical-disease metaphor tends to locate people's problems and needs within the person, obscuring social processes in which the person is embedded. In contrast, the ecological perspective provides an adaptive, evolutionary view of human beings in constant interchange with all aspects of their environment.

In the complex transactions between people and environments, upsets in the usual adaptive balance or goodness-of-fit often emerge. These upsets represent the stress generated by discrepancies between needs and capacities, on the one hand, and environmental qualities on the other. Stress arises in three interrelated areas of living: life transitions (developmental and status changes, crisis events); environmental pressures (unresponsive organizations, social networks or physical structures); and maladaptive interpersonal processes of relationships and communications. These stresses in living provide the field of social work with a unique and responsive social purpose: to strengthen adaptive capacities of individuals and primary groups, and to influence environments so that transactions promote growth and development. This conception of social purpose shapes the features of the life model, including problem definition, client and worker roles, phases of helping, assessment, and professional action.

How people's needs or predicaments are defined determines in large measure what will be done about them. If their needs and predicaments are located in the interface between person and environment, then professional intervention is directed to the reciprocal processes in that interface. Goals will refer to a strengthened adaptive capacity and increased environmental responsiveness.

In the life model, the client–worker relationship is regarded as transactional: each brings to the encounter the influence of the interacting forces in his or her own life space. Both worker and client are affected by social definitions of their respective statuses and roles, agency structures and functions, and professional perspectives. Distorted communications or maladaptive relationship patterns may appear in the client–worker interaction that create barriers to the helping process. They are often defined as client resistance, when in fact, they are transactional in origin.

The model of practice is phasic. Its processes and operations constitute three phases: the initial, ongoing and ending phases. In the initial phase, the worker prepares herself to enter the client's life by considering the objective and subjective possibilities. In the first and subsequent sessions, she uses exploration and contracting skills to develop mutual agreement with the client on the nature of the need and objectives, and on planning the focus and tasks involved in the client's life transitions, environmental issues, and maladaptive interpersonal processes. Professional skills are required in the flexible use of individual, group, and family modalities; the engagement of organizations, social networks, and physical structures; and the use of temporal arrangements such as duration, pacing, and frequency of service. In the ending phase, the worker prepares for and carries out the termination process.

As in any systematic approach to social work practice, interventions in the life model are continually guided by assessment processes. From the objective and subjective facts, the worker makes tentative inferences which are continuously tested and reformulated in the light of client responses and evaluation of interventions and outcomes. To understand fully another person and situation, the worker must also possess the empathy to "hear" and understand another human being. Thus, professional assessment requires an integration of the scientific and artistic traditions—the rigor of a scientifically-oriented practitioner and the creative artistry of a compassionate participant.

In helping people with stresses in living, the social worker carries out various professional roles, each with its repertoire of skills. These roles and skills are embellished by the worker's individuality and creativity. Professional purpose, knowledge, and skill are integrated with personal style throughout the helping process.

Notes

1. William E. Gordon, "Basic Constructs for an Integrative and Generative Conception of Social Work," in Gordon Hearn, ed., *The General Systems Approach: Contributions Toward an Holistic Conception of Social Work* (New York: Council on Social Work Education, 1969), pp. 5–11; Harriett M. Bartlett, *The Common Base of Social Work Practice,* (New York: National Association of Social Workers, 1970).

2. See, for example, Charles Gillispie, *The Edge of Objectivity, An Essay in the History of Scientific Ideas* (Princeton, N.J.: Princeton University Press, 1960); Gerald Holton, *Thematic Origins of Scientific Thought: Kepler to Einstein,* (Cambridge, Mass.: Harvard University Press, 1973).

3. See, for example, René Dubos, "Science and Man's Nature," *Daedalus* (Winter 1965), 94:223–44.

4. J. T. Fraser, *Time, Passion, and Knowledge* (New York: Braziller, 1975); Masao Watanabe, "The Conception of Nature in Japanese Culture," *Science* (January 25, 1974), 183:279–82.

5. Kenneth Boulding, *The Meaning of the Twentieth Century* (New York: Harper & Row, 1964); Peter Drucker, *Landmarks of Tomorrow* (New York: Harper & Row, 1959).

6. Werner Heisenberg, *Physics and Beyond* (New York: Harper & Row, 1971).

7. Floyd Matson, *The Broken Image* (New York: Braziller, 1964); Albert Camus, *The Myth of Sisyphus and Other Essays,* Justin O'Brien, tr. (New York: Knopf, 1955).

8. See, for example, Theodore Roszak, *The Masking of a Counter Culture: Reflections on the Technocratic Society and its Useful Opposition* (Garden City, N.Y.,: Doubleday Anchor Books, 1969).

9. See, for example, Gerald Holton, ed. *Science and Culture* (New York: Houghton Mifflin, 1965); Robert M. Pirsig, *Zen and the Art of Motorcycle Maintenance* (New York: William Morrow, 1974); Margaret Mead, "Towards a Human Science," *Science* (March 5, 1976), 191:903–9.

10. W. H. Murdy, "Anthropocentrism: A Modern Version," *Science* (March 28, 1975), 187:1168–72.

11. Carel B. Germain, "An Ecological Perspective in Casework Practice," *Social Casework* (July 1973), 54(7):323–30; E. H. Auerswald, "Interdisciplinary vs. Ecological Approach," *Family Process* (September 1968), 7:202–15; Salvador Minuchin, "The Use of an Ecological Framework in the Treatment of a Child," in E. James Anthony and Cyrille Koupernik, eds., *The Child in His Family* (New York: Wiley, 1970), pp. 41–57; James G. Kelly, "Ecological Constraints on Mental Health Services," *American Psychologist* (June 1966), 21(6):535–39; Donald H. Blocher, "Toward an Ecology of Student Development," *Personnel and Guidance Journal* (February 1974), 52(6):360–65.

12. The use of metaphor in a professional practice is examined by Carel B. Germain, "Social Casework" in Harleigh B. Trecker, ed., *Goals for Social Welfare, 1973–1993* (New York: Association Press, 1973), pp. 125–37.

13. See, for example, René Dubos, *Man Adapting* (New Haven: Yale University Press, 1965); René Dubos, *So Human an Animal* (New York: Scribner's, 1968); Theodosius Dobzhansky, *Genetics of the Evolutionary Process* (New York: Columbia University Press, 1970); Paul Weiss, "Biological Basis of Adaptation," in John Romano, ed., *Adaptation* (Ithaca: Cornell University Press, 1950), pp. 3–21.

14. Hartmann suggests there are three processes of human adaptation: the autoplastic (change of self), alloplastic (change of the environment), and the seeking of new environments. Heinz Hartmann, *Ego Psychology and the Problem of Adaptation* (New York: International Universities Press, 1958), ch. 2, "Adaptation," pp. 22–37.

15. The pioneer investigator in the field of human stress is Hans Selye. See his *The Stress of Life* (New York: McGraw-Hill, 1956). See also Harry S. Abram, *Psychological Aspects of Stress* (Springfield, Ill.: C. C. Thomas, 1970); Joseph E. McGrath, ed., *Social and Psychological Factors in Stress* (New York: Holt, Rinehart, & Winston, 1970); Richard S. Lazarus, *Psychological Stress and the Coping Process* (New York: McGraw-Hill, 1966); Sol Levine and Norman Scotch, eds., *Social Stress* (Chicago: Aldine, 1970).

16. See Alex Gitterman and Carel B. Germain, "Social Work Practice: A Life Model," *Social Service Review* (December 1976), 50:601–10; and Carel B. Germain and Alex Gitterman, "The Life Model of Social Work Practice," in Francis J. Turner, ed., *Social Work Treatment* 2nd rev. ed. (New York: Free Press, 1979).

17. Some researchers and theorists in the field of stress suggest that the critical factor in stressful life events is change—change that poses new kinds of demands upon the person. See, for example, B. S. Dohrenwend and B. P. Dohrenwend, eds., *Stressful Life Events* (New York: Wiley, 1974). For a critical assessment of research design and methodology in studies of the role of stressful life events in the etiology of illness, see Judith G. Rabkin and Elmer L. Struening, "Life Events, Stress, and Illness," *Science* (December 3, 1976), 194:1013–20.

18. See, for example, C. Murray Parkes, "Psycho-social Transitions: A Field for Study," *Social Science and Medicine* (April 1971), 5:101–5.

19. For a discussion of the impact of social class upon worker–client interac-

tion, see Dale G. Hardman, "Not with My Daughter, You Don't," *Social Work* (July 1977), 20(4):278–85; Alice Overton, *Clients' Observation of Social Work* (St. Paul, Minn.: Greater St. Paul Community Chest and Councils, 1959); J. M. Rosenfeld, "Strangeness Between Helper and Client: A Possible Explanation of Non-Use of Available Professional Help," *Social Service Review* (March 1964), 38:17–25. For discussion of the impact of race upon worker–client interaction, see George P. Banks, "The Effects of Race on One-to-One Helping Interviews," *Social Service Review* (June 1971), 45:137–46; Shirley Cooper, "A Look at the Effects of Racism on Clinical Work," *Social Casework* (February 1964), 54:252–58; Alex Gitterman and Alice Schaeffer, "The White Professional and the Black Client," *Social Casework* (May 1972), 54:280–91. For discussion of the impact of gender upon worker–client interaction, see Frederick J. Duhl, "Changing Sex Roles—Concepts, Values, and Tasks," *Social Casework* (February 1976), 57:87–92; Sanford N. Sherman, "The Therapist and Changing Sex Roles," *Social Casework* (February 1976), 57:93–6.

20. John E. Mayer and Noel Timms, *The Client Speaks* (New York: Atherton Press, 1970). See their "Clash in Perspectives Between Worker and Client," *Social Casework* (January 1969), 50:32–40; Anthony N. Maluccio, *Learning From Clients* (New York: The Free Press, 1979).

21. Dorothy F. Beck and Mary Ann Jones. *Progress on Family Problems: A Nationwide Study of Clients' and Counselors' Views on Family Agency Services* (New York: F.S.A.A. 1973); Howard J. Parad and Libbie G. Parad, "A Study of Crisis-Oriented Planned Short-Term Treatment: Part I and Part II," *Social Casework* (June 1968), 49:346–54 and (July 1968), 49:418–26.

22. Erica Chance and Jack Arnold, "Effect of Professional Training, Experience, and Preferences for Theoretical System Upon Clinical Case Description," *Human Relations* (August 1960), 13:195–214; Martin Lakin and Benjamin Lebowitz, "Bias in Psychotherapists of Different Orientations: An Exploratory Study," *American Journal of Psychotherapy* (January 1958), 12:79–86.

23. For example of assessment as a moment-to-moment process, see Harry J. Aponte, "Diagnosis in Family Therapy," in Carel B. Germain, ed., *Social Work Practice: People and Environments* (New York: Columbia University Press, 1979), pp. 107–49.

24. An attempt to achieve insight is often less effective than the provision of opportunities for action that lead to the development of skills and a sense of personal competence. Indeed, insight may follow rather than precede behavioral action. For elaboration, see Allen Wheelis, "How People Change," *Commentary* (May 1969), pp. 55–66.

25. Anthony N. Maluccio, "Action as a Tool in Casework Practice," *Social Casework* (January 1974), 55:30–35.

26. In reviewing the question of professionalism, Allport urges professionals to be less rigid and to trust their "friendship" motives. Gordon Allport, "The Limits of Social Service," in J. F. Russel, ed., *National Policies for Education, Health, and Social Services* (New York: Doubleday, 1955), pp. 194–213. Mullin hypothesized that more than technique is required for success in treatment. Rather, the helping person

is seen more as a person exerting personal influence than as an expert applying techniques. Edward Mullin, "Differences in Worker Style in Casework," *Social Casework* (June 1969), 50:347–53.

27. Carl Rogers, "The Characteristics of a Helping Relationship," *On Becoming a Person* (Boston: Houghton Mifflin, 1961), p. 50.

28. Reynolds makes an important distinction between standardized techniques and professional artistry. Bertha Reynolds, *Learning and Teaching in the Practice of Social Work* (New York: Farrar & Rinehart, 1942).

2

The Initial Phase

ENTERING INTO a person's life space and its field of forces requires delicacy, knowledge, compassion, careful planning, and skill. We think of the initial phase as having two parts, preparation and entry. Preparation has both cognitive and affective components; entry comprises exploration and contracting. Preparation and entry are each approached differently according to whether the social work service is sought, proffered, or imposed.

Preparation

Cognitive and Affective Preparation

Before even seeing the client, the worker prepares herself to deal with the client's objective and subjective concerns. The client's objective reality is considered through examination of the data so far at hand—however minimal they may be—and tentative evaluation of their potential impact on the client's situation and on the initial encounter of worker and client.

Betty, a 16-year-old white girl from a working-class community telephones a community mental health center to ask for help with feelings of depression. She explains to the intake interviewer that she does well in school, has girl friends, but no boy friends. She is unhappy about this and wonders what's wrong with her. She feels ugly and fat. She even hates to be with her friends because they're so happy. She says she gets along better with her mother than her father.

He resents her getting older and says things that hurt her. He makes fun of anyone she likes, and teases her when a boy doesn't call. She longs for last summer when she had a close relationship with an older boy (age 20). She is given an appointment to see a social worker two days later.

Before seeing Betty for the first time, the worker reflects upon theoretical issues such as the adolescent struggle with dependence and independence, the resurgence of earlier feelings toward parents, the preoccupation with self, the need for acceptance as a desirable person, and the need for heterosexual and same-sex relationships; and social and cultural pressures on the mid-adolescent. She considers the strong motivational factors in the self-referral, and weighs the depression and such biological features as hormonal bodily changes and obesity. She seeks to anticipate her own responses to adolescent concerns and to possible provocative behavior so that she will be alert to the danger of slipping into a parental role, or of assuming authoritarian or belittling attitudes. She reflects, too, on the differing advantages of individual, family, or group modalities, and of planned short-term or open-ended service.

The client's subjective reality was considered through a process of anticipatory empathy,[1] or viewing through the client's eyes her life situation and her perceptions of their initial encounter. Moving into another's frame of reference in this way represents a critical measure in engaging a client. To accomplish this task, a four-step process is suggested: 1) identification, through which the worker experiences what the client is feeling and thinking; 2) incorporation, through which the worker feels the client's experiences as if they were his own; 3) reverberation, through which the worker evokes life processes of his own which facilitate understanding, and; 4) detachment, through which the worker engages in rational, objective analysis.[2]

A new worker in an agency serving the blind found it difficult to understand many behaviors of her clients, and she appeared aloof rather than concerned and involved in her contacts with them. While observing a sewing group, she was encouraged to wear a blindfold and to participate in the activity. She writes of her reactions:

> There were several instructors in the room; I could not determine who was speaking. Several times I answered

> questions that were not addressed to me, and I felt very embarrassed. Other times, I spoke to the person next to me, only to receive no response. I felt frightened to have my comment met by silence. Still other times, we interrupted each other, talking simultaneously. I had always attributed blind persons' interruptions to poor self-control, but suddenly, I realized how difficult it is to converse without visual cues. Finally, I experienced many distortions: time went by ever so slowly, and waiting was unbelievably frustrating. The instructor would say, "I'll be there in a minute"; I would not know whether she forgot, or whether I should ask again and risk an impatient response. I began to realize that there were several ways a blind person could get attention—aggressively, repetitiously, pleadingly, seductively—precisely the same behavior that has frightened me and alienated me from my clients.

Role playing is an excellent way to recreate in the pre-encounter the experiences of another, increasing the worker's receptivity to the client's perceptions and covert messages at their first meeting. Role playing can facilitate the steps of identification and incorporation. In identifying with the experience of another, the worker must also, through reverberation, call up memories of his own similar experience, at the same time separate his experience from that of the client. The worker must be aware of his own feelings and thoughts, so that he can anticipate his characteristic patterns of handling certain situations or his likely responses to particular kinds of people, situations, and problems. Finally, the worker must pull back from the empathetic steps of identification, incorporation, and reverberation to achieve the distance required for objective analysis of the client's situation and need. The fourth step of detachment in objective analysis is based upon professional knowledge and its integration with the available data, and their anticipated meanings for the client. The four steps of empathetic preparation provide a guide for entering the client's life situation.

Another worker describes how she prepared herself to meet with Mr. Sachs, who was facing the imminent loss of his wife to cancer.

> In preparing for the initial interview, I considered how I would introduce into the conversation various concerns Mr. S might have. I also tried to anticipate various reactions. The interview itself confirmed my anticipated perceptions. However, I stopped short of dealing with his wife's approaching death. I failed to invite discussion in this area. I was aware of what I was doing at the time, yet I continued to avoid the painful subject, thus undermining my intention to help. In preparing for my interview with Mr. S and his possible reactions to his wife's death, I hadn't considered my own reactions. I had "forgot" to consider how the loss of a loved one would make me feel.

While the worker used identification and incorporation to anticipate and predict the client's responses, inattention to the reverberation of her own feelings and reactions resulted in an unhelpful interview. Contrast this with the following experience of a worker who prepared herself to empathize with her client and to anticipate her own likely reactions.

Mrs. Georgio, a 38-year-old mother of two children, was operated upon for metastasized cancer. She had asked the social worker to talk with her husband, because he is confused and anxious.

> I told Mr. G I was a social worker and had spoken to his wife on two occasions and was interested in knowing how he and the children are getting along. Mr. Georgio raised several questions concerning his wife's care, which I answered. He then began talking about her first admission five years ago for a mastectomy. When his wife discovered what had happened, she looked at him and asked if he still loved her. He said of course he did, that if it had made any difference to him, he would never have given permission for the surgery.
>
> After the operation they had counted the years, for they knew after five years they could be more hopeful of a cure. He said Mrs. Georgio had not experienced any trouble until last year, when she had a hysterectomy. The doctor then told him the situation was grave. Mr. Georgio had

asked the doctor for an estimate of how long his wife could expect to live. The doctor had said he had seen some women live one year, and others as long as twenty years after they had reached this point. Mr. G commented that this hadn't been much help to him. I remarked that one of the most difficult things is not knowing what to expect, and having to live with this uncertainty.

His wife was not afraid of death, he said. She talked about it frequently and thanked God for letting her spend five more years with her family. I wondered how it was for him, and he said it is much more difficult for him to bear, to watch her go through all of this. I asked if he and his wife are able to talk together about their feelings. He said yes, they have a marvelous relationship, because they have been happy together for eighteen years.

The worker's preparation to understand a client's situation and his feelings about it needs to be flexible and multi-dimensional rather than rigid and linear. A young worker assigned to an elderly client, for example, needs to prepare to "hear" and to deal with possible expressions about their age difference. At the same time, she must be careful that the anticipatory preparation does not become a preconceived "script" in which the age difference becomes an automatic issue. Effective empathic processes remain open to additional data and impressions, and it is important to avoid stereotypes and predetermined conceptions.

Degree of Client Choice

An important factor in the preparation process is the degree of choice available to the actual or potential client in accepting or rejecting a service. A service may be sought, proffered, or imposed.[3] People *seeking* social work services are experiencing stress in some area of their lives. These clients seek help, presumably of their own accord, though presumably not without ambivalence and not without some pressure from others.

People invited to use social work services may or may not be experiencing stress in some area of their lives. Services may be *prof-*

fered, for example, to hospital patients screened by the social worker or other staff for special needs, or to residents in a low-income housing project as a population-at-risk for whom a new social work program has been designed. Services may be proffered to individuals, families, or groups designated by the environment as in need of service, such as retired members of a labor union or an adolescent group in a settlement house. In proffered services, the worker reaches out and offers a service. She may find interested, uninterested, or neutral respondents.

People also have services *imposed* upon them, usually after their behavior has created problems for others. Such involuntary clients enter the social work arena at the suggestion, pressure, or even the coercion of other individuals and organizations. Often they themselves do not acknowledge a need for help and they may not be experiencing discomfort beyond their immediate resentment at having to be involved. People who have social work services imposed on them include those under court mandate to obtain evaluative screening or rehabilitative counseling, natural parents attempting to regain or maintain custody of their child, and people in total institutions such as prisons, mental hospitals or residential treatment centers where choices in day-to-day functioning are extremely limited.

These differences in how the service is initiated—whether sought, proffered, or imposed—have implications for the way the service is carried out, and how social worker and client involve themselves in the initial phase.

Services Sought. In addition to the anxiety, despair, or concrete needs that propelled the person or family to the agency, additional stress is often created by the act of seeking help.[4] In a society that values individualism and self-reliance, seeking help may imply personal inadequacy and loss of control over one's affairs. Intermingled with the resulting sense of shame or anger, or even fear of how one will be received by the social worker, is a sense of hope that the need will be met, the problem solved, and the predicament eased. Thus, many clients face the initial session with mixed feelings. To varying degrees, they both want and dread help. The ambivalence may be accompanied by a fear of the unknown that lies beyond the door of the agency, generated by such phenomena as stereotyped ideas about social workers, culturally patterned attitudes toward help, and feelings derived from past experiences with persons in authority.

There are variations in these ideas and feelings, but the ambiguities inherent in the situation generate anxiety in most clients. Sensitive preparation enables the worker to create a welcoming atmosphere and to elicit client concerns, expectations, apprehensions, and confusions. A clear explanation of agency services and resources at the outset decreases ambiguity and relieves anxiety; the client is more likely to feel sustained, and to view worker and agency with some confidence.

A student was assigned to a former client returning to the agency for help with numerous problems. The student began by reviewing the case folder:

> After reading the folder, I had misgivings about working with Mrs. Stein. Early entries pictured her as a physiological and emotional invalid. One label after another was used to describe this one human being: cerebral palsy, chronic paranoid schizophrenic, legally blind, mentally retarded, foster child. As I read, I felt myself becoming emotionally removed, hiding my fears in diagnostic speculations. Then I allowed myself to be curious about the person rather than the labels. This time, her ''story'' as a human being unfolded. I found myself feeling Mrs. Stein's sense of being overwhelmed, alone, and scared. I began to sense her inner strength and her capacity to endure despite numerous traumas. I pictured her sitting in the chair next to me, and I wondered what she would be like, and how she would react to me. If I were Mrs. Stein, I might be curious about why I was getting a new worker. She might feel that the change of workers was her fault, a reflection of her unworthiness. She might be angry and upset about beginning anew with another social worker. At the same time, she might be curious about me and hopeful that I could help. As I anticipated her possible reactions, several opening strategies occurred to me for explaining how I was assigned to her, eliciting her understanding of why the other worker left, listening for her feelings about

starting with someone new, sharing with her what I know about her situation, inviting her to bring me "on board" her present situation and needs.

The student's sensitive preparation resulted in effective engagement. A lack of preparation and understanding, however, could have led to Mrs. Stein's provocative and prolonged testing of the worker, nonverbal expressions of anxiety, lack of communicativeness, or deciding not to return.[5]

Services Proffered. To reach out and invite a potential client to use a proffered service requires careful preparation. The identification of need and the selection of clients must reflect a felt concern, or an interest within the community. Genuine concern and responsiveness to the potential client's perceptions of her situation must be reflected in the introductory correspondence, telephone, or personal contact. Defining the service in clear and direct terms for the potential client is particularly important so that there is no hidden agenda to arouse suspicion. The service must be proffered in terms that fit the client's values and life style.

A hospital social worker, for example, was asked by nursing staff to talk with Ms. Butler, a 60-year-old, unmarried, black woman. Ms. Butler, who had worked all her life as a domestic, had been admitted to the hospital a month earlier for a severe circulatory disorder related to chronic diabetes. Gangrene required the amputation of her foot, and shortly afterward, the further amputation of her leg to the knee. The nurses described her as hostile and uncooperative. She refused to talk to them and to follow medical orders, and the nurses regarded her as a serious management problem.

The worker considered these data intellectually and affectively. He reflected on the double assault of losing a limb, piece by piece. He considered Ms. Butler's likely responses to the psychic and physical pain. He thought of her anger, grief, and the fear of losing still more, even life itself. He considered the additional impact of age and the age-specific tasks related to loss of both the work role and financial independence now looming before her. He reflected on the fact that Ms. Butler was black, while all the physicians, nurses, and social workers were white. He wondered also about the patient's available social supports. Finally, he allowed himself to anticipate his own feeling responses to the pain of the patient.

By such cognitive and affective processes, the worker prepared to enter Ms. Butler's life experience, connecting to her view and perception of the experience, rather than identifying with the staff's negative judgments. He was able to relate to the immediate anger that greeted him because he was prepared for it and understood its sources. He conveyed his empathic concern, and she accepted his offer to help in dealing with her immediate and concrete needs.

Service Imposed. Many of those whom social workers seek to serve are "captive," involuntary clients. They confront an organization and its representatives who have the authority and power to require the use of a social work service. Where the authority represents a legal mandate, the service may be imposed as a condition for escaping an undesired status of juvenile offender, parolee, or probationer. Service is frequently a prerequisite for achieving a desired status of adoptive or foster parent. Service may be imposed as a condition for having a natural child returned, or for receiving methadone maintenance, or homemaker service. While a service may be proffered, the authoritarian nature of the agency creates ambiguity for the client about the degree of choice. A welfare recipient may feel compelled to accept a group service for fear of jeopardizing the assistance grant. A housing tenant may accept service for fear of being dispossessed. Hospitalized mental patients, residents of geriatric facilities or child care institutions may fear negative sanctions if they refuse service. While freedom of choice may be declared by agency and worker, the potential client experiences the opposite.

The initial contact with a captive client requires special preparation. The worker must take into account that he or she represents an environmental threat, even an obstacle, to a client's desired ends. Preparation has to be attuned to potential responses to the imposed service. Some clients may find the service congruent with their own definition of needs and aspirations, and cooperate immediately. Other clients may seem, on the surface, to cooperate in order to obtain a positive evaluation. Often, the unprepared worker then reacts to being "manipulated," and is unable to initiate discussion of the obstacle between them. Other clients oppose the worker through such aggressive behaviors as subtle insults and verbal attacks, or such passive behaviors as exaggerated compliance and guilt-inducing statements. In response, the unprepared worker may become immobilized or punitive.

If the worker has prepared for potential client responses, she will be able to define the service in terms to fit the client's perception of reality (e.g., "you feel that the teachers are picking on you") and his adaptive patterns. Two social work students, assigned to a mental hospital, were asked to form pre-discharge groups of schizophrenic patients who had been institutionalized for over twenty years. The purpose was to help the patients with their feelings about now having to leave the hospital. One student described her efforts to anticipate the patients' reactions to the proposed service.

> A part of them would like to leave the hospital. It isn't a pleasant place, yet it's been home for twenty years. The ward is their world and they have achieved acceptance and security. It has protected them from outside pressures. They probably are scared of leaving and losing its protection. It would be dysfunctional to offer a service for "talking about your feelings about leaving the hospital." That would be a major threat to them, to be defended against. They might even regress in order to justify their need for staying in the hospital.

With her field instructor, the first student reformulated the purpose, focusing upon visits and trips to the community. She felt the patients might find it easier to experience the community than to talk about it. Even talking about leaving might be made easier by actually leaving the hospital for short periods. The group visited foster homes and began to deal with their concerns in the context of their real-life community experiences. Gradually they were able to make individual decisions and plans about the future.

The group led by the second student followed the original purpose. The members engaged in regressive behavior, and assured their continued hospitalization.

In forming a group, whether the service is proffered or imposed, part of the preparation is concerned with group composition. Available knowledge indicates that homogeneous groups are more apt to be cohesive and to offer immediate support and mutual aid than heterogeneous groups. The latter, more than homogeneous groups, are apt to be vital, intense, and insightful, provided they overcome the tensions associated with diversity.[6] In preparation, the worker considers these comparative advantages in order to form a group that will have both stability and vitality. An additional consideration is the intensity of the felt need. When a group of people share a sense of acute and common need, they are better able to absorb differences in background. Diabetic patients, for example, experience profound common concerns. Therefore, as a group, they will probably accept diversity in their backgrounds and situations.

No group member should be isolated on a significant characteristic. One black member in a foster mothers' group for example, or one male in an adolescent group, may be uncomfortable. A "Noah's Ark" principle is useful to keep in mind in group composition: people should be matched, at least two-by-two, on behavioral and demographic characteristics. In preparing for a group service it is helpful to list variables of age, sex, race, religion, residence, social class, and problem/need, and to decide which ones are to be met on a uniform basis, and which by diversity among members.[7] Latency age children, for example, often require homogeneous grouping on gender and geographic variables, while adolescents may benefit from diversity on these two variables.

Entry

Exploration

Initial sessions are critical in the helping process and affect ultimate outcomes. People seeking services are applicants until they accept the agency service and the agency agrees to provide it. Only then do they become clients, users, or consumers of services. People invited to use the agency service become clients only when they agree to a need for it and agree to the specified conditions. When service is imposed, the captive client's participation and acceptance of the service is equally necessary. Even continuing clients, when transferred to new workers, must agree to reinvolve themselves. Professional skills in entry are essential to gain people's acceptance of and engagement in social work services. In fact, studies of early client dropout attribute the phenomenon to workers' lack of empathic concern, unresponsiveness to client needs and expectations, failure to communicate hope that the predicament can be eased, and lack of planning with the client for meeting the problem–need.[8] Helping people to use services therefore represents a critical task for the social work practitioner.

If the *client has sought the service* by initiating the contact, the worker establishes a welcoming climate of courtesy, support, and acceptance, and communicates his interest and respect verbally and nonverbally. He is sensitive to accepted social amenities and seeks to provide an uninterrupted period for the client by minimizing telephone or other interruptions. He arranges his office or meeting area so that it will be comfortable and as attractive as possible, with pictures, plants, or other interesting objects.

The worker invites the client "to tell her story" and to elaborate her concerns and needs. The opening needs to be nonthreatening, yet must invite specific responses. He may ask, "Can you tell me what concerns have brought you here?" Such a question focuses attention, yet gives the client latitude in replying. The use of the term "concerns" may avoid the more negative implications of "problems."[9] As the client responds, the worker watches for nonverbal messages that may indicate anxiety, depression, guilt, or relief. He notes what is left out and what is stressed, and any discrepancies between verbal and nonverbal behaviors, as when a mother smiles while complaining about the child's behavior.

The worker seeks further detail that will clarify and amplify the material through questions directed to the what, how, and when: "Can you tell me more about that?" "What happened then?" "How did you respond?" "When did this happen?" Where necessary to help the client continue, the worker may make supportive statements: "That was rough." "You were hurt very badly." "Most parents would be worried about that." Questions that ask why should be avoided, as they are often experienced as either challenging or accusatory, and they elicit justification and rationalization. Asking the client *why* she is depressed, may be taken as an implication that there is something inappropriate in her feeling, or that she is required to produce an insightful answer. The question of why is usually unanswerable, and interferes with the client's spontaneous discussion of her concerns.

Beginning with the problem/need itself, the worker seeks to develop a mutual assessment of where the problem is located and how it manifests itself. Together, social worker and client consider the problem's onset, duration, and intensity, what has been done about it so far, and with what results. By maintaining balance between a focus on the felt need, and responsiveness to verbal and nonverbal cues, the worker encourages the client to tell her story in her own way. This allows worker and client to gain a beginning sense of the interplay of forces within the client's life space. The worker may then be able to tentatively confirm the client's own definition of her need, or pose an alternative definition for the client's consideration, or suggest further exploration at a subsequent time to clarify the nature of the problem. Together, they may examine then, or a bit later, what each believes might be helpful, including the objectives to be sought. At this point, the worker needs to describe and explain the agency's function and services, and to define his own role and purpose with respect to the client's need, as it is understood so far. The explanation must be concise, explicit, and clear.

Inviting the client to tell her story in no way suggests that immediate needs, especially of concrete nature, are not met until all the facts are in. On the one hand, the worker must guard against being frozen into inaction by a perceived need for more and more facts. Prolonged periods of study and evaluation or screening and diagnosis, during which responsive action is deferred, means that the client receives limited help with her initial problem. She may become frustrated or alienated, and drop out from service. Yet, the worker must also guard against acting prematurely and intervening without sufficient understanding of the nature of the need or problem, or of what will be most helpful. While false reassurance or hurried action may allay the worker's own anxiety, it is often inappropriate and not helpful to the client. Thus, the worker seeks a balance between meeting immediate, pressing, concrete needs, and exploring the complexity of the situation. He strives also to reach an early agreement with the client to work together on mutually defined objectives, to arrange a referral to a more appropriate service, or to end the contact.

If the *agency initiates the contact by reaching out,* or developing a new service, or *imposing a mandated service,* the worker must begin by defining the agency's service and his role before inviting the client to present and discuss her concerns. The worker takes initiative to explain agency services and professional functions clearly and explicitly. It is especially important to be direct and clear about purpose, and to avoid the use of professional jargon. One must take care neither to disown nor to defend the agency in the face of negative client responses.

The worker has to be particularly careful to avoid imposing a covert or "hidden" agenda, in which he speaks of one service, but intends to deliver another. In a psychiatric hospital providing service to adolescent patients and their families, for example, social workers were expected to interview parents for the ostensible purpose of securing developmental histories of their children. The latent purpose, however, was to engage parents in treatment as clients. A worker reflects upon his struggle with this agenda:

> In my first contact with Mr. and Mrs. Dalton, I explained to them that the hospital provides parents with regular interviews with a social worker so that the family can help by providing us with information about developmental and family history and recent events in the patient's life, we can inform the family about the patient's progress and answer their questions, and the family can help us with discharge plans, especially where the patient will live with the parents or have close contact with them.
>
> Mr. and Mrs. Dalton readily accepted my invitation and agreed to provide the necessary data. In subsequent sessions, however, they resisted my efforts to treat them. The more I tried, the more they resisted. I had never openly acknowledged the covert aim. I was too uncomfortable to state directly that in this instance they may be part of their son's problem.

Naturally, most parents worry about being blamed for their children's illness, and the extent to which their own difficulties will be exposed. The covert agenda mobilizes their defense system, closing off engagement possibilities. Contrast the Daltons' experience with that of the parents of a 16-year-old girl recently hospitalized as schizophrenic following her attempt to strangle her 4-year-old foster sister.

> After greeting Mr. and Mrs. Parker, I discussed the purpose of our getting together and mentioned that mothers and fathers often have worries about how their children became ill and also what happens to them in the hospital. They may also wonder what to expect when their child goes home for the weekend. I said I would like to help them with any worries and questions they may have, and at the same time, I needed their help with our trying to understand Linda.
>
> Mrs. Parker responded that Linda had had no troubles, no temper tantrums, no feeding problems. "We always thought she was a happy child and it's hard for us to understand what went wrong. I want to know what went wrong, what caused this to happen? Can you tell us, or don't you know? Or do you know and won't tell us?"
>
> I replied, "There hasn't been enough time for us really to understand how this all came about, but I will always share with you anything I know. Right now, we want you to know that in this type of illness there is usually no single factor, no single experience, that one can point to as the cause. There may be biochemical factors in this illness which we still don't understand. There can also be emotional experiences that only Linda may have perceived to be significant. She might have been feeling pressure and building up anxiety, and you and I need to understand that, too."
>
> Mr. Parker noticeably relaxed and shared some recollections about when he first began to suspect that Linda was having trouble.

A direct statement about the natural worries that all parents have is both reassuring and inviting. It relieves the parents' fears of negative judgments and blame. In contrast, a covert agenda creates barriers to client–worker communication and diminishes the worker's and agency's credibility.

Social workers' discomfort about intruding into the privacy of people's lives, or their ambivalence about leaving the safety of the office can be easily communicated to clients. A worker might demonstrate reluctance by offering a service mechanically, without the enthusiasm of genuine involvement, and investment. Out of discomfort, another might focus on forming a positive relationship, intending to gradually ease into the "serious" business later. This assumes wrongly that the relationship is the goal of the work, as though it were the solution to the problem. It overlooks the fact that a relationship emerges out of the quality of the work done together, and is a vehicle through which the work proceeds. If the worker is preoccupied with forming a "good relationship," attention and energy will be deflected away from the client's concerns and will interfere with the worker's ability to help.[10] In offering a group service to a group of orthopedically handicapped children, or to a group of adolescents in foster care, for example, honesty and clarity of purpose demand that the social worker be secure enough to refer directly to the common tasks the groups face as physically handicapped children or as foster teenagers. Without this, the ambiguity will block the children's understanding of why they are there and how they can use the group. Yet, some workers fear that such candor will interfere with the relationship when, in fact, it helps create mutual trust.[11]

After defining the agency's service, the worker invites and waits for client responses so that misunderstandings or inappropriate expectations can then be explored and clarified. The client is encouraged to consider the agency's services and the worker's function in the light of his concerns; the worker explores clues that point to doubts or ambivalence about becoming engaged with the agency, the worker, and the proposed service modality. Honesty and openness in communication are thus established at the outset, and the way is open toward achieving a tentative common understanding. When client and worker agree about the nature of the problem, they are then ready to consider and explore the salient areas in the client's life situation that are relevant to goal-setting and problem resolution.

Exploration to reach mutual understanding is more difficult with the *involuntary client who denies need.* Here, the effort must be directed to finding a common ground between the stress experienced by the environment, which resulted in the referral, and some area of discomfort in the client that fits social work purpose and the agency's function. In some instances, this common ground can only be formulated as helping the client get the worker and the agency ''off his back''; that is, helping the prisoner or the mental patient achieve the tasks that will make it possible for him to move out of the institution, helping the neglectful parents to improve their child care so they may be free of agency surveillance, or helping the delinquent adolescent to achieve the tasks that will release him from clinic attendance and/or probation. Frequently, this involves a sequencing of objectives in accordance with client priorities. In the case of neglectful parents, for example, their own personal needs of a concrete nature must be met before they can think about and respond to the needs of their children. In a prison setting, prisoners often require help with day-to-day experiences in their harsh environment before they can deal with the tasks of preparing for the outside world.

Exploration or the concern of an inquiring mind, together with the caring heart, marks the skilled and effective practitioner. Exploration is a process that continues through the life of a case, with humility and recognition that one can never fully know another human being. While it pervades the entire process, the need for accurate problem definition requires at the outset a preponderance of exploratory activities on the part of worker and client. As we saw in chapter 1, defining the problem accurately is critical in determining what is done about the problem, need, or predicament in which the client finds himself. It must be accomplished as early as possible, even though the definition may shift as new facts emerge and the work goes on. In a service profession, as contrasted with a science or an academic discipline, the practitioner deals with uncertainties, or at best, probabilities. He must, therefore, be prepared to take risks into the unknown where need requires it, but always with as much thoughtful analysis and assessment of situations as are possible at the moment when intervention is required.

A complex epistemological issue is inherent, however, in the ecological perspective. On the one hand, the perspective requires an understanding of the client's life space broad and holistic enough to aid in defining the problem accurately, sifting out the important factors that social work intervention can affect, and locating the personal strengths and situational assets which can be engaged for problem resolution. Yet, the immediacy and pressing nature of the stresses that bring people to social work preclude the broad and deep scanning of the field of systems that holism seems to imply. Moreover, it is questionable whether one can understand the whole (the life space) before one has understood the parts and their interrelationships. Yet, if one begins with the parts, one may miss the emergent properties of the whole.[12]

Three concepts that are useful in dealing with this dilemma of the exploration process are relevance, salience, and individualization.[13] The way in which the problem itself is defined determines the direction and content of exploration. Thus, relevance of information is related to the nature of the problem or predicament, and it is this relation that guides the inquiry and shapes the observation and collection of data on which the exploration rests. If a set of circumstances is defined as a personality disturbance, as in the medical model, the data collected and interpreted will be of a particular nature. If the same set of circumstances is defined as the outcome of transactions between the person and various elements of his social environment, as in the life model, the data collected and interpreted will be of a different nature.

Salience refers to the dominant features of the client's felt need and of the life situation as guides to exploration. One does not review exhaustively the total life space, but particularizes its features according to the salient transactions affecting the presenting request/need. While the worker remains receptive to historical material, for example, he does not regard it as essential for understanding the present. Historical explanations tend to take on the character of self-fulfilling prophecies—what has been determines what is and what will be. Historical material tends to be selective in the questions asked by the worker or the answers provided by the client. Historical material given later by the client as it assumes significance for him, however, represents a different process at work from the worker's routine collection of social history at the outset. Given later, history serves client need; collected early, it serves agency need.

Individualization seeks to maintain a constant focus on the whole person as a unique entity, including the social context in which he is embedded, as one seeks to gather relevant information concerning the salient features of the need.

Contracting

Contracting refers to the process through which the client and worker reach a shared definition of the problem and an explicit mutual agreement about their goals, tasks, respective roles, and terms of work. A social work contract should be characterized by mutuality and clarity. For understanding and agreement to be mutual, both worker and client have to participate in problem definition, exploration and assessment, the setting of priorities, and the planning of initial strategies. A client's statement of need or an agency's offer of service does not represent a mutual agreement until client and worker have reached an explicit understanding about their foci and methods. For the understanding and agreement to have meaning, they have to be specific and clear. This requires a partialization of the client's service requests or identified needs, as well as the agency's service resources and expectations.[14]

A mutually and clearly established contract serves important functions. It reduces some of the power discrepancy between client and worker at a time when client is under stress and vulnerable to manipulation or misuse of agency and professional authority. Contracting engages the client's motivation and cognition in setting goals and tasks, and in assuming responsibility for working on them. Moreover, it develops reciprocal accountability for problem definition, assessment, planning, and intervention which provides a base at termination for assessing accomplishments, planning future directions, and evaluating service outcomes. Most immediately, contracting gives structure and focus to the work, decreases anxiety associated with fear of the unknown and the ambiguity inherent in beginnings, and mobilizes energy for work.

In the contracting process, client concerns are considered within the framework of problems in living. Foster adolescents invited to participate in a group, for example, can be helped to sort their concerns into: environmental issues, including school, foster care agency, and peer group; life transitional issues, including identity concerns related to foster status, race, and gender; and interpersonal issues, including communication and relationship problems in the natural and foster families. The worker and client develop and specify priorities among the various concerns identified, creating a sense of mutual purpose, focus, and direction. If the purpose and direction of the work are unclear or unspecified, the worker and client will struggle with persistent ambiguities. A lack of structure and focus causes immediate anxiety and distance between worker and client. A newly formed adolescent group illustrates this problem.

> I then stated that they had common interests and concerns, like most teenage boys, and said that their presence would give them an opportunity to discuss these concerns. I emphasized the fact that it was their group and it would, therefore, be their decision as to what they wanted to talk about. B entered . . . sat down without taking his coat off. I asked if they had any questions. Each of them said no.
>
> After a long period of silence, I asked if they were in favor of attending the meeting when they first heard about it. Y said that he wasn't. F said he didn't mind coming. I asked if they would like to talk about girls, and there was a long period of silence. . . .

The worker left undefined the agency's service and his role. He made no effort to elicit the members' understanding about purpose, function, common interest, and concerns. Their foster status was unrecognized, probably generating anxiety about a hidden agenda, such as re-placement. His invitation to "talk about girls" was met with a bewildered and alarmed silence when identification of common tasks had not been established. Contrast this with the worker's ability subsequently to offer a simple and clear statement of service purpose, roles, and general concern.

> I stated that I was a social worker with the Department of Welfare, but I would not be visiting their homes or schools because they had their own social workers for that purpose. I also mentioned that all the boys in the group are foster kids and that their concerns and problems are quite common. I paused, and there was silence. I said: "How about it, are you concerned about your own parents, foster parents, and about who you are and where you come from?" M said: "About our own parents, Mr. B . . . the only thing that bothers me is that they tell you

> about them." I asked M what he meant. He said: "After you live in a foster home from the time you were a baby and think that you are living with your own parents, your social worker comes by one day and tells you that the people you are living with are not your real parents." I replied that it is a rough deal and asked if the others felt the same way. F said he always knew he was a foster child and knows the reason. F wanted to know why M was a foster child, and said he didn't have to answer if it were too personal. M said he didn't mind telling the group. He then asked me if I had ever been downtown near the W——— Department Store. I said I had been in the area a couple of times. He asked F the same question and F said yes. M continued: "Well, there is a man who sells pretzels in front of the store all year round." He hesitated, smiled and said, "He's my real father." Though M smiled as he informed us of this, there were no smiles from the other boys . . . M continued to tell his story, the others listened, exchanged observations, and then moved into a discussion of fathers' drinking, what drinking means to them, etc.[15]

While the worker's offer of service and asking for response may have been somewhat awkward, his directness reduced the youngsters' anxieties about his role and motivation. Their commonalities as foster youth, and their shared developmental, environmental, and familial concerns provided common reference points. Their energy was released for mutual engagement, and the work began.

When a sense of mutual focus, purpose, and direction becomes clear, the worker can then help to develop mutual tasks for client and worker. A ten-year-old boy, Ken, had been placed in a treatment institution because of disruptive behavior in school and at home:

> Ken and I reached agreement that we would focus on his discharge, getting him back home with his parents. Ken agreed to discuss with me any concerns or problems arising in the placement (cottage, school, peers, staff), or at home, during visits. Ken's objective was to avoid any situation that could delay his return home. He asked me to

> help him deal with the cottage staff, and to get a change of program activities from the recreation department. After exploring these issues, I sensed a validity to his assessment. We planned how to proceed, and decided I should accompany him to meet with them. We then decided to use our session to rehearse what he wanted to say to the staff, and agreed that I would contact them beforehand to prepare them for his efforts.

The worker recognized that Ken had primary responsibility for task accomplishment. She assumed responsibility for providing the necessary conditions that would help assure Ken's accomplishment of his task, such as securing resources and intervening with staff.[16] She also explored Ken's expectations of her so that a clear and mutual understanding of respective role responsibilities could be established. Together, Ken and the social worker specified their goal, developed a structure for their work, and identified mutual tasks related to the goal, and to developmental, interpersonal, and environmental concerns.

Contracting requires particular skills used differentially according to age, sex, cultural norms, cognitive styles, level of social functioning, and agency setting. Children, for example, often require an informal, low-keyed approach, with spontaneous responsiveness to their styles and rhythms of interaction; several sessions may be required before a contract is explicit or acknowledged. Adults with impaired cognitive or social functioning require direction and structure, so the worker may be quite active in helping the client to articulate problems–needs, goals, and tasks. In exploring and contracting with a group of mentally retarded adults, for example, the worker assumes an active, orchestrating role. She defines common tasks, and links individual members to them. The worker occupies a central position of influence, encouraging interaction, gradually building it from dyads to triads, and from there to the group as a whole. Clear and simple tasks, such as making coffee together, provide a climate of security for the members. Clarity and mutuality in such a group evolve slowly because purpose, tasks, and the structure for work are not easily developed. Time and attention must be given to the exploring and contracting processes over the life of the group. The worker may need to refer frequently to joint purpose and respective tasks. From time to time she may also need to elicit the clients' views about their work together to the degree possible.

Adults with a greater degree of autonomy, self-esteem, and confidence usually require minimal direction and structure.[17] The worker must guard against dampening cognitive action by taking over too much of the contracting, as though she lacked confidence in the clients' abilities and strengths. Extending open-ended invitations to set the terms of the work provides individuals and groups with opportunities for decision-making and action. With an adoptive parents' group, for example, the social worker invited the members to define the group's purpose, set priorities, and specify the tasks and conditions for work. She assumed a supportive, guiding role, seeking to promote the environmental conditions for group-directed functioning. She began by suggesting possible purposes for the group.

> By way of opening this first group meeting (of a series of four), I remarked that the couples had been parents for a matter of months now . . . many of them are still in the early stages of parenthood and are trying to make adjustments required of them in their new roles as parents. We in the agency thought it would help them if they could get together and share their thinking and their experiences in their new roles, what this new experience has meant to each of them, what adjustments have been necessary, what unexpected problems have been encountered, and what they anticipate in the future. What did they think?
>
> They began first with the joys and then moved to some adjustments in life style, including babysitting problems. As they shared some of these things, one or two referred tentatively to their concerns about feeling inadequate as parents.

Contracting includes attention to the advantages and disadvantages of individual, family, or group modalities, or some combination of them. This is a difficult area of decision-making. Organizational constraints and rationalizations, expressed as "we don't have a room big enough," "we're not set up to supervise work with groups or families," "our clients are not interested in groups," etc., inhibit the worker's flexible response to need and the exercise of professional judgment. But also criteria for selection of modality are lacking. Theory and research to guide the practitioner in the selection of the family modality as opposed to the individual modality are limited. Nor are there explicit criteria—beyond custom, tradition and the influence of the medical model—for the selection of the individual over the family or group modalities.

The definition of the problem itself may be a useful factor in the choice of modality. If the problem is located by worker and client in the area of family relationships and communication, family structure and boundary processes, or family tasks and functions, then the usefulness of the family modality needs to be considered. The living unit related by blood, marriage, or association is the natural modality of choice except where specifically contraindicated (as in an older adolescent's struggle for autonomy, perhaps, or a marital partner's firm decision to terminate a troubled marriage). Within the living unit itself the sibling, the marital, or parent-child subsystems may represent an appropriate focus of attention. A combination of family, subsystems, and individual contacts can be helpful, depending upon the nature of the problem, the rhythm and tempo of family life, life tasks of the family, and the developmental tasks of individual members.

There are few criteria guiding the selection of the group modality for individual clients. Nevertheless, where members share a common set of life concerns and tasks, the group modality provides multiple opportunities for human relatedness, mutual aid, and learning task-related coping skills. The worker can help the client to consider entering a group in place of, or in addition to, individual sessions. In many agencies, individual services are assumed at the outset, whereas agency and worker should be open to exploring with clients the relative advantages of family, group, and individual modalities.

In contracting with families and groups, members' perceptions of their problems and needs may be disparate, so they may not agree about problem definition, goals, and tasks. The worker will need to help the members develop mutual understanding of each others' views of the situation, and their hopes about it. By her supportiveness, the worker helps each member attend the sessions despite the pain or threat and, once present, to express his or her views. When consensus develops, it is possible to establish priorities among the identified concerns, to clarify goals, and to set tasks.

Time is a significant aspect of service to be considered in contracting. Crisis theory underscores the importance of rapid response to need and suggests the usefulness of brief, focused, and immediate service with frequent sessions as needed until the crisis is past. Research indicates that even aside from crisis situations, planned brief services to individuals and families in many instances are associated with more positive outcomes and more positive views of the service than open-ended temporal arrangements.[18] Experience suggests that in time-limited groups, the time factor helps the members to focus quickly on their concerns, and to maintain purpose and direction. In settings where there is a frequent turnover of clients, the advantages and disadvantages of a short-term group of one or two sessions must be weighed against those of a continuous group having changing membership. A short-term group creates a sense of immediacy and urgency; a continuing, open-ended group provides an opportunity for experienced members to assist newer members.

In contracting, account must be taken of the different ways people experience time according to age, culture, physical, and psychological states.[19] Unless these variations are taken into account, agencies and institutions may be out of phase with their clients. In work with the physically ill, for example, the fevered patient's accelerated sense of time might require that contracting reflect quick responses to patient requests for service. The fact that time passes slowly for the young and speeds by for the old has implications for contracting and planning. In work with children, placement decisions, planning, and the frequency and duration of sessions must be geared to the child's orientation to present time and his limited awareness of future time. Mutual aid is not easily established in children's groups where meetings are held only once a week, so that more frequent sessions are desirable. Young children usually benefit from short sessions of less than forty-five minutes.

Contracting with the elderly must take into account the aged person's sense of fleeting time, so that delays or postponements are scrupulously avoided. Depending on the members' physical and emotional states, most adult groups, even those for the elderly, can sustain work on group tasks in sessions of one and one-half to two hours' duration. Frequency depends upon members' and worker's resources and capacity. Open-ended groups with changing membership gain more from frequent meetings than do time-limited groups. Crisis groups, such as those for the recently widowed or post-surgery patients, benefit from several sessions a week, at least until the crisis is past.

Cultural orientations to time affect people's regard for punctuality, their interpretations of long waits, their attempts to prolong or to shorten interviews, and the value they place on the past, present, or future. Such variations need to be considered during the contracting process—and throughout the contact—in planning the respective responsibilities and tasks of client and worker. Without such consideration, there is a danger that the client will be viewed as resistant or unmotivated, and the worker will be viewed as uncaring and uninterested.

Interviews with individuals are generally thought to be most productive when kept to an hour's duration or less, although this idea has become somewhat ritualized into the fifty-minute hour once a week, and is sometimes rationalized on the basis of transference and dependency phenomena. It seems wise to remember that stressful life events and processes do not easily accommodate themselves to agencies' and institutions' temporal structures, so that meeting more frequently or less frequently, for longer than an hour or less than an hour may be helpful. Temporal arrangements made by worker and client in contracting or in later changes and re-contracting should, to the degree possible, fit the nature of the problem, the agreed-upon goals, and the client's own temporal resources and orientations rather than organizational convenience or ideology alone.

The social worker and client must, in contracting, also consider the options available in the locale of service. Home visits, office visits, and other sites such as school, work place, playground, library, senior citizen center, hospital waiting room, park bench, tenement stoop, automobile or any other point in the client's life space offer advantages and disadvantages that need to be weighed.

Problem definition, goals, tasks, roles, conditions, modalities, and temporal arrangements may be evaluated, re-evaluated, and renegotiated as the work continues. Contracting and re-contracting as integral parts of the helping process are flexible, dynamic and continuous processes that must remain sensitive to changes that occur. In concrete services or crisis-oriented services, in particular, there may be an interest by both client and worker in continuing their work after the limited goal has been achieved. Re-contracting will be required to encompass a different set of needs with different goals and tasks:

Helen, age 17, white, unmarried, high school senior, was seen in an abortion clinic. She was brought in by her mother for her second abortion in six months. Despite Helen's sullen, monosyllabic, and seemingly indifferent mien, the situation appeared to be a crisis because Helen was in the twelfth week of pregnancy, requiring a major (saline) procedure. It was clear that Helen was having serious school, peer, and family problems, but the contracting process was limited to her immediate need for information and support in the three sessions available before the abortion.

After the abortion, the worker offered continued service based on her perception that Helen was concerned about her situation. Helen responded to the worker's invitation to return, saying there were a lot of things going on in her life and she needed someone to talk to. Together, worker and client identified new problems, set new goals, and began to gather new data needed for their joint understanding. In the process, a new agreement was reached to work on Helen's relationship with her boyfriend. Although both client and worker recognized the connections between this relationship and her family and school problems, "we decided to take up each specific problem or issue, one at a time, and Helen and I agreed that her relationship to her boyfriend was a good place to begin. Not only is he a major figure in her life, but their relationship has many ramifications, including the two abortions."

Throughout the helping process, an important task for the worker is to seek client feedback. Such questions as, "Are we working on our agreed upon goals and tasks?"; "Is our style, rhythm, and pace of working satisfactory, or should we change any aspect?"; "Are we fulfilling our mutual responsibilities?" can elicit the necessary information from the client. In this way, potential tensions and incongruences are identified and can be handled before they become serious obstacles to communication, and focus and direction are maintained.

Finally, there are the intangibles of practice, difficult to specify or to conceptualize, which represent the subtle nuances of human interaction. They provide context and meaning. As worker and client participate in the entry phase, the client has to experience the worker's faith and commitment to the helping process, and a sense of hope that their joint effort will be beneficial. This happens when the worker truly believes in what she is doing. In the entry phase, as in all aspects of the helping process, knowledge and skill must be blended with personal style, creativity, and commitment.

Case Illustrations

John Fein

John Fein, 23-year-old, lower class Jewish man had received a dishonorable discharge from the army because of his behavior. He and his family had been known to the family agency for a number of years. John stammered and as a child he experienced ridicule from other children. He learned to cope primarily through withdrawing from peers and by occasional aggression. When John returned from army service, his parents became alarmed because his aggression turned toward them and he began to have fights on his job. Mrs. Fein requested the agency's help for her son. An experienced worker who had known John as a teenager reached out to him by letter and telephone. He arrived at her office looking quite sad.

> I greeted John. I described my conversation with his mother, sharing her concerns and my desire to be of help to him. He responded, "I am tongue-tied, I can't talk to you." I responded that I knew it was difficult, but encouraged him to share his concerns. He exclaimed, "Well, I have a picture in my mind. I am sure your picture is different from mine. We don't see the same picture." I encouraged him to tell me about his picture. Hesitatingly he responded, "It's a big city," and then he withdrew into silence.
>
> After a short period of time, I asked him if he were in the picture. He explained, "No, I don't like the city. People are not communicating. Everybody is going the same way. It's hard to live in that kind of environment." He no-

ticed that I looked puzzled and commented, "You don't understand, do you?" I asked him to have some patience with me, that I was really trying to understand him and would need his help.

He said, "Okay, let me give you another example: Suppose you're in the army, you want to get into a building, and a soldier is guarding the entrance. How would you get in without using violence?" After thinking a while, I stated that indeed this was a difficult problem, and that I probably would go to the commanding officer and try to get a pass. John became silent. I asked, "What's the matter, John? Try to tell me what you are thinking right now." He slowly responded, "I would never have thought of that answer. I would have . . . " Gently, I said, "I think you are asking how you can do something without pushing or hitting."

After a silence, he described fights he had had recently on his job, with his sister, and with his mother. He exclaimed, "Authority tells you what to do. You don't want to do it. You see it another way." I asked, "Who is the authority, John?" He responded, "Oh, the army, work, school, parents." I said I was beginning to understand—he is having a lot of trouble explaining to these authorities his ideas, what he wants—they don't understand him. So he had to do something—shout, push, anything.

His facial movement suggested that I was with him, so I continued, "John, I want to help you with these troubles. You are helping me understand what hurts you, what you are unhappy about." He responded with much feeling, "Yeah, I want to be happy; but, do you know what happiness is? It's like when you've got an old shirt full of holes and somebody gives you a new shirt—then you are happy."

I said, "John, I think people have holes inside of them, too." He exclaimed, "Yeah—like loneliness, boredom, being scared." I responded, "That's right, John, you need help with those holes—it's not as easy as getting

> a new shirt.'' He asked me if I could repair his holes. I suggested that he could be his own builder, and that I want very much to help him with these holes as they affect his job and his relationships with his friends and parents. He replied, ''Yeah, I am starting to see what I can talk to you about . . . I had no idea when I came . . . my troubles at work and home . . . maybe you'll understand me.''
>
> I supported his understanding, suggesting we could meet every week at this time. I told him that I would try very hard to help him deal with these authorities. Sometimes, he might think, I'm one of those ''authorities'' who didn't understand, but I said I hoped he would try to tell me when that happens. He stood up, after I said our time was up, and shook my hand, stating, ''That's a deal. See you next week—same time, same day, same station.''

The worker decodes John's cryptic messages. She encourages him to share his picture, struggling to understand, and to enter his life space. She requests his assistance in the decoding process, and demonstrates her increasing cognitive and affective comprehension of his life stresses. She is creative in clarifying their roles and specifying tasks in dealing with friends, parents, etc. Her warmth, caring, and willingness to risk sets the tone for the beginning interview.

Mrs. Grattan

Mrs. Grattan, age 43, telephoned the family agency asking for help for herself and her five children, ages 6 to 17. She and her husband had been divorced for a year, and he had since remarried. While the children present no problems at school, their behavior at home is very difficult. Following visits with their father, the children are even more unmanageable. Mrs. Grattan cried on the telephone, and said she felt completely overwhelmed. The children know she is asking for help, but the oldest boy, who will be going to college in the fall, refuses to participate. An appointment was made for the following week for the family to be seen together. In the interval, the worker considered the many stresses the family is under. Mrs. Grattan's change in status from wife to divorcée, particularly as she faces the developmental tasks of the middle years, her impending ''loss'' of the oldest son, coupled with the loss of her husband; the developmental tasks faced by each of the children at their various stages of adolescence and childhood, now made more complex by the loss of their father; and, finally, the impact of that loss on family structure and functions. The worker recorded the first session:

> There was silence in response to my question if they understood why they were here, and if they could tell me what they understood to be the reason why they had come. When there was no immediate response, I commented on the possibility that they felt strange and uncomfortable coming to a strange place and talking to someone like me whom they did not know. I told them the name of the agency, who I was, and what I was here for. There was then a lengthy dialogue between Mrs. Grattan and John (age 15) about the arrangements for coming and John's feelings that the whole problem was the fault of Gary (age 17), who was not present. John said, "I can handle myself, there's no reason for me to be here, what other problems are there? It's just that you cry like you're doing now, and you and Gary can't get along." Tearfully, Mrs. Grattan looked at John and said, "You know what my concerns are," and he shrugged. I commented, "I don't know, and maybe the other children don't know, so can you say more about what is worrying you?" Mrs. Grattan looked at Margaret (age 6) and said Margaret has a problem going to school and clinging to her mother. I asked how long Margaret had been troubled about school and leaving her mother, and Mrs. Grattan said that it started after the divorce.
>
> I wondered if the divorce and everyone's reaction to it was something we should discuss. John said, "Oh that, I have no feelings about it." I expressed a little surprise at this, and commented that most children, even a boy of 15, would have some feelings about his parents getting a divorce, and the father not being in the home. John said he might have at first, but he was too busy now to think about it. There was then another dialogue between John and his

mother about his feelings and his activities. I said that most of the exchange so far had been between Mrs. Grattan and John, and I wondered about the other children. No one said anything, and I turned to Eliot (age 11) and asked what he thought about coming here. He just shrugged. I asked him if he had comments about what his mother and John had talked about, and he shrugged again. Then I told him I was interested in how he felt about the divorce and the fact that his father was not living at home. He said he didn't know, he's getting used to the idea. I wondered if he missed his father. He said, "Why should I miss him, I see him." John and Eliot then argued about the way that Eliot fights with Margaret and Betsy (age 8). Eliot said the girls are silly and make a lot of noise and bother him. If they would leave him alone, he wouldn't bother them. I looked at Margaret and Betsy and asked if they did bother Eliot? Betsy shrugged and moved further down in her chair. At this point, John defended the girls and said to his mother, "You don't know how to handle them because you always end up crying." Mrs. Grattan said there is something wrong when all this is going on in a family, and she mentioned her concern about Betsy, who has nightmares, wakes up crying and screaming, "No, mother, don't do that." She doesn't know what it is that Betsy is afraid of. Everyone turned and looked at Betsy and I said it looked as if we were all expecting her to tell us if she knew what she was afraid of. She shrugged and said she didn't know. In response to some comment from me, she did say she misses her daddy.

I said how difficult it is for everyone in the family when there is a divorce, and even though members of the family accept it, a divorce can still make everyone feel very angry. Very often, children feel more angry at the mother than at the father. John denied this, and Mrs. Grattan said there was truth in this, even though the children had been told why the divorce had to be. I added that very often the mother gets concerned about the children and feels less able to manage now that she is alone. Mrs. Grat-

> tan nodded vigorously. I also said that many times both adults and children feel sad and a sense of loss which are painful feelings, but many times what they express instead is anger and dissatisfaction. Perhaps they need to talk about their sadness and the fact that they miss their father, and we could do this here.
>
> I told them I would see them again as a family, and that I hoped Gary would join us. I explained that I felt it best to see their mother alone next week. The week after that we would all meet together, so we could sort out the feelings everyone has about the divorce and about their father not living with them anymore. I asked what they thought of this plan. The children nodded their acceptance, except for John who said he had no reason to come because he didn't have any problems. I said I knew he felt that way, but he is a member of the family too, and I would like to have him come to the next family interview. I also commented that he is probably resentful that Gary can refuse to come, and yet he comes, and I expressed appreciation for his willingness to cooperate, even though he didn't think it was necessary. With that we said goodbye, and Mrs. Grattan smiled through her tears and said she would see me next week.

In asking for the children's understanding of why they were there, the worker wishes to clarify possible misconceptions, relate to any fears, and to note the ways in which Mrs. Grattan did or didn't prepare the children. When they don't respond, she recognizes their discomfort openly, and then clarifies the nature and function of the agency, and what her role is.

As Mrs. Grattan and John argue about the arrangements for coming, the worker picks up on Mrs. Grattan's statement about her concerns. At the same time she attempts to draw in the other children by legitimizing their need to know mother's concerns. Mrs. Grattan's reference to Margaret's troubles having begun after the divorce is used by the worker to focus on the divorce and what it has meant to each member. She recognizes John's resistance and attempts to reduce it by suggesting that pain about the divorce is a natural feeling.

She attempts to bring in the other children, but it is hard going, as she invites first one and then another to share their feelings. The children are unable or unwilling to do this, and she again suggests their probable feelings of sadness and anger. This, she hopes, will pave the way for the children to use subsequent sessions. She indicates this will be the purpose of their meetings together, and suggests that the family discomfort lies in the tasks related to the loss of the father. She asks for and receives their acceptance of the plan. Her commendation of John's cooperation, despite his anger that Gary has avoided coming, and her expectation that all family members will come, are also important parts of the initial contracting.

Sensing Mrs. Grattan's high level of anxiety, the worker made a professional judgment to see her alone the next week, but conveyed her respect for the children by sharing next steps with them. The exploratory process will continue in order to clarify the nature of the problem and the interacting forces contributing to the problem. It is not yet clear, for example, whether the difficulties in family relationships and communications came into existence with the divorce, or whether there are other factors involved within the sibling and the parent–child subsystems. Strengths within the social context will need to be identified. Nevertheless, in this first interview, the children's feelings are supported, the mother's difficult tasks are recognized, and the beginnings of engagement can be observed.

A Group of Cardiac Patients

A social worker in a Veterans' Hospital had invited eleven cardiac patients to form a group.

> After the refreshments and introductions, I said—as I had explained to each one of them individually—that they were invited to participate in a four-session group for patients with recent heart attacks. The staff believed they could be helpful to each other in dealing with their reactions, concerns about hospitalization, illness, and what the future had in store.
>
> Bill indicated that it was the specific problem of work which worries him the most. Mario, Hector, and John agreed. In an agitated way, Bill continued, "If the doctor

won't let me go back to longshoreman's work, what can I do? It's been twenty-seven years of my life and I always put in an honest day. Now the doctor says give it up. What kind of bullshit is that? Doesn't he realize that I have family and financial obligations?'' Lenny agreed, stating angrily that the doctors didn't care that a medical recommendation could destroy a man's life.

I asked if they were mostly annoyed about what their doctors said, or how they said it, or both?

Hector explained that he thought it was a doctor's responsibility to make work recommendations in order to protect health, no matter what the economic consequences were. He, for example, has ended up on relief, and that's been hard to swallow. Bill responded with intensity that no doctor was ever going to do that to him, and he let out a barrage of angry words. Mario suggested that Bill was doing what he has stopped doing—taking out the anger at the doctor's recommendation on his own heart. Hector said he understood Bill's being fighting mad because he, also, is having a hell of a time living with his ''bum ticker.'' He is just beginning to calm down and realize that it will never be the same. Bill shook his head in disbelief, ''How can I be calm, I have a family to take care of?'' Lenny explained that he also has a family, but getting excited and upset will only lead to another heart attack. Andy supported Bill, adding that this was certainly hard for a family man. Peter exclaimed, ''But shit, commonsense will tell a man that health is the only important thing and everything else has to become second.'' Most members agreed that if they let themselves get excited or experience too much pressure, they would only hurt themselves.

Bill became angry again, telling group members that they had to be as dumb as the doctors to be forgetting their problems. Bill's eyes teared as he shouted, ''If the doctor says give up longshoreman work and truck driving where I feel like a real man, what am I going to turn to? Who is going to hire me? What good am I?'' Lenny suggested Bill calm down. Mario suggested Bill talk to his boss and ask about a light job. Bill felt insulted by the suggestion and shouted that he has pride and isn't going to degrade himself and tell the boss to pity him . . . to give him crumbs . . . to kiss his ass. What kind of man did Mario think he was, anyway? Mario answered, "I think you are a good man and I respect you. I know a wounded animal has to fight for his brood. But Bill, you have brains, you have to listen to your body and accept its limits. It takes a man to talk to your boss about lighter work."

I suggested that it seemed some of them have made peace with their hearts, while others were still fighting it. Either way, I realized how much pain they were under.

Peter implored Bill to take it easy, to accept his heart condition. Bill insisted that his boss wouldn't give him light work because it would raise insurance rates. He described his boss as being "between sweat, shit, and the floor," that he wasn't a man. At this point, Bill began to sob. The air was heavy with painful silence.

Several of the members tried to change the subject, but I encouraged the others to share their struggles. Walter referred to the mortgage and his family's food needs. Hector talked about his pension and how it helps. In a disgusted tone, Bill wanted to know what he was going to do with an $80-a-month pension.

Mario spoke quietly, but firmly. "Bill, I can see you are a big man, strong, and you can beat anybody here in a fight, but I'm gonna tell you something, you gotta stop crying and be a real man, that means accept what is, do what has to be done, face the facts. You want to help your family, you ain't gonna help them by killing yourself. You have to cut down on your expectations, do what the doctors say, and start to build a new life."

Everyone waited for Bill's reaction. He stared at Mario as if trying to decide what to do. After a while, he said, "I guess I could sell my home and buy a smaller one. My oldest son can go to work." Peter put his hand on Bill's back, saying that it was much better to be a live father than a dead one. Hector agreed, suggesting that they were all afraid of the same thing, but handle it differently. Each man then spoke of how he had changed or planned to change life styles and habits, of his fears, and the group members' common objective: "Life!" Bill said how helpful the guys have been. He continued, "I'm a man, and I'll do what has to be done. I'll even talk to my wife about working, and you know how hard that is for the Italian race." Peter responded that as a black man, he learned a long time ago about wives going to work, and it didn't make it any easier.

At the end, I asked what they thought of our first meeting, and many said it was helpful to see that others struggle with the same kinds of problems. Mario's comment caught the essence: "It's like we are in the same boat trying to keep from drowning. Talking can help us to stay afloat." We agreed on the place and time of our next meeting.

The worker's simple, straightforward statement of the group's purpose, her reference to their common concerns and her interest in their feedback is all the group needed to begin developing its own processes of mutual aid. The intensity of feelings and concerns associated with heart attacks propels the group into work, requiring minimal assistance from the worker. Ethnic diversity in the group's composition (Black, Irish, Italian, Puerto Rican, Jewish) provides richness and vitality to their helping efforts. The time-limited nature of the service, related to the crisis of heart attack, is an added dynamic in the group's willingness to move quickly into their common tasks of dealing with life and death fears, concerns about their families' well-being, their ability to work, and their self-images as "whole" men.

Summary

Before even seeing the client, the worker prepares himself to engage the client. He examines available data and develops tentative inferences about the client's situation and their initial encounter. Through anticipatory empathy, he views the client's perception of reality through her eyes. This is accomplished through processes of identification, incorporation, reverberation, and detachment. Preparatory understanding needs to be flexible, multi-dimensional, and open to subsequent data and impressions, and never stereotypic.

An important consideration in the preparation process is the degree of choice available to the actual or potential client in accepting or rejecting a service. The act of seeking help may be stressful. Sensitive preparation enables the worker to create a welcoming atmosphere and to elicit client concerns, expectations, apprehensions, and confusion. In reaching out to a potential client, the proffered service must reflect a felt need. Introductory correspondence, telephone or personal contacts need to communicate genuine concern and responsiveness to the potential client's perceptions of her situation. Imposed services require special preparation. The worker must take into account that she may represent a potential threat or obstacle to the person occupying an undesired status—such as the parolee—or seeking a desired status—such as an adoptive parent. The client's perceptions and expectations need to be considered in preparing to enter his life space.

Initial sessions are critical to the helping process and affect ultimate outcomes. A worker's entry skills enlist the potential client's acceptance of and engagement in social work services. If the client has sought the service, the worker invites the client "to tell her story," to elaborate her concerns and needs. The worker establishes a climate of courtesy, support, and acceptance, responding to the client's verbal and nonverbal messages. Beginning with the problem–need itself, the worker seeks to develop a mutual assessment of where the problem is located and how it manifests itself. Together, social worker and client consider the problem's onset, duration, and intensity. If the agency has initiated the contact by offering or imposing a service, the worker begins by defining the agency's service and his role clearly and explicitly. He invites and waits for client responses, so that misunderstandings or inappropriate expectations can be explored and clarified. Honesty and openness in communication are set forth at the outset, and the way is open for achieving a tentative common understanding.

Through processes of exploration and contracting, client and worker reach a shared definition of the problem and an explicit mutual agreement about their goals, tasks, respective roles, and terms of work. These processes serve important functions in reducing some of the power discrepancy between client and worker. The client's motivation and cognition are engaged in assuming responsibility for involvement in the helping process to the degree possible. A structure and focus is provided to the work, and this decreases anxiety associated with ambiguity inherent in new experiences. And reciprocal accountability for the method and content of the work is established.

Skills in exploration and contracting are adapted to age, sex, cultural norms, cognitive styles, level of social functioning, and agency setting. The degree of direction and structure varies with client need. The worker, for example, may be quite active with cognitively impaired clients in helping them to articulate needs, goals, and tasks. In contrast, adults with a high degree of autonomy, self-esteem, and confidence usually require minimal direction and structure, so the worker may extend open-ended invitations to articulate needs, goals, and tasks.

Modality and time are significant aspects to be considered in the initial phase. Criteria for selection of modality are sparse. In many agencies an individual service is assumed at the outset, despite the need to consider with clients the relative advantages of family, group, and individual modalities. Research into the time dimension indicates that short-term services are associated with positive outcomes and positive views of the service more often than are the open-ended temporal arrangements. The time limit helps client and worker to focus quickly on pertinent concerns, and to maintain purpose and direction. To the extent possible, temporal arrangements should fit the nature of the problem, the agreed upon goals, and the client's own temporal orientations and resources.

Problem definition, goals, tasks, roles, modalities, and temporal arrangements may be evaluated, reevaluated, and renegotiated as the work continues. Exploration and contracting are flexible, dynamic, and continuous processes. Throughout the helping process, the worker invites the client's reactions to the tasks and method of their work. Tensions can then be identified and handled before they become serious obstacles.

Notes

1. Zanger defines empathy as the knowledge of another person acquired by experiencing his feelings. See Allyn Zanger, "A Study of Factors Related to Clinical Empathy," *Smith College Studies in Social Work* (February 1968), 38:116–37.

2. Pauline Lide, "Dynamic Mental Representation: an Analysis of the Empathic Process," *Social Casework* (March 1966), 47:146–51.

3. We are indebted to Professor Irving Miller for the formulation.

4. David Landy, "Problem of the Person Seeking Help in Our Culture," *Social Welfare Forum, 1960* (New York: Columbia University Press, 1960), pp. 127–45.

5. Perlman attributes the one-third dropout rate before the second interview to poor communication between worker and client. See Helen H. Perlman, "Intake and Some Role Considerations," *Social Casework* (April 1960), 41:171–76.

6. For a review of research on group composition, see Henrietta Glatzer, "The Relative Effectiveness of Clinically Homogeneous and Hetergeneous Psychotherapy Groups," *International Journal of Group Psychotherapy* (July 1956), 6:258–65; P. Hare, E. Borgatta, and R. Bales, eds., "Group Size and Group Composition, Coalitions, and Subgroups," *Small Groups* (New York: Knopf, 1965), pp. 490–500; Margaret Hartford, *Groups in Social Work,* (New York: Columbia University Press, 1972), chapters 4, 5, 6; R. Paradise and R. Daniels, "Group Composition as a Treatment Tool with Children," in Saul Bernstein, ed., *Further Explorations in Group Work* (Boston: Boston University Bookstore, 1970), pp. 29–45; Fritz Redl, "Art of Group Composition," in S. Schulze, ed., *Creative Group Living in Children's Institutions* (New York: Association Press, 1951), pp. 79–96; William Schutz, "On Group Composition," *Journal of Abnormal Social Psychology* (March 1961), 62:275–81; Irving Yalom, *Theory and Practice of Group Psychotherapy* (New York: Basic Books, 1970), pp. 156–79, 180–207.

7. Group composition scales have recently been developed. See Harvey Bertcher and Frank Maple, "Elements and Issues in Group Composition," in Paul Glasser, Rosemary Sarri, and Robert Vinter, eds., *Individual Change Through Small Groups* (New York: Free Press, 1974), pp. 186–208.

8. John E. Mayer and Noel Timms, *The Client Speaks* (New York: Atherton Press, 1970).

9. Kadushin identifies the subtle differences in opening statements and how they may determine the interview's direction. See Alfred Kadushin, *The Social Work Interview* (New York: Columbia University Press, 1972), p. 132.

10. Alan Keith-Lucas, *The Giving and Taking of Help* (Chapel Hill: University of North Carolina Press, 1972), pp. 484—50.

11. For further discussion and illustration, see Alex Gitterman, "Group Work in the Public Schools," in William Schwartz and Serapio Zalba, eds., *The Practice of Group Work* (New York: The Columbia University Press, 1971), pp. 45–56; and Joan Shapiro, "The Entry Phase in Social Work With Slum Hotel Residents," *Transcending Fear of the Stranger* (New York: United Neighborhood Houses, monograph, 1958), pp. 1–18.

12. For different points of view concerning the problem of wholes and parts see, for example, Ernest Nagel, "On the Statement, 'The Whole Is More Than the Sum of its Parts,' " in Paul F. Lazarsfeld and Morris Rosenberg, eds., *The Language of Social Research* (Glencoe, Ill.: Free Press, 1955), pp. 519–27; Robert S. Weiss, "Alternate Approaches in the Study of Complex Situations," *Human Organization* (Fall 1966), 25(3):198–206; René Dubos, "Science and Man's Nature," *Daedalus* (Winter 1965), 94:223–44; Abraham Kaplan, *The Conduct of Inquiry* (San Francisco: Chandler, 1964), pp. 80–82.

13. Carel B. Germain, "Social Study: Past and Future," *Social Casework* (July 1968), 49(7):403–9; Beulah Roberts Compton and Burt Galoway, *Social Work Processes* (Homewood, Ill.: Dorsey Press, 1975), pp. 275–91.

14. The discussion on contracting draws on: Tom A. Croxton, "The Therapeutic Contract in Social Treatment," in Paul Glasser, Rosemary Sarri, and Robert Vinter, eds., *Individual Change Through Small Groups* (New York: Free Press, 1974), pp. 169–83; Charles Garvin, "Complementarity of Role Expectations in Groups: The Member–Worker Contract," *Social Work Practice, 1969* (New York: Columbia University Press, 1969), pp. 127–45; Werner Gottleib and Joe H. Stanley, "Mutual Goals and Goal-Setting in Social Casework," *Social Casework* (October 1967), 38(8):471–81; Anthony N. Maluccio and Wilma Marlow, "The Case for the Contract," *Social Work* (January 1974), 19(1):28–36; Sonya L. Rhodes, "Contract Negotiation in the Initial Stage of Casework Service," *Social Service Review* (March 1977), 51(1):125–40; William Schwartz, "The Social Worker in the Group," *The Social Welfare Forum, 1961* (New York: Columbia University Press, 1961), pp. 146–71; and Brett Seabury, "The Contract: Uses, Abuses, and Limitations," *Social Work* (January 1976), 21(1):16–21.

15. Edited practice excerpts reprinted with permission of the author and the American Public Welfare Association: William Schwartz, "Group Work in Public Welfare," *Public Welfare* (October 1968), 26:343.

16. Elliot Studt, "Social Work Theory and Implications for the Practice of Methods," *Social Work Education Reporter* (June 1968), 16:22–4, 42–6.

17. For a discussion of the worker's role with different types of groups, see Norma C. Lang, "A Broad Range Model of Practice in the Social Work Group," *Social Service Review* (March 1972), 46:76–89.

18. William J. Reid and Anne Shyne, *Brief and Extended Casework* (New York: Columbia University Press, 1969).

19. For a fuller discussion of biological, psychological, social, and cultural time, see Carel B. Germain, "Time: An Ecological Variable in Social Work Practice," *Social Casework* (July 1976), 57(7):419–26.

3

The Ongoing Phase: Life Transitions

THE WORKER'S AND client's entry into the ongoing phase assumes that they have reached a degree of shared, though tentative, understanding about the nature of the problem, the solutions or objectives to be sought, and the possible means for achieving them. In discussing practice in the ongoing phase, we recognize that help was already taking place in the initial phase, and that features of the initial phase may well continue in the ongoing phase. Problems and needs, for example, may be redefined, objectives may shift, and the helping means may change as new information, energy or resources become available to one or both participants. This chapter will present the knowledge and skills of the social worker in helping people deal with the stresses arising from developmental changes, status and role demands, and crisis events, which people face as individuals or in primary groups. In the first section, stresses associated with developmental changes, status and role demands, and crisis events are examined. In the second section we discuss the function, roles, and skills of the social work practitioner. In the final section, we present more complete case illustrations, analyzing skills of practice and summarizing the elements of the ongoing phase.

Life Transitions as a Source of Stress

Developmental Changes

Over the course of a lifetime, the human being proceeds through biologically determined changes. Regardless of the historical time or the geographic place, the physiological and biological changes of infancy, childhood, puberty, adulthood, and old age are universal. Depending upon the culture, some or all of these changes may also be recognized and marked in socially patterned ways as life stages, carrying particular duties and privileges. The biology is universal, the cultural definition is not. Adolescence, for example, has been recognized as a stage in the life cycle in our own society only since the late nineteenth century.[1] It is not so recognized in all societies. In some cultures, puberty marks the entry into the rights and responsibilities of adulthood, with no intervening period or stage. The value placed on particular stages of biological change also varies across cultures. In the traditional societies of the Orient, for example, old age was a venerated stage. In our society it is a dreaded stage, and those who are old are largely cast outside the activities of the society.[2]

In a complex technological society such as ours, biological development over the life cycle has become more complicated by an overlay of socially and culturally imposed expectations, constraints, and opportunities, so that developmental changes need to be understood within the context of transactions between the developing individual and his environment. The young adolescent, for example, is confronted by major biological changes including rapid physical growth, altered proportions among bodily structures, and profound hormonal changes that trigger the appearance of secondary sex characteristics and new awareness of sexuality. These biological factors elicit changing responses and challenges from the environment. Thus, the adolescent must cope with inner and outer perceptions of the biological changes that affect his self-image, goals, activities, and his relations to parents, school personnel, peers, and others. Concurrent with the biological changes, the adolescent is thrust into the "teenage culture," with its peer pressures and expectations, and into a new form of educational experience imposed by the change from the small elementary school to the large, diverse, and impersonal middle or junior high school with different expectations for academic performance and behavior.[3]

The nature and quality of the adolescent's past life experiences and relationships, whether the adolescent is a male or female, in good health or poor health, influence the nature of the demands, the responses to them, and the coping resources available. The social class, religion, and ethnicity of the adolescent's family, whether they are poor, working-class, or middle-class; Jewish, Catholic, Protestant, Moslem, Buddhist, unaffiliated or nonreligious; and whether black, Hispanic, native American, Chicano, white, or Asian-American—all such characteristics will affect the adolescent's experience differentially in both subtle and blatant ways. The character of the physical setting—whether the adolescent lives in a rural, suburban, or urban area; in a foster home, an institution, or his own home; in a deteriorating slum, a residential district or a public housing project, with or without the amenities of parks, playgrounds, recreation and service facilities—all will have a bearing on the young person's passage through the life transition of adolescence and how he and his family cope with its major adaptive tasks.

All developmental stages across the life cycle present biological changes interacting with psychological, social and cultural forces, and physical settings, posing particular demands and creating varying degrees of stress. The dynamic, interacting processes of biological growth or decline, emotional, cognitive and perceptural development, learning, and socialization and acculturalization have been conceptualized by Erikson as occurring in epigenetic stages of development.[4] Successful completion of the life tasks presented at one stage lays the foundation for successful resolution of life tasks at the next stage. Faltering on the tasks at one stage may create difficulties at a later stage.

Using the idea of "cogwheeling" between the generations, Erikson sketches a reciprocal responsiveness in the meeting of needs. Through responsiveness to the child's needs, for example, parents meet their own age-specific needs for generativity. Through responsiveness to the parents' caretaking, the child meets his own need to develop basic trust in himself and his environment. The institutions of the society and the culture, however, must also be responsive to the needs of the developing individual across the life cycle. For parents to nurture infants, for example, the society must provide them with responsive economic, social, educational, and health care structures. Thus, at any point in the life cycle, there are mutual phase-specific adaptive tasks to be met by the developing individual and by his environment, if personal growth and social benefit are to accrue.

When all goes well, the *innate* adaptive potential is released, including the muscular–skeletal structures, cognitive–sensory–perceptual structures, memory and language structures. *Acquired* adaptive capacities are also developed. Erikson conceptualizes the acquired qualities as trust, autonomy, initiative, and industry, in the four stages of infancy and childhood; identity in adolescence; intimacy and generativity in young and middle adulthood; and integrity in old age. These global qualities can be understood as comprising such adaptive capacities as human relatedness, self-regulation, the self-image and self-esteem, coping skills, talents, goals–ideals, and interests. Thus, adaptation represents a joint achievement of individual and environment in reaching a goodness-of-fit between adaptive skills and qualities, the progressive forces in the person, and growth-supporting properties and structures of the environment.

Life being what it is, however, things don't always go well. Stressful environments providing excessive or insufficient biological, sensory, cognitive, emotional, or social stimuli—or the exceptional tasks arising from such biological factors as congenital handicaps, illness, and injury—may make task resolution at a particular stage extremely difficult, or even impossible. Erikson believes that where a stage is not traversed successfully for whatever reason, there may be residues of distrust, shame, guilt, or inferiority (the antonyms of positive achievement in childhood), identity diffusion (the antonym of positive achievement in adolescence), self-absorption, stagnation, or despair (the antonyms of positive achievement in adulthood and old age). These residues interfere with the development of acquired adaptive capacities, and make adaptation that much more difficult.

Robin, age 13 and black, is the oldest of several children. She had been beaten, abused, and neglected by her own mother, and two years ago she and two young brothers, ages 3 and 7, were placed with a rigid, puritanical foster mother. Robin is not doing well in school, has no girl friends, and is given undue responsibility for looking after her brothers. She has few opportunities for interchange with the world beyond her foster home and the school, except for a not-quite-real relationship with a neighborhood boy whom the foster mother describes as a "Don Juan type" who is sure to get Robin into trouble if she continues to associate with him. Robin had experienced rapid pubertal changes, and is the tallest and most physically mature girl in her class. She feels awkward, ugly, knows little about sex or personal hygiene, and her teacher has complained of her odor.

Robin is an unhappy and despairing youngster. Very little in her life has gone right, and now she faces the difficult psychological, social, and biological tasks of adolescence with few environmental supports. From the Eriksonian perspective, the central task of establishing identity, difficult at best, is excessively stressful for this youngster. Identity formation requires the gradual synthesis of biological givens, such as sex, race, bodily structures and appearance, and innate needs and drives,with the acquired interests and capacities, significant identifications with family members and others. Such a synthesis arises from a sense of continuity between one's past and one's aspirations for the future.

Robin, however, was rejected, unloved and even abused by her own parents, and her self-image is that of an unlovable person. She is a foster child, bearing a stigmatized label that makes her different from all youngsters who live happily or unhappily with their own families. And, she is also black in a white-dominated society that devalues blackness. Her early and rapid pubertal changes set her apart from classmates, so that she feels even more different. She has had no loving adults with whom to identify, and understands little or nothing of the profound biological and emotional changes she is experiencing. She has no girl friends at a stage when peers are essential for successful resolution of life tasks. She has a rigid, ungiving foster mother who can not allow Robin the needed opportunities for autonomous actions and decisons. Living constantly in terror of being rejected and ejected from the only home she now has, Robin is afraid to assert herself or declare her needs and to deal with issues of dependence and independence, a critical task for the adolescent. Confined to home and to responsibility for the care of her little brothers, Robin is also denied the opportunity of widening experiences in the physical and social world so important for the cognitive, emotional, and perceptual tasks of adolescence. While the social worker will seek to engage the adaptive capacities that Robin has acquired in the course of her difficult life, and all the innate strivings toward growth, the residues of mistrust, shame, guilt, and inferiority from earlier life stages will need to be taken into account.

Cognitive development also occurs in a sequence of stages that is thought to be the same across cultures, but specific content at each level may be different in different cultures. Although environmental nutriments or inputs are required by the cognitive structures, knowledge and learning come not just from perception of those environmental stimuli (accommodation), but from taking action in the environment (assimilation).[5]

People have different cognitive styles which are related to particular emphases in cognitive development.[6] Human beings translate their sensory perceptions into a model of the world along three dimensions of cognitive development. The earliest appearance of cognition is an *enactive* representation of the world. This is typical of the preverbal stage in the child, in which there are no words to describe what is perceived and acted upon. This form of cognition remains through life. One can't, for example, learn to play tennis by reading a book. Tennis strokes have to be demonstrated by action, and then the learner undertakes to practice the action. Thus, learning by doing, learning through action, is one mode of cognition.

The second dimension of cognition is an *iconic* representation of the world that develops a model of reality through summarizing images. The images come from the sensory apparatus and are cognitively organized into patterns and pictures. One goes beyond the information given by the senses, and organizes the perceptions into patterns and pictures.

The third mode of cognition is *symbolic* representation, by which one organizes the world through symbols such as words, concepts, constructs, and theories. These modes are thought to proceed developmentally. People generally master all three to some degree, although one or the other may become the individual's dominant intellectual style. Some people think and learn more readily by doing; others think and learn by the use of pictures, visualizations, and other graphic modes. Still others think and learn more readily by the use of language and ideas, and through verbal and written materials.

People can experience stress related to cognitive functioning when cognitive powers are damaged or impaired through injury, illness, or deprivation of sensory and intellectual stimuli. Stress may also arise as the result of rigidity of one's intellectual style that does not permit flexibility in problem-solving. Others may find it difficult to cope with conflicting cognitive styles that can occur, for example, in the classroom between teacher and pupil, in the medical setting between physician and patient, and in the social work setting between worker and client.[7]

Just as individual developmental changes have been conceptualized as bio-psycho-social life stages with reciprocal adaptive tasks for individual and environment, work is advancing on identifying stages of family development with their associated tasks.[8] These stages are shaped by cultural, social, biological, and psychological pressures and resources, forming themes of family life. In general, the family is viewed as beginning with the coming together of two individuals from different families of origin to create a new family. Following the arrival of the first child, there is a stage of child-rearing, followed by a stage of children leaving home, a stage when the parents are once more alone together, and finally the stage of the dissolution of the family beginning with the death of one partner and ending with the death of the other. This general framework does not take into account such forms as childless families, one-parent families, or other arrangements, for which there are as yet no developmental scheme.

Rhodes has identified seven sequential, cyclical, multi-generational stages of family development, each with phase-specific tasks.[9] The initial phase of forming a dyadic relationship is characterized by the task of establishing intimacy that is based on the realistic perception of each other's traits and attributes rather than on an exaggerated, idealized, or intensely romanticized image. Success at this phase depends, in part, upon the degree of each partner's emancipation from childhood ties to his or her own parents, and the readiness to accept responsibility for one's self and for offering support and love to the other. Roles must be defined, positive complementarity established, responsibilities assigned, and patterns developed for satisfactorily carrying out the functions of a two-member interactional unit. These tasks include division of labor. decision-making, economic arrangements, friendship and kin relations, conflict resolution, recreation, religious affiliation, etc. This is a difficult stage, because so much accommodation is acquired to reach a successful "fit" in emotional, sexual, economic, and developmental spheres—no matter how well the partners thought they knew each other before they set up their household, and no matter how carefully they anticipated possible differences and strains. The stage can be made more difficult by such unforeseen events as job loss or illness. Depending upon how well each partner resolved her or his own earlier life tasks, each may bring certain unrealistic or distorted expectations and perceptions, and regressive or arrested needs into the relationship, which then interfere with the achievement of intimacy. Disillusionment, disappointment, and conflict may arise, instead.

Where this stage and its tasks are traversed reasonably well, the new family is reasonably well-prepared for the demanding tasks of the child-bearing years. These include the opening up of a two-member system to include a third (and later, more) members. A three-member system is frequently an unstable system in which possibilities for maladaptive coalitions and alliances are present. This stage requires the parents to continue giving to one another while moving somewhat apart to include the baby. It requires that they cooperate in meeting the needs of the baby. To do all of this, the parents must be prepared to replenish the supplies to each other that are now diminished by constant giving to the helpless and dependent baby, and/or their other young children. These same tasks, when faced by a one-parent family represent a severe adaptive burden, since the parent who is alone receives no replenishment and support from the other parent for her or his needs. At the same time, social and institutional supports for the one-parent family, such as day care facilities, are not yet adequate in our society.

Mrs. Charles, age 27, mother of two children, ages 5 and 2, has asked for help with marital problems. She thinks that her being a closed instead of an open person has created the problems. Now her husband is undecided about staying in the marriage. He stays out all night, and doesn't tell her where he's been. She is unsure if she loves him, and feels she should have left before the children arrived, as the marriage was troubled then. She believes she is a weak person, and has said that she married to get away from home. She was never close to her own parents, and even feels closer to her husband's mother than she did to her own mother. She has always been fearful and unsure of herself, and never felt she could hold a job that paid a decent salary, so she took menial jobs.

In the next interview, Mr. Charles came with his wife. He said he felt that his wife had never been concerned about him, and always pushed him away sexually. He felt that everything else came first: the children, her friends, even her knitting. He felt pushed out, so now he is involved with someone else. He's not yet sure what he will do, but thinks that things may be too far gone to save the marriage. Four years ago he had an affair which his wife knew of, but didn't do anything about it. He doesn't understand why she puts up with his staying out all night and running around. He admits that he would never put up with her doing this to him.

While Mr. Charles was relating all of this, Mrs. Charles was sobbing. When the worker asked Mr. Charles how he felt about Mrs. Charles' crying, he said in a detached and unfeeling way that he was used to her tears. Later, as Mrs. Charles talked about how her husband humiliates her, he smiled. When the worker commented on his detachment, he said he thinks there is a way to get to him, but his wife will have to find this out for herself. He added that he wants his wife to put him on a pedestal.

The Charles family is in the childbearing and preschool years, when the family task is to achieve mutual replenishment between the parents, as opposed to their turning inward. It is clear, however, that part of the present difficulties are due to Mr. and Mrs. Charles' failure to successfully complete the tasks of the first stage. Instead of achieving intimacy based upon realistic perceptions of each other, each attempted to parentify the other. Mrs. Charles had not emancipated herself from her own family, and so she sought mothering from her husband. He, in turn, sought from his wife parent-like limits on his immature behaviors. As a result, little or no mutuality and reciprocal need-meeting developed. Both are like hungry children seeking food in an empty cupboard. Hence, their present task of replenishing each other so they may nurture their children is much more difficult. Each has few inner resources from which to give to the other. And each makes demands upon the other which are unrealistic and childlike, leading to further disillusionment, rather than to intimacy. Each turns inward to a concern for the self alone, rather than outward, toward the other, for reciprocal need-meeting.

As in Erikson's schema for individual stages and tasks, a family framework suggests that where the family's tasks at one stage are not successfully met, certain residues or dysfunctional alternatives are carried over to the next stage, increasing the adaptive burden on all members. As with individual development, the family's successful task achievement depends upon adequate social and institutional supports and nutriments from the environment and the family's adaptive interchanges with the physical and social environment. Beyond the tasks of intimacy for the new family, and replenishment during the childbearing years, family tasks include individuation during the school years; failure in this task leads to the maladaptive alternative of pseudo-mutuality. Families with teenagers must achieve companionship within and outside the family, or be left with the residue of isolation; families in which children are leaving face the task of regrouping, and failure to achieve this task results in the binding of, or the premature expulsion of the adolescent. In the post-parenting phases, the family, now reduced to the original pair, must achieve the tasks of rediscovery and mutual aid, or be faced with residues of despair and uselessness.[10]

In addition to the struggles to meet these various family tasks, the developmental tasks and needs of individual family members may conflict at particular stages of family development. A family with an adolescent child may experience more than the expectable amount of stress around such issues as separation and autonomy, sexuality, education, vocation, or values.[11] The tasks of parents and child in dealing with these issues may clash because of conflicting needs. Parents' efforts, for example, to keep the child within the family circle may be generated by the pressures of sexual imbalance in their marriage, disappointments about their own achievements, or their confusions and fears in the value realm. These individual needs may make their tasks at this stage of family development difficult to resolve and increase the difficulty experienced by the adolescent in his tasks of establishing a separate identity and autonomy. The resulting stress may become unmanageable for either the parents or the child, or both.

Although more compressed in time and space than the family, natural and formed groups also proceed through phases or transitions that pose characteristic tasks. These may lead to problematic issues which, if unresolved, prevent the group from moving ahead. When the phases are successfully traversed and the tasks adequately handled, the group will have succeeded in establishing a system of mutual aid. Without resolution of the tasks at each phase, however, mutual aid cannot emerge, develop, and be sustained. Garland and his colleagues have delineated five stages in social work groups: preaffiliation approach and avoidance, power and control, intimacy, differentiation, and separation.[12] During the group's first phase, members' ambivalences about involvement with one another and with the worker are expressed through approach and avoidance behaviors. Members are preoccupied with the worker's authority, and seek her approval or search for her vulnerabilities. Early in the development of children's groups, for example, members may run in and out of the room, moving toward and away from involvement and testing the limits of permissible behavior. They may call the worker "teacher," since the classroom provides an initial frame of reference for the new situation. As a worker tells it:

> In a fourth grade boys' group meeting in the school, Ronnie asked if the group always had to take the same seats. I said it didn't matter to me, they could sit wherever they want. At this, Lenny asked if I could tell them where to sit. And, when I mentioned that we might try talking without raising hands this, too, was a bit hard for them to get used to, even after I told them that I'm not a teacher and this isn't a classroom. This seemed to really take them by surprise. After the group put together a set of rules, Len was the first to suggest how to enforce the rules—put the offender in a corner for five minutes. The group continually tested me. Allan called Carl a name, and Carl retaliated, and both looked at me for a reaction. Members kept getting up to walk around the room, looking behind the curtains, at the lights, etc.

As the members feel safer with each other, much of their vacillation about entering into the group's purpose and tasks wanes. They move toward involvement and develop some comfort in their interactions with one another and with the leader. Issues of power and control then come to the fore. The members attempt to define and formalize their relationships, and to develop a status hierarchy. Where the worker belongs in the hierarchy is often a central issue. Some members may want to place her at the top, others at the bottom.

Such discrepancies may create polarized subgroups, or lead to periods of rebellion and stress.

> Peter tells Ronnie to shut up, and warns him that he will have to go back to the classroom. Several minutes later, Ronnie tells Chuck he "better stop foolin' around. . . ." As meetings continue, Len emerges as the assistant social worker–authority figure, with much resentment toward him building in the group. Cliques have been forming over the past four meetings. Allan always takes a seat next to Len and agrees with everything Len says. Peter formed a dependent alliance with Bob, and Ronnie continues to sit next to me. Chuck always sits down alone, seemingly aloof from everyone else. The members have continued to challenge me—they fool around, pay little attention, complain about my advice and my action on their behalf, tell me in no uncertain terms they would rather be doing other things at the meetings. Yet at the same time, they want me to discipline them, help solve problems, protect them from attack by others, and provide them with a degree of structure.

Gradually, as the members assure themselves of the worker's willingness and ability to maintain a safe balance between control and autonomy, they move to a new level of involvement with her and with one another. They are ready for the transitional tasks of intimacy, differentiation, and ultimately, separation.

> Ronnie and Allan sat down together. They've gotten very friendly both at meetings and in class, as reported by the teacher. I asked what the group wanted to do, and they decided to draw with magic markers. Ronnie asked if the group could talk at the same time and told about a problem he had with the principal, who threatened to put him back in the third grade. He said he's been behaving well in classes, and the group disagreed. Ronnie took the disagreement well, agreeing with the group to some extent. Previously, he would have told them to shut up or would have set up a defense against their involvement.

The developmental stages confronted by individuals have a biological base, and the associated tasks arise out of the biological pressures interacting with the expectations, opportunities, and obstacles posed by the culture, and the social and physical environment. Developmental stages of the family do not have a biological base, although they may arise in connection with biological changes of individual members. They are, in a sense, analogous to the biologically-based stages of individual development, and they, too, carry an overlay of cultural, societal, and other environmental influences affecting the tasks of each stage. In groups, however, the transitional phases and tasks may perhaps be reflective of real-life processes only as they emerge in such natural groups as neighborhood gangs. With formed groups, while no less observable, the phases and tasks appear to emerge as artifacts of the group modality itself. It is clear that in both natural and formed groups, the phase-related tasks can lead to tensions; the tasks may not be completed, and the group may not be able to move ahead in its purpose, failing to achieve a mutual aid system. Where this happens, members tend to withdraw from one another or exploit one another, creating further stress.

Status Changes and Role Demands

Human action takes place in a social, cultural, and physical context comprising a variety of social systems, such as the family, peer group, social network of significant people in the life space, and bureaucratic organizations and social institutions. The action is influenced by personal and interpersonal processes, and is regulated and patterned by cultural norms and values. It is located in a physical space or structure. The complexities of human action derive from the interplay among the social systems, the personalities, and the cultural and setting influences.

In every social system to which the individual belongs, she occupies a social status; each such status comprises a set of interrelated roles.[13]

Mrs. Cain occupies the status of ADC mother in the welfare system. In that status, she carries the roles of welfare recipient and system negotiator. In her family, Mrs. Cain occupies the status of single parent, and carries the roles of mother, abandoned wife, daughter, and sister. In her religious affiliation, she occupies the status of church member, and carries the roles of choir singer, Sunday School helper, and Bible class student. She also has other statuses in still other social systems.

The various expectations exerted upon Mrs. Cain with respect to her statuses and roles may conflict with one another and compete for her time, energy, and interest. She has to balance, as best she can, the diverse status and role responsibilities imposed by each of the social systems to which she belongs, taking into account her motivations and capacities, her cultural beliefs, norms and values, the relative significance of the statuses and roles to her, and the limitations or opportunities provided by the various physical settings in which she is involved. These dimensions are associated with societal and cultural forces, status and role transitions and changes, properties of the status or role itself, and characteristics of the person occupying the status, or of partner in a role relationship. We will consider each dimension in turn.

Societal and cultural factors include rapid social change and the consequent impact of either ambiguity or rigidity in status–role definitions, and class and ethnic influences on role definitions. Part of the socialization process over the life span is directed to preparing children and adults for their social roles. In time of social change, when sex roles, family roles, and even work roles are changing rapidly, the socialization process is very difficult for many parents, and role choices and role responsibilities become increasingly difficult for youth and adults. This is because the future is more uncertain in a complex technological society, and what is sound preparation for future demands appears less and less predictable.[14] At a more subtle level, the culture itself is undergoing profound changes in the norms and values that pattern the expectations and perceptions of status and role performance. We are aware of some of this cultural change, but much of it is out of our awareness, thus making preparation for future roles still more difficult, and the requirements of present roles still more ambiguous. The very social systems that are composed of a web of statuses and roles are also changing rapidly so that the definitions of statuses and roles within them will have to change, but they are usually slow in doing so. Cultural lag of that sort can lead to conflict about what is "right and proper," and who is to make the decision about what is "right and proper." New family forms inside and outside the institution of legal marriage, new forms of contraception, changing ideas about authority and power, the push for greater control over their own lives by ethnic groups, women, youth, workers, the aged, handicapped, and others, all affect the structure of family systems, school systems, health care systems, work systems, professional systems, etc. But, until the perceptions and expectations regarding the rights and responsibilities inhering in statuses and affecting role performance become very much clearer in these and other social systems, then status–role demands are likely to be significant sources of stress for people.

Many statuses in our society are devalued, and those who occupy them are subtly or openly considered to be "outsiders."[15] These include the stigmatized statuses of prisoner, parolee, probationer, abusing parent, alcoholic, drug abuser, and the devalued statuses of mentally ill person, handicapped person, poor person, foster child, and welfare client. Persons occupying such statuses and roles often carry a heavy adaptive burden, since they must fulfill their status and role tasks associated with other social systems while coping with the stress generated by the exceptional demands of the stigmatized or devalued status.

Transitional changes in status can also be stressful. Sometimes they accompany biologically induced developmental changes, and their tasks are then almost indistinguishable from developmental tasks. A person may relinquish the status of worker and its associated roles, and assume the status of retiree at the same time that he is dealing with the developmental tasks related to aging. This may not always be the case, however, for a retiree may have dealt with many tasks of aging prior to retirement, or he may not be faced with them until some time after retirement. Where they do coincide, however, there is apt to be added stress. In our society, for example, the onset of puberty and its associated tasks often coincides with the new status of junior high student and its many new role demands, thus increasing the likelihood of stress.

There are times when assuming a new status and its related roles comes too early in the life cycle, or too late, so that the potential for stress is increased. A young adolescent who becomes a parent, a young child who is not ready for day care, an old woman who must take on parenting tasks, the oldest child in a bereaved or other one-parent family who must care for younger siblings, all may face strains between developmental tasks and role tasks.

The stress associated with assuming a new status and its impact on other statuses and roles is illustrated in the first meeting of a group of disabled men with a social worker in a rehabilitation center. Each member has a new status, "handicapped person," and he doesn't yet know what the roles associated with this status are likely to be, nor how his familial, work, and other statuses and roles will be affected. He can be expected to bring his cognitive abilities, perceptions, and other adaptive capacities, and his social and cultural experience to bear upon the tasks associated with the new status. The worker has just explained that a purpose of the group might be to help one another deal with being handicapped:

> Mr. Collins asked the group, "What do you do when people call you freaks?" Someone asked what he meant, and he said, "Odd—not like other people."
>
> Mr. Pallas said that was ridiculous—no one would think of them as freaks. Only a crazy idiot would. Mr. Collins said he was wrong, and gave an example where a girl he knew said she wouldn't have anything to do with him because he has lost a leg. Mr. Pallas said, jokingly, that he was past the stage of being a girl chaser. Some group members smiled, and Mr. Collins grinned. Several patients spoke up and said they didn't feel like freaks. Mr. Pallas said he felt "like a man," a complete person, even without his two legs. Mr. Garren related in detail how he talked with his children about his amputation and showed them the stump, so they would know just what was going on. He felt that teaching people about this was how he, and others like him, wouldn't be looked at as freaks, because people would understand better.
>
> The worker asked Mr. Sciappo, who had received his limb eight days ago, how his visit home had gone last weekend. Mr. Sciappo launched into a description of how his wife insisted on doing things for him, and the minister hadn't wanted him to make the trip to church. He wasn't sure how to handle all of this, and wondered what the

> group thought. Mr. Chaiklin said, "You got to tell them no, when people want to do something for you, which you can do yourself." In Mr. Sciatto's situation, Mr. Chaiklin would explain to people that it's no good to have someone wait on you. The worker asked, "How come?" Mr. Chaiklin said, "You got to feel you can keep independent, not lean too much on others."

As the group continues, each member will struggle to cope with the new status that poses profound and multiple demands and conflicts with the responsibilities and privileges of other statuses and roles. Each must handle the grief and anger at the loss of a valued body part or function and develop a new self-image, must test out the reactions of loved ones and strangers, and must deal with issues of dependence and independence. The acceptance and support of the social worker will facilitate the development of a group process or mutual aid system in which the patients can serve as successful role models for one another as they share their experiences in their families, in dealing with physical and psychic pain and the trials of prostheses, and in their efforts at vocational rehabilitation.

In addition to being subject to societal and cultural forces, transition and changes, statuses and roles have properties of their own that sometimes lead to unmanageable stress for people.[16] Status and role properties include the *size* and *diversity* of one's set of statuses or of roles, and the relative *ranking* of each status or role in the eyes of others and one's self.

As the life space expands over the life cycle until old age, the individual assumes more statuses as he becomes affiliated with more social systems beyond the family. Sometimes these are in addition to existing statuses, thus increasing the size of his set, and sometimes they are in place of former statuses. Each such addition or change means new tasks or demands that may result in stress if they conflict with the demands and responsibilities of other statuses and roles. The tasks involved in the work roles of parents, for example, may conflict with tasks related to their marital roles or parenting roles. The status of single person or divorced person may conflict with the status of parent. Not only did Mrs. Cain, the single parent mentioned in chapter 1, have to carry the roles of both father and mother in the sense of fulfilling their different tasks, but if she pursues romantic interests or activities consonant with her status as single person, she may experience conflict or even guilt with respect to her status as parent. The status of social work student involves several roles which frequently present conflicting demands and responsibilities: she is an advisee, a supervisee, her clients' social worker, and her teachers' student. She may have other statuses as well, which conflict with the demands and expectations of the social work student status: wife, parent, daughter, part-time clerk, etc..

The person who occupies too few statuses or roles is subject to a different kind of stress. An urban housewife without other statuses and roles that provide adequate outlets for her talents and interests may become depressed. An elderly individual, subject to a decline in the number of statuses and roles customarily occupied, may suffer an existential void. Some statuses such as widow and widower have painful meanings and carry painful tasks. People living in rural areas may not have the competing demands of large status and role sets and may therefore experience inadequate stimulation.

Ranking, as a property of statuses and roles, involves factors of prestige, power, and access to resources that differentiate among statuses and their relative location in the social structure. Thus, the statuses of employer and employee, parent and child, banker and borrower, guard and prisoner carry ranking factors that lead to inequality and strains in the role relationships connected to such statuses. This is the case, also, in former conceptions of the statuses of social worker and client. Since a higher rank carries with it the power to make one of a lower rank conform to one's wishes or influence, it was considered desirable to reduce the power differentials in the social worker–client relationship as much as possible. Hence, relationship factors of mutuality, reciprocity, accountability, and contracting are emphasized in contemporary practice.

Characteristics of the person occupying the status or carrying the role may also lead to stress. A status change or the demands of a role may be beyond the coping range, or the person may not be motivated to carry out the status or role responsibilities. Personal characteristics can also lead to a lack of fit between role partners. Instead of reciprocity in expectations and need-meeting, one partner in a marriage may seek to make a parent instead of a spouse of the other. If the other partner accedes to the demand, which is usually covert, the resulting negative complementarity may work satisfactorily until the arrival of children upsets it, because of new role demands. Occasionally, there are role reversals, as when a very immature parent expects to be cared for and nurtured by her young child. What used to be termed role reversals in marriage, however, may now represent changing lifestyles!

Several personal characteristics affect the way one handles the demands and expectations of his various statuses and roles. These include not only cognitive abilities and style, motivations, and adaptive patterns, but also perceptual capacities. The clarity, acuity, and accuracy of such perceptions, including the awareness of one's own needs and the needs of others, affect understanding of the expectations attached to his statuses and roles, and awareness of how he is performing in them. Conversely, the clarity, acuity, and accuracy of the perceptions of others—including role partners—affect their demands and expectations, and their assessment of an individual's performance, and of the way one handles the various demands, conflicts, and expectations.

The perceptual–sensory apparatus in the human being is affected by biological factors of age and physical condition and by cultural, social, and psychological factors. Sensory–perceptual decline in old age, for example, is often compensated by actions which violate the norms for role behavior. An elderly patient in a geriatric facility may alienate residential staff by seeking physical contact and closeness in order to compensate for loss of sensory acuity. Because this is regarded as inappropriate behavior for the role of patient or resident, young staff feel intruded upon, and may move physically to keep the elderly at arm's length. In a similar effort to make up for sensory losses, an aged person may prefer living space in which furniture and other objects are within easy reach and sight. To younger family members, such spatial clutter may be perceived as sloppiness, and inappropriate to the status of parent or grandparent.[17]

Cultural factors associated with social class, ethnicity, and other subgroup affiliations affect the ways in which people organize and interpret their perceptions of both internal and external stimuli, including status and role demands and expectations. For example, assuming the role of patient and developing a complementarity with the role of physician is affected by the perceptions of both partners of what is expected. A Puerto Rican patient, for instance, has different perceptions—culturally based—about the value of folk medicine, including herbalists and spiritualists, and about the value of scientific medicine than does the physician.[18] Unless the Puerto Rican's perceptions are taken into account, the physician's efforts to cure or alleviate a condition may end in failure: mutual expectations concerning role responsibilities and appropriate behaviors were not met.

States of emotional or physiological stress may lead to perceptual distortions because external or internal stimuli are ignored, blocked out, or misunderstood. Hence, people who are prone to projecting their own anxiety-laden ideas onto others, for example, will have difficulty in perceiving accurately what is expected of them in their various statuses and roles and in assessing accurately their own role performance and that of their role partners. From a different perspective, functioning in an environment that presents insufficient external stimuli to the sensory–perceptual apparatus can lead to the person's autistic preoccupation with internal stimuli, thus interfering with the performance of role tasks. Pressing physiological needs can also influence perception by affecting which stimuli are attended to and the degree of sensitivity and discrimination with which they are attended. If, for example, one is chronically hungry, or without shelter or physical protection and security, or is lacking other biological necessities, the acuity of one's perceptions of external or of other internal stimuli will be adversely affected. This may be the case among some neglecting parents whose own unmet basic biological needs interfere with their attending perceptually to the expectations attached to their status as parents.[19]

Crisis Events

Distinctions between stress and crisis have not yet been made clear by theorists and researchers. Presumably, the distinguishing features of crisis are its time-limited nature, and its immediacy and enormity. The principles of crisis intervention that have been developed in practice, however, are equally applicable to all types of stress, and we will return to this point later. In general, it can be said that not all stress partakes of the nature of crisis, but all crises are stressful. From this point of view, it is clear that any of the other life transitions which we have conceptualized as developmental changes and status role demands, may, in particular instances, take on the character of a crisis.

Thus, crisis events refer to sudden changes that have an immediacy and enormity about them. They are experienced as disastrous and overwhelming, and tend to immobilize people. They often represent losses of the severest kind, such as loss of a loved one; loss of a job; loss of health or bodily integrity through sudden severe illness or injury; loss of cherished hopes, as in the birth of a defective child, or in the failure to achieve a desired goal, such as college entrance or reciprocated love in a romantic attachment; and sometimes the loss of a house or other treasured object. As indicated above, threats to the self-image and to psychic stability, aroused by developmental or status–role demands, may reach the level of crisis, as in peer pressures toward sexual activity or drugs exerted in adolescence, the assumption of a new status involved in a job promotion, or becoming a first-time parent. Presumably, for most people in these situations, there is stress of varying degrees, but it is more manageable or endurable and less overwhelming than it is for those who experience these situations as crises. The state of crisis also arises from natural disasters and their impact on people's lives, safety, possessions, livelihoods, interpersonal attachments, and the meanings attributed to their surroundings.

A crisis also represents a situation in which ordinary adaptive patterns are not adequate, so that novel solutions or coping skills are required. Coping, in contrast to more ordinary adaptive behavior, is the response to change that requires new behavior, change that very likely ". . . gives rise to uncomfortable affects like anxiety, despair, guilt, shame, or grief, the relief of which forms part of the needed adaptation. Coping refers to adaptation under relatively difficult conditions."[20]

There is an opportunity for growth inherent in the nature of crisis as a challenge to be mastered. But also inherent is the hazard of regressed functioning if the tasks in resolving the crisis are not successfully completed.[21] Human beings cannot long remain in the state of extreme discomfort implied by crisis. The painful anxiety and/or grief elicits protective measures sooner or later, so that crisis is also thought to be time-limited. Some observers have suggested six to eight weeks, at most, for the crisis itself,[22] although stress may continue for some time after the crisis has passed. The crisis caused by the death of a spouse is time-limited, but the long and stressful process of mourning will continue for a year or more. The stressful tasks involved in the new status of widower, and the role changes involved, will continue long after the crisis of bereavement has subsided.

In response to crisis events, people may initially respond by rigidifying their defenses, but these may then be quickly and briefly relaxed. Defenses are adaptive strategies such as denial, projection, repression, rationalization, etc., which people use unconsciously to ward off the threat of anxiety.[23] Defenses are not necessarily pathological, depending on the situation, how they are used, and for how long a period. The defense of denial, for example, can be highly adaptive in the event of sudden loss or grave injury. Such a response allows for continued functioning while the person gradually lets bits and pieces of the threatening reality into his awareness. In this way, the risk of being immobilized by anxiety and depression at the outset is warded off, and some problem-solving can begin.[24] While defense at the outset may be adaptive, in the long run the person must come to terms with the crisis event—the loss, the injury, the illness—and face periods of depression, secure necessary information, strengthen social ties, construct a new self-image and make future plans.[25]

Mr. Morris, a 66-year-old black man, had worked in the construction trade all of his life, supporting himself and his three sons, one of whom he put through college. They are married now, and he lives alone. His wife deserted him and the three sons twenty years before. Mr. Morris has been in the hospital several months following vascular surgery.He had been confined to a wheelchair for one year previous to this, eagerly looking forward to the promised surgery which was expected to restore his ability to walk. He worked hard in physical therapy, and is now able to walk cautiously with a cane. He has been looking forward to returning home with the ability to maintain himself independently once again. He has just been told by the doctors, however, that he will never walk well and will soon have to return to the wheelchair. He is to be discharged and will need homemaker services. He was very upset, but quickly assumed the position that staff was not helping him to secure normal walking ability. Mr.

Morris refused to consider homemaker services, saying they would be unnecessary if staff would only do their job. In an effort to prove the staff wrong, he worked overzealously in physical therapy, suffered a fall, and became very anxious.

At this point, Mr. Morris is in a state of crisis precipitated by the severe threat to his valued sense of independence posed by the doctors' prognosis and recommendations.[26] The initial use of denial which enabled him to continue working hard in physical therapy is no longer adaptive. It is interfering with coming to terms with his physical limitations and with planning for immediate and future needs. In order to master the crisis, Mr. M will need to express and to tolerate his feelings of discouragement, grief, and sense of loss. In order to do this, however, he will need help in achieving cognitive and perceptual clarity about what has happened to him and what the many implications are. When this is done by a sensitive social worker with attention to Mr. M's many strengths, and within a context of support and understanding, he can begin to relax the denial and air his feelings. Only then will he be ready to begin considering the usefulness of homemaker assistance as a way of advancing his own interests and sustaining remaining areas of independence. It is imperative, however, that such help be provided at the point of crisis, and not some time later.

Social Work Function, Roles, and Method

The Worker and Life Transitions

With people experiencing stresses that arise from life transitions, the professional function of the social worker is to help them meet the particular life tasks which, in their culture, are associated with developmental stages, status and role demands, and crisis events. For the most part, the environmental aspects of the worker's activities in carrying out this function are considered in chapter 4, but the reader is asked to remember that we make this separation only for purposes of the analysis, so that the complexities of practice can be presented in a reasonably systematic way without, we hope, distorting the realities of practice.

The environment represents a critical force in life transitions.

The development of adaptive skills, for example, requires adequate preparation and training in culturally acceptable problem-solving skills by the society's training institutions including family, school, religion, recreational organizations, mental hospitals and prisons.[27] When schools, for example, fail to meet the learning needs of children who then drop out, such children are ill-equipped for adaptive functioning in an industrialized society. De-institutionalizing mental patients before they have developed coping skills to meet the demands of life in the community, or before coping resources are provided within the community, dooms the patients to bleak and despairing lives as marginal outsiders in the community, or to eventual return to the institution after still another failure.

Adaptation also requires motivation to grapple actively with stress, but it is the environment that provides incentives for motivation, and it is the environment that rewards or punishes coping behavior.[28] A medical patient in a hospital who actively seeks information about his condition and treatment regimen is too often defined by staff as an acting-out, difficult patient. The patient's attempts at coping are not valued; they are punished rather than rewarded. He may then regress to being a "good" patient, passive and docile.

The social worker's function, then, is to help people move through stressful life transitions in such a way that their adaptive capacities are supported or strengthened, and the environment's responsiveness to coping needs is increased. This professional function can be further specified by casting it into the various roles of the social work practitioner in helping with life transitions. These are the more expressive role of *enabler,* and the more instrumental roles of *teacher* and *facilitator*.

In order to deal effectively with problems in living, people must have some degree of psychic comfort by maintaining at least minimal control over such threatening affects as grief, rage, shame, guilt, and despair that can immobilize them. Psychic comfort also includes some minimal degree of self-esteem and self-confidence, or trust in one's self and in others.[29] Successful coping also requires both the motivation to cope, and some hope that melioration of problems–needs can be achieved. In the role of *enabler,* the social worker carries out the tasks of promoting and sustaining or strengthening people's motivations to deal with the stress associated with life transitions through skills of eliciting, identifying, and managing feelings; responding to signals of distress; providing legitimate support; identifying transactional patterns; legitimizing concerns; validating strengths; conveying hope; reducing ambivalence and resistance; providing rewards for coping efforts; partializing problems; and maintaining focus on the work.

An important component in adaptation and in the management of stress is problem-solving behaviors. Successful problem solving includes the following steps: recognizing the problem or need; scanning its nature, likely consequences, and the tasks it poses; considering alternative solutions and likely outcomes of each; selecting the goal(s) or solutions; planning the actions to be taken; undertaking the actions; evaluating the outcome, and returning to adaptive balance, or planning next steps for additional work on the problem.[30] In the role of *teacher,* the social worker, in general, carries out the function of teaching adaptive skills through clarifying perceptions; providing pertinent information in the appropriate cognitive mode and at the appropriate rate for effective cognitive–perceptual processing; offering advice or suggestions; identifying alternatives and their likely consequences; modeling desired behaviors; and teaching the steps in problem-solving.

Effective coping depends not only on one's self-esteem, self-confidence, and defense repertoire, but on the freedom to take action and to make decisions with sufficient time for developing such adaptive strategies. Human beings, like other organisms, have a built-in need for effective interaction with the environment. Repeated experiences in which this need is satisfied lead to feelings of competence. While competence motivation may be covered over or dampened by harsh environments, it can be mobilized and supported by imaginative provisions of opportunities for action. And finally, effective coping requires willingness and ability to turn to the environment for information, resources, and support, maintaining appropriate degrees of dependence and independence.[31] People must have their basic needs met without fear on the part of others (including social workers) that this somehow creates dependence. Reciprocity, the give-and-take of human relatedness over the life span, suggests that maturity means being free to be either dependent or independent as the situation realistically requires. In the role of *facilitator,* the social worker, in general, carries out the tasks of assuring freedom of action, and mobilizing and supporting capacities for competence through skills in providing opportunities for successful action and decision-making; in defining tasks and mobilizing the environment supports, including the information and resources needed for successful task accomplishment; in regulating the pace and rhythm of the work; and in managing issues of passivity and dependence–independence.

Professional Method

The principles and skills of helping which draw on professional purpose and knowledge are used to carry out the functions and roles of the social worker. The principles include respect for cultural and other differences, a focus on strengths, mobilization of human relatedness and support to the sense of identity, autonomy, and competence. The skills include an array of communication, relationship, and problem-solving activities. How each worker carries the roles and performs the skills is a function of her professional philosophy, ideology, and knowledge—all filtered through her own individuality, creativity, and experience. In this section, we focus on practice skills, presenting brief practice excerpts to illustrate how the social worker helps individuals, families, and groups to deal with the adaptive tasks of stressful life transitions.

Developmental Changes. Developmental changes often create internal and interpersonal stress. The worker needs to invite discussion of difficult and painful material where pertinent, and to legitimize the clients' concerns and reactions. Because some issues may be defended against in a maladaptive way, and others may be culturally taboo, sensitive timing and appropriate persistence are required.

A group of ten girls, ages 11 to 14, have been meeting with the social worker at the settlement house for almost a year, as part of a delinquency-prevention project. The girls, eight Puerto Ricans and two blacks, live on the fringe of a Spanish-speaking ghetto, and all of their families except one are on welfare. The work of the group is directed to the tasks of adolescence, and is particularly focused on racial and sex-role issues in identity formation.

Over a period of several months, the worker felt the girls had some concerns about developmental issues of sexuality. Her attempts to explore their feelings brought immediate closure and retreat. While the members provided various cues of interest and intense anxiety, the cultural taboo for Puerto Rican girls and parental admonitions against open verbal expression of sexual matters inhibited exploration. During this time, the worker attempted to convey her acceptance and respect of their feelings, and to separate the universal and natural aspects of sexual interests from the anxious feelings attached to talking about them. One meeting began with discussion about the birth of a neighbor's baby. Suddenly and dramatically, the members shared their questions and anxieties, and were able to begin to use the worker's help.

> Kathy asked if it was true that we had eggs inside. I replied yes, and Tata began shouting that they had been talking about periods and that stuff at school, and added that they called it hygiene or something. This was said in a disgusted tone as if to indicate "hygiene" was a cover-up. I replied that I had noticed they got upset when we talked about such things. I asked if they had a question time when they could ask questions about sex. Judy replied, "Hell, yes, but who's going to open their big mouth?" Again there was laughter. I said it must be very hard for them since, like most girls, they probably had questions they wanted to ask, but they couldn't do it there.
>
> Tata explained further about the health class, saying the teacher had said fresh things. I suggested it must be hard to understand just what she was saying, especially if they felt upset about her even talking about it. Kathy repeated her question about the eggs really being there, and I said they were there in every girl, but the egg came out once a month, since it wasn't going to grow into a baby. Kathy said the hygiene teacher had said it was where a baby came from, and I agreed with this, adding it was terribly small like a little seed, but that the baby started from that. I asked if it weren't amazing that people as big as we are started from such little things. Tata said she had never known this, and Judy said that was why you had to stop fooling around with boys when you got your period. I

didn't reply. Lydia declared emphatically that she knew the boys were listening at the door when the teacher asked those fresh questions.[32]

The girls' own internal pressures, their interpersonal experiences, and their advance in age propel them into verbalizing their concerns. The worker proceeds slowly at their own pace and is mindful of the cultural constraints. She begins by recognizing with them their upset in talking about sex. This frees them to elaborate their concerns. Several of the girls begin to talk quite freely, and the worker consistently attempts to legitimize their interests. This helps to decrease their anxiety and guilt, and loosens the restraints on their adaptive need for knowledge. Skillfully, she universalizes their interest in declaring that, like most girls, they have questions. Throughout, she is careful to stay in tune with their anxiety level and to be responsive to individual concerns.

In all these respects, the worker is utilizing the skills of the enabler role. Her greatest impact in the excerpt, however, comes from the role of teacher, in which she clarifies the girls' misperceptions and provides them with pertinent information, in terms they can understand, and at a pace matched to their readiness. She also moves beyond the level of biological facts and expresses for them the feeling of awe at the wonder of reproduction. Their fears are beginning to subside, so that work can continue at the cognitive, perceptual, and feeling levels on the particular adolescent tasks related to sexuality, and what it means to be young women at this time and place. The delicate task for the worker is to steer a course between helping the girls relax culturally-based taboos and superstitions, while not violating cultural norms for sex-role behavior. Her intent is to strengthen their adaptive capacities in their environments.

In helping people to anticipate and prepare for developmental changes, the worker's initial efforts may be met with resistance. Through lending emotional support and providing information, through legitimizing, universalizing, and partializing the concerns, the worker can help the client reduce the resistance and move ahead. These skills, integrated always with genuine concern, interest, and a sense of timing, are particularly essential for helping people with difficult developmental tasks. One of the developmental tasks of the elderly, and of the very old especially, is to anticipate and prepare for death. Within the Eriksonian framework, the ending of life is indeed a life task.

Mrs. Mannheim is an 87-year-old widowed woman living in a housing project in a rubble-strewn, fire-gutted, dangerous neighborhood where the elderly are easy prey to muggers. She demonstrates adaptive strengths in taking care of her apartment and preparing simple meals. Even her denial of aging has so far not been maladaptive. Recently, however, the student–worker has sensed in Mrs. Mannheim some beginning concerns about the aging process, her own death, and what is going to happen to her.

> 11/9—At one point, she showed me pictures taken of her with a policeman last year after her mugging. She remarked, with surprise, "Look at those wrinkles and that skinny neck." She began to laugh. I said she sounds a little surprised. She looked at the pictures of herself again, laughed, and said, "It's hard to believe that's me." She quickly changed the subject. While she was talking about beautiful places, Mrs. M said how pretty the cemetery is where her husband is buried. I asked where she is to be buried. She said that she had a plot next to his. . . .
>
> 11/30—She talked a lot today about her dead sister. At one point, she mused over her own age of 87. She said, "Am I really 87? Where did the last 50 years go?" She began telling me about interviews on television with people in their 90s and 100s. I said some people do have very long lives, and maybe she's hoping she will live as long as they. She nodded and said, "I'd like to make it to 90."
>
> 12/14—At one point, Mrs. M talked about giving away her dishes. "I could drop down dead tomorrow and they (the neighbors) would come in and take everything." I said, "You're worried about what will happen to your treasures?" She said, "Well, I

would like them to go to my family—my niece and her daughter.'' I wondered if she would like my help with this, and she responded that she would.

As I was marking on her calendar the day of our excursion, Mrs. M said, ''I hope I'm alive, I don't want to die yet.'' I put my arm around her, and we walked to the door.

1/25—I asked Mrs. M if she had heard anything about Beth (a friend). When she shook her head no, I said, ''I have something to tell you about Beth. She died on Friday.'' Mrs. M gasped and clasped her hands together. She looked stunned, and said, ''I feel bad for her. You know, she said she was going to die, she was always talking about death. Well, at least she was with her people. What about her apartment and furniture? I guess her family will take care of it?'' I said, ''It's upsetting to hear about the death of a friend.'' Mrs. M said, ''Well, I hope she rests in peace. That's what I hope for all the dead, that they rest in peace.'' A little later, Mrs. M and I were looking through her photographs, and she came across one of her dead sister. She said, ''Imagine, who would think that I'd be alive and I'd outlive my sister?'' I said she sounded surprised. Mrs. M looked at the calendar and said, ''Yeah, I'm 87.'' I said, ''Sometimes it feels like life is speeding by.'' Mrs. M replied, ''Let's face it, we all have to go sometime. As long as I can get out of bed and walk I'm okay.''

The worker was aware that along with the remarkable and endearing strengths of Mrs. M there was a growing concern about what would happen to her should she fall ill and not be able to do her ''routines,'' and what would happen to her treasured belongings should she die. Hence, there was a delicate task for the worker in steering between the danger of undermining the denial that helped keep Mrs. M going in the face of unspeakable isolation, and the helpfulness that could be extended in planning arrangements for her death. The worker handled the delicate distinction between denial as coping and denial as avoidance by the gentleness with which she probed under Mrs. M's protestations of strength. The worker utilized most opportunities to invite further comment in these areas, making particularly good use of Mrs. M's pleasure in reminiscing over family photographs. In the exchange about Beth's death, the worker's legitimate intent was to help Mrs. M recognize her grief and to mourn the loss of her friend. It might also have been helpful, perhaps even more so, to pick up on her own agonizing concerns: "I guess you worry about who will be with you?" Or, if this is too threatening, as it might be, "I guess you worry about what will become of your things?" At the same time, one might reach out with human touch as this worker so often did, putting her arm around Mrs. M, and verbally expressing her caring and concern as well.

A common lay attitude is that one should not bring up such a frightening subject as death, especially to a very old person, or to a terminally ill patient. This may be, in part, a rationalization to cover the discomfort all of us have with the subject because of conscious and unconscious fears and attitudes toward our own dying. This beginning student was sensitive and deeply compassionate in her attempts to help Mrs. M deal even more adequately with her life tasks, and especially the tasks of preparing for the end. This assures Mrs. M that the worker is strong enough, and she herself is strong enough to talk about the relative nearness of death without either of them being frightened or overwhelmed by anxiety. Indeed, our own practice experience suggests that many old people, in good health or poor health, feel comfort and relief when they can talk with someone about their wishes regarding funeral arrangements, disposal of their belongings, insurance, and related concerns.

Throughout the contacts, though not in these particular excerpts, the worker's steady concern was to help Mrs. M move out to her relatives and reestablish linkages with them. Similarly, knowing Mrs. M's pleasure in excursions, she took her on walks; they visited favorite stores and places of interest. The worker was especially careful to prepare for holiday activities, knowing well the impact of holidays on the lonely and isolated. Throughout the helping process, the worker moves easily between and among the roles of enabler, teacher, and facilitator, as the situation requires. She keeps always in mind the nature of the life transition and its tasks, the nature of the environment, Mrs. M's strengths and her ambivalence and resistance, and the degree of mutual trust in their relationship. Thus, she probes gently and retreats, sometimes wisely, and sometimes unnecessarily. She teaches the facts of aging; she provides support and validates strengths; and, in very important ways, she brings human pleasures into Mrs. M's restricted life. The emphasis is on action. Together they look at photographs while Mrs. M reminisces. Together they walk and visit the botanical garden; together they celebrate Hanukkah and Passover.

Status Changes and Role Demands. Status changes and role demands are often accompanied by ambivalence. Separation involved in the placement of a child in foster care or of an elderly parent into congregate care may stimulate feelings of grief, guilt, or relief. Any change in status may reawaken earlier and still unresolved conflicts and ambivalences. The worker needs to comment on the presence of these feelings, clarifying their nature, and distinguishing between past and present experiences. In this way, the person's doubts and hesitancies become understandable to her, freeing her to act on the positive side of the ambivalence. If this is not done, there is a danger that the negative side and all its angers and resentments, most of which may be out of immediate awareness, build up and intensify, interfering with adaptive action. The following excerpt illustrates help with ambivalent feelings that are related to a perceived threat to a highly valued status:

Mr. and Mrs. Eaton, a lower-middle-class black couple, are the parents of a 17-year-old daughter, Mary, who has been a severely disorganized and suicidal patient in a university-based psychiatric hospital for over a year. She has just been discharged to a foster home. Doctor W had felt that at this point in Mary's treatment, she could not return to her parents. At their request, and with Mary's consent, placement was arranged in the home of family friends after assessment by the social worker. Immediately following the placement, Mrs. Eaton came in for her weekly interview with the social worker. (Father and mother were seen separately, as well as together, and occasionally with their daughter and Doctor W.)

Mrs. Eaton said Mary moved to the Smiths' the day before yesterday, and I asked how it went. "Mary saw twin poster beds in her room and said, 'I like this.' She had been reluctant to go over there, so I was at least glad for that! She's going to be spoiled. She's not even missing me so that I could at least comfort her." [All said in a jocular fashion.] Mrs. Eaton said she called Mary the next morning at 11, and she was still in bed, but called her mother back in a gay mood.

Mrs. Eaton added that her husband is a changed man, he's so relieved. I didn't pick up on this, thinking Mrs. E's feelings were uppermost, so I referred back to how is she feeling about all this? She said she is so happy, she can sleep now, she knows Mary is safe, the problem is solved. I wondered about Mrs. Smith—is she happy too? Mrs. Eaton said, "Mrs. Smith is too happy." I asked her to tell me about that. Mrs. Eaton explained, "It's selfish of me, I'm just piqued, I'll get over it."

I wondered if maybe she was feeling a little fear, too, a fear that she might lose Mary. Mrs. E responded that she could give her up to college or give her up to a man. I said yes, but this situation is a little different, this is another mother–person. Perhaps Mrs. E is afraid that Mary will see Mrs. Smith as a better mother? Mrs. E said she guessed she has to admit she's jealous, and she wonders if I think she's silly? I said I thought it was very understandable. Mrs. E then said, "I need you to talk about this, I can't mention it to my husband, he'll only say forget it—and my neighbors and friends wouldn't understand. I could only have told my sister [a beloved mother–figure, now dead]. I don't even think Dr. W would understand—he would talk just like a doctor. Do you see psychiatry in what I'm saying?" I said I saw pretty basic human nature, maternal human nature.

Mrs. E continued, "But I should be happy that Mary's problem is working out well—and I *am* happy for that." I said, "You're happy for that, and at the same time you're frightened you're losing your child?" Mrs. Eaton

> said that was it, and she supposed "It's like loving your husband and at other times hating him, yet going on living, like we've talked about before." I said it was a little like that, except now she's having two very different feelings at the exact same time. She replied, "Yes, and it's making me miserable, except now that I've talked about it and faced it, and not gone on shoving it away I do feel better." I mentioned that talking about it can help, but I wondered if there wasn't something else required too —looking at it and trying to see just what the feeling was all about? Mrs. Eaton replied, "I have to face the fact I'm jealous. I couldn't stand staying there last Monday, I had to leave even though Mrs. Smith asked us to visit. I was hurt that Mary didn't phone, didn't need me to comfort her. Maybe she'll tell Mrs. Smith all her problems, and Mrs. Smith will be her mother."
>
> I wondered if she wasn't saying how frightened she is that she could be losing her child. Mrs. Eaton said yes, and I said, "This is a parent's hardest task. Mary is reaching the stage of development where she no longer needs the kind of protection and nurture you have given her. She will need you and love you just as much, but in a different way. Doctor W feels it is easier for Mary to meet this stage and to attain her full health again in another home." Mrs. E nodded, looking unhappy. I said, "It isn't going to be easy for you—it wouldn't be for any mother."

In the role of enabler, the worker helps Mrs. E to recognize her conflicting feelings around Mary's new situation. The worker accepts them as natural and understandable, but needing to be worked on. This helps Mrs. E begin to accept the doctor's decision and all that it means. As this work continues, she will be less likely to sabotage the plan wittingly or unwittingly. The worker clearly aligns herself with the positive side of the ambivalence, the part of Mrs. W that is happy because her child is better, while not condemning the negative aspects. The tasks in coping with this threat to her parental status and mothering role have been defined within the larger context of the family's developmental tasks related to adolescence. One can expect that Mrs. Eaton is ready to work on them with the worker's support and encouragement, even though the ambivalence will continue to manifest itself painfully from time to time. One other reason for the effectiveness of this particular interchange lies in the worker's staying from the outset with Mrs. Eaton's own feelings, and not picking up on the statements related to her husband's and her daughter's responses to the events under consideration.

Always, in helping people with problems in living, including life transitions, it is important to convey a sense of realistic hope. With hope, people take action and strive toward achieving goals. Without hope they become apathetic, despairing, and unable to move forward. Hope seems to be a necessary condition for help to be effective, although it is not sufficient in itself to cause a person to change. It has been said that hope and discomfort need to be in a particular balance to provide motivation for working on one's problems and needs.[33] This balance refers both to moving positively toward a goal, and escaping from a painful or uncomfortable state. If neither the worker nor the client has any hope of change, then it seems likely that no change—except, perhaps, for the worst—can be achieved, and the contact is best terminated before it begins!

Despite the importance of hope as a lever of action, it sometimes happens that a client resists involvement in the worker's expression of hope, or positive expectations, or focus on strengths. This is usually the person who is drawn to the passivity of the patient role, and feels an ambivalent tug to remain in it.

Mrs. Duggan, age 45, white, Catholic, was referred to the family agency following her discharge from the psychiatric hospital where she had received electro-shock treatment during her six-week stay. She had been hospitalized twice before in the three years since her divorce. She was receiving alimony and child support for a daughter, age 16 and in school, and a son, age 20, employed at odd jobs. Mrs. Duggan was still struggling with the complex tasks in her loss of one status and assumption of the less valued status of "divorced woman" and its associated roles. The worker planned to see mother and children together, but the children refused to come, and, while Mrs. Duggan expressed some concern about the children she was most worried about herself. She viewed the problem as arising from people who had failed her—her family, the psychiatrist, welfare, etc.—and was mired down in feelings that the world had let her down. The worker's view of the problem was that Mrs. Duggan's self-esteem, confidence, and coping abilities had been severely shaken by the divorce and several related events. The worker writes;

> I took a very positive, optimistic approach that things could go better and that she could get her feet on the ground if she were willing to work at it with me. At first, Mrs. Duggan vacillated between wanting to go back to the hospital and wanting to struggle to make it on the outside. When she indicated she would try the latter, she added it would take forever to solve her problems. I did not accept this, and said that I felt we could expect some definite progress within two months.
>
> Early in our discussions, I let Mrs. Duggan know there was really nothing I could do to change her past, and that spending a great deal of time talking about the past wasn't going to help change her present and future. It was a hopeful sign when, in the fourth session, she could stop herself short and bring herself from complaints about the past to talk about what she was doing now. She also tended to spend time talking about what others should do for her, and I continually shifted it back to what she can do for herself. At the same time, I let her know that I'm not asking her to make these efforts all on her own, that I will stick with her.
>
> In my discussions with Mrs. Duggan, I didn't accept her description of herself as very sick, or as needing a psychiatrist, or as needing to return to the hospital. Now (two months later), she is no longer bringing this up. She appears relieved by my taking the position that she had been overwhelmed by a combination of circumstances, and by my impression of her that she can learn to function adequately as a person, mother, and head of the household. Mrs. Duggan has now come up with two goals that she has set for herself and that she wants my help with. One is resuming her role as head of the household. Although the children continue to assume much responsibility in this

> area, there are indications that Mrs. Duggan is gradually taking over some of the responsibilities of the parenting role. The second area relates to the family's poor financial condition. Mrs. D sees herself as ultimately being able to work. At this writing she has been out on one job interview, but is still apprehensive about moving into that area yet.

Here we see worker and client struggling to withstand the pull of the regressive forces. As Bandler suggests,[34] the progressive forces are stronger and the worker, as enabler and facilitator, allies herself with them, clarifying the nature of the stresses and the tasks necessary to cope with them, and regulating the pace of expectations in line with Mrs. Duggan's capacities, level of self-esteem and psychic discomfort.

An important set of practice skills in helping people deal with status and role demands are those connected to the teaching role. Sometimes teaching involves the provision of information and other cognitive stimuli on which effective adaptation and coping depend; sometimes it involves engaging the cognitive powers in a problem-solving process; and sometimes it involves both. Earlier in this chapter, we discussed the three modes of cognition: the enactive, iconic, and symbolic.

Ideas about cognitive development do not deny the affective and irrational in human beings. But they offer an additional area in which social workers can be helpful to all clients, and most especially to those who have had little opportunity to exercise their cognitive powers, to make decisions, and to solve problems successfully. Many clients, victimized by unemployment, illness, discrimination, poor housing, and dehumanizing contacts with service systems, have had little in their lives to encourage a positive outlook toward developing new means of coping. Part of the social worker's responsibility in providing the conditions that will support successful task resolution includes not only focusing on strengths and offering support, but also includes furnishing information in the cognitive mode in which it is most useful and at the pace at which it can be assimilated.

Social workers presently use modes of cognition beyond the verbal and symbolic, as in role play or role rehearsal, play therapy, psychodrama, family sculpting, and the use of eco-maps and genograms with clients.[35] The consequences of variation in the cognitive styles between worker and client, and how to overcome such cognitive barriers, have not received much attention.

If we attend to the cognitive elements in the client–worker relationship with the same care that we attend to the emotional elements, we can help people cognitively to restructure their perceptual world, thus enriching their adaptive capacities. Communication is facilitated when the social worker develops awareness of clients' cognitive styles and of his own. The following example shows a creative social worker working with a Mexican-American family, to help them cope with their many serious life problems, and particularly their statuses as parents and their familial roles.[36] The A's had come to the agency's attention after an accusation of incest against Mr. A by Mrs. A's oldest daughter, Lucinda, age 13. Both Mr. and Mrs. A had experienced a lifetime of poverty. Both had been separated from their parents in early childhood and had received little substitute parental care or nurturance. They, in turn, had been unable to establish loving and reciprocal need-meeting relationships with each other or with their seven children. Both parents had longstanding serious health problems. The family lived in a public housing project in an urban area and was receiving public assistance. Four years earlier, they had lived in a small southwestern town and had worked as farm laborers.

The worker reports that she visited the home frequently, working with anyone who was available. Much time was spent in meeting concrete needs and requests and in discussing the family's current problems. Much of the work with Mr. and Mrs. A was modeled on how parents raise well-adapted children, modified to take into account Mr. and Mrs. A's chronological ages. This approach was designed to enable each to meet needs and to accomplish life tasks not resolved at earlier stages. While not conceptualized within the framework of cognitive theory, the following brief excerpt from the ongoing phase nevertheless illustrates the use of cognitive styles.

> "Searching for a way to give Mrs. A some tangible experience of problem-solving, I struck upon the idea of involving her in putting together jigsaw puzzles. As we worked on the puzzles together, I compared the pieces in

> disarray on the table to recent family difficulties: disagreements with Lucinda and her husband were frequently used as examples. On some occasions, we viewed the pieces as apparently disparate and isolated occurrences—which fitted together perfectly to form a mighty quarrel, before our eyes. On other occasions, we viewed the pieces as the various elements of the solution of a problem. The nature of my work with Mrs. A was determined in large measure by two facts: she was overwhelmed by problems, and she had been deprived of experiences through which she might have developed a capacity to reach solutions. Putting together jigsaw puzzles gave her the experience of conceptualizing problems in a tangible context. And it was hoped that she could come to parallel this activity in her day-to-day living. It was hoped, moreover, that the gratification she received from solving the puzzles would lead her to seek a similar gratification in solving her family problems."[37]

The worker also describes the use of other skills related to the enabler and facilitator roles. She describes the progress made by the family, and she concludes that meeting dependency needs, communicating hope and positive expectations, and providing opportunities for task mastery stimulated a growth response in Mr. and Mrs. A. We would agree; but, using cognitive theory, let us return to the excerpt for an examination of why such a seemingly simple idea as a jigsaw puzzle had its own powerful impact.[38]

Worker and client communicated in the *iconic* (pictorial) style, and the *enactive* (doing) style. The pieces of the jigsaw puzzle were used by the worker to represent pieces of the family puzzle, and, on both the level of jigsaw and family, she demonstrated that the pieces of the puzzle could be put together to make a coherent picture out of disastrous chaos. Within the emotional context of a consistent, giving, hopeful, and expectant relationship, the worker engaged the cognitive functions of Mrs. A at the iconic and enactive levels and, by making the connection between puzzle and family, helped her move to the *symbolic* mode, a higher level of cognitive integration. Put another way, the worker as teacher provided information needed for mastery in a form that could be processed and understood, with patience for the time needed to develop the coping skills (problem-solving) at the symbolic level. Mrs. A's adaptive capacities were enhanced, her self-esteem stimulated, her motivation and sense of competence mobilized through action that had both cognitive and motoric elements.

Crisis Events. Crisis is thought to create a particular openness to the environment. People in crisis tend to reach out to others for help and guidance; others in the environment tend to reach out to the person in crisis. A neighbor, for example, reaches out to another who has sustained a loss, although as neighbors they may not have had much previous contact. Members of the extended family may rally around a member in crisis regardless of their feelings about her before the crisis. This reciprocal openness suggests that the social work practitioner should make every effort to utilize, mobilize, strengthen, and support these linkages, helping the person to reach out to the environment and the environmental figures to reach out and sustain the person.

Mrs. Talbot was seen by the social worker in a large, private, voluntary psychiatric hospital. Her father had just been hospitalized for an agitated depression. He had lived with Mr. and Mrs. Talbot and their two school-age sons, following his divorce from Mrs. Talbot's mother several years earlier. Since the father's insurance will cover only 4 to 6 weeks of hospitalization, the social worker wishes to engage Mrs. Talbot in discharge planning at the outset. In the first interview she discovered that Mrs. Talbot was very anxious, guilty, and angry. She felt completely unable to cope with the demands her father was placing on her through his telephone calls and during her visits with him, and at the same time handle the situation at home and on her job. She was clearly in distress and feeling overwhelmed. Excerpts from the second session follow:

> Mrs. T appeared anxious again—her hands were shaking—but she was pleasant and friendly. I asked how she was, and she said okay. I then asked if she had seen her father over the weekend, and she said she visited him Sunday, along with her brother. It was a good visit, and she

was glad her brother came. She continued that her father was mad that she wasn't alone. She doesn't know why, but feels it's because he thinks she's his wife. He called her this morning two or three times. Mrs. T began going off on tangents and expressing her annoyance at father's demands. I asked what had happened between them on the phone. He told her he missed her. She said, "I don't miss him, but I'm relieved he's being taken care of. When he called the second time I thought, oh God, I hope he doesn't start this again!" I said I could see she felt very burdened by his calls, and added that the doctors are exploring the possibility that his confusion may be organically caused. Her response was, "They can't do much about it then?" I explained that the possibility was now being explored, and he would continue to be observed, talked with, and would undergo tests. I told her she could call Dr. Blanchard (he had suggested I do this), and she took his number.

I asked if she had thought of plans for her father when he leaves the hospital, and she said her husband had already suggested placing him in a foster home. She feels placement will be necessary, and I stressed that we don't yet know if her father's problem is organic. We talked about other possibilities, such as his having a homemaker, etc. From her response, it appears that she is amenable to any situation, so long as he's not in her home and she does not have to bear responsibility. I asked about who we can depend on in the family to help plan for the time her father leaves the hospital. Mrs. T said no one else would do anything, and began to complain that her sisters don't call her or her father. Her brother is willing to help and will meet with me. She said she's angry with all of them. I remarked that it sounds like she sees herself as bearing the whole burden. She perked up and said, "You're right. I'm always doing the work." I wondered why she had, when she had a large family. She said, "What can I do? They won't do anything." I asked her if she had asked them to help. She said that they know what's happening and won't call. I made a concrete suggestion that she call her sisters and mother (she had mentioned her mother's interest), and tell them she'll need their help to plan for their father when he leaves the hospital. We discussed this a bit. She felt they might all come to meet with me when the time comes.

She then asked what to do about her father's calls. I told her he might be too confused to realize he had already spoken to her the same morning, and suggested she tell him she was glad to hear from him, but couldn't talk now and would call him the next day. She said her response to him had been to refuse to listen to him, and just hang up. I pointed out that knowing people care is probably important to him, and suggested she convey this, while setting limits with him at the same time. She said she'd try. Mrs. T volunteered that he must feel bad not hearing from her sisters. I said he might, and commented that if they called him or wrote, he wouldn't need her so much, and she could feel less burdened. We discussed this for a bit, and I tried to point out how she could give up some of the work and let her family take over some of it. This would give her father more contacts, and give her some relief. She liked this, and said she'd call the family this week, including her father's sister and brother. Then she asked, 'Suppose they don't want to call?' I said we could talk about this when we meet again, but wondered why she thinks that will happen. She said they're 'fed up.' I then asked if her husband will get involved in plans for her father. She answered that he won't have him live with them, and went on about his strong feelings in the matter. I said it might be a reality that father would not be best off with them, and we may have to accept that and look at other possibilities. I asked if her husband had always felt this way about her father? She said only recently, with his illnesses.

I then reviewed our talk about calling her sisters, mother, aunt, and uncle, and limiting her contacts with her father without cutting him off totally. I said I'd call her brother and set up a joint appointment for next week. She

> smiled and said she felt much more relaxed. I smiled and said she looks calmer. We made an appointment for our next session the day after tomorrow.

Here we see the beginning efforts of the worker to clarify for Mrs. Talbot the nature of the situation, and to facilitate her cognitive integration of the factors involved and the tasks needing to be done. She allows for expression of the associated affects, makes concrete suggestions, and attempts to restore the linkages within the family network. She remains clearly focused on the presenting problem, and provides immediate relief of the anxiety by her direct, problem-solving approach. At the end she summarizes their interview, which also aids the cognitive structuring. Because the worker helps Mrs. Talbot to set limits with her father and to reach out for help from her family, Mrs. Talbot already feels less anxious, and may now be able to deal with her father less angrily, thus feeling less guilty as well. It is clear that Mrs. Talbot welcomes the suggestions and feels that the worker is helping her to decide how to proceed.

Over the next few weeks the worker's continued use of skills in the enabler, teacher, and facilitator roles helped Mrs. Talbot to organize herself, perceive her conflicting roles more clearly, set priorities for herself, and ask for the help and involvement of other family members. The provision of information, and the giving of advice and suggestions, supported her coping efforts. At the end of the contact, Mrs. Talbot had recognized her need for help with feelings related to earlier familial experiences that had made this crisis particularly difficult. She accepted a referral to the family agency.

The particular skills conceptualized for crisis intervention are illustrated in this case. They are based upon a rapid, initial response and a directive approach, and include the following: helping the client achieve a cognitive grasp and mastery of the situation through focusing on the crisis event and clarifying the attendant circumstances; reducing the anxiety, and placing irrational responses in a rational context; creating a climate of hope and confidence; re-establishing the client's sense of autonomy; making use of interpersonal and institutional resources; and using time limits as a dynamic in strengthening coping and in avoiding regressive behavior.[39] These skills are helpful not only in crisis situations but in the stresses that arise from any life transition, because they utilize the life processes involved in adaptation.

Case Illustrations

Mrs. Kaminsky

Mrs. Kaminsky, age 81, had been admitted to a geriatric residence two years earlier after a fracture of the hip that made return to her own apartment unfeasible. She was a difficult resident, assaultive toward a roommate, incontinent (non-correctable), depressed, agitated, and constantly complaining to nursing and medical staffs about her health. After prolonged conflict with a second roommate, Mrs. Kaminsky was moved to another building in the complex, where she could have a private room. Mrs. Kaminsky was not only dealing with the biological and emotional demands of advanced age, but now had the additional life task of adapting to a new social context. She was very afraid of the change, the loss of her familiar surroundings, and the relationships she had formed with staff and residents, poor as the relationships were. She did, however, accept the opportunity for change, with the hope that a single room would bring her some comfort. The worker writes:

> Fortunately, the first day on which Mrs. K arrived on the sixth floor coincided with the day of the weekly floor meeting. I introduced myself to Mrs. K as the social worker. In a whining way, she spoke of the despair she was feeling. "They all hate me on this floor. They are all German, and I'm not, so I'm not good enough for them." I recognized with her the sense of loneliness and the strangeness she is feeling, and we talked about how frightening it is to come into a new situation where she knows no one. After a bit, I mentioned to her that many women on the floor are not German and, in fact, some were born in Russia just as she was. Mrs. K brightened a little at this, and seemed surprised. I asked her if there had been floor meetings on her other floor, and she said yes, she had attended them. I invited her to come to our meeting this eve-

ning. Mrs. K began to use her whining voice again, and said she would like to come, "but they all hate me." I asked what had happened today that had made her feel that way. She said nothing had happened, she just felt that way. I again acknowledged the feelings of helplessness and confusion she was feeling because she doesn't yet know anyone, and I again invited her to come to the meeting. She said, acceptingly, "If you think it's all right, I'll come to the meeting."

When the group meeting began, I said we had a new resident, and introduced Mrs. K to the others. Mrs. S wished her good luck, and Mrs. B graciously said she hoped Mrs. Kaminsky would be happy on the floor. During the meeting, Mrs. K was quiet but involved. After the meeting she remained in the day room and engaged in conversation with two residents.

In the days that followed, Mrs. K continued to voice the alienation she felt as, "They all hate me." She whined like a child, stayed in her room, and refused to participate in occupational therapy, the same behaviors she had manifested on the previous floor. I continued to point out that Mrs. K was feeling strange and lonely, and that this is expectable in a new situation. I reminded her it was going to take time to feel at home, and within a week or so, Mrs. K had no difficulty expressing to me her need for help in adjusting to the new floor. Together we agreed to work on alleviating her sense of being "foreign" on the floor, so she could find a new niche for herself. My job would be to help her understand and participate in the formal systems (nursing, dietary, medical, occupational therapy) and the informal systems (the ward culture of norms and customs, relationships, etc.) around her. I assumed that Mrs. K's effectance motivation could be mobilized, and an opportunity soon presented itself in a situation which Mrs. K viewed as hopeless and herself as helpless. This was the matter of her social security checks. Mrs. K said she has no money and she doesn't know what she can do about it. I asked what she did before, when she found herself in

> need of money. "I went downstairs to get it, but I am so mixed up about where I am, I don't know how I would get to the place where I used to go." I said that now she is in a different building, so it is easy to understand how she might have lost her sense of where the accounting office is located. I offered to go downstairs with her so she will know how to get to the office from the new building. When we arrived at the accounting office, Mrs. K told me, "This is where I used to come when I needed money." There were many other residents in the accounting office, and Mrs. K became increasingly upset, worrying she wouldn't know how to sign for the money. I asked her what she remembered about signing for the money before. She said she remembered, and we talked about how she did it. She didn't think she could do it now, and I reassured her that Mr. A will tell her what she has to do. When it was Mrs. K's turn, she sat next to Mr. A and, in her whining voice, said she didn't know what she was suppose to do. He instructed her how to sign, and Mrs. K then seemed very pleased that she managed to negotiate this transaction. We talked about her success in doing something for herself that she had thought she was unable to do.

At every opportunity, the worker continued to acknowledge the reality of Mrs. K's feelings of loss, fear, and despair, and to focus on her adaptive strengths.[40] As the worker continued to point out the various stresses Mrs. K was experiencing in the new environment, Mrs. K's own perceptions became more accurate. As the worker clarified the nature and impact of the stresses, Mrs. K's own cognition came into play as she developed cognitive understanding of what was happening with her. Both cognitive and perceptual functions were engaged in the coping tasks. The opportunities created by the worker for Mrs. K to take action on her own behalf and to have a positive effect on her environment, restored Mrs. K's self-esteem and sense of competence.

> As the work proceeded, I frequently observed Mrs. K in the day room talking with other residents. She continued to attend the group regularly, and although she remained a

passive member, she always stayed on afterward to chat with the others. She made a more consistent effort to use the toilet at regular intervals in order to minimize the incontinence and attendant discomfort. For the first time in the two years of her residence, she began attending the occupational therapy group, and enjoyed making a pillow. She required my continued encouragement because of her visual difficulties, but took pride in her work. She negotiated independently for new eyeglasses, and was particularly pleased with herself, and with my commendation of her success. In our interviews, the regressive and demanding behaviors continued to recede, and Mrs. K began to enjoy reminiscing with me about her earlier life, and even recalled how at the beginning of our contact she used to stay in her room and was afraid to leave the floor. Her level of functioning seems higher now than it had been before the move, even though at stressful moments, she still resorts to whininess and even to speaking in Russian.

Without the social worker's help, it is likely that Mrs. Kaminsky would have closed off exchanges with her environment to such a degree that her functioning would have regressed still further. The use of action in the enhancement of the self-image and the provision of opportunities for cognitive mastery and autonomy seemed to make the difference. Mrs. K's anxiety and tension had been eased so she was ready to undertake action, and the actions were relevant to her life situation. Tasks were related to her own demands, so that by participating in them Mrs. Kaminsky began to meet her own demands without resorting to manipulative, regressed behaviors.[41] The worker was careful to provide the necessary environmental conditions for Mrs. Kaminsky's successful task achievement by intervening with staff and residents to increase their sensitivity to Mrs. K's needs and feelings.

The relationship with the worker, at a time when Mrs. Kaminsky was experiencing extreme threats from her environment, led Mrs. K to reach out in new ways for other interpersonal relations which, in turn, led to new responses from staff and fellow residents in a continuing spiral of increased self-esteem.

A Group of Head Start Mothers

After addressing a church meeting on parent–child problems, a social worker received a request from five Head Start mothers for services from the family agency she represented. The mothers were offered group service of ten sessions which could be later extended if sufficient interest emerged. They contracted to work on shared life tasks in their relationships with men. Initial exploration had revealed that almost all were either single or separated, most were receiving welfare, several were involved with alcoholic men, and most found themselves either overly involved with or estranged from their mothers or, in one instance, a teenage daughter.

> 3d session: Shirley asked Betty why she left home when she did, wondering why it was so bad there. She added that she wanted to know because she too left home in her teens. Betty replied that she feels she is an outsider in her parents' home. She has one sister, age 19, who she feels is favored by her parents; she is "the perfect one." Her parents created a very close-knit circle of dependency between themselves, her sister, and her sister's boyfriend. Betty just doesn't fit in, nor does she want to. She added that she feels they are "sick," as they never go out and all stay together all the time. They never want to watch her daughter for her, though they protest that they love her. She was very angry, and I commented on this. Betty said she was just fed up and wanted to get away from them.
>
> Carolyn observed that she comes from a similar home, except that she was enmeshed in the dependency until she went to college, met her husband, and got married. She revealed that she and her older sister are only 11 months apart in age. Her sister still lives with her parents, and runs their home for them. She added that she could identify with Betty, and could understand her hurt, even though her situation wasn't as deplorable as Betty's.
>
> Anne opened up at this point, and talked about her unhappy childhood. She remarked that her father was "an old-fashioned Italian," who verbally and physically abused his wife and children. Her parents divorced when

she was 17. She did not speak to her father for 8 years after that. She described herself as being very passive and shy, quiet, and frightened. She said that it has been very difficult for her to handle her mother since then, as she feels guilty that her mother is all alone.

Her father remarried and has another family. Her mother retreated into herself. Anne openly talked of her distrust of men, saying her father never gave her any love or good feelings. She spoke of her fear of dating new men, and her anxiety about what they want of her.

Shirley intervened and said she knows Anne very well, and revealed they call one another whenever they are feeling anxious. Shirley feels that Anne avoids meeting new men, and spoke of how they got together in the Parents Without Partners group. Betty interrupted to ask about this group, sharing her desire to get out and meet people. She has not gone out in over a month.

I asked Anne and Shirley if they would take time after the meeting to give Betty the information, saying I felt we were getting away from some very real issues here. I brought the women back to focusing on why we were here, and noted that I felt a lot of feelings had been shared, and it seemed they all had much in common. I wondered how they saw it.

Shirley said, "It seems we all have a problem with our mothers." The rest of the women agreed. I asked Shirley to elaborate if she could. She spoke of her own inability to separate from her mother, and her resentment of her. She said she still has difficulty communicating with her mother, and revealed that each needs to term the other "sick." I related to the ambivalence, referring empathically to the difficulty in letting go and the need to stay angry with her mother. Betty didn't comment, but looked moved. I noted her nonverbal communication, saying she looked as if she knew what Shirley was feeling. She said she did, but she wasn't going to bother trying to get along with her mother any more; it is futile.

Time was almost up, and I commented we had talked

> about some central feelings of all the members. I credited their openness and willingness to share deep feelings with one another and with me.

In this session, the worker makes sure that each member has a chance to participate, and she helps them maintain focus when they veer off to a tangential discussion of the Parents Without Partners group. She doesn't permit Shirley to stop with a general statement, but asks for elaboration. This is important to do, because generalizations can cover complex feelings and distort the specifics in individuals' situations. The worker also called attention to ambivalent feelings, but does not yet align herself with either side of the ambivalence. Instead, she invites the group to work on it, but unfortunately, the time is up. This is a theme that undoubtedly will reappear and will need to be identified by the worker as requiring group attention.

At the end of the session, the worker credits the members' motivation by commending their willingness to share their feelings, and recognizing their hard work.

> 4th Session: Shirley said that she had seen three men on three separate occasions during the week. They were all old friends, with whom she had already had relationships. She revealed that she felt very low this week, and seeing these guys didn't help. She added, "I don't really feel like telling any more." Anne responded, "Go on, tell them the rest." Shirley replied, "You know already."
>
> At this point, I intervened to break through their alignment, which was keeping out the rest of the group. I observed that we all knew that she and Anne were good friends outside of the group, but what they were doing now was unfair to the rest of us. Either Shirley wants to share her feelings with all of us, or not; it wasn't right for her to play verbal games with Anne. Shirley replied, "You're right," and proceeded to reveal her painful feelings. She described herself as feeling "used, empty, and alone." She shared with us the fact that although these men held no future for her (they are all alcoholics), she

> still needs to turn to them for security, but in the end she feels used.

Here the worker's intervention, confronting Shirley and Anne with their avoidance of work, served to move them on. It might have been still more helpful had she asked the group for their response to the game-playing. In any case, Corinne responded to Shirley compassionately and asked her,

> "Do you ever feel like these are the only men you can attract, and wonder why you look for these men?" Shirley answered quietly by nodding her head affirmatively. Corinne went on to say she felt like this when she dated in the past, and added that she went through two alcoholic marriages. She described her first husband as a physically abusive man, and her second as an emotionally abusive man. She said, "Now I look out for myself; my heart no longer rules my head." She spoke of her present relationship with her first husband [he rents a room in her house] as one of purely business, and said it's good for the children to have him there. She denied there was any conflict in the home, and said the children see him as "Daddy," and do not question her lack of relating to him. I questioned her about this, but she refused to discuss it, and said, "There are lots of marriages where the husband and wife don't sleep together, and the children are aware of it, and don't see anything wrong with it." No one else challenged her. She then turned to Carolyn, who sat to her left and said, "Now it's your turn."
>
> Carolyn spoke of her relationship with Tom, and told how she is really worried about him, as he has resumed heavy drinking. She is trying to get him to see a social worker from the welfare department, but he refuses. She again spoke of her therapeutic work on her own growth as an individual, and expressed how difficult it is for her to reach out to Tom now. She is trying to cope with her anger and resentment. Anne interjected, "But I wonder how you feel, exposing your children to him when he is drinking? I

couldn't handle that. That's why I left my husband.'' Carolyn said she is fearful of what Tom will do to the children, as he has been threatening her that he will tell their oldest daughter [age 10] that she is illegitimate [Carolyn was six months pregnant when they were married]. The members all felt that Carolyn must protect her children. Anne asked, 'How long has he been drinking?'' Carolyn replied, ''Just two and a half months; he was sober for nine months.'' To which Anne said, ''That's a shame!''

This comment set off a torrent of tears in Carolyn. She broke down and cried, ''That's just it. There's so much potential there. If you could only have seen him when he wasn't drinking—that's the Tom I love. I still love him!'' Her pain was excruciating, and filled the room. No one could respond. I reached across and put my hand on hers, and said she had shared her feelings with us, and it had touched us all deeply. I wondered if she ever let Tom see this side of her, and let him see how much she loves him? [She had previously told us that he calls her a robot, a machine with no feelings, which he resents very much.] She wept, then dried her eyes, and said she knew what I meant, and it was very hard for her to show Tom this side of her, or anyone else, for that matter. She said she felt better, but it hurt her to let these feelings out. I looked around the group and saw that Carolyn's pain had enveloped them all.

I turned to Shirley, sitting very rigidly in her chair, her face void of emotion, her hands tightly holding the arms of the chair, and said, ''Shirley, you seem very upset.'' She replied, ''I can't respond to this; I'm afraid if I move, I'll cry too.'' I said that was okay, we are all feeling Carolyn's pain. At that Shirley began to weep, and said, ''I know how she feels, and it just hurts so much.'' Anne could not respond, but just sat quietly in her chair, looking pained. Corinne looked as if she were holding back her tears, and was trying at the same time to kid herself out of her pain. She commented, ''Carolyn makes me remember, and I don't want to." She said she feels as Carolyn does about her own [second] husband, but he's remarried now, still drinking, and there's no use dwelling on those old feelings. She mused aloud, "How many times do you have to put yourself through this?" I commented gently, "Perhaps as often as it takes to get through it."

It was time to stop, and everyone said they were feeling depressed, but also good about getting so close. Even Corinne said, "We have a common bond here." Everyone agreed. I told them that I felt we had talked about important things tonight, and commended them for staying with the difficult work. Corinne tried breaking the mood and chided, "Next week I want to talk about my daughter." I said, "Fine."

In the second excerpt, the worker helps the group members stay with anxiety-laden areas, even when the pain is palpable. The mutual support system is strong enough to sustain the members, and it is important that this work should continue, in the light of the group's purpose. The worker is responsive to nonverbal signals, and seeks to have them converted into verbal expressions, which advances the work and aids in coping and problem solving. She is particularly skillful in noting and interrupting a beginning coalition between two members that, if permitted to continue, could interfere with mutual aid.

With Carolyn, the worker raises a tentative question about a possible maladaptive pattern of marital interaction, and Carolyn accepts it. The tentativeness of the question permits Carolyn adequate room to avoid the issue if she were not yet ready to deal with it. Comments and questions related to material that may be out of the client's awareness for the moment, or just below the surface, are best couched in such a tentative and questioning way, and they are raised only after one is quite sure of the accuracy of one's observation. And, finally, we see that the worker is not afraid to offer the comfort of physical contact when the situation calls for it. In helping this group of unhappy, even depressed, women deal with their status and role tasks as separated spouses, single parents, and adult daughters, the worker draws primarily on the skills of the enabler role to facilitate a mutual aid system and problem-solving activities.

Summary

Developmental stages across the life cycle arise from biological changes interacting with psychological, social and cultural forces, and physical settings. Each stage poses particular demands and can create stress. When a developmental stage is not traversed successfully, difficulties may be experienced at a subsequent stage because of residues of distrust, shame, guilt, inferiority, identity diffusion, etc. Families and formed groups may experience stress in completing one stage and meeting the challenges of a new one. Where a family's or group's tasks at one stage are not successfully met, maladaptive residues are carried over to the next stage, increasing the adaptive demands on all members.

Status–role demands and transitions can also be stressful. Societal definitions of statuses and roles are changing rapidly. People experience ambiguous expectations and perceptions. Some may have too many statuses that then conflict and compete for their time and energy. Others may have too few statuses and experience insufficient stimulation and purpose. Personal characteristics such as perception–cognitive abilities and styles, motivation, and adaptive patterns affect the way status–role demands and expectations are perceived and handled, and the degree of accompanying stress. Moreover, many statuses in our society are devalued and stigmatized; persons occupying such statuses carry an additional adaptive burden. Finally, transitional changes may coincide with developmental changes as puberty coincides with entry into junior high school, thus intensifying stress. Transitions may come too early in the life cycle, as in adolescent pregnancy, or too late, as with the grandparent who must assume the parenting function, increasing the potential for stress.

Crisis events are sudden changes characterized by the immediacy and enormity of coping tasks. They often represent losses of the severest kind in which ordinary adaptive patterns are inadequate. People in crisis tend to use defenses such as denial, projection, and regression to ward off the grief and anxiety. Initially, these defenses are adaptive because they permit continued functioning. When prolonged, however, they may become maladaptive because they interfere with effective coping; stress is prolonged.

With people experiencing stress in life transitions, the social worker's function is to help them move through the transitions by supporting or strengthening their adaptive capacities and increasing the environment's responsiveness to coping needs. This professional function draws on the roles of enabler, teacher, and facilitator. In the role of enabler, the social worker carries out the tasks of promoting, sustaining, and strengthening people's motivation to deal with life transitional stresses. She uses such skills as eliciting, identifying, and managing feelings; responding to signals of distress; providing legitimate support; identifying transactional patterns; legitimizing concerns; validating strengths; conveying hope; decreasing ambivalence and resistance; accrediting coping efforts; partializing problems; and maintaining focus.

In the role of teacher, the social worker carries out the tasks of teaching coping skills through clarifying perceptions; providing pertinent information in the appropriate cognitive mode and at the appropriate rate; offering advice or suggestions; identifying alternatives and their likely consequences; modeling desired behaviors; and teaching the steps in problem solving. Finally, in the role of facilitator, the social worker carries out the tasks in assuring space and time for adaptive action and the exercise of competence. He uses professional skills to provide opportunities for successful action and decision making, to define tasks and mobilize environmental supports, regulate the pace and rhythm of the work, and manage issues of passivity and dependence/independence.

Notes

1. Joseph Kett, *Rites of Passage* (New York: Basic Books, 1977).

2. See, for example, Jules Henry, *Culture Against Man* (New York: Random House, 1963).

3. Beatrix A. Hamburg, "Early Adolescence: A Specific and Stressful Stage of the Life Cycle," in George V. Coelho, David A. Hamburg, and John E. Adams, eds., *Coping and Adaptation,* (New York: Basic Books, 1974), pp. 101–26.

4. Erik H. Erikson, "Growth and Crises of the Healthy Personality," in Erik H. Erikson, *Identity and the Life Cycle: Psychological Issues,* Monograph 1 (New

York: International Universities Press, 1959), 1(1):50–100. The usefulness of the Erikson conception for the social worker lies in its dual emphasis on person and environment, which fits nicely with the profession's social purpose and with an ecological perspective; and its addition of a temporal dimension to the concept of life space. A lifetime or life cycle is viewed as a succession of life spaces that shift and change over time, thus issues of time and space inhere in life transitions. Erikson's action emphasis on tasks fits nicely with the life model's practice emphasis on action. Despite its usefulness, however, Erikson's conception does not deal adequately with the variations due to social class, ethnicity, and gender. Thus, the specifics in the framework may not always be entirely relevant to many users of social work services who face different sets of challenges, different environmental structures, opportunities, and obstacles. And finally, it is important to remember that all such frameworks, both individual and family, are based on group data and may or may not fit any particular individual or family. When used cautiously, however, the framework can be useful in locating points of stress and providing task focuses for the helping process.

5. Jean Piaget, *The Origins of Intelligence in Children* (New York: International Universities Press, 1952).

6. Jerome S. Bruner, *Toward a Theory of Instruction* (Cambridge, Mass.: Harvard University Press, 1966), ch. 1, "Patterns of Growth," pp. 1–21.

7. While we introduce cognitive development and cognitive styles in the context of developmental changes, the reader should bear in mind that cognition is an integral part of all human functioning and, therefore, of adaptive efforts to deal with all life transitions, interpersonal exchanges, and environmental interactions.

8. Otto Pollak, "A Family Diagnosis Model," *Social Service Review* (March 1960), 33(1):19–31 exemplifies early attempts. A more recent developmental scheme is provided by Patricia O'Connell, "Developmental Tasks of the Family," *Smith College Studies in Social Work* (June 1972), 42(3):203–10.

9. Sonya L. Rhodes, "A Developmental Approach to the Life Cycle of the Family," *Social Casework* (May 1977), 58(5):301–11. While basing her framework on the nuclear or two-parent family, the author believes it may prove, with modifications, to be applicable to other family forms such as single-parent, extended, newly formed second families, and communal families.

10. *Ibid.*

11. Frances Scherz, "The Crisis of Adolescence in Family Life," *Social Casework* (April 1967), 48(4):209–16. Families frequently experience stress at any stage of family development whenever the tasks are beyond the coping capacity of the family, or the environment fails to provide the resources needed for successful task resolution. Status changes and role demands may cause stress for the family as a whole in addition to the individual member involved. Families, like individuals, also experience crisis events. When the stress becomes unmanageable, families frequently turn to or are propelled toward social agencies and social workers for help.

12. James Garland, Hubert Jones, and Ralph Kolodny, "A Model of Stages of Development in Social Work Groups," in Saul Bernstein, ed., *Explorations in Group Work* (Boston: Boston University School of Social Work, 1968), pp. 12–53

13. By social status, we mean a cluster of norms defining expected behaviors of the person occupying a particular position within a particular social structure. See Robert K. Merton, *Social Theory and Social Structure* (Glencoe, Ill.: Free Press, 1968). For the social worker, the concepts of status and role are useful because "status" requires the practitioner to consider the structure and functions of the particular social system of which the status is a component. "Role" requires him to attend to the transactional aspects of action, because a role implies a role partner–for example, husband–wife, mother–child, teacher–pupil, patient–doctor, tenant–landlord, etc.

14. See, for example, Alvin Toffler, *Future Shock* (New York: Random House, 1970); Margaret Mead, *Culture and Commitment* (New York: Natural History Press, 1970). Despite the ambiguities, however, some clarity does exist about the tasks involved in some current statuses and roles, and research is available about cultural differences. The findings provide useful general guides to social workers and clients who are working together on the stresses associated with particular status changes and role demands. See, for example, Rhona Rapaport, "Normal Crises, Family Structure, and Mental Health," *Family Process* (1963), 2(1):68–80, discusses the tasks in becoming a spouse; Rudolf H. Moos, ed., *Human Adaptation* (Lexington, Mass.: Heath, 1976), contains papers on tasks related to a variety of statuses and roles.

15. See, for example, Howard S. Becker, *The Outsiders* (New York: Free Press, 1963); Edwin M. Schur, *Labeling Deviant Behavior* (New York: Harper & Row, 1971); Erving Goffman, *Stigma: Notes on the Management of Spoiled Identity* (Englewood Cliffs, N.J.: Prentice-Hall, 1963). In our society, there may be no real escape from certain stigmatized statuses. While one is expected to strive toward vacating such a status, one can really only assume a similar status such as ex-criminal, ex-mental patient, ex-alcoholic, ex-addict, etc.

16. See William Goode, "A Theory of Role Strain," *American Sociological Review,* (August 1960) 25:483–96; Neil Gross, Ward Ruson, Alexander McEachern, *Expectations in Role Analysis,* (New York: Wiley, 1958); J.D. Snock, "Role Strain in Diversified Role Sets," *American Journal of Sociology* (January 1966), 71:362–72.

17. Alton J. De Long, "The Micro-Spatial Structure of the Older Person: Some Implications of Planning the Social and Spatial Environment," in Leon A. Pastalan and Daniel H. Carson, eds., *Spatial Behavior of Older People* (Ann Arbor: University of Michigan–Wayne State University Institute of Gerontology, 1970), pp. 68–87. At the other end of the life cycle, there are differences in biologically-based stimulus threshholds. Some newborn infants, for example, are more responsive to tactile, auditory, and visual stimuli than others, and this can affect the mother–infant transactions in positive or negative ways. See Anneliese F. Korner, "Individual Differences at Birth: Implications for Early Experience and Later Development," *American Journal of Orthopsychiatry* (July 1971), 41(4):608–19.

18. See, for example, Horacio Fabrega, Jr., "The Need for an Ethnomedical Science," *Science* (September 19, 1975), 189:969–75; Alan Harwood, "The Hot–Cold Theory of Disease, Implications for Treatment of Puerto Rican Patients," *Journal of the American Medical Association* (May 17, 1971), 216(7):1153–58.

19. While we discuss perception in the context of status changes and role demands, the reader should bear in mind that, as with cognition, perception affects all human functioning, including the ways in which people deal with the stress of developmental tasks, crisis events, maladaptive interpersonal relationships, and environmental tasks. The human being's perceptual–sensory apparatuses process external stimuli through the senses of sight, hearing, smell, taste, and touch. They process internal stimuli through kinesthetic (muscle) and organic (organ systems) senses. The receiving and processing of stimuli is affected by biological, emotional, learning, cultural, and social factors.

20. Robert W. White, "Strategies of Adaptation: An Attempt at Systematic Description," in Coelho et al., *Coping And Adaptation,* pp. 47–68. In White's view, successful adaptation requires: securing adequate information about the environment, neither too much nor too little, and in a form that can be understood; maintaining an internal equilibrium that will permit using information and taking action; maintaining freedom of movement in order to use one's adaptive strategies flexibly.

21. Lydia Rapoport, "Crisis Intervention as a Mode of Brief Treatment," in Robert W. Roberts and Robert Nee, eds., *Theories of Social Casework* (Chicago: University of Chicago Press, 1970), pp. 265–311.

22. L. Rapoport states that Dr. Gerald Caplan "suggests that six weeks is a usual time limit." Rapoport, *iid.,* p. 287.

23. While we discuss defense and coping in the context of crisis events, it is important for the reader again to bear in mind that these processes, like the other adaptive capacities of cognition and perception, apply to all human functioning and affect how people deal with all problems in living.

24. The work of Hamburg and his colleagues with seriously injured and ill patients illustrates the adaptive nature of denial. "At first, there are efforts to minimize the impact of the event. During the acute phase there tends to be extensive denial of the nature of the illness, its seriousness and its probable consequences. Such avoidance defenses appear to serve a useful function in preventing the patient's being overwhelmed, and permitting him to make a more gradual transition to the exceedingly difficult tasks that lie ahead." David A. Hamburg and John E. Adams, "A Perspective on Coping Behavior," *Archives of General Psychiatry* (1967), 17:277–84.

25. In other kinds of situations, such as severe visual and hearing impairments, the continued use of denial is often an effective coping strategy that seems to lead to the development of new skills, compensatory sensory capacities, and successful striving to maintain the accustomed level of functioning. In still other kinds of situations, however, denial at any stage may lead to additional stress, as when it is used by a substance abuser to shut out, perhaps permanently, the painful reality of the addiction. Motivation to deal with that reality is then effectively blocked.

26. According to Rapoport, "Three interrelated factors produce a state of crisis: 1) one or a series of hazardous events which pose some threat; 2) a threat to current or past instinctual needs which are symbolically linked to earlier threats that result in vulnerability or conflict; and 3) an inability to respond with adequate coping mechanisms . . . A threat may be directed to . . . an individual's sense of integrity or autonomy." See Rapoport in Roberts and Nee, *Theories of Social Casework,* p. 277.

27. David Mechanic, "Social Structure and Personal Adaptation: Some Neglected Dimensions," in Coelho et al., *Coping and Adaptation,* pp. 32–46.

28. *Ibid.*

29. Robert W. White, "Motivation Reconsidered: The Concept of Competence," *Psychological Review* (September 1959), 66:297–333.

30. John Dewey, *How We Think* (New York: Heath, 1933). For a concise, practice-oriented discussion of Dewey's ideas, see Belulah Compton and Burt Galaway, eds., *Social Work Processes,* (Homewood, Ill.: Dorsey Press, 1975), pp. 234–35.

31. Robert White, "Strategies of Adaptation . . ." and David Mechanic, "Social Structure . . ." both in Coelho et al., *Coping and Adaptation.*

32. Adapted from a case record, *The Wanderers* (Pre-teen Project: United Neighborhood Houses, New York City), mimeo.

33. See Lillian Ripple and Ernestina Alexander, *Motivation, Capacity, and Opportunity* (Chicago: University of Chicago Press, 1964); Helen Harris Perlman, "In Quest of Coping," *Social Casework* (April 1975), 56(4):213–25.

34. Bernard Bandler, "The Concept of Ego-Supportive Psychotherapy," in Howard J. Parad and Roger R. Miller, eds., *Ego-Oriented Casework: Problems and Perspectives* (New York: Family Service Association of America, 1963), pp. 27–44.

35. See, for example, Frederick Duhl, Bunny Duhl, and David Kantor, "Learning, Space and Action in Family Therapy: A Primer of Sculpture," in Donald Block, ed., *Techniques of Family Psychotherapy* (New York: Grune and Stratton, 1973); Ann Hartman, "The Use of Family Sculpting in Teaching Systems Concepts," (paper presented at the Annul Program Meeting, Council on Social Work Education, Chicago, March 4, 1975), mimeo.; Philip J. Guerin, Jr., and Eileen G. Pendagast, "Evaluation of Family System and Genogram," in Philip J. Guerin, Jr., ed., *Family Therapy: Theory and Practice* (New York: Gardner Press, 1976), pp. 450–64.

36. Evelyn A. Lance, "Intensive Work With A Deprived Family," *Social Casework,* 50(8):454–60.

37. *Ibid.*

38. Jerome S. Bruner, *Toward a Theory of Instruction* (Cambridge, Mass.: Harvard University Press, 1966), pp. 10–12.

39. See Rapoport in Roberts and Nee, *Theories of Social Casework,* for further discussion of crisis intervention as a model for practice.

40. Meanwhile, the worker recognized that the residents on the floor were threatened because the usual balance had been upset when Mrs. K came in to occupy the room of a high-status resident who had recently died. In addition, she had brought with her a reputation of being difficult to live with, and she was an offensive presence because of her incontinence. The worker utilized the skills discussed in the next chapter to influence staff to be more responsive to Mrs. K, and she worked to help the residents recall their own reactions and feelings when they first came on the floor so they, too, would be more receptive and patient with Mrs. K.

41. Anthony N. Maluccio, "Action as a Tool in Casework Practice.," *Social Casework,* 55(1):30–5.

4

The Ongoing Phase: Environmental Problems and Needs

THE ENVIRONMENT IS dynamic and complex. It comprises many kinds of systems, each with its characteristic structure, level of organization and spatial and temporal properties. The *social* environment comprises human beings organized in dyadic relations, social networks, bureaucratic institutions and other social systems including the neighborhood, community, and society itself. The *physical* environment comprises the natural world of animals, plants, and land forms, and the built world of structures and objects constructed by human beings. The social and physical environments are related to each other in complex ways. They form a unitary system that we separate here for the purpose of analysis. The social environment is shaped by the physical setting. An open classroom manifests a different kind of social structure, for example, than a classroom in which the desks are fixed to the floor in long rows so that pupils face the teacher but not one another. Conversely, the nature of physical settings is changed by social interactions through the impact of urban layouts, building design, wilderness use, etc. Both the physical and social environments, including the economy and polity, interact with the knowledge, beliefs, sentiments, values, and norms of the culture.

Embedded in physical and social environments and their political and economic structures, individuals and primary groups continually experience environmental challenges, opportunities, and obstacles to adaptive functioning. Some of these upset the goodness-of-fit and lead to undesirable or even unmanageable stress. This chapter examines interactions between people and their social and physical environments, and describes and illustrates social work function, knowledge, and method in helping people deal with problems and needs arising from environmentally induced stress, or from the lack of environmental resources and supports.

Environmental Processes as Sources of Stress

The Social Environment

Contemporary society is characterized by the ubiquity of complex bureaucratic *organizations,* including health, education, and social service organizations. Such structures are themselves embedded in social and physical environments. They affect and are affected by political, economic, and cultural forces. Changes in political and economic life influence society's definitions of social problems and its institutional responses. At times, society and its institutions are responsive to the problems associated with poverty. They are more willing to consider structural inequality, and they are more open to problem definitions and services oriented toward societal change. At other times, self-reliance is highly valued, deviance is harshly treated, and problem definitions are oriented toward changing people.

Initially, a social welfare organization (including health, education, and social service organizations) is established with social approval and financial support from private and/or public funds. Once established, however, the organization must maintain a balance among the pressures exerted not only by its funding sources, but by legislative bodies, regulatory agencies, the community, changing definitions of social need, and new knowledge and technologies that continually pose the threat of organizational obsolescence. At the same time, the organization must seek to maintain an adaptive balance among its internal parts: the service users, professional and occupational groups; the various departments that compete for organizational status and prestige; and formal and informal systems. Once established, the way the organization defines its function and boundaries has a profound impact on the experiences of applicants and service users.[1] A social work agency, for example, may define its function in terms of methodological distinctions of group, individual, or family services. Applicants must fit their problems to the agency's method instead of the agency providing methods fitted to applicants' needs. Other organizations may define their function in terms of changing people, with little account taken of the complex interactions between personal and social variables. In some schools, for example, pupils are referred to social work services as disruptive or disturbed children because teachers find them unmanageable. The practitioner is expected to help such children adjust to the school environment, leaving little time for other professional activities. By acquiescing in this definition of function, the social worker overlooks the need to intervene at the classroom level, family level, educational policy and procedural level, or community level. Yet, any one or all of these levels may be creating or sustaining the problem.[2] An unanticipated consequence of defining the functions this way is to stigmatize the service. This adds another label to the dysfunctional labeling process present in the school system, and increases the pupil's stress. Preventive help to all children and their families in their transactions with the educational system lies outside the boundary of the social worker in such a school system.

Like all social systems, the organization gradually evolves a social structure of statuses and roles for the division of labor. If roles are narrowly or rigidly defined, they constrict professional function and have a negative impact on service, thus increasing stress for service users. The function of hospital social workers, for example, may be defined as discharge-planning. This definition deprives patients and their families of social work help with the psychological and social stress of illness and disability. When the narrow function is combined with a restriction against case-finding, and exclusive reliance on physician referral for discharge planning, the social worker enters the situation too late for adequate planning. Her acquiescence in the restricted definition of function helps to maintain the existing social structure and its rigid subsystem boundaries between social workers and physicians. Such barriers to good patient care create stress for patients and families, rather than decreasing it. Stress may be created by organizational boundaries in other ways too. Some agencies locate their services away from the life space of those they seek to serve, thus inhibiting client use because of transportation costs, babysitting costs, or social intimidation by an unfamiliar geographic area. An agency's gatekeepers, such as telephone operators, receptionists, and intake personnel may be unwelcoming and gruff.[3]

Its physical aspects may be unattractive and uncomfortable; long waits may be imposed.[4] These boundary-maintaining functions, by undermining the dignity and self-esteem of service users, increase their stress.

Boundaries of other organizations may be not firm enough and are too easily penetrated. Mental hospitals, for example, may not help prospective patients explore alternatives to institutionalization.[5] Children may be taken into substitute care without sufficient effort to keep them in their own homes, or at least in their own neighborhoods and schools so that all ties to their families and environments will not be broken. This is the tragic effect of financial policies that compensate private agencies on the basis of numbers of children placed, but not on the basis of work done with natural parents to preserve families.

Intra-organizational boundaries between subsystems may interfere with stress reduction. In some hospitals, social workers may cross professional boundaries to consult with psychiatrists or other physicians, while little or no traffic across the boundary in the opposite direction occurs. In such instances, patients and families do not have the benefit of the social worker's unique contributions to medical diagnosis and treatment based upon her knowledge of psycho-social-cultural factors in illness, disability, and stress.

Intra-organizational boundaries can be too loose, particularly in those interdisciplinary settings where useful role distinctions are blurred. The distinctive contribution of the social worker may be lost in the general welter of "everyone can do everything." Clients are confused by ambiguity in professional function, and stress is increased by the competitiveness among helpers that overly relaxed interprofessional boundaries can generate.

Inter-organizational boundaries may also create stress for service users. In order to eliminate duplication and fill service gaps, organizations develop a division of labor among themselves. Where boundaries are drawn unrealistically, or where there is a lack of linkage mechanisms to assure effective referral and pickup of service, some clients become lost and do not receive needed service. An aged person in need of medical care may be deemed ineligible by a clinic because of his medicare policy, yet he may lack money to activate the policy. A mental patient discharged from a state hospital having no after care program may be denied service by a family agency because of poor prognosis, weak motivation, or other reasons.

In order to carry out its function, and to manage external and internal pressures which continually threaten its stability, an organization develops structures, policies, and procedures. These, in turn, have both positive and negative effects on those who use the organization's services and on those who, through a professional practice like social work, attempt to carry out the organization's mission.

An authority structure is needed to allocate responsibility and coordinate tasks. It provides a chain of command through which decisions are made about what is to be done, who is to do it, and how and when it is to be done. Authority is vested in stratified positions and legitimized through the dispensing of rewards and sanctions.[6] While such a structure is essential to organizational functioning, it also can be a source of stress for the service users and rank-and-file employees. Some authority structures are overly rigid: they reward conformity, discourage innovation, and block horizontal and vertical communication. They are then unable to respond to changing conditions and needs, or they may interfere with the practitioner's ability to respond to client need. In the latter instance, the practitioner providing the service may, for example, have little or no access to policy details while being responsible for critical decisions regarding eligibility. The layers of authority may become so numerous, or communication channels so clogged, that the time span in decision making discourages both practitioner and client from pursuing individualized needs or even common entitlements. Instead of stress being decreased by the service, it is increased. In other instances, authority structures may be too flexible; they allow inappropriate discretionary power to practitioners having minimal accountability. The client is then vulnerable to a worker's individual whim, prejudice, or narrow interpretation of service provisions; stress is increased.

In order to standardize its practices, the organization develops a set of policies and procedures to assure all service users of fair and neutral treatment without regard to personality traits, race, sex, age, social status, and kin and friendship ties. Policies and procedures proliferate over time as circumstances change or exceptional situations arise.[7] They tend to take on a life of their own, become reified, and take precedence over client need and the organization's avowed goals. The organization begins to operate in ways that support its own needs, as defined by interest groups within the organization or in its environment. A set of latent goals and functions then displaces the avowed or manifest goals and functions. An agency may, for example, gradually create an increasingly complex set of intake procedures, such as a lengthy triage in a neighborhood mental health center. This effectively screens out those citizens whose environmental problems do not permit them to wait for several weeks for service. At the same time, it leaves a group of highly motivated applicants whose reality problems are not so intractable as to interfere with staff interest in long-term psychodynamic psychotherapy. The consequences of such latent functions are generally unrecognized; originally, they may have been unintended. Even when recognized, however, they tend to continue because they serve organizational needs—in this instance, professional interests and ideologies. The triage, originally intended to help applicants move into service, creates stress for them instead.[8]

Some organizations demand strict adherence to policies and procedures: the ''manual'' supersedes the applicant's or client's needs and interests. Exceptions represent feared precedents as individual needs are held hostage to bureaucratic needs. Some organizations use procedures and policies to deny needed services. A welfare agency, for example, may use numerous procedures such as long waits and complicated forms that serve to discourage applicants, delay service, and block referrals. Still other organizations may not formalize or codify practices, and the individual is subjected to non-uniform practices and to the idiosyncratic judgments of workers. Whether procedures or policies are insufficiently formalized or over-formalized, they represent a potential source of stress for clients.

Beyond such formal structures and their latent functions, informal structures also develop within organizations. These may support the organization's responsiveness to client need or subvert it. The informal system that evolves within the work group itself develops its own culture of values, norms, and expectations, and its own structure of rewards and sanctions. Because the informal system influences what the members do and how they view themselves, the organization, and its clients, it affects responsiveness to client need.[9] Just as the formal structures socialize each organizational member to the agency's culture, the informal system socializes the member to its own culture. Formal and informal sanctions influence the member to accept formal and informal structures and processes as immutable. The following example of work with a group of blind persons illustrates this process.

> Several times, I heard members complain about the cafeteria situation. Today, Bill was very angry, shouting to the aides, ''Help us with lunch!'' After some ventilating about this in our later meeting, the group went on to another subject. It is clear this is a frustrating experience for them, and it's too bad nothing can be done about it.

The worker limits her intervention to ventilation of feeling and expresses no curiosity or concern about the situation. The culture of both the formal and informal systems values psychological intervention and devalues environmental intervention, so the worker accepts the situation as unchangeable; the clients' feelings of helplessness are reinforced and their stress is increased. The professional ideology of the agency can effectively eliminate any consideration of alternative approaches to the diverse and emerging needs of its clients. The informal system may actually exert pressure toward conformity with the organization's own norms and practice, and disapprove of creative or innovative approaches by staff members.

In an agency where staff morale is low and there is dissatisfaction with personnel practices and working conditions, the informal system may support scornful, punitive, or uncaring attitudes toward clients as displacements of feelings aroused by the authority structure of the agency itself. Anita Dorsey, age 34, came to a private child welfare agency requesting temporary placement for her expected baby, due in four months. The baby's father had left her and she had no money or job. A friend was willing to provide shelter until the baby was born. Ms. Dorsey wanted to organize herself, find work, get a suitable living arrangement for herself and the baby, and find someone to mind the baby while she is out at work. The worker writes:

> After the first interview, I felt she was confused and unrealistic about the meaning of the baby for her and her plans for herself and for the baby. Yet she is concerned

> about the baby's well-being. During the next two interviews, Ms. D continued to be uncommunicative, and was very reluctant to answer my questions pertaining to her feelings, her family, her relationship with the putative father, or her past life. She was indignant because she felt I was overlooking her real problem. She said her problem was that she is expecting a baby and does not have the means to provide for it; this is the only thing that worries her, and she asserted that it was useless to discuss anything else. She was obviously angry and suspicious of me, and refused to give more information because she did not see how it could help her.

In this instance, the professional ideology of the agency assumed the primacy of intra-psychic phenomena in people's needs. But more importantly, because of widespread dissatisfaction with working conditions, the informal system supported harsh attitudes toward clients. Workers rationalized their attitudes by blaming clients for their resistance. In this instance, services were withheld on the grounds that the client was uncooperative and not amenable to help. She was referred elsewhere. The formal system's ideology and the informal system's attitudes combined to create stress for the client.

In many different ways, then, organizational structures and processes may be dysfunctional for the users of service by failing to reduce stress, increasing it, or withholding services and resources. People's interactions with the organizational environment are a critical arena for the social worker. In helping his client to secure services from an organization other than his own, the worker's task may be difficult but is not unusually hazardous. The task is more delicate when he seeks to influence his own organization in order to secure the services or resources required by his client and withheld by the agency. Particular kinds of knowledge and skill are required so that neither client nor worker is placed in jeopardy. Not only is the worker's professional autonomy, responsibility, and accountability affected by the very processes that are stressful to clients, but issues of job security, agency loyalties, and professional reputation may be involved. Above all, the social worker's responsibility and accountability to his client, with recognition of the vulnerability inherent in the status of client, must be constantly and unflinchingly observed. As we shall see later in this chapter, the matter of feasibility and hazard to either client or worker must be carefully and mutually assessed.

Increasingly recognized as an important element of the social environment is the client's *social network,* defined as the linkages among a set of significant others, including kin, friends, neighbors, work mates, and acquaintances. What distinguishes the concept of network from the concept of relationship is the notion that the characteristics of the linkages themselves affect the social behavior of the various persons involved in the network.[10] The interaction between two or more persons in the network can influence the behavior of others in the network. In the case of social work practice, the interaction within the client's social network can affect what happens in the client's use of service.[11] Whether or not a person even applies for social work service and, having applied, whether he remains connected to the agency and worker, often depends upon what the members of his social network think of his applying for formalized help, of social workers, or of the agency itself. Formed groups, since they comprise a set of unrelated strangers coming from very different networks, sometimes experience difficulty reaching agreement on goals and tasks. Unwittingly, perhaps, they may be following agendas of invisible persons who exert influence on how each participates.

People's social networks can be supportive environmental resources, and serve as important instruments of help. They provide emotional resources for meeting the need for human relatedness, and for recognition and affirmation. They also serve as mutual aid systems for the exchange of instrumental resources such as money, services, housing, etc. Within the network, there may be members who quite consciously and purposively serve as effective informal helpers of others, making it unnecessary for those others to seek out institutionalized services.[12] In certain kinds of problems such as one involving sexuality, the person may be reluctant to turn to her network because of the sensitive nature of the problem, or the restrictive or repressive norms operating within the network. Should the person then apply for and receive social work services, the network's norms regarding sexuality may make it impossible for her to continue with the social worker. In such a situation, the network is adding to the stress experienced by the client.

Networks may be maladaptive in other ways. They may reinforce deviance, holding to values that contravene the healthy or normative strivings of the client. A member of a drug-oriented network or a delinquent network may seek to modify his values and aspirations and terminate his affiliation. Yet, the network may exert a strong negative force, leading to unmanageable stress. Similarly, some families have difficulty withstanding the influence of peer networks on their younger members, or the unwanted interference by kin networks on the day-to-day functioning of the family. Some networks are subject to internal exploitative and competitive processes, and these undermine the person's sense of identity and autonomy. A network may have rigid boundaries that isolate the client from growth experiences beyond the close-knit network relations. Some networks have ill-defined boundaries, and are so loosely knit that they are actually unavailable for concrete or psychological support. In these situations, networks create stress.

The lack of any viable network is also a source of stress for many persons. Some residents of low-cost, high-rise housing projects, while they find their housing otherwise satisfactory, experience stress because of the lack of physical provision for the formation of social networks.[13] This is especially true for tenants whose former neighborhoods have been lost to redevelopment. Although slum areas may be physically deteriorated, many such areas do have strong social networks with natural helpers who perform important functions in sharing resources, meeting coping needs, etc. Part of the sense of loss, and the grief and anger experienced by displaced residents of redevelopment areas is traceable to the breakup of these natural networks, thus adding additional stress to already stress-filled lives.[14]

Life cycle events of age changes, school changes, marriage, migration, job promotion or job loss, sickness, death, etc., interrupt or dissolve linkages to others. Such losses can be devastating, because the sense of self and of individuality is dependent upon involvement with others. Some of the psychologically most painful and stressful experiences of humankind are those of loneliness, isolation, and unwanted distance from others.[15] This is true even when a person has learned to fear human attachments, as in some kinds of emotional disturbance. Anxiety, separation, and death on the one hand, or engulfment, intrusion, and loss of a sense of self, on the other hand, may underlie such fear of attachments, yet the pain of loneliness continues.

In old age, friends and kin die, one's activities are curtailed, and the acquisition of new networks is limited. Loneliness and isolation can undermine the sense of self, interfere with the need for love and attachment, and ultimately even the connectedness to the environment that maintains autonomy. Women appear to make greater efforts than men to establish and maintain friendship and kinship networks, although this may change as women spend increasingly longer segments of their lives in gainful employment. For elderly men, however, the death of a spouse frequently means even more than the stress of the lost attachment. The widower has also lost the social ties which were maintained by his wife. This can be a potent source of stress and may even be compounded by a concurrent loss of the work role and the network created at the work site.

Social and geographical mobility also affect network relations, even though the telephone may help to preserve the basic connections. This is a particularly difficult loss for the poor. But even in the case of the middle-class Claytons (chapter 1), we saw how their move disrupted the supports available from kin, friends, and neighbors. Mrs. Clayton, in particular, felt bereft and lonely, unloved, and uncared for. Mr. Clayton, on the other hand, achieved some social integration through his job, which provided affiliation with a new social network. So too, did the adolescent sons forge new linkages in school. Mrs. Clayton, like many other middle-class women uprooted by the exigencies of their husbands' careers, was alone and isolated in what was no doubt an attractive home in an attractive suburb. She did not have a personal physician in a time of acute illness, apparently did not know her neighbors, and was prevented by illness from actively establishing new ties through work or social activities.

The Physical Environment

In order to consider the complex transactions between people and their physical settings, we distinguish between the *built world* and the *natural world*.[16] The natural world comprises climatic and geographical features; landscapes and seascapes; diurnal, seasonal, and annual rhythms and cycles; and cosmic and lunar influences.[17] The built world includes architectural structures, an almost infinite variety of objects; communication, media, and transportation systems; and arrangements of physical space and of the objects and structures within it. The natural and built aspects of the physical environment shape each other and, together, they affect and are affected by the social environment and by the culture.

Social processes and culture govern which aspects of the natural world and the built world will be internalized to become important components of the self concept, and even of the culture itself. The sense of place is incorporated to become part of an individual's or a group's cultural identity. In the United States, for example, regional aspects of this identity, such as characteristics peculiar to the Far West, New England, the South, the Midwest, the Eastern Seaboard, or the Northwest, mingle with attachments to specific areas—city, mountain, shore, or plain—and their associated value orientations and historical traditions. The stress caused by the uprootedness that is part of geographic mobility is attributable, in part, to the sense of being torn away from such an identity base, whether urban or rural.

Cities develop a special character and meaning for their inhabitants as the result of physical layouts, patterns of social interaction, and cultural values. The ambience of one's own neighborhood is influenced by the physical aspects of its streets and buildings, the social interaction of neighbors, cultural sentiments and life styles, and the structure of the city in which it is embedded. The stress that is caused by redevelopment, for example, arises not only from the loss of social networks, as mentioned earlier, but from the loss of familiar and cherished places and structures that comfort and protect, and are part of one's individual and group identity.

The design of dwellings is influenced in part by the character of the physical setting, including climate, and in part by cultural styles and meanings. The interior design and decoration of the dwelling is thought to symbolize one's self-image as the self viewed from within, while the building's façade symbolizes the self displayed to others.[18] The structure and design of high-rise, low-income housing appear to violate culturally and psychologically determined aspects of the self-image. Such housing is a warehouse symbol of lost identity, rather than a personal symbol of the unique self.[19] It gives the tenants no safe territory on the ground, and no defensible territory within. Parents have no way to watch over the outdoor play of their children from their apartments, and all tenants lack the means of surveillance, and hence control, over such public areas as lobbies, elevators, fire stairs, and open exterior spaces.[20] All are prey to muggers and thieves. The vandalism and lack of care in housing projects may represent the tenants' angry responses to the stressful assaults on their identity and dignity as separate and unique personalities, and lead to further social, psychological, and even physiological stress. Other physical structures such as mental hospitals, prisons, schools, and residential facilities for the aged or the very young, reflect similar social and cultural processes which dehumanize and devalue society's "outsiders," and pollute the physical and social environments.

Social and cultural processes influence the uses, arrangements, and responses to physical space. They may be maladaptive and therefore stressful. How space is allocated—its location and size and contents—communicates status differentials in work sites, social agencies, and in homes. Constrictions in available space are related to problems in density and crowding.[21] The arrangement of open and closed spaces in institutions, treatment cottages, and schools invites or discourages particular behaviors in children.[22] The arrangement of furniture and other objects in mental hospitals and geriatric facilities promotes or discourages social interaction among the residents. Ward "geography" in any inpatient setting either supports or inhibits patients' shifting needs for privacy, on the one hand, and for socializing, on the other.[23]

The presence of color, varied textures, thermal and olfactory cues increases nutritive stimulation to the sensory-perceptual apparatuses of patients or residents in total institutions. The absence of such stimuli in bleak, bland, and unchanging environments has a negative effect on coping and adaptation, and leads to stress. The residents' orientation to space and time, their sense of identity, and relatedness to others may deteriorate or be lost altogether. Young children may receive too much or too little sensory-perceptual stimulation, thus impairing their cognitive and emotional development. Infants raised in hospitals and other institutions where there are insufficient sensory and perceptual stimuli, little consistency in handling, and no opportunity for a continuing relationship, often display this kind of retardation in development.[24] Sensory deprivation experiments with college students reflect the temporary loss of autonomy from inner autistic experiences, bordering on the psychotic, that can occur among "normals."[25]

Objects made by humans are endowed with special meaning by cultural values and personal experiences, and become incorporated as significant aspects of the self-image. From the transitional objects of infancy to the treasured objects of childhood, adolescence, and adulthood, their loss or destruction is experienced as a threat to the self, and may cause stress. Such objects are also used as symbols of rank and status. When access to the society's opportunity structure is blocked, closing off legitimate means to culturally approved goals—including the acquisition of objects—some individuals resort to illegitimate means or retreat into stressful states of withdrawal, disorganization, or physical illness.[26]

The natural world, too, has a greater impact on human functioning than most of us realize. Studies of accidents, suicides, crimes, psychiatric hospital admissions, and even rates of social interaction have shown suggestive associations with one or the other climatic feature.[27] It seems likely that barometric pressure, wind, excessive temperatures and humidity, and seasonal variations in climate influence the moods and behavior of people, and contribute to stress. Their influence is probably mediated by physical states, social learning, social cycles such as vacations and work schedules, and proximity to others. The influence of the natural world may be intensified in poor rural areas where climatic features are less controlled, and where life styles expose residents to the elements and to greater distances from neighbors and other social stimuli.

Lifestyles may reflect the opportunities and obstacles presented by the physical environment. Landscape features such as islands, mountains, coasts, deserts, lakefronts, and marshlands have differential effects on lifestyles and identies. The Puerto Rican migrant to a northern mainland city, for example, must contend not only with cultural, social, political, and economic differences, but also with the differences he meets when leaving a self-contained tropical island and entering a seemingly limitless continent, and a city located in a temperate zone with marked seasonal changes in climate. If the migrant comes from a rural area of Puerto Rico, the impact of urban life is all the more stressful. In the United States, similar stresses may be encountered by Native Americans or by Chicanos who move to the urban centers of the north, by blacks migrating from the south, and by rural whites from Appalachia.

The natural environment has a temporal texture in its alterations of day and night, seasons, and annual rhythms as the earth journeys around the sun. Such rhythmic variations have been entrained in all forms of life through adaptive processes over evolutionary time. Biological rhythms in human beings such as REM sleep, hunger cycles, pulse, and respiratory rhythms reflect these terrestrial cycles. Temporal cycles imposed by schools, hospitals, social agencies, and even work arrangements may conflict with fundamental biological rhythms and cause physiological and psychological stress.[28]

Air, water, food, and other critical aspects of the physical environment are now endangered by interaction with the technology of human culture. Ingestion of lead by young children living in substandard housing with peeling paint is a striking example encountered by many social workers in their daily practice. Plants and animals, part of the physical setting along with man, may be defined by cultural values and human needs as useful, dangerous, supportive, unimportant, endearing, or symbolic. As valued possessions, pets may be part of one person's or family's social network, but sources of stress to neighbors or others.

Social Work Function, Roles, and Method

The Social Worker and the Environment

We have seen how organizational and network processes in the social environment, and processes related to the natural and built features of the physical environment, and their interactions, may create stress in people's lives, or otherwise add to their adaptive burdens. With limited power and limited awareness of their rights, some service users may become resigned to the unresponsiveness of various organizations' services. Because of cultural or psychological influences, other persons may be unwilling or unable to use organizational resources that are actually available and responsive. Thus, the social worker's attention and actions must be directed to the behavioral interface between individuals, groups, and families, and the organizations on which they depend. The focus is on helping clients make use of available resources and on influencing organizations to provide responsive services. The relations between an organization and its community, as seen in its own formal structure, policies, and procedures, and in its informal, social and cultural system all offer possible areas in the interface for providing effective help or influencing.

Similarly, the worker's attention and action must be directed to the behavioral interface between the individual, group, or family, and its social network. Mobilizing or strengthening "real life" ties, finding new linkages and re-establishing old ones, enlisting the aid of natural helpers, and helping clients disengage from maladaptive affiliations represent interface areas for improving transactions between clients and their networks.

The worker's attention and action must also be directed to aspects of the physical environment in rural or urban life which alone, or in concert with social processes, creates stress for the individual or primary group. Efforts can be directed toward adequate housing and furnishings; help with territorial needs; increasing perceptual and sensory stimuli in total institutions; manipulating spatial arrangements, design, and use; attention to the temporal aspects of family and institutional life; provision of opportunities for growth and renewal to urban dwellers in the natural world of countryside, seashore, park, or for rural dwellers in the built world of a nearby city such as museums, concert halls, etc.; and the use of pets and plants.

In the discussion that follows, it is important to remember that there must always be mutual assessment and agreement concerning the desirability and practicality of the client's assuming the responsibility or a degree of responsibility for the tasks involved in influencing social and physical environments. Where the client's knowledge, experience and physical state permits, his taking action on the environment is an important means of enhancing coping skills. Where worker and client agree that the client's own action is not feasible, then the decision must be made as to whether the end can best be attained by worker and client together taking action, or by the worker alone, with the client continually apprised of the process.

The professional function can be specified by casting it into the three roles of the social work practitioner specific to helping with environmental processes. These are the *mediator, advocate,* and *organizer* roles.[29] We again remind the reader that work with environmental issues is usually concurrent with work on life transitions, so these roles are used in tandem with those of enabler, facilitator and teacher. All come into prominence and recede in a fluid way, again and again throughout the service contact, as circumstances and client needs and interests require.

Continuous processes of problem definition, exploration, and contracting will disclose the source of maladaptive interactions between client and organization, between client and network, or between client and physical environment. If, for example, the problem of inadequate environmental supports manifests itself in the individual's, group's or family's unwillingness or inability to use available organizational or network resources, the social worker's role, in general, will tend to be one of those discussed in the previous chapter. The worker may assume the role of teacher, for example, if the client has insufficient knowledge of the availability of resources and services, or the role of facilitator if the client requires experience and help in using them. The role of enabler may be used if there are psychological or cultural resistances to using the service or seeking the resources, or if fear of the unknown or unrealistic concern for independence contribute to the inability to use available organizational or network resources.

In most instances, however, the problem is not located in the client's inability to use the social environment. Instead, it may lie in distorted communications or interactions between client and organization or client and network. In the role of *mediator* the social worker, in general, carries out the function of helping client and social system reach out to each other in more realistic, rational, and reciprocal ways[30] through the collaborative skills of intercession, persuasion, and negotiation.[31]

More frequently, the problem actually lies within the organization itself, or within the network. It may lie even with persons outside the network—landlord, physician, or creditor, for example—who are nonetheless significant figures in the client's social environment. The organizational problem may arise from any of the organization's various structures and functions. If the collaborative skills of the mediator role do not accomplish the desired end, the social worker, in general, may carry out the function of influencing the organization to be more responsive by assuming the *advocate* role and calling upon the adversarial skills of pressure, coercion, or appeals to third party intervention. The latter may include use of media, mobilization of group, neighborhood, or community processes, and involvement of the legislative, fiscal, or regulatory agencies in the organization's environment.[32]

What has been said about the use of the enabler, teacher, facilitator, mediator, and advocate roles in person–organizational issues holds also for person–network issues. Within the network there may be unresponsive or punitive individuals whom the worker in the mediator role must seek to engage on the client's behalf for greater understanding of the client's needs or for securing emotional or material resources of various kinds. There may be kin, friends, or neighbors whose direct relationship with the client is maladaptive or whose relations with other members of the network exert undesirable pressures on the client. The worker must seek to engage these persons, too, on the client's behalf. Certain authority figures who may or may not be members of the network sometimes have unresponsive or punitive attitudes toward a client. Such persons as a landlord, policeman, creditor, physician, or others may need to be approached in an attempt to increase their understanding of the client's needs and responses, or to secure concessions, delays, access to rights and entitlements, etc.

Where the client has no network, or where she seeks to disengage herself from her present network, the worker may arrange to introduce her to existing networks of neighbors, fellow tenants, or to institutionalized sources for potential affiliation and personal participation such as parent–teacher associations, church-sponsored groups, etc. Or, the worker and client may decide on referral to a self-help group, such as Parents Without Partners, Alcoholics Anonymous, or one of the many medically oriented self-help groups, as a network substitute and/or a task-oriented experience for improved coping.[33] In all these instances, the worker uses the skills of enabler, facilitator, mediator, and advocate. Where there are no networks or network substitutes in the client's life space, the worker may take on the role of *organizer*. Alone, or with clients and colleagues, and usually with agency support, the worker undertakes to organize an informal network or a more structured self-help group. In both rural and urban settings, he may help clients and others with similar interests or concerns to form a telephone network among elderly neighbors, a babysitting exchange among young mothers, a student visitation service to shut-ins, groups and workshops for special interests, such as nutrition, parent–child relations, health, etc.. The skills involved in organizing efforts include assessment of need through survey techniques, such as canvassing all the neighbors on a block or in a high-rise building; mobilizing motivation and interests; identifying and supporting natural leaders; locating and securing resource persons, and providing for physical arrangements; using media and other public relations techniques to publicize the program and to engage the interest of local churches, shopkeepers, and other local business people in serving as sponsors, providing supplies, etc..[34]

In working with problems arising from the physical environment, the helping roles of enabler, facilitator, and teacher are appropriate when the client's lack of information, fearfulness, or inability to use or respond to the natural and built worlds is involved. The influencing roles of mediator and advocate are appropriate when service systems, or powerful individuals in the social environment such as a landlord, must be influenced before the physical environment can be manipulated for a better fit with the client's need. The organizer role is utilized where the mobilizing of group or community efforts is deemed necessary in order to have an impact upon the physical environment in either its natural or built aspects.

The social worker's professional function in the environment area, then, is to help people use the adaptive and coping resources of their social and physical environments that are available and accessible to them. When such resources are missing, inaccessible, denied, or withheld because of maladaptive organizational and network processes or inadequate physical settings, the professional function includes influencing those processes to be more responsive to client need.[35] We are now ready to examine how professional functions and roles with respect to environmental problems and needs are translated into a method of helping and influencing.

Professional Method

The dual functions of helping people use their social and physical environments for their adaptive needs and coping resources, and influencing those environments to be more responsive to client need, draw upon professional purpose and knowledge. They call for a range of practice principles and skills. The practice principles include maintaining a continuing vigilance with regard to the impact of environmental variables on clients; keeping sensitively attuned and open to clients' overt and masked requests for help with environmental issues; maintaining clarity about the legitimacy and primacy of this area for joint client–worker attention and action; and being scrupulously concerned that there is client participation when possible, and that the client has given his or her informed consent. The practice skills include an array of communication, organizing, collaborative, problem solving, and adversarial activities across a range of social work roles. In this section, we focus on practice skills, presenting brief practice excerpts to illustrate how the social worker helps individuals, groups, and families deal with organizations, social networks, and aspects of the physical environment.

Organizational Environment. Organizational resources may be present in the client's environment, and the organization may be accessible and ready to be of service. Yet, the client is unable to use the service—although he needs it—because of fear, lack of knowledge or experience, culturally determined resistances, or other personal issues. The worker's task, then, is to help the client reduce his fear, relax the resistance, and/or acquire the necessary knowledge and experience to enable him to make use of the available service. Thus, the worker's purpose is to help both client and organization reach out to each other. In doing this, roles of enabler, teacher, facilitator, and mediator may all be used in tandem, as the following case situation illustrates.

Alfredo Collazi, age 24 and epileptic, had been known to the rehabilitation and physical medicine outpatient unit of a university hospital. He had been considered by the staff to be severely disturbed as well as epileptic. After many months of intermittent contact, he was discharged from the unit as being no longer in need of its services. He and his parents, with whom he lived, refused a referral either to a family agency or community mental health center, saying they needed no help. Several months later, Mr. Collazi, the patient's father, called the clinic social worker and said Alfredo's bizarre behavior had become steadily worse and something had to be done for everyone's protection. Because of the unit's continuing concern for its former patients, the social worker agreed to make an immediate home visit.

> There was much anger and open quarreling between the parents. Mr. C frequently told his wife to shut up when she interrupted, but he would quickly defer to her taking over. He was disheveled and distraught, and very fearful of what Alfredo might do. Mrs. C constantly depreciated and disparaged her husband. Alfredo sat in a corner of the room looking withdrawn and unhappy. He did not respond to my greetings or my attempts to engage him in the discussion. Mrs. C was intrusive with him, telling him not to smile, not to talk to himself, not to smoke. He did not respond to her. I tried to relate to Mrs. C's desire that her son get better, and to support Mr. C's attempts in this direction by raising the possibility of hospitalization. To her husband, Mrs. C said angrily, "If you get rid of my boy you'll have my corpse on your hands!" To me, she talked of her feelings concerning Calhoun State Hospital and Alfredo's earlier experience there. When I accepted these feelings as understandable, Mrs. C made a frantic attempt to find reasons why hospitalization is out of the question. Finally, Mrs. C said she might let Alfredo go to University Hospital. Insurance has been exhausted, however, and there are no other financial resources. We then talked a little of what treatment is like at various state hospitals, and left it that the family would think more about the situation, and I would investigate treatment possibilities.
>
> During the next two days, I spoke with the chief of the inpatient psychiatric service at University Hospital. No free beds were currently available. He agreed to hold the next one for Alfredo, but expected this to involve a long wait. Thinking Mrs. C might consider day care, I spoke with the admitting psychiatrist of Barrows Center. She knew the patient and family because of an earlier referral, and felt Alfredo was not a suitable candidate because of

brain damage and extremely hostile behavior. She also said Mrs. C had been disruptive in the contacts, is hopeless, and would interfere with any treatment plan formulated by Barrow. She was adamant in refusing to consider admitting Alfredo. I next consulted with the State Department of Mental Health, then with Calhoun State Hospital where Alfredo had been before, and with Vinson State Hospital (the "star" of the state system). In a three-way conference, it was mutually agreed that residential zone requirements would be waived so that Alfredo could enter Vinson.

I then visited the family, and both parents presented a united front, saying the patient had improved and was on the road back to health. This soon broke down and they quarreled about how sick he really is, with Mr. C urging his wife to consider hospitalization. I described the admission process worked out for Vinson and some of the treatment facilities there, and suggested the parents talk with Alfredo to see how he feels about hospitalization, presenting it to him as a means of getting better. Mr. C took hold of this and said he would talk to Alfredo, while Mrs. C persisted in viewing this as "throwing Alfredo away," because only she can give him everything he needs.

Later, Mr. C called to tell me that Mrs. C refused to accept Alfredo's need for care, but he was now ready to take action on his own. Alfredo was becoming increasingly violent, breaking furniture, attacking his mother, exposing himself, saying he was God. Mr. C said he would bring Alfredo to Vinson by taxi, and I suggested he explain to his son what he was doing and why, as it is apparent that Alfredo is himself asking for help. I then spoke with the social worker in the pre-admission unit at Vinson, and she and the admitting physician agreed to see Mr. C and Alfredo on their arrival. As it turned out, Mrs. C came also, and the admission went well. The staff handled the family with sensitivity, and the parents were pleased with what they experienced. They agreed with me that seeing the hospital social worker on a continuing basis might be

> helpful, but they were not interested in a referral to the family agency.
>
> From time to time, Mr. C called me because of his wife's threats to take Alfredo out of the hospital. Each time, I recognized with him how well Alfredo was doing in the hospital, but also how difficult the situation is for his wife and himself. I continued to commend the parents, saying they had done the right thing, despite the difficult separation. This appeared to help Mr. C, so that he was able to continue dealing with his wife's anger and despair. She had refused to talk with the hospital social worker soon after the initial meeting, and both parents continued to decline a referral to the family agency, but their informal connection to the rehabilitation unit seemed to sustain them to some degree.

In this situation, the various parts of the psychiatric service system were engaged by the social worker until a satisfactory plan could be worked out. Fortunately, Vinson Hospital was receptive to the needs of the patient and family from the outset. The difficulty was posed by the patient's mother, whose maladaptive relationship with her son (and her husband) interfered with the family's use of available resources. The situation was made more difficult by the isolation of the family from any support systems. They had long ago cut themselves off from kin, were shunned and feared by neighbors, and were too suspicious of community agencies to make use of them. On the other hand, their long experience with the staff of the rehabilitation unit during the neurological work with Alfredo provided a weak but viable link to draw the family into the larger service system during this period of crisis. From the standpoint of University Hospital's formal policies, Alfredo and his parents were really not eligible for further service because there was no presenting medical problem. Nevertheless, the informal system of the rehabilitation unit, reflecting the leadership of the physiatrist in charge, maintained a firm commitment to former patients even after formal connections had been severed. It was this commitment of the informal system that permitted the worker to respond to the cry for help.

He used the skills of the enabler role to help Mr. C support his wife, to reduce Mrs. C's anxiety at least enough to permit her to tolerate Alfredo's hospitalization. The most significant contribution, however, lay in the worker's own network of organizational resources, upon which he could draw as needed. Most effective social workers, beginning with their entry into practice and continuing over the years, construct systems of inter-organizational relationships. Through processes involving the exchange of professional favors with staff members of other organizations; the gradual accrual of respect from others for one's competence and commitment to client need; and interpersonal skills in dealing with other organizations, a worker builds a resource file. This takes note of the many formal and informal structures in one's urban or rural community and of the people within them whom experience has shown are likely to be the most responsive to appeals for service. These structures and their personnel shift remarkably over short time periods so that constant updating and searching are needed. Resource files that are developed by the agency, or published centrally within the community, can form a useful base for the individual worker's file, but can never substitute for it. Most especially, such formalized files cannot substitute for the professional exchange of favors or for building a professional reputation.

The worker's role is quite different in situations that involve distorted or maladaptive transactions between the client and the service system. In these instances, the mediator role comes to the fore. While the work may include elements demonstrated in the Collazi case, such as support and/or use of resources, it rests particularly on the collaborative skills of intercession, persuasion, and bargaining. The effectiveness of these skills depends, in part, on familiarity with the client's situation, careful assessment of the organizational components in the problem, and knowledge of organizational properties and operations. In the following illustration, a nursing home group is meeting with the social worker, and the members are discussing their concerns about the food:

> Mrs. Schwartz said she thought we should spend time talking about all the things that go wrong during meals. Mr. Ball agreed, saying that the food is lousy and the ser-

> vice is lousy. If he didn't have to eat to survive, he wouldn't even bother going to meals, he said. Several other members nodded. I asked the residents to say specifically what was bad about the food and service.
>
> Mrs. Schwartz brought up the subject of napkins: they either arrive wet on the trays or they're given out at the very end of the meal, which defeats the purpose. I could understand how annoying this is, and said so. Mr. Silverman broke in, declaring that the silverware is often missing from the trays. By the time the missing pieces are given to the residents, the food is cold. He sighed and said, "For all they care, we can eat with our hands." Mrs. Schwartz commented that it would be logical for the dietitian to send up extra silver, so the aides could replace the missing pieces right away. Mr. Phelps then said they often get different food from what they ordered. Mrs. Schwartz confirmed this, saying she doesn't know why they put things on the menu if they have no intention of giving them to the residents. They pretend to give you a choice, but in the end they give you whatever they damn please. I said it must be frustrating, and asked whether substitution happens often, and with what kinds of dishes—main dishes or smaller items? Mrs. Schwartz said it usually happens with things like dessert—you order ice cream and get jello. . . .

The worker helps the members to specify their concerns, which not only increases her understanding of the problem, but theirs as well. Once the concerns have been identified, the worker will need to involve the group in assessing the complexity of the problem the concerns represent. She must help them determine what resources and supports are available for work on the problem, and then determine their joint motivation and readiness to deal with the issue. Risks and potential consequences must be examined because it is imperative that intervention be based on the members' knowledgeable consent. Alternative goals and strategies must be explored, the various tasks structured into manageable steps, and a clear division of labor mapped out. In this instance, the worker also involves the members in helping one another to carry out their respective tasks, using role play to rehearse and prepare for all eventualities.

> I said, "So, you have three specific dietary complaints: napkins that are either wet or not given out until the meal is almost over; missing silverware; and the substitution of items that you've selected from the menu. I wonder if you have any ideas about what we might do about these problems?" Mrs. Liebner asked, "Who could we speak to?" Mrs. Schwartz responded, "We could meet with Miss Jackson (the floor dietitian)." I asked other members what they thought. Mr. Goldstein said, "Talking to the dietitian won't help." Mr. Lazar agreed, "No one will listen to us any way, so why bother." I wondered if they were fearful of possible reprisals by staff. It seemed, however, that the major obstacle was their sense of hopelessness. I suggested it was worth a try, and I would like to help them improve the kitchen situation. Mrs. Schwartz again suggested inviting the dietitian. Mr. Hirsch and Mr. Price supported the idea, and several others agreed. I said, "Okay, how do you think we should go about extending the invitation to her?" Mr. Silverman said, "You go as our representative, and invite her." This led to a discussion of the strategic advantages and disadvantages of my doing it or of a member's inviting her. We decided that a positive response was more likely if I extended the invitation. We rehearsed what I would say to her.
>
> I then asked them how we should go about presenting their concerns when the dietitian comes. Mr. Silverman suggested we make a list of the concerns and read off the items. This was agreed upon, and I asked who would begin the meeting and read the list. Mr. Goldstein said that as the group leader, I should. I responded that I could, but I felt it was important for the dietitian to hear directly from them about their experiences. Mrs. Schwartz volunteered

> to start the meeting off. We role-played what she would say. Mr. Silverman volunteered to offer specific examples of his own experiences. Others volunteered to share theirs. We then considered possible responses of the dietitian and how to handle them.

Before she herself approached the dietitian with the group's request for a meeting, the social worker prepared herself for the encounter. She attempted to put herself into Miss Jackson's shoes, to consider the likely impact of still another pressure on a busy, harassed staff member, and some possible responses Miss Jackson might make to the request. She considered how best to present the request without stimulating resentment toward the residents, and with a view of engaging Miss Jackson in collaborative problem-solving efforts. This reflection enabled the worker to develop sensitivity to Miss Jackson's possible personal and professional concerns. It enabled the worker to feel confident regarding the need for persistence, firm persuasion, and bargaining should the dietitian prove to be resistant to the worker's intercession and mild persuasion. Through this process, the worker was able to begin in a positive, expectant way by assuming initially that she and Miss Jackson have the same concern for residents' needs.

> I said, "The group members have been discussing their dietary problems, and they feel it will be very helpful to have your input—so they have asked me to invite you to our next meeting." She said she didn't know if she could make it. I responded that I knew she was very busy. She explained she is responsible for several floors, and it's hard to find time for everything. I acknowledged it was, but added that the group members really feel she can be helpful to them, especially since their concerns are quite specific. She asked me what their complaints are, and I mentioned several. She smiled and shook her head. I said, "I imagine you're really tired of hearing complaints, especially when you're working so hard." She responded, "You're not kidding." There was a pause, and she asked me what time the meeting would be. I told her, and she

said she would come, but cautioned that she could stay only until 3:15. I said that would be fine, and expressed my appreciation.

In her mediating role, the worker conveyed her understanding of the dietitian's perspective and commiserated with her difficulties. At the same time, she persisted in stating the clients' need for Miss Jackson's assistance, and clarified their concerns for her. In such efforts to intercede, the worker must be willing to risk tension and even conflict, yet to persevere despite barriers or setbacks. In this instance, her perseverance succeeded, and Miss Jackson came.

The group was assembled when Miss Jackson and her supervisor, Mrs. Hart, entered. After sitting down next to me, Mrs. Hart said she thought it might be helpful if she joined us. I said we appreciated her coming. I began, as we had agreed, by stating the general purpose of the meeting, and suggested Mrs. Schwartz share the first concern. While she was somewhat intimidated by Mrs. Hart's presence, Mrs. Schwartz began by asking who was responsible for wiping the tables. Miss Jackson said she usually clears them before each meal. Mrs. Schwartz observed that they are often dirty. Miss Jackson explained she is sometimes rushed, and cannot always get to every table. She assured the group she will try to correct this problem. Group members said they would appreciate it. There was a pause, and I asked if anyone else wanted to say something about this particular problem? A few shook their heads. This was the prearranged cue for Mr. Silverman to ask about the pieces of silverware missing from the trays. Miss Jackson said this was a problem on many floors, because those who loaded the trays are often negligent. Mrs. Hart broke in, saying that from now on, she would have two extra sets of silverware sent up. I asked the members if they felt this was a good solution. They all agreed. Mr. Phelps said he would like to know why he gets jello every day when he hates it, and orders other desserts. Miss Jackson asked him if he had dental problems. He said no. She explained that when a dessert on the menu has to be changed at the last

> minute, they substitute applesauce or jello. Mr. Phelps said he prefers applesauce. Miss Jackson took note of his request. I asked why substitutions have to be made. Mrs. Hart explained that when menus are made up, the department assumes a certain item will be obtained. When it isn't available, or they run out of a popular dish, substitutions are made. Mrs. Schwartz said she could see how these become problems. After discussion of how the residents could be given some choice, we moved on to the issue of napkins. The meeting ended with Miss Jackson agreeing to return in a month for evaluation of the extent to which the suggestions have been implemented.

The changes were, in fact, immediately implemented and became institutionalized. Members felt a sense of accomplishment, and they were then more willing to work on other environmental tasks.

In this instance, the transactions between the service system and its residents had become unintentionally distorted. The residents, fearful of asserting themselves to the appropriate authorities, had continuously but ineffectively complained to the dietary aides, thus increasing their own sense of powerlessness and hopelessness. Meanwhile, the dietitian was vaguely aware of inefficiencies, but since she already felt overburdened, and no one had approached her directly, she had rationalized the situation on the grounds of her work load. After mobilizing the group's interest in taking action with respect to their own life space, the worker used the skills of interceding in requesting the dietitian's meeting with the residents and persisting in her request. In the meeting she served as a catalyst, helping both sets of participants, essentially receptive to each other, to reach accord on the issue. Had the dietitian been less willing to come, or had she or the group been antagonistic, other skills would have been brought into play. Here, however, the worker used the least amount of pressure needed to bring about the desired outcome. She assumed from the outset, and correctly so, that there was a basic consensus of goals between the dietary department and the residents, and that she needed only to help both relate more adaptively to the other, thus improving their transactions.

Effectiveness in the mediating role depends, as it does in other professional roles, on accurate assessment based on adequate information, careful weighing of alternative solutions, and possible strategies and tactics for achieving them. The worker must always have the client's informed consent and his direct involvement to the greatest degree congruent with age, physical state, capacities, interests and life style, and the nature of the organizational problem. Unsuccessful attempts to influence organizational elements are almost always the result of overlooking the need for information, accurate assessment, feasible objectives and strategies, or client consent and involvement.

In our earlier example of the social worker working with a group of blind persons concerned with cafeteria conditions, an interesting opportunity arose for the worker to have an organizational impact regarding this concern. She and other staff were invited to meet with the program committee of the board about agency issues. She requested and received permission to report on the cafeteria situation. She writes:

> I decided not to mention the upcoming board presentation to the group or to involve the members in the process. If I did accomplish something, this would demonstrate to them that I was committed to helping them and was competent in doing so. If I failed, I would not have incurred their anger nor would I feel guilty for raising their hopes and then letting them down.

In effect, the worker blocked communication between clients and powerful agency representatives, leaving both parties uninformed and uninvolved. The group members could have been helpful in developing the presentation by providing anecdotal material and rehearsing the actual presentation. Various strategies might have been explored, such as utilizing the persuasiveness of the clients themselves in making their own presentation. The worker's stance, however, was self-protective, since neither agency nor clients then had a stake in the plan. Thus, there was no potential for criticism. In fact, her plan failed, and no one knew. But no one gained—not the agency, not the clients, not the worker.

When the social worker seeks to influence an organization on the clients' behalf, but without their informed consent and involvement, he conveys a lack of faith in the clients' ability and strength. Doing "for" rather than "with" clients—where it is not necessary—can add to their sense of powerlessness and increase their apathy, instead of supporting and developing problem-solving skills and a sense of competence.

> Ms. Hill told me that an orthopedist had been to see her and said the casts should come off, but he hadn't yet taken them off. After clarifying for her that the removal of the casts was a way of checking her progress periodically and not a permanent removal, I asked if she would feel comfortable in speaking with the doctor about why the casts haven't been removed. She shrugged in a childlike manner, and said, "I don't think I could do that. I don't understand what he says. Would you do it for me?" I said I would.

Ms. Hill wasn't invited to describe the specifics of her interaction with the doctor, or her concerns about understanding him. By moving prematurely to speak to the doctor, the worker encouraged client regression and reinforced her sense of helplessness. After the worker's contact with the doctor, Ms. Hill's legs were examined, but another delay occurred. As Ms. Hill became increasingly depressed, the worker realized the importance of involving her in working on the problem.

> I asked if she could think of ways for us to find out about the delay and try to prevent it from recurring in the future. She thought a moment, then said, "Well, maybe you could go speak to him again and make him come down here. When he comes, I need you here—I can't speak to him myself." I asked her what concerned her about speaking to him. She responded that she doesn't understand his foreign accent. She added that he also wouldn't listen to her—she doesn't know how to talk to doctors. I told her that I could understand her concern, as the doctor is difficult to understand. But, I added that I thought it important for him to hear her concerns and fears directly from her; this might make him feel more responsible for her than if a social worker just talked to him about another pa-

> tient. She could understand this. We spent the rest of the time figuring how we would go about it. I was to set up a three-way conference, and she would share her fears and specific questions at that time. We rehearsed our mutual tasks, and she was pleased and animated.

While doing "for" a client is certainly more preferable than ignoring environmental problems, "doing with" a client invites her particpation in important life tasks. Because of differences in power relationships, the worker often has to intervene on behalf of clients, but his actions need to be guided by the principles of client consent and involvement, where possible.

In dealing with organizational personnel, the worker's knowledge of relevant laws, policies, research findings, technical procedures, and professional jargon within her field of practice is a critical source of influence.[36] Mrs. Frome, an elderly resident of a nursing home, had been seen several times by a competent ophthalmologist. She was unable to obtain information from him, and she feared she was becoming blind. The social worker in the nursing home began by consulting Mrs. Frome's medical record in the clinic, noting the doctor's diagnosis of choriodial sclerosis.

> I went to the medical library, and checked texts on ocular diseases. I found that the problem is primarily in the artery at the retina. In many cases, there isn't complete deterioration or loss of vision, because only a portion of the retinal artery may be implicated.

This knowledge provided the worker with the means to communicate effectively with a more powerful figure in Mrs. Frome's environment.

> I called Dr. Williams and introduced myself. He said he had received my note, and had reviewed Mrs. Frome's record this morning. He asked what I wanted to know. I replied that the major concern was her prognosis. He briefly reviewed the medical situation, clarifying for me the location of the sclerosis. I told him I had reviewed the literature and had read that the loss of vision is not always complete. I wondered about Mrs. Frome's vision loss. He

> asked what books I had read, and said he was impressed by my "homework." He believes that with no other signs of physical deterioration, such as heart disease, Mrs. Frome will be able to continue functioning adequately on the minimal-care floor. I mentioned Mrs. Frome's emotional state and her fear of blindness, and asked him to share his prognosis with her. He said that since I had been willing to read medical books, he would be willing to do a little social work!

The doctor respected the professional interest and effort of the social worker. The worker's comfort with medical language provided a context for communication and helped connect the physician to his patient's concerns.

The collaborative skills of the mediator role are generally used effectively by beginning with intercession, the most economical method in terms of time, effort, and other resources, and proceeding as needed through the increasingly costly skills of persuasion, bargaining, and negotiation. Used in this way, collaborative skills may be successful not only in the communication problems between client and organization, but in the more difficult problems that lie within the structures, practices or personnel of the organization itself. Occasionally, however, these skills are not effective enough to gain the desired outcome in organizationally based problems or even, as occasionally happens, in problems of communication between client and organization. When collaborative efforts fail, it is then necessary for the social worker to consider the usefulness of the advocate role and its adversarial skills of pressure, coercion, and appeals to third party intervention. These activities, in contrast to those of collaboration, are far more costly in time, effort, and other resources, and are used after the more economical skills have failed. In the role of advocate, just as in the role of mediator, the processes of data gathering, assessment, and planning are critical. If they are overlooked, there is a risk of not only failing to secure the needed services or resources for one's client, but of endangering the social work practitioner's future efforts to influence the organization or its personnel by firming up their resistance and undermining his own reputation for competence.

The following example illustrates the transition from the mediator role to the advocacy role. It also illustrates some missteps along the way, caused by the worker's neglecting to secure necessary information.

> Mrs. Thomas, a 25-year-old black woman with two children, came to a community service agency requesting help in obtaining SSI benefits for her daughter, who suffered from cerebral palsy.
>
> She explained that her daughter is eligible for additional assistance under a recent federal law, but she has not succeeded in obtaining the benefits. Mrs. Thomas said her daughter's claim had been approved, but she had received no checks. When she went back to the local Social Security office, she received an emergency grant of $100. Still no checks came. When she went back again, she was told she was not eligible. Since then, she has moved to another district, but has continued her efforts through the local Social Security office in the new neighborhood, again to no avail.
>
> Mrs. Thomas and I agreed to work together on the problem, and we decided she would bring in all her documents, and I would call the Social Security office.
>
> When Mrs. Thomas returned with the documents, we went over them. Then I telephoned the local office, identified myself, and described the problem. The staff person responded that Social Security doesn't handle that kind of problem and we should try welfare. I suspected he was wrong, and I challenged his assertion. He said, "Listen, we can't help you." I asked to speak to a supervisor. She took the phone, and again I described the problem. I fared even worse with the supervisor, who said that cerebral palsy does not qualify Mrs. Thomas' daughter for benefits. I said, "Are you sure?" The supervisor responded with a firm yes. I thanked her and hung up.

The worker had made a crucial error in contacting the organization before acquiring knowledge of Social Security policies and organizational structures. His effort was undermined because his lack of knowledge encouraged agency personnel to assume an intractable position. Fortunately, however, the worker and client were undaunted, and they set about learning the rules regarding disability claims. The worker obtained the SSI manual and studied its contents with the client. Several sections seemed to establish Mrs. Thomas' eligibility, so they decided to retrace Mrs. T's earlier attempts. The worker called the first Social Security office.

> I related the problem. The staff person listened without much interest and referred me to the current office. Playing a hunch, I said I understood records of initial claims were held in the original office. He then referred me to the records representative, Mr. Ross, who turned out to be responsive. He asked for documentation, and I said that Mrs. T had received an emergency grant from that office, so her claim must have been accepted. Mr. Ross agreed to look into the matter further. He later called back and said the application had been initially accepted and processed. He believes a large retroactive sum is due, and outlined the steps to be taken. I thanked him for his help.
>
> I was elated and called Mrs. Thomas to tell her the good news. She was excited and hopeful she would get the checks soon. We talked about the steps involved, and she felt she could do this alone. I encouraged her to do so, and affirmed her competence.

One month later, however, Mrs. Thomas advised the worker that she still had not received a check, and she asked the worker's help. They discussed the steps she had gone through, and agreed that the worker would again telephone the local Social Security office.

> Mr. Ross was not in, and I spoke to another person. I informed him of the situation and asked him to find out what had happened. After a few minutes he returned, saying Mrs. T's grant had not been processed because she first had to go to the welfare department and notify them of the large retroactive benefits she would receive, which she would then be obligated to turn over to welfare (Mrs. T had been receiving welfare for her daughter in the in-

> terim). I asked if this were agency policy, because the SSI manual did not mention formal collaboration between the two organizations. The staff person insisted it was policy, and Mrs. T could not receive checks until she fulfilled the requirement. I asked him to mail me a copy of the policy, and he refused to do so. I then asked to speak to his supervisor, who confirmed the policy, and who also refused to forward or even to read the policy statement over the phone.

Up to this point, the worker had depended upon the collaborative skills of interceding by requesting, pleading, and persisting with staff members. Also, he attempted to persuade by informing, instructing, clarifying, explaining, and arguing with agency's staff. He also used the negotiating skills of sympathizing, placating, and bargaining to the extent that the situation allowed. Still the organization withheld the funds Mrs. Thomas was entitled to. The Social Security office appeared to be totally unresponsive. It denied Mrs. T's rights by not informing her of the basis on which benefits were denied. After consulting with Mrs. Thomas, the worker decided that he must go beyond the mediating role to the advocacy role, utilizing the adversarial skills of pressure and coercion. He began with pressure—that is, with threats and challenges, rather than the more costly coercion.

> After searching, I found a lawyer whose expertise was in welfare and Social Security legislation. He explained to me that the agency has no right to withhold payments from clients because of informal agreements with the Department of Welfare. This practice is clearly illegal. He offered to intervene, and I said I would first discuss the matter with Mrs. T and get back to him, if necessary. I expressed our appreciation.

Mrs. Thomas decided that she and the worker should make one more effort before turning the matter over to a lawyer. She preferred to avoid legal escalation, fearing reprisals. So they prepared for another telephone contact, rehearsing and selecting the worker's approach.

> I asked to speak with the supervisor, and brought him up to date on our previous contacts with the office. I said Mrs. T and my agency had retained a lawyer, who informed us that under the law the daughter was the legal recipient of the disability allowance. Therefore, Welfare had no claim to the retroactive payment. I informed him that we were presently prepared to seek a fair hearing, and the lawyer wished to move to a class action. I continued that this was Mrs. T's and my agency's final effort to handle the matter ourselves, before seeking legal redress. The supervisor asked for a half hour to look into the matter. When he called back, he apologized for a misunderstanding and announced that the claim had been processed. I asked for a specific commitment, and he said that Mrs. T would receive her first check and all retroactive benefits within three weeks. She did, indeed.

As frequently happens, the bureaucratic organization's formal policy is more responsive to client need than are its actual practices. What seemed to be the real lever of change in the situation was the threat of legal challenge. It is often the case that individual members of organizations are responsive to the threat of crisis, making it unnecessary to go further. The worker's decision to move beyond the collaborative strategies of interceding, persuading, and placating, to the adversarial strategies of pressure and threat was effective in securing his client's entitlements. His entrance into the situation, especially as he gained in knowledge and competence in the two roles, lent weight to the cause of a vulnerable client. The unfavorable balance of power was corrected in some measure. Mrs. T received her entitlement, and experienced the satisfaction that comes from taking effective action on one's own behalf.

When collaborative persuasion and negotiation are ineffective, the worker needs to involve the client in considering adversarial tactics of threat and challenge. In turning to these tactics, however, worker and client must understand that the risks increase. They must consider their respective vulnerabilities. Group services usually diminish the potential risks and increase the likelihood of success. People gain strength and security from being with others in similar situations. In the process, the stigma associated with a particular status is alleviated as members come to realize that problems defined as individual and psychological are frequently collective and social in nature. Having greater visibility, group action gains institutional attention and concern, and militates against individual isolation and reprisals. Client groups can express their grievances through various forms of protest such as sit-ins, vigils, marches, rent strikes, picketing, the use of mass media, and engaging the interest of a political figure, etc. These actions are intended to increase clients' bargaining power to induce organizational responsiveness. At times, the mere threat of adversarial action and its potential consequences may be sufficient.

In dealing with organizational obstacles, the problems are frequently overwhelming, the tasks complex, and the process frustrating. The client may experience feelings of despair and futility. The worker must invite the client to express his doubts, hesitations, fears, and resentments. The worker must also provide realistic support, encouragement, and hope. In pursuing the environmental objectives, he has to be responsive to feelings and internal needs. In other words, he must not forget the person in the process. Whatever the strategies, the worker continuously takes into account the possible consequences for the client. People can be hurt by practitioners having benign intentions, but using dysfunctional interventions. Clients' rights and self-interests must not be overlooked in the pursuit of a professional cause or a class action. Through their full participation, however, service users do become educated to environmental structures and procedures, and develop increased competence and control over their life situations. Clients must be involved in all the steps involved in influencing organizations to be more responsive.

The Social Network. This is a relatively new environmental concept for social workers, and its incorporation into everyday practice has only just begun. Yet, its essential aspect has probably characterized social work practice since its beginning. The settlement movement, for example, was conceived by its founders as good neighboring. The college students and youthful professionals who became settlement house residents sought to be friendly neighbors to the poor among whom they lived. They wanted to help their neighbors organize themselves to improve the quality of neighborhood life through mutual help. Now, a century later, there is growing recognition of the importance of natural helpers in people's lives—not only neighbors, but kin, friends, and work mates, as they coalesce into social networks.

Network channels of communication and mutual aid can become blocked so that access to emotional or concrete resources is cut off. There are certain people who are at-risk of emotional or social isolation, including the bereaved, the separated and divorced, the single parent, the newcomer, the isolated elderly, the friendless and the shut-ins and certain rural populations. Social isolation is the loneliness felt because of unwanted distance from others, or lack of a social network. Emotional isolation is the painful loneliness caused by the loss or absence of a specific attachment to a loved person. Some persons are in double jeopardy, suffering the loneliness of both forms of isolation.[37] To deal with these painful needs, worker action needs to be directed toward mobilizing or strengthening the real-life ties between the client and significant others, re-establishing old linkages, or helping the client find and develop new ones.

Neighbors, since they are in frequent face-to-face contact, are particularly suitable for helping the person with immediate and short-lived tasks.[38] Because the network of neighbors has a shifting membership in our mobile society, neighbors are usually most helpful in immediate emergencies ranging from the trivial to the catastrophic. They may lend and provide resources (a ride to the store, using the telephone, watching the baby, and providing information about neighborhood customs and resources). Unfortunately, the presence of such natural helpers has usually been given scant notice and, at times, professional involvement has been discouraged. One of us, while a student in child protective services some years ago, encouraged an interested older neighbor and Mrs. Reese, a neglected and neglectful young mother of four small children, to strengthen their relationship. The motherly neighbor, who had older children of her own, provided contacts with friends and other neighbors, teaching in marketing, housekeeping, and child care, all of which had a significant impact on Mrs. Reese's sense of competence and self-esteem. The neighbor found pleasure in her companionship with Mrs. Reese and the children. A reciprocal, affectionate real-life relationship grew up between the two women. Nevertheless, the student was cautioned against such an "inappropriate approach" in which the neighbor must surely be using Mrs. Reese for her own neurotic needs! Some natural helpers may have neurotic motivations, but such persons apparently are exceptions.[39] In most instances, if the helper is exploitative, she is not likely to retain her status as helper in the network.

Natural networks of neighbors are often found in mutiple-unit dwellings. In single-room-occupancy hotels, tenanted by the "outsiders" of society—the isolated elderly, recipients of public assistance, discharged mental patients, addicts and alcoholics—natural helping networks are present. Informal leaders look after the frail, managing their checks, caring for them when ill or drunk, and seeing that they take their medications, keep their clinic appointments and report to the welfare center as required. Occasionally, they provide a needed bottle of wine. Although functioning marginally themselves, these natural helpers make it possible for their neighbors to cope and survive in a harsh environment.[40] The worker has to take special care not to undermine the influence or the role of informal helpers because of the danger of disrupting the delicate balance within the network.

In an agency located in a large public housing project in a deteriorating urban neighborhood, the worker reports:

> Mrs. M, an elderly woman who lived across the hall from the agency, turned out to be a matriarch in the community. Well respected, she functioned naturally as a broker amongst people in need. She cared for children on a daily basis and frequently sent their mothers in to us for social service help. She also began to send friends who needed jobs to see "what we could do." She allowed herself to depend on us, but we soon saw that many depended on her.
>
> We had elderly clients who were alone and isolated. Some had incomes slightly above the Medicaid level due to a small lifelong savings, which they would not part with. We were able to convince some to pay a small fee for a homemaker on a part-time basis, and we used ourselves as screeners for the people Mrs. M sent who were interested in caring for the elderly in this way. Our use of Mrs. M and her friends in this way enhanced her position, met the employment needs of the friend, and also met the

> physical and social needs of some of our most isolated elderly clients. And so it was that whenever a client with some leadership in the community was involved, her own social network was served. As we recognized her natural position, she became an outreach agent for us and services were developed to meet the needs that she helped uncover.[41]

In residential neighborhoods, a worker may locate natural helping resources by various means.[42] The staff at a community center may know of such persons. Sometimes operators of the local tavern, laundromat, beauty parlor, grocery store, or drug store can direct the interested worker to these helpers. The settlement worker, bartender, postman, bodega proprietor, barber or hairdresser, and druggist may themselves be significant natural helpers. The social worker can collaborate with such natural helpers in order to extend their circle of influence, and increase their scope. He also seeks to sustain the clients' connections to neighborhood helpers where such connections already exist.

Extended kin networks maintain affective ties and exchange resources, even across geographical distances. Although kin may move apart, their connections are usually maintained by rapid communication and transportation systems, so that kin networks are characterized by permanence. In the case of Puerto Rican migrants, for example, many return to the island regularly to participate in the life events of birth or death or to replenish affective supplies. They may send regular remittances to family members who have remained behind, or reciprocally depend upon them for material aid, advice, encouragement, and love. On the mainland, many form replacement networks for the very close networks they knew on the island. In addition to culture shock, climatic shock, and problems of unemployment, Puerto Ricans must deal with the stress of loneliness and homesickness. To do so, most try to live near kin and friends who may have migrated before them. They establish mutual aid systems for exchange of money, food, baby-sitting services, etc. Another network is the "hometown club" which offers connectedness to all those who come from a particular island town. The club provides a sense of identity and belonging through a range of activities that recapture island ties.[43] Additionally, such uniquely Puerto Rican institutions as bodegas, botanicas, and mediums serve important network functions in Puerto Rican communities.[44] Without such networks, the level of stress experienced by migrant families would be even greater than it is. These attachments and linkages are important resources for the worker and client to mobilize, draw upon, and strengthen. In the same way, other groups of poor migrating to the urban center—Chicanos, native Americans, blacks, and whites from Appalachia—often have extended kin networks or neighborhood helpers in the new area who can be encouraged to expand their emotional support and concrete help.

Whether near or far, kin are most suitable for tasks requiring long-term commitment, such as help during illness and periods of financial stress.[45] The social worker may need to help her client to approach the kin network and to influence them to be responsive. At times, the kin network may need to be mobilized as a natural support system to work collaboratively on problem-solving, thus extending the potential for coping resources. The worker may help the network to become more effectively integrated for greater support, reassurance and solidarity.[46] The use of such graphic modes as kinship maps, sociometric diagrams, genograms, and photographs with individuals, groups, and families helps to re-awaken old ties, develop a sense of continuity, identify sources of stress and mobilize resources to master "collective" problems.[47]

Friendships lack the permanence of kinship networks, and usually the frequent face-to-face contact of neighbors, but they rest on bonds of affection and regard developed through free choice. Friends may be located in various primary groups—work, religious, social, and recreational. Each such group represents a source of potential friendship ties for affective and instrumental support.[48] Friendship networks appear to be most helpful by serving as consultants in such shifting matters as behavioral norms, dress, life styles, and modes of relating to peers, work group, and authority figures.[49] The worker can help the client to assess friendship resources and to examine potential obstacles to their use such as concern about imposing on them, embarrassment, or reluctance to risk rejection.

Ancillary networks, such as self-help groups, are important resources to people. Developing now in all areas of life, the earliest and perhaps the best known self-help groups are Alcoholics Anonymous, Synanon, and Parents Without Partners. Self-help groups are found in medical areas (colostomy groups, cancer groups, Mended Hearts, Living!), in mental health (Recovery, Inc.), and in criminal justice (The Fortune Society). They are often formed around minority statuses such as women's groups, gay groups, ethnic and religious groups, and for counseling purposes such as Widow-to-Widow programs.[50] Each such group is like a recycling process in which people take active roles in decreasing the very stresses or problems that victimized them, and so improve their own environments.[51] Human beings have a need to give as well as to receive, and in helping others they help themselves. Mutual aid and self-help serve to enhance the dignity and competence and hence the functioning of the participants. They are real-life processes, rather than clinical processes. Their focus is on coping and adaptation rather than illness, on action rather than passivity, and on progressive rather than regressive forces in people. At times, clients require help in finding self-help groups and other ancillary networks. They may experience difficulty in using these resources and need encouragement and support to facilitate their participation. Occasionally, the networks themselves are insufficiently responsive and the worker must mediate or advocate with and on behalf of the client in order to increase their receptivity.

When communities lack ancillary networks, the worker can organize them with the cooperation of his agency. Often self-help groups can be established around a common concern, interest or task.

In a low-income project located in a major city and housing approximately 18,000 people, for example, the social workers recognized that new tenants feel confused, lost, and isolated. Getting used to the neighborhood, meeting neighbors, and adjusting to project life are important adaptive tasks. The social workers decided to provide an opportunity for new tenants to construct a social network for mutual aid that would help them develop a sense of belonging. Each new tenant received a letter of welcome, announcing a meeting for new tenants. Escort and baby-sitting services would be available. An appointment for a home visit by the social worker and a member of the tenants' association was offered.

> Mrs. Peterson invited us in. I introduced myself and Mrs. Charles, stating that we had come to welcome Mrs. Peterson to the community, and to invite her to the meeting for new tenants. Mrs. P said she would like to come so

she could get to know some people. Mrs. Charles described how she had made some friends at these meetings. Mrs. Peterson said it is difficult to live alone in a new community. She comes home from work and doesn't know what to do with herself. She particularly appreciated the availability of an escort service, and we worked out a time for her to meet the escort.

At the meeting, new tenants were introduced to each other informally over refreshments. Then, as the ten new tenants settled down, I suggested we begin our meeting. I re-introduced myself and Mrs. Charles, and told the group that everyone present moved into the project last month. Since they are all new they probably have similar concerns, such as getting settled into their apartments, getting used to the "big" landlord, finding their way around to shops, hospitals, clinics, welfare center, and schools. It isn't easy to make all these connections, I said, and so we thought they might be helpful to each other in doing all this. We can also discuss any problems they might be having in the process, and Mrs. Charles and I will try to help.

Mrs. Rolph complained about malfunctioning appliances and a crack in her window. She had spoken to the secretary and left a message for the project manager to no avail. Mrs. King suggested she call the manager directly, and told of her own positive experience doing that. Mrs. Rolph was surprised that the manager took calls. Mrs. Charles encouraged her to call him. The message was clear: "Make yourself heard and you'll obtain service."

Mrs. Peterson told how she had been knocked down in the lobby and how she fears the teenagers she sees hanging around the project. Several nodded and referred to what they are doing to protect themselves, such as never going on the elevator alone. Out of this discussion, the tenants decided to coordinate activities, such as going to the subway and shopping together. They exchanged phone numbers and were pleased with the sense of security this gave them. Mrs. Charles also explained the function and operations of tenants' patrols. Mrs. Santiago then told of

> her difficulty in registering her children for school. Several members explained the necessary steps and Mrs. Valdez offered to act as interpreter.

The linkages through which the worker connects people in need of others became helpful influences in their daily lives. Here a "life line," a mutual aid system, was created through which people's common human need for social contact and interpersonal commitments were realized. In a similar way, adolescent hot lines, suicide and drug lines, and youth peer-counseling seek to make up for the absence of caring and helpful neighbors, kin, or friends. They are a source of help and support in threatening life situations or for difficult life tasks.

Like his urban colleague, the rural social worker must focus on the community as well as on the individual, family, or group. But because institutional resources in the social environment are generally more limited in rural settings, the rural social worker often must engage in a wider range of activities in order to engage the community itself, as the following example suggests:

> When a social worker was assigned to a small mental health center in a rural town 150 miles away from the nearest city, he decided his first task was to learn about the community and to let them learn about him. He met with the mayor, the county commissioners, the school principals, church officials and the state legislators from the area. He planned his coffee breaks at the local drugstore when the town's two policemen and the county highway patrolman were usually there. He visited the county welfare office, the Visiting Nurse Association, and the American Indian boarding school at the edge of town. In each instance, he let people know that he was now living and working in their area and that he was interested in helping with human needs and problems.
>
> Very soon, the social worker was told about the problems of alcoholism, about the teenage group that was harassing the boarding school children, and about the drug problem at the boarding school. Several families talked with him about the lack of summer employment for teenagers. He was asked by the Visiting Nurse Association to visit some of their patients to help the nurses understand the family dynamics in situations where the medical regimen was not being

carried out. Several people called on him to obtain help for a retarded child or an aged parent.

By the end of his first year, this enterprising rural social worker was providing consultation to the boarding school, the VNA, and the welfare office as well as accepting referrals from them. He was conducting several weekly groups on parenting skills. He had involved the school officials, county commissioners, shopkeepers, and police in planning and carrying out a summer recreation and employment program for adolescents. He initiated a volunteer program to assist patients who were returning home from the State mental hospital. And he was arranging a series of community educational programs on alcoholism with the assistance of an alcoholism specialist from the state office.[52]

This social worker was keenly aware of the impact of people–environment transactions on adaptation, stress, and coping in rural areas. He understood his function to include mobilizing, supporting, and utilizing the strengths of the community itself as well as those of the individuals, families, and networks comprising the community. He was as skilled in the creation and provision of environmental resources as he was in working with individuals, families, and groups on issues in life transitions and maladaptive interpersonal processes. What he clearly understood is that focusing on the second function alone would have undermined the strength of the rural community in dealing with its own needs and problems. It was probably his clarity about this that enabled him to engage the community as quickly as he did. Rural communities are even more likely than urban communities to view the newcomer—and especially a professional—with distrust and skepticism.

Good practice always attempted to improve aspects of the physical environment in order to help the client. Little of such work, however, was recorded in agency materials or included in textbooks, probably because its importance was underestimated. It was viewed more as a function of common sense than of professional knowledge and skill. With the advent of a conceptual framework that relates the levels and textures of the physical environment to the social environment and to the culture, the important role of the physical environment in growth and adaptation is clarified. It will, we suspect, hasten the development of more sophisticated practice principles concerning people's interaction with the physical environment. The following section presents one attempt to sketch out what such principles might encompass.

Built World. Until recently, the built world was considered a fixed or given feature of the life space, a static backdrop against which people's lives were played out.

> I had been seeing my upper-middle-class adolescent client for six months. We talked of the severe problems she has with both parents in achieving an age-appropriate independence. I think this work together will ease her school situation and her relations with peers. Recently, I became interested in practice issues regarding physical environments, and I asked Mary to draw me an interior map of the house where she lives, indicating the traffic patterns of family members within the house, and their joint and separate use of the various rooms. It was only then I learned that while Mary and her younger sister have their own bathroom, several necessary plumbing connections had never been installed. Nothing had ever been done in the years the family owned the home to make the bathroom usable for these sixteen- and fourteen-year-old girls. Instead, the girls use the parents' bathroom, and they must go through their parents' bedroom for access to it. Neither the parents nor the girls have privacy. I was horrified to think I had never thought to ask simple questions about basic living arrangements that have such an influence on functioning. Mary and I are now working on how we can deal with this issue in a non-threatening way to achieve her parents' agreement to install the needed fixtures.

This example highlights the necessity for taking the physical setting into account during the exploration process in the initial phase of helping. In this instance, the physical environment—space and its uses—reflected the reciprocal problems these parents and daughters had in separating and in establishing necessary distance for the development of autonomy. The problems in this enmeshed family will not, of course, be solved by the installation of plumbing in the bathroom, but it can help start the needed process of differentiation between parents and children. Fortunately, money for the needed installation is no problem in this affluent family. Where physical environmental constraints are combined with urban or rural poverty, however, the problems can be all but intractable. But with imagination, perseverance, knowledge, skill, and compassionate concern, the social worker can help her client change seemingly unchangeable aspects of the phsycial environment.

Issues of unsafe housing and overcrowding come to the fore in the social work task of helping with stressful aspects of the environment. The social worker needs to take into account the meaning of privacy and overcrowding to particular individuals, families, and groups. It is sometimes possible to make suggestions of how to establish areas of privacy within a home or even within a small rural or urban apartment through the use of screens, containers for private belongings, arrangements for having one's own time for access to an area set aside for privacy. In the case of unsafe housing, it is sometimes possible for the client, or the client and social worker together, or the worker on the client's behalf, to secure the needed corrections to housing violations by appeals to the landlord, the municipal health department, or the housing department. The use of existing tenant groups or the formation of tenants into pressure groups are important processes to invoke when ordinary request procedures are ineffective. Occasionally securing needed furnishings or the replacement of a defective stove or heater, for example, can be achieved through calling upon the cooperation of another social agency. Often, however, unsafe housing requires the search for other quarters and, similarly, the stress of overcrowding can only be overcome by moving to more adequate shelter. For those who are poor, or who for other reasons have limited mobility, it is usually necessary for the worker to participate in finding suitable housing, arranging for moving costs and needed furnishings, and assisting with the adaptation to the new dwelling and the new neighborhood. In some instances, natural helpers can be located for tasks of improving the physical environment as shown in the following example.

A family agency, through its growing interest in outreach services to the aged poor, placed several social workers in a low-income housing project in which there was a large concentration of older residents. The social workers had many concerns about the loneliness and isolation of the aged residents, their need for apartment repairs, and the lack of interest in their aged neighbors among the younger residents. Since the management would not undertake the tasks of repair, one worker set about building systems of mutual aid which she hoped would create a more nutritive social environment in addition to improving the physical setting.

> Miss Carroll, an elderly white resident, was very eager to have her apartment painted. She had no relatives to help and was quite stymied in how to get the job done. I tucked this piece of information away in my mind. My contacts with one of the young black residents indicated he needed money to buy winter clothes for his children. At the same time, I learned he had worked at one time as a painter. The task was to relate the two on the basis of the mutuality of their needs.
>
> The first meeting was pleasant. Miss Carroll did not seem perturbed by the fact that Mr. Allen was black, although the aged—largely a white group—experienced some tensions about the multi-racial composition of the project, and expressed fear of adolescent and young adult residents. Miss C and Mr. Allen got along well together and arrived at some mutual decisions. The date for the painting was put off several times, however, and Miss Carroll was quite disappointed. Finally, the date was set and Miss Carroll began to prepare for the event, taking dishes off the shelves, clothes out of closets, etc. At this point, Mr. Allen began to weaken, and it seemed as though he might back out. I began to think I would have to paint the apartment myself! His objections seemed to revolve around his image of an older person: "She's very particular. She won't like the way we do it, and we'll have to do it over again. She'll feel overwhelmed by my sons who are going to help me. She'll be afraid to have us black men in her apartment." I tried to help Mr. Allen sort out the facts of the situation. Finally, it was arranged. Mr.

> Allen's wife decided to come and help and to provide womanly contact for Miss Carroll. In addition, I planned to drop by to see how things were going.
>
> Things went quite well. When I arrived, Miss Carroll was confused by all the activity, but was bearing up. I invited her out for a while, and an interesting interchange occurred. Mrs. Allen whispered to me, "Don't you think she will be afraid to leave us here in the apartment alone?" I asserted my own trust in them, and said it was all right. It was a touching moment, for it was as though they had not been trusted often before.
>
> The work was finished and the apartment was done satisfactorily. Mr. Allen was paid slightly more than he had asked for the job, and was able to buy a second-hand washing machine and begin purchases for winter clothing. He seemed pleased he had been able to do this for himself rather than having to try charitable organizations. It was difficult, however, to make the minor touch-ups Miss Carroll wanted, although he did return and lay her rug for her when it came back from the cleaners. For this he would take no money. Finally, after several unsuccessful attempts to get him to clean paint from the floors and other minor things, I took the job in hand and did it myself. There was much humorous discussion with my colleagues about whether this was really a part of a social worker's job! I thought the whole process from beginning to end was indeed a part of the social worker's job. The apartment is quite lovely, and Miss Carroll is delighted with her new environment. We hope Mr. Allen will receive other requests and we feel that such contacts can lessen some of the tension between white and black residents and between the generations.[53]

Such work in the physical environment requires considerable investment of time and effort on the part of the social worker. Agency case loads do not always permit such investment. Social workers therefore need to alert administrators and policymakers to the importance of the social work function in such necessary but often overlooked areas, and its implications for preventive work.

With growing knowledge of the impact of design, materials, and spatial arrangements in dwellings and institutions, practitioners are increasingly aware of what they can do to intervene in the built world for its active support of adaptation and coping. It has been discovered, for example, that carpeting psychiatric wards where severely regressed patients were housed had a positive effect on problems of incontinence.[54] Increasing the quantity and quality of perceptual stimuli through sensory therapy has improved the functioning of aged residents in geratric facilities.[55] The provision of closed and open spaces on a purposeful rather than accidental basis is helpful to children in treatment cottages. In a residential facility where a former dining hall was converted into a set of social worker offices around a central unused, unfurnished central space, children waiting for their appointments engaged in boisterous, aggressive, and acting-out behaviors. When the central, open space was provided with area rugs, and chairs and tables were arranged in conversational groups, much of the undesired behavior ceased.

In institutionalized dwellings, such as mental hospitals, geriatric facilities, children's treatment cottages, and general hospitals, crowding problems can be often acute. Patients or residents may, because of spatial arrangements and the placement of furniture, have little or no opportunity for social interaction. Conversely, they may have little or no opportunity for privacy. An optimally nutritive environment provides opportunities for both interaction and privacy as needed and desired by the institutional resident. The social worker who is aware of the impact of physical settings on people's functioning will be constantly alert to the need for rearrangement and restructuring of space and furniture. She will engage the participation of staff and patients in considering alternative arrangements to reduce stress and to enhance adaptation.

A state hospital, concerned about the lack of social interaction and the apathy of the patients on a female geriatric ward, redecorated the day room. Attractive new chairs, walls painted in vibrant colors, and a tile floor with an interesting design changed the room's appearance remarkably. Still the patients did not interact with one another and remained apathetic.

A consultant who was called in noted that the beautiful new chairs were placed side by side along the walls of the room, making it difficult for the women to converse, as they sat shoulder to shoulder. In addition, four chairs were placed around the four sides of each of the pillars in the room, making conversation impossible. The women sat all day staring vacantly. The consultant rearranged the chairs into conversational groupings around new small tables.

For the first few days thereafter, several women, acting as self-appointed monitors, pushed the chairs back against the wall where they had been for so long. Others complained they couldn't find their own chairs. Magazines and vases of flowers were then placed on the tables to lure the residents to the conversational groupings. At first, these disappeared as patients took them into their own rooms, but gradually they remained as the patients became used to the new arrangements, began to interact and to enjoy their interaction and their new environment.[56]

The initial unhappiness caused by changing the "right way of arranging the chairs" reflected the patients' sense of having lost what little control they possessed over their environment. That stress might have been avoided by engaging the participation of the patients in the planning process from the beginning. The engagement of institutional residents in planning for their own physical setting which is, for many, their total life space, requires the special skills of the social worker's organizer role. Community and staff support must often be solicited, motivation must be aroused, opinions surveyed, and arrangements for successful task achievement provided, as illustrated in the following example.

> Rainier House, a home for the aged, is located in a small city and has about 40 men and women residents, most of whom are in their 70s and 80s. They are ambulatory and basically self-sufficient. The building itself is a deteriorating mansion located in what fifty years ago was an exclusive section of town. The interior is oppressive, with dimly lit corridors and rooms of institutional green. Time lies heavily on the residents. Their eyes are downcast or vacant as they wait for the next dose of medicine, the next meal, the next day, and for death itself. The board, increasingly concerned with the plight of the residents, initiated a successful fund-raising campaign for a new Rainier House that was to be completed within two years.

At about this time, I was engaged as a social work consultant. I soon noticed that board members were deeply involved in tasks related to the new facility. The executive director was immersed in plans, budgets, and programing, and the staff talked excitedly of their new surroundings. But the residents seemed only to watch the clock on the hall wall, oblivious to the exuberance that surrounded them. Residents typically responded to my remarks about the new home with a cynical, "If I live that long."

In staff groups and with administrative personnel I began to raise the question, "Why aren't the residents as excited about the new house as you and the community are?" The growing realization that the residents themselves had never been invited to participate in planning for their own residence led to my suggestion that involving them might stimulate their interest and promote their adaptation to the tasks of moving and finding a new niche. I also suggested that rekindling the dormant creativity of the residents through involvement in planning might spread and develop to other constructive tasks that could make their lives more fulfilling in their new living situation.

A "town meeting" of all the residents, staff, board and significant members of the community was organized. A lively discussion regarding architectural plans, decorating, and services took place. Out of this grew several working committees charged with various responsibilities related to making Rainier House a pleasant place in which to live. Inclusion of the residents on these committees had a reverberating effect on the less involved or more disabled residents by heightening their interest and stimulating their suggestions. Activities such as tours to the new site and consultations with the architect and decorator were arranged to enhance the direct involvement and participation of the residents. Interest and action replaced apathy and lethargy in the resident community. Joined now in a mutual set of tasks with staff and others, the elderly residents regained a sense of dignity, autonomy, and competence by participation in their own destiny.

Through the skill of the social worker in organizing the interest and support of all the relevant participants, the residents became connected to their physical setting in a way they had not been previously.

The physical setting provided by one's own agency is often an area in which the social worker may take action that will improve its negative influence on the users of the agency's services. Dismal, unattractive, cluttered and even dirty surroundings communicate to clients that they are considered unworthy and reinforce their feelings of powerlessness. The practitioner can engage the interest of colleagues and other staff in improving the agency's environment through decorating walls with pictures and posters, adding plants and magazines, rearranging some chairs into groupings that permit interaction and other chairs into more isolated positions. Typically, small private agencies provide for the comfort of their clients. But, even the reception areas of larger agencies such as welfare offices and public hospitals can be restructured to support self-esteem, to be humanizing rather than de-humanizing places, if the staff is sufficiently alert to the impact of the physical setting and sufficiently imaginative to make creative suggestions for ameliorative measures. Bureaucratic processes may thwart such efforts in which instances the worker must undertake the procedures of organizational influencing as described earlier in this chapter.

Natural World. The field of child welfare has probably made the greatest use of this environmental level. Social workers in urban areas frequently take children, and often with their mothers, on expeditions and picnics to the countryside, the seashore, or to the city park and zoo. Those formerly designated as group workers, in particular, made imaginative use of natural settings for camping experiences, hikes, and other outdoor activities that refresh the spirit and renew the sense of wonder and beauty. Such activity helps to establish the sense of competence and self-esteem as children and adults learn to care for themselves in the out-of-doors and to share the give and take of intimate living in which mutual aid is required for survival. The provision of experience in the world of nature for urban children and their mothers has a long history, dating back to the fresh-air camps operated by the settlement houses, and continuing through the later youth organizations, community centers, and the camping movement. In contemporary life, wilderness experiences and organized camping are provided to mental patients, disturbed youth, the blind, diabetics and others with serious physical disabilities, and the elderly.[57]

Finding one's way through the complex urban environment, and locating and using its physical, social and cultural resources is an essential skill for participation in modern technological societies for both rural and urban residents. It is part of what is meant by "social competence."[58] Discharged mental patients, particularly those who are de-institutionalized after lengthy hospitalization, frequently lack the basic skills needed for moving through the physical environment of their small town or large city. Residents of the inner city are often fearful of leaving their own neighborhoods bounded as such areas are by ethnic and class status. Wherever geographic mobility is limited by poverty, fear, or lack of knowledge or experience, then adaptive potential is also limited. Adaptive capacities are enhanced by enriched physical and social environments, so that constraints on freedom of movement, on exposure to new experiences, and on the access to varieties of information inevitably constrain the quality and variety of coping skills that develop.

We have discussed how social workers can help people learn to negotiate organizational environments, a coping skill that is also essential for adaptive functioning in today's world. Similarly, social workers can help people learn to negotiate the physical world, both natural and built. For clients whose life experiences have been limited to neighborhood, institution, or rural town, social workers can teach the skills involved in freely traversing a widened home-range, and in absorbing, responding, and using its cognitive and sensory–perceptual stimuli.

For children and their mothers, for teenagers, for the elderly, and for discharged mental patients of all ages, trips around the city by bus, trolley, subway, or ferry are "learning by doing." Visits to libraries, musical events, museums, public gardens and zoos may be as helpful in developing adaptive capacities as the same number of hours spent in office or home interviews. Part of the growth that emerges from these activities and experiences is related to the relief they bring from urban or rural isolation, the stress of overcrowded dwellings, the lack of sufficient and safe play space, and the presence of environmental stimuli that may be excessive, noxious, or lacking in diversity.

In addition to the provision of rural and urban experiences, social workers frequently make use of animals and plants to enrich the lives of their isolated and lonely clients. Caring for a pet or a plant can sustain relationship capacities and a sense of purpose and achievement. A bird or a plant, for example, that needs and responds to care and attention, can bring joy and a sense of being needed to an elderly person or a disabled child. Pet dogs, introduced as companions to mental patients, have succeeded in inducing improved functioning in many instances where more conventional therapy had failed. In some mental hospitals and general hospitals, social workers have prevailed upon administration to provide horticultural therapy for patients of all ages and types of disability. Other social workers in housing projects have interested tenants in beautification projects. Adolescents in one such project had little to do but "hang out," and harass others. Through the helping activity of an imaginative social worker and project manager, they became engrossed in the activity of gardening and the importance of their gardens, and then in general repairs and upkeep of the project.

Case Illustration

Mrs. Misvankas

Mrs. Misvankas, a 70-year-old Greek woman, was hospitalized with a uterine cancer (not terminal). She was referred to social services by Dr. Bass, a respected private physician. Initially, the request was for arranging transportation; later, the need for home care help was apparent. Mrs. M defined the most pressing concern as the lack of knowledge about her condition; she wanted to know what was medically "wrong" with her.

In an effort to cope with their own feelings and to "protect" the patient, the doctors, nurses, and family behaved as if nothing was wrong. At the same time, Mrs. Misvankas was receiving some cobalt therapy, suffering severe anxiety attacks before each treatment. The discrepancy between the extreme medical treatment and the denial of concern by significant others increased the expectable stress of illness and hospitalization.

Mrs. Misvankas told the worker about her worry. While she was fairly certain she had cancer, she felt that knowing the truth had to be better than what she was imagining. The worker said that the hospital policy permitted only doctors to communicate medical diagnoses and suggested that Mrs. Misvankas ask the doctor to explain her condition. The worker helped her to prepare for the contact by having her write down the specific questions she wanted to ask. After meeting with Dr. Bass, Mrs. M was even more frustrated because he told her not to worry and quickly left the room. Mrs. Misvankas told the worker of her despair, and urged her to intervene with Dr. Bass. Since the worker did not know Dr. Bass, she decided to consult first with the nurses for ideas on how to proceed, and to enlist their support. The nurses had previously informed the worker that Mrs. Misvankas was impossible to deal with during her anxiety attacks, and this provided a base for the worker's appeal.

> I said, "You know, you and I have been trying to help Mrs. Misvankas with her anxiety but she still seems very troubled. She says she becomes anxious while wondering what's happening to her, and maybe if she knew exactly what's wrong with her she could rest easier. I have been thinking about calling Dr. Bass to discuss it. What do you think about the idea?" Mrs. Allen said, "I'm for anything that lessens Mrs. Misvankas' anxiety. It's hard to take." And Ms. Blair said, "We don't usually give diagnoses. I don't know if Dr. Bass will like it."
>
> I wondered why she thought he might not like it and she said she felt he wouldn't want to upset the patient. Mrs. Allen agreed, adding that Mrs. M is already upset. On the other hand, she thought that while lots of doctors might not like it, perhaps Dr. Bass wouldn't object. So I asked what she thought made him different. She said, "In this case, he has just delivered Mrs. Misvankas' great-granddaughter here and he had four generations of patients from the family here, so you can bet he cares." Mrs. Blair

> then said, "Talking to the family might be your best bet. Dr. Bass really does care about his patients' lives, but he may be too busy to get involved."
>
> I told them they had helped me in how to approach Dr. Bass, and Mrs. Allen indicated that if I wanted them to be there when I talked to the doctor I could let them know.

The worker's previous contacts with the nurses had created an atmosphere of mutual trust and respect. They now provide helpful information about the doctor, the family, and they offer their own support. With Mrs. M's agreement, the worker discussed the situation with her daughter, who did not want to tell her mother the diagnosis herself, but agreed to take an active role in requesting that Dr. Bass share the medical diagnosis and prognosis. Daughter and worker decided that it would be wise for the daughter first to make a family request. If necessary, the worker would follow up. The daughter reported that the doctor remained uncommitted but agreed to consider the request. The worker then called him.

> I introduced myself as the worker assigned to take care of the transportation referral he had made for Mrs. Misvankas. I said I had been also helping her with her concerns about radiation treatments and reactions to them. "Her feelings about not knowing what's wrong with her and fearing the worst keep coming up. She looks to me to tell her, but, of course, I can't discuss the medical aspects of her illness."
>
> Dr. Bass responded, "What's going on here, first Mrs. Misvankas, then her daughter, now you? I have thought about talking to her but I'm not convinced that it would be a good thing." I wondered if it was contraindicated medically, but he said that wasn't the problem. "It is just that she's such a nervous woman and there's no telling how she'll react."
>
> So I said, "That's where I come in. I could help her with any reactions and I can also help the family to provide the necessary support." Dr. Bass said—somewhat sarcastically, I thought—"You mean you'll deal with it?"

> I said that I could, because I do think Mrs. Misvankas will do much better knowing than not knowing. He agreed that was a possibility, and said he'd get back to me.

While the worker had hoped to make some suggestions on the method of presentation (including the possibility of her presence), she was caught off guard by the doctor's abrupt ending of their telephone conversation. Even though initial contact had been established, the worker's area of professional competence specified, and the doctor's responsibility acknowledged, no commitments had been made. After several days, the worker decided to try again.

> I told Dr. Bass I wanted to talk with him again about Mrs. Misvankas. "I have an idea I'd like to share with you. As we discussed last time, I don't work on the medical and you don't work too much on the emotional and yet they are connected. I thought we might team up to help Mrs. Misvankas. I have heard that doctors and social workers in other hospitals work together on these kinds of situations. How about if we go together to speak to her about what's happening to her?"
>
> Dr. Bass said he has heard of what I had described, and he thinks it would be best if we also involve the family. I agreed this was an excellent suggestion and wondered about Mrs. M's daughter. Dr. Bass thought she could be helpful. But then he expressed concern about how long the meeting would take. He mentioned his busy schedule, and said he might not be able to stay long. I thought he might have to spend enough time to answer Mrs. M's questions about taking care of herself, her treatments and medication, activities, and nutrition, but that this might not take very long. Dr. Bass then suggested we arrange to meet with Mrs. M and her daughter the following Monday at noon. He said he was seeing the daughter in his office today and would tell her.
>
> I thanked him and added that I thought it would be extremely helpful to Mrs. Misvankas and that I would help her organize her questions in preparation for his visit. I also suggested that we meet for a few minutes beforehand.

> He agreed and said he would call me when he arrives at the hospital.

The worker's persistence and persuasiveness broke the cycle of denial. They also decreased the power of the norms by which only the doctor is believed to know what's the best for the patient, and the patient conforms and internalizes anxiety, relatives stand by helplessly, and the social worker is limited to support and concrete tasks. Here the worker expressed a shared professional interest in the patient and appealed to the doctor's latent interest in team methods.

> The actual meeting took place on schedule and was relatively low-keyed. Dr. Bass meticulously explained the medical conditions, specifying concrete issues related to uterine cancer and its physiological impact. His prognosis was somewhat guarded, but positive. He answered Mrs. Misvankas' questions factually and with a caring manner. When he left, Mrs. Misvankas cried and was consoled by her daughter. In the days that followed, her moods shifted from anxiety to depression, to despair, to anger, to mourning, and to beginning acceptance.

In subsequent contacts, the worker encouraged Mrs. M to use her doctor fully, helping her to ask if her fading eyesight meant the cancer was spreading. She helped her to find meaning in her present life, encouraging her to crochet a sweater for the new grandchild. She supported realistic adaptations, assisting in the move to the daughter's home for convalescence. Using the skills of the mediator role, the worker helped patient, physician, family, and staff to communicate openly and honestly. By having greater control over the forces impinging on her life, Mrs. M could then draw on her own adaptive potential and cope more effectively with the tasks involved in treatment and convalescence.

Summary

The presence of complex bureaucratic organizations is pervasive in contemporary life. How organizations define their function and boundaries has a profound impact on the experiences of clients dependent upon them. Clients are sometimes required to fit their problems to the agency's purpose and method rather than the agencies' being responsive to the clients' needs. At times, the agency's definition of its purpose and services stigmatizes the user of its service by emphasizing pathology and deviance. An organization's social structure of statuses and roles for the division of labor may be another source of stress. Some social work roles are defined narrowly or rigidly, and constrict professional function. Others are defined broadly and loosely and provide minimal accountability and standardization of practice.

Policies and procedures proliferate over time. They tend to develop a life of their own, taking precedence over client need and the organization's goals. Some agencies demand strict adherence to policies and procedures, using the "book" to deny needed services. Other agencies may not formalize or codify practices sufficiently, which subjects the client to capricious judgments and practices. In these and other ways, organizational structures and processes are dysfunctional for users of the service. Such features increase clients' stress by subjecting them to dehumanizing procedures or by withholding services and resources.

Social networks are an important source of strength in rural and urban life, but they also have the potential for creating stress. Some networks may have rigid boundaries and isolate the client from the outside world. Other networks may have loosely knit and poorly defined boundaries, and are unavailable to the client for concrete or emotional support. Many persons belong to no networks and experience isolation and loneliness. Life transitions such as divorce or job change can mean lost attachments and loneliness. In old age, network relations diminish and the acquisition of new networks is limited. In adolescence, the values and practices of the peer network may exert a negative influence.

The physical environment of city, town, or rural area also influences human behavior. Geographic mobility may create stress as the person leaves behind a familiar identity base. One's sense of self is derived in part from familiar and cherished places and structures that comfort and protect. The design of public housing, mental hospitals, prisons, and schools may dehumanize and devalue people.

How space is allocated—its location, size and arrangement—may discourage social interaction or limit privacy. It may encourage withdrawal or acting-out, and communicate negative values. The absence of color, varied textures, thermal and oflactory cues creates a bland environment, and can interfere with coping and adaptation.

In order to help in the stress that arises from organizations, social networks, or physical settings, the social worker's attention and actions must be directed to the behavioral interface between individuals, families, groups, on the one hand, and social networks, organizations, communities, and physical environments, on the other. The social worker's professional function is to help people use their adaptive and coping capacities to obtain available and accessible environmental resources. When such resources are missing, inaccessible, withheld, or denied, the professional function is to influence those structures and processes to be more responsive to client needs. The social work roles of mediator, advocate and organizer are used to carry out those functions.

In the role of mediator, the social worker helps clients and environmental representatives reach a greater reciprocity through the collaborative skills of intercession, persuasion, and negotiation. In the role of advocate, the worker calls upon the adversarial skills of pressure, coercion, or appeals to third party intervention. In the role of organizer, the worker organizes rural or urban community groups to deal with environmental deficiencies. The skills involved in organizing efforts include assessing needs; mobilizing motivation and interests; identifying and supporting natural leaders; locating and securing resource persons; and facilitating mutual aid.

Notes

1. For further discussion of this point see Elaine Cumming, *Systems of Social Regulation* (New York: Atherton Press, 1968).

2. Alex Gitterman, "Social Work in the Public Schools," *Social Casework* (February 1977), 58(2)111–18.

3. Cumming, *Systems of Social Regulation.*

4. Brett Seabury, "Arrangements of Physical Space in Social Work Settings," *Social Work* (October 1971), 16(4)43–49.

5. D. L. Rosenhan, "On Being Sane in Insane Places," *Science* (January 19,

1973) 179:250–58. See also "Letters to the Editor," *Science* (April 27, 1973) 180:358–69.

6. When authority is assigned to only a few positions, the structure is said to be centralized; when authority is divided among various levels and positions, the structure is said to be decentralized. See Jerold Hage and Michael Aiken, *Social Change in Complex Organizations* (New York: Random House, 1970), pp. 18–21.

7. Organizational structures having many procedures and regulations are said to be highly formalized. See Hage and Aiken, *Social Change* pp. 21–23.

8. Merton refers to this process as goal displacement. The organizational mechanisms become ends in themselves. The instrumental value becomes a terminal value. See Robert Merton, *Social Theory and Social Structure,* 2d ed. (New York: Free Press, 1957), pp. 199–200.

9. Peer group pressure supported by such informal sanctions as ridicule and ostracism reinforce the norms of the informal structure. The reward for conformity is interpersonal prestige and influence. These internal processes represent the "grease" that lubricates the formal machinery, and they have a potent impact on the delivery of services.

10. J. Clyde Mitchell, "The Concept and Use of Social Networks," in J. Clyde Mitchell, ed., *Social Networks in Urban Situations* (Manchester, England: Manchester University Press, 1969), p. 2.

11. John Mayer and Aaron Rosenblatt, "The Client's Social Context," *Social Casework* (November 1964), 45(9)511–18.

12. Alice Collins and Diane Pancoast, *Natural Helping Networks* (New York: National Association of Social Workers 1976).

13. W. L. Yancey, "Architecture, Interaction, and Social Control: The Case of a Large-Scale Public Housing Project," *Environment and Behavior* (March 1971), 3(1):3–18.

14. See, for example, Marc Fried, "Grieving for a Lost Home," in Leonard J. Dull, ed., *The Urban Condition* (New York: Simon and Schuster, 1963), pp. 151–71.

15. See, for example, Robert Weiss, *Loneliness, the Experience of Emotional and Social Isolation* (Cambridge, Mass.: M.I.T. Press, 1973).

16. This distinction is made for analytic purposes only. To view the distinction as real would reinforce the dichotomy between human beings and the environment which the ecological perspective seeks to eliminate. All organisms change the physical environment and are changed by it. What man does to the physical environment to mold it to his needs is as much a part of nature as the reef-building of the coral polyp.

17. Rudolph H. Moos, *The Human Context* (New York: Wiley 1976), chs. 2, 3.

18. Clare Cooper, "The House as Symbol of the Self," in H. M. Proshansky, W. H. Ittelson, and L. G. Rivlin, eds., *Environmental Psychology,* 2nd ed. (New York: Holt, Rinehart & Winston, 1976), pp. 435–48.

19. *Ibid.* See, also, Carel B. Germain, "Space, an Ecological Variable in Social Work Practice," *Social Casework* (November 1978), 59(9):515–22.

20. Oscar Newman, *Defensible Space* (New York: Collier Books, 1973).

21. Irwin Altman, *The Environment and Social Behavior* (Monterey, Calif.: Brooks/Cole, 1975). Altman has developed a paradigm for understanding how people regulate their interaction with the social environment. He identifies and describes the various personal and spatial mechanisms people use to control their openness or closedness to others. When the mechanisms are ineffective, more interaction or less interaction occurs than is desired. Too much interaction is experienced as crowding. Too little interaction is experienced as social isolation. Both are unpleasant.

22. Barker has shown how behavior changes across physical and social settings. Roger Barker, *Ecological Psychology* (Palo Alto: Stanford University Press, 1968).

23. Humphrey Osmond, "Function as the Basis of Psychiatric Ward Design," *Mental Hospitals* (Architectural Supplement) (1957), 8:23–29; Robert Sommer, *Personal Space* (Englewood Cliffs, N.J.: Prentice-Hall, 1969).

24. See, for example, Sally Provence and Rose Lipton, *Infants in Institutions* (New York: International Universities Press, 1962).

25. Philip Solomon et al., eds., *Sensory Deprivation* (Cambridge: Harvard University Press, 1965).

26. Robert Merton, *Social Theory,* pp. 185–92.

27. Rudolf Moos, *The Human Context,* ch. 3. See also W. Michelson, "Some Like It Hot: Social Participation and Environmental Use as Functions of the Season," *American Journal of Sociology* (1971), 76:1072–83.

28. Carel B. Germain, "Time: an Ecological Variable in Social Work Practice," *Social Casework* (July 1976), 57(7):419–26.

29. In delineating these functions and roles involved in work with environmental issues, we are limiting our discussion to practice efforts on behalf of a particular client whether the client is an individual, a group, or a family. The social worker's function and role actually go beyond this single-client focus to encompass the impact of organizational network, or physical environmental variables on all actual or potential service users. This important function, that moves from case to cause, will be discussed in chapter 7.

30. William Schwartz, "On the Use of Groups in Social Group Practice," in William Schwartz and Serapio Zalba, eds., *The Practice of Group Work* (New York: Columbia University Press, 1971), pp. 3–24.

31. Charles Grosser and Brenda McGowan, "Case Advocacy Practice," (paper presented at the National Conference of Social Welfare, San Francisco, May 1975), p. 32, mimeo.

32. *Ibid;* see also, Charles Grosser, "Participation and Practice," in Carel B. Germain, ed., *Social Work Practice: People and Environments* (New York: Columbia University Press, 1979), pp. 305–25.

33. For a discussion of self-help groups see Arthur Katz and Eugene I. Bender, *The Strength in Us* (New York and London: New Viewpoints, A Division of Franklin Watts, 1976).

34. For an example, see Sr. Mary Paul Janchill, "People Cannot Go It Alone," in Germain, *Social Work Practice,* pp. 346–61.

35. Brager has distinguished between skills of helping and skills of influencing. See George Brager, "Helping vs. Influencing: Some Political Elements of Organizational Change," paper presented at the National Conference of Social Welfare, San Francisco, May 1975), mimeo.

36. Irving Miller, "Presentation," (Alumni Conference, The Columbia University School of Social Work, November 3, 1973), mimeo; Alex Gitterman, "Social Work in a Public School," *Social Casework* (February 1977), 58(2):111–18.

37. Weiss, *Loneliness*, pp. 18–20.

38. Litwak's and Szelenyi's analysis of functions of primary group structures, on which we draw, refers only to the categories of neighbors, kin, and friends. See Eugene Litwak and Ivan Szelenyi, "Primary Group Structures and Their Functions: Kin, Neighbors, and Friends," *American Sociological Review* (August 1969), 34(4):465–81. Other observers include other categories of persons. See Elaine Cumming, Ian Cumming, and Laura Edell, "Policeman as Philosopher, Guide, and Friend," *Social Problems* (Winter 1965), 12:276–86; Matthew P. Dumont, "Tavern Culture, the Sustenance of Homeless Men," *American Journal of Orthopsychiatry* (1967), 37(5):938–45.

39. Collins and Pancoast, *Natral Helping Networks*, p. 28.

40. Joan Shapiro, *Communities of the Alone* (New York: Association Press, 1970).

41. Judith Lee and Carol Swenson, "Theory in Action: A Community Social Service Agency," *Social Casework* (June 1978), 58(6):351–70.

42. Collins and Pancoast, *Natural Helping Networks*, pp. 117–19.

43. Maria Correa, Working paper prepared for a doctoral seminar in advanced practice, Columbia University School of Social Work (Fall 1976), unpublished.

44. See, for example, Stanley Fisch, "Botanicas and Spiritualism in a Metropolis," *The Milbrook Memorial Fund Quarterly* (July 1968), 46(3):377–88.

45. Litwak and Szelenyi, "Primary Group Structure." Leichter's research in an urban Jewish family agency showed that within an Eastern European Jewish population, vertical and horizontal kinship ties were a prominent element of families' environments. While the agency staff tended to view familial connections and exchanges as evidence of immaturity and untoward dependence, and sought to change the relationships, the research established that such ties are an important source of strength and mutual aid. See Hope Leichter and William Mitchell, *Kinship and Casework* (New York: Russell Sage Foundation, 1967). Similarly, Burruel and Chavez declare that a young Chicano adult living at home may be labeled passive–dependent on the assumption that he or she has been unable to separate from the parents and home when, in fact, this is normal expected behavior in the Mexican–American culture. Interventions directed toward the individual's emancipation from the family can create guilt and stress if mishandled. See Grace Burruel and Nelba Chavez, "Mental Health Outpatient Centers: Relevant or Irrelevant to Mexican Americans," in A. B. Tulipan, G. Attneave, and E. Kingstone, eds., *Beyond Clinic Walls* (University, Ala.: University of Alabama Press, 1974), pp. 108–30.

46. Speck and Attneave have pioneered in this approach. See R. Speck and C. Attneave, *Family Networks: Retribalization and Healing* (New York: Pantheon

Press, 1973). See also Carolyn L. Attneave, "Social Networks as the Unit of Intervention," in Philip J. Guerin, Jr., ed., *Family Therapy, Theory, and Practice* (New York: Gardner Press, 1976), pp. 220–31; Carol Swenson, "Social Networks, Mutual Aid, and the Life Model of Practice" in Germain, *Social Work Practice,* pp. 213–38.

47. Philip J. Guerin, Jr., and Eileen G. Pendagast, "Evolution of Family System and Genogram," in Guerin, *Family Therapy,* pp. 450–64; Ann Hartman, "The Diagrammatic Assessment of Family Relationships," *Social Casework* (October 1978) 59(8):465–76.

48. Weiner, Akabas, and Sommer have made productive use of the work site as an arena of help and of fellow workers and union representatives as sources of help. See Hyman J. Weiner, Sheilah Akabas, John Sommer, *Mental Health Care in the World of Work* (New York: Association Press, 1973).

49. Litwak and Szelenyi, "Primary Group Structures." See also Beatrix A. Hamburg, "Early Adolescence: A Specific and Stressful Stage of the Life Cycle," in G. V. Coelho, D. A. Hamburg, and J. E. Adams, eds., *Coping and Adaptation* (New York: Basic Books, 1974), pp. 101–24; Joyce Ladner, *Tomorrow's Tomorrow, The Black Woman* (New York: Archer Books, Doubleday, 1971), pp. 109–24. See especially pp. 114–18.

50. Katz and Bender, *Strength in Us*.

51. Gordon Hearn, "Human Recycling," University of Oregon School of Social Work (no date). Mimeo.

52. Adapted from Karen Vice Irey, "The Social Work Generalist in a Rural Context: An Ecological Perspective." (paper presented at the Annual Program Meeting, Council on Social Work Education, Boston, March 1979), Mimeo, University of Oklahoma School of Social Work, Norman, Oklahoma.

53. Adapted from Mary Francis Libassi, "The Elderly in Charter Oak Terrace" (Master's thesis, University of Connecticut School of Social Work, 1973), pp. 80–3. Mimeo.

54. F. E. Cheek, R. Maxwell, R. Weisman, "Carpeting the Ward: An Exploratory Study in Environmental Psychiatry," *Mental Hygiene* (January 1971), 55(1):109–18.

55. One such program has been developed at Metropolitan Jewish Geriatric Center, New York.

56. Robert Sommer, "Small Group Ecology in Institutions for the Elderly," in Leon A. Pastalan and Daniel H. Carson, eds., *Spatial Behavior of Older People* (Ann Arbor: University of Michigan) – (Wayne State University Institute of Gerontology, 1970), pp. 25–39.

57. Charles Cataldo, "Wilderness Therapy: Modern Day Shamanism," in Germain, *Social Work Practice,* pp. 46–73.

58. Thomas Gladwin, "Social Competence and Clinical Practice," *Psychiatry* (1967), 30:30.

5

The Ongoing Phase: Maladaptive Patterns of Interpersonal Relationships and Communications

IN DEALING WITH life transitions and enviornmental issues, families and groups may encounter obstacles caused by their own patterns of communication and relationships. Some families and groups are flexible enough to change their patterns for more adaptive functioning. They need no help. Others will be caught in disjunctions between the societal–cultural structure and their life tasks, in which inner and outer demands require new forms of coping, a demand that generates stress because the family or group hasn't recognized the need for change. In such instances, the family or group will need modest help in revising its usual patterns of relating and communicating. In still other situations, extreme forms of maladaptive patterns are present which threaten the continuity of the family or group or are already reflected in the labeling of one or more members as deviant. Because of the rigidity of such patterns, help may need to be directed to changing the structure of the family or group itself.

Since both families and formed groups are collectives, they share some interpersonal processes. Nevertheless, they are also characterized by very important differences. The family is bound together by ties of kinship and by legally defined rights and responsibilities. Its members have a shared history and most likely a shared future independent of their relationship to a social work service. By contrast, the formed group lacks these attributes, and typically, comes together to work on specified tasks common to the members, under the aegis of an agency, and for a limited period of time.

This chapter presents the knowledge and skills of the social worker in helping families and groups deal with maladaptive patterns of relationship and communication. Throughout the chapter we take into account both the similarities and the differences between families and formed groups. In the first section, family and group structures, functions, and processes are examined. In the second section, we discuss the social worker's function, roles, and skills in helping the family and group to change maladaptive patterns that interfere with the tasks of life transitions and environmental issues. In the final section, we present more complete case illustrations, analyzing skills of practice and summarizing the elements of this dimension of the ongoing phase.

Maladaptive Interpersonal Processes as Sources of Stress

The Family: Functions, Structures, and Processes

Increasingly, the family is being viewed as a system of interacting parts contained within a boundary that separates family from nonfamily.[1] Like all social systems, the family structure organizes the individual members into a network of statuses and roles so that the system may fulfill its functions. The essential functions that seem to cut across various family structures, cultures, and historical eras are the procreation and socialization of children. To these basic functions might be added such instrumental survival functions as securing a livelihood, shelter and protection, and such expressive functions as meeting members' needs for nurturance, acceptance, security, and realization of potentialities. Families have additional functions of connecting their members to the outer world of society and the culture. In modern life, former family functions such as education, socialization, and health care have gradually been assumed in whole or in part by other social institutions. This has meant that families have had to develop structural means and channels for connecting their members to these institutional systems. Families have not necessarily undergone a net loss of functions, however, since they must often assume new functions in place of the former functions. This happened, for example, when romantic love became the base for and a continuing function of marriage. Former functions are occasionally returned to the family, though in a somewhat changed form. A contemporary example of such a returned function may be occurring with the new emphases on child birth and dying as family functions rather than hospital functions.

Most theorists of the family agree that its universal primary functions are the procreation and socialization of children. Such theory has not yet taken account, however, of the growing numbers of families that elect to remain childless. This family structure is meeting with increasing social approval because of environmental and population pressures and a humanistic concern that individual options be available and positively sanctioned. Homosexual families may also fall into the childless structure, although many such families have children from the partners' previous heterosexual unions, and some are now adopting children.

The nuclear family structure of two legally married parents of the opposite sex and their children is historically and geographically less prevalent in the world than the traditional extended family consisting of more than two generations and horizontally related kin. As an ideal type, the nuclear family structure appears to be of recent origin, having been generated by the Industrial Revolution, and is found mainly only in the industrialized societies of the West. While responsive to the demands of industrialization, urbanization, and urban housing, the nuclear structure is an undermanned, and therefore weak, organization for the complex functions it carries. In particular, it is exceedingly vulnerable to loss of one parent, because the entire system rests on the marital pair.

This family form faces pressures and adaptive demands that may exceed adaptive limits. A strain on this type that is becoming significant concerns the mobility that was heretofore considered a unique strength of the nuclear family structure. In many middle-class families, the constant uprooting in response to corporate demands and/or to the personal quest for achievement and success places stress on the wife, in particular, and on the children to some degree. In dual-career families, the stress may be of a different order, as decisions are made in favor of one or the other spouse's career location, or even in favor of geographically separate households. In the suburbs, families may suffer from the long daily absence of the employed parent(s), social isolation, heavy indebtedness, and other pressures. Such structural arrangements may adversely affect the nature of the relationships and communication patterns within the family which, in turn, creates new discomforts and adds to the stress of life transitions and environmental issues.

While still dominant in the United States, the nuclear structure is beginning to lose ground as its variants proliferate and new family forms appear. Single-parent families, augmented families, reconstituted families, extended families, and communal families possess structures different from the nuclear form, and confront different tasks and different environmental opportunities and limitations.[2]

The increasing numbers of one-parent families of the never-married, the divorced, separated, or widowed, for example, carry unique burdens in addition to the functions shared with other family structures. Among female-headed single-parent families, the common characteristic is poverty. In general, women earn less than men in comparable jobs. Most women, however, are in lower-paid unskilled jobs, or are out of the labor force altogether for a variety of reasons. Relatively few such families receive child support from fathers. Thus, women must support themselves and their children on inadequate wages or welfare. It is becoming clear that the disadvantages for the millions of children living in such families derive as much from the conditions associated with poverty as from the family structure itself. One-parent families also suffer from a severe shortage of hands: the single parent must double for the other parent, or cast an older sibling in that role. Problems are posed in household management, child care, personal respite, and personal fulfillment. Society has not yet developed institutionalized solutions that are quantitatively and qualitatively adequate to meet these adaptive needs. Thus, adaptive demands may exceed the adaptive limits of many one-parent family structures. Maladaptive patterns of relationships and communications need to be understood within the particular structural context, for help to be effective.

Less is known about the stresses related to other family structures, such as the reconstituted (the joining of two parents with both sets of offspring from prior unions) and the communal families, but it is likely that their unique tasks, in addition to functions shared with all families, hold the potential for creating stress that will influence interpersonal processes. In addition, the very newness of these forms and the lack of environmental supports for their special needs, suggest that the actual establishment of adaptive relationship and communication patterns may be difficult in and of itself. In any family structure, we view the pattern of relationships and communications developed by the family as the means through which it seeks to fulfill its functions, including those related to the needs of the individual members, the needs of the collectivity, and the demands of the environment.

Within the view of the family as a system of interacting parts, attention must also be given to the subunits of its structure. In the nuclear structure, these are the marital, parent–child, and sibling subsystems, differentiated on the basis of age, sex, and relationship. Theoretical and practice attention in the social work field have been chiefly directed to the marital subsystem, on the assumption that it strongly influences the parent–child system. Some independent attention has been given the latter subunit, chiefly in the area of variations attributable to social class and ethnicity. At another extreme, practitioners have sometimes dealt with the parent–child subsystem as though it were unrelated to the marital subsystem, commonly leaving the father out of the service program. These deficiencies are undergoing correction as practice incorporates the systemic view of the family and its parts. This view includes the sibling subsystem as an important structure in family life and as a possible site for intervention. In addition to the dyadic and even triadic relationships among the children, the children as a group serve important educational, socializing and expressive functions for one another and for the parents, and instrumental functions in the family's connections to the outside world. The sibling subsystem remains strongly influential throughout the life span of its members.[3]

Over a period of time the family evolves structurally related means for dealing with issues of authority, power, decision-making, and task allocation. These are lodged in the subunits of the family structure, helping to shape the patterns of relationships and communication and, reciprocally, being influenced by them. Characteristic patterns develop within each subunit that may or may not be different from those of the family as a whole or from those of other subunits. In some families there may also be subsystems which can be either relatively permanent, quite temporary, or even shifting, such as coalitions and alliances that cross over the age and sex boundaries of the other subsystems, usually in maladaptive ways. Other family structures may have different or additional subsystems. In the augmented family, a variant of the nuclear family, other related members, such as grandparents, aunts and uncles, or non-related members, such as lodgers or friends, live in the household. While such household members may serve important instrumental functions, as in providing substitute child care for a working mother, they sometimes participate in maladaptive alliances that lead to maladaptive patterns of relationships and communications.

Mrs. Bardwell requested counseling because of her inability to cope with her daughter's behavior. Helen is 13 and has just returned to her mother after three years in a residential treatment center. She refuses to obey, has friends that Mrs. Bardwell considers bad influences, and spends little time at home. Mrs. Bardwell's sister, Mrs. Clark, lives on the floor above in their two-family home, and is charged with supervising Helen in her mother's absence.

> I asked Helen and her mother to give me some idea of Mrs. Clark's role. Helen became rigid and raised her eyes to the ceiling in a nonverbal expression of the hostility she feels toward her aunt. Mrs. Bardwell defended her sister, saying she is very helpful and comes down to stay with Helen when Mrs. Bardwell is not at home. Helen said she is mean, and when Mrs. Clark is present, Helen avoids her by not talking to her. In exploring this relationship, I learned that Mrs. Clark spends much time in the household even when Mrs. Bardwell is home; she orders both Helen and her mother around, and takes over Mrs. Bardwell's parenting functions. She often prepares their meals and decides what they will do on weekends. As we clarified their feelings toward Mrs. Clark, Mrs. Bardwell and Helen both expressed their resentment. Helen carried this further, explaining to her mother, almost desperately, that she wants care and direction from her rather than from her aunt. Mrs. Bardwell expressed the hope that she can tell

her sister to be less bossy, although she also expressed her fear that she is incapable of parental functioning.

In this instance, the relative is intrusive, adversely affecting the relationship and communications in the parent–child system.

Subunits, the interacting parts of the family structure, are demarcated by subsystem boundaries. Where such boundaries are neither firm nor clear, they can be sources of maladaptive relationship and communication patterns that interfere with individual and family life transitions or with environmental issues. The boundary between the marital and the sibling subsystems (or the single-parent and sibling subsystems) must be clear and firm, so that children are free to work out issues of sharing, rivalry, loyalty, gender identification, and reciprocal socialization without parental interference. The boundary between the two parts of the parent–child subunit must be clear and firm in order to sustain parental authority. Yet, the boundary must also be appropriately permeable in order to sustain the needs for nurturance and mutality between parent and child.

In a similar fashion, the family as a whole must establish and sustain a clear, firm, yet permeable boundary between itself and the environment. If this boundary is too firm, there will be insufficient interchange with the environment. Such a family may rely too heavily on interaction among its own members at the expense of personal autonomy and social competence. If the boundary between family and environment is unclear or too loose, members will lack clarity about who and what belongs inside and outside the family, and hence, will be unclear about role responsibility and expectations. They may experience independence, but may lack a feeling of belonging and a sense of family identity. Autonomy is gained at the expense of connectedness.[4]

Thus, in many ways the various functional and structural elements of the family can become sources of maladaptive interpersonal patterns of relationship and communications. The scapegoating sequence, seen so frequently in distrubed family situations, is an apt example. Systemically, the scapegoating of a child declared deviant or symptomatic by the family enables the parents to avoid looking at their own conflicted relationship. Their negative feelings toward each other are displaced onto the child, uniting the parents so that the marital conflict is contained and the balance of the marital subsystem is protected. The child learns to carry the deviant role and elicits criticism. While parents criticize the behavior, their communications tend to reinforce the deviance. The stability of the marriage, and hence the family's constancy is preserved, but disorganization in the child is promoted.[5] His development suffers. Thus, what appears to be good for the system may be poor for one of its parts.

Mrs. Smith had brought her son Billy, age 10, to a child guidance clinic. She had complained that he disobeys his parents, wets his bed, and his school performance is poor. He does excel in reading, and spends all of his time reading while in the house.

Mrs. Smith is an attractive, light-skinned black woman. She completed the tenth grade, wishes she had more schooling, and wants her children to have a good education. She would like to move to a better neighborhood in the northern city to which the family migrated ten years earlier.

Mr. Smith is a dark-skinned black man, with a sixth grade education. He has trouble supporting his family because laboring jobs are sporadic. He would like to move back to their rural Georgia community, as he feels life here is too fast. He asserts that "book learning" is for girls, and he wants his sons to be active, tough, and masculine.

Mr. and Mrs. Smith hold conflicting perceptions of each other. Mrs. Smith feels her husband is inadequate as a breadwinner, husband, and companion. He sees her as too demanding and ambitious. These conflicts never surface, however, as the Smiths don't voice their dissatisfactions to each other. Instead, they focus on the trouble they are having with Billy. Mrs. Smith is disappointed in his school performance, bed-wetting, and his provoking his father's anger. Mr. Smith is disappointed in his son's lack of interest in activities other than reading. While they don't agree about the nature of their son's problems, the parents are united in their mutual concern about him. The conflicting messages from the parents reinforce Billy's deviance. His mother criticizes him for making his father angry, yet encourages his reading, which produces the father's anger. She presses him to achieve in school, while his father denigrates this goal.

Billy provides the avenue for the discharge of marital tensions that might otherwise threaten the stability of the family system. The marital conflict centers on role expectations of the male, and Billy's characteristics make him a good symbolic substitute for the conflict. He is the oldest male child, and is tall, thin, and dark like his father. He is isolated in the family, with two younger sisters, 8 and 7, who are very close to each other, and a brother who, at 4, is too young to be a companion.

Other maladaptative communication processes, such as double-binds, ambiguous or conflicting messages, and monitoring of interactions by one member also may serve to keep the family system in a precarious balance. Yet they are dysfunctional at both the collective and individual levels.

The Liggett family is being seen in a family agency because of the school's concern about the withdrawn behavior of the oldest child, Harry, age 9. Communication within the Liggett family seems to follow a uniform pattern. In the family sessions, Mrs. Liggett is the first to state the family's position on a given topic. Mr. Liggett usually supports his wife in her assertions. The children are then asked, usually by Mrs. Liggett, to express their feelings and thoughts, which are then negated. What is interesting is that Mrs. Liggett seems constantly to monitor the communications and to cue the behavior of the other members. Mr. Liggett participates in this process by letting his wife take the lead. As a result, there is very little real interchange and sharing of feelings in the family. Whatever gains Mr. Liggett experiences by keeping silent are offset by the sense of loneliness and helplessness he shows within the family. The children, especially Harry, suffer from a lack of understanding by both parents, and they often appear lonely and scared. Mrs. Liggett, by taking the major responsibility for communication and relationships in the family, receives little emotional support from her husband. She, too, is lonely and isolated. Yet, she continues the monitoring and her family permits it to continue since it maintains the family's precarious balance against the threat of intimacy. It is dysfunctional for the individual members and interferes with the family's resolving the many environmental issues facing it or completing their transitional tasks.

Maladaptive communication processes are transactional phenomena. The victims in such vicious cycles are not simply victims. They participate in the process not altogether helplessly, but because of certain consequences. From the standpoint of the victim, the process justifies his helplessness and at the same time gives him exquisite control over the family system. The symptom or behavior, and its part in the communication and relationship processes with the family, represent a transactional process, and both system levels must be understood and handled if change is to be effected. Together, the functions, the structural elements, and interpersonal processes represent the life style of the family through which it develops its own set of values, norms, and perceptions that tend to shift and change as the family develops over its life cycle. Indeed, where the family cannot change its structures, functions or interpersonal processes in response to environmental and internal changes, it may be in trouble.

The Formed Group: Functions, Structures, and Processes

A formed group comprises individuals who come together under agency auspices to work on life task(s) which they have in common. Like the family, the group is regarded as a system of interacting parts enclosed within a boundary. Its primary functions are to establish and maintain a nutritive interchange with its environment and a mutual aid system among its members, so that individual potential for growth is released. When successful in these twin tasks, a group may be said to be in adaptive balance. When that balance is upset by internal or external sources of stress, the group attempts to regain balance by various coping means. Some re-balancing efforts are maladaptive. Even though they may temporarily reduce stress, they create additional group problems, and lead to maladaptive communication and relationship patterns. Such interpersonal processes can also emerge from formational and structural elements as well. In any case, they inhibit individual adaptation.

Formational elements include size and composition. Groups can be too large or too small and thus provide inadequate opportunities or excessive demands for intimacy and task involvement. These compositional factors can skew interpersonal processes.[6] Groups that are overly homogeneous may lack vitality. A group whose members are all depressed, for example, may find its communications stifled. A homogeneous group may be unable to absorb a member who deviates from group norms on important personal attributes. A group of light-skinned Puerto Rican girls with one black member, or a parents' group with one father may not be able to assimilate the different member.

On the other hand, groups that are too heterogeneous may lack stability because members with limited interests or concerns in common may find it difficult to relate to one another. In latency groups, differing behavioral trends may skew interpersonal processes as some members act out and others withdraw.

The degree to which a groups's interpersonal processes become patterned, and the quality of these processes, also depend on the length of the group's life, its purpose—for example, educative or therapeutic—and the stability of its membership, for example, open-ended or closed.[7] All formational factors can be important sources of maladaptive interpersonal processes, and need careful attention in the course of forming the group.

In order to fulfill its function, the group evolves a social structure and culture which mediate between environmental demands and the group's needs, and between the group's demands and the individual's needs. The social structure represents a network of roles through which responsibilities are allocated, decisions are reached, and relationships and communication patterns established. These roles may shift and change as the work continues, and as the group passes through stages of its development. Some group structures are too loose and others are too tight for adaptive interchanges to take place within the group, and between the group and its environment. In a group that is too loosely structured, individual autonomy may be valued, but the members do not experience a sense of identity and support that comes from group solidarity. Members are not sufficiently integrated into a structure so that decisions are difficult and tasks are not completed. The patterns of relationship and communication in a loosely structured group may not permit involvement in developmental or environmental issues. In a group that is tightly structured, over-involvement of group members with one another lead to patterns of relationship and communication that limit nutritive interchange with the social environment. The price for belonging is a reduction in individual autonomy.

A group's social structure and its accompanying patterns of relationships and communications lead to the emergence of a group culture. Out of their individual beliefs, knowledge, and value orientations, the group members develop a set of group norms regarding rights and responsibilities, modes of work, and styles of relating and communicating. Shared beliefs and orientations toward activities and task performance, quality and style of interaction, and physical and verbal expressions of feelings are enforced by normative sanctions. They unite group members and integrate their behaviors. Norms that are rigidly defined and/or punitively enforced, however, pose problems for members seeking to develop and maintain individuality and a degree of autonomy. They may create maladaptive patterns of relationships and communications. Children of religious orthodox families, for example, may experience painful conflict between parental expectations and the group's norms. The violation of norms that prohibit certain behaviors often poses a serious threat to group survival, and generates powerful sanctions leading to expulsion, ostracism, or scapegoating.

A natural-friendship adolescent girls' group valued interpersonal loyalty. One member, Gladys, violated a group norm by flirting with and kissing another member's boyfriend.

> As Rita walked into the meeting room, she said hello, walked past Gladys and slugged her hard on the side of her face, and continued walking to an empty chair, casually greeting everyone on the way. After a period of giggling and indirect conversation, Rita began to rant at Gladys, bawling her out for kissing her boyfriend at a party over the weekend. Everyone else joined in on the attack. It seemed Rita's boyfriend flirtatiously asked Gladys for a kiss. And indeed, she kissed him twice. Rita continued her angry tirade as Gladys attempted first to deny and then excuse her behavior.

Where group norms are ambiguous, members may become anxious and engage in continuous testing of the leader and the group to establish guidelines. Whether they are ambiguous or clear, norms may be unevenly enforced, reflecting preferential treatment and double messages, and creating rivalrous patterns of relationship. Members may subscribe to discrepant personal norms regarding morality, logic, and attractiveness. Such discrepancies can also create maladaptive communication and relationship patterns.

Both the structure and culture of the group are influenced by environmental properties including societal, community, agency values and norms, and environmental opportunities and limitations. Group members may respond to environmental limitations with apathy, which then militates against their use of whatever resources are available within the group and environment. Others may respond by turning inward and displacing their anger and frustration onto the group members. In school groups composed of minority children, for example, the children may internalize teachers' negative judgments of their intellectual abilities and potentials and project such judgments onto one another. Thus, societal, community, and organizational conditions affect group life and may create maladaptive communication and relationship patterns.

Interpersonal processes are also affected by stages of group development. Tension and maladaptive communication arise from discontinuities among the members relative to their personal developmental tasks or to group developmental tasks. In a group of latency girls, one member may already be dealing with the biological and social tasks of early adolescence, which pose communication and relationship problems for her and for the group as they take each other's measure. In another group, most members may be ready for the group's developmental stage of interpersonal intimacy, but their relationships and communications are adversely affected by one member's continuing preoccupation with testing the worker's authority. Thus, group developmental factors are potential sources of interpersonal stress and maladaptive behaviors.

Maladaptive interpersonal patterns in formed groups are often expressed in such relationship and communication processes as factionalism, monopolism, scapegoating, withdrawal, and ambiguous, indirect communications. While these processes are usually dysfunctional for most members, they serve a latent function, often unrecognized and unintended, of maintaining a group's equilibrium. Thus, they can be best understood by focusing on the functions they serve for the individual member and for the group as a whole.

When *factionalism* becomes a fixed pattern of relations, the subsystem of clique or alliance provides its members with greater satisfaction and sense of identification than is experienced by the total group, a desirable outcome for the clique. Subunits are usually composed of members with similar interests, concerns, and interpersonal orientations to authority and intimacy. Members who are similar tend to find, or drift, toward each other, seeking security together. When subunits are fluid and responsive to group developmental phases, they serve important support functions. However, when they become frozen—inflexible and exclusionary—they usually represent sources of maladaptive interpersonal patterns. Subunits' exclusionary features isolate and reject other group members and threaten the constancy of the group. Autocratic attitudes of the indigenous or professional leaders encourage the promotion of such subunits as a way to obtain security and protection from punitive interaction with the leader.[8] The members then compete for the leader's attention and for improved status for themselves at the cost of the unaffiliated members. This protects the subsystem members against threat, but undermines the status and security of the nonaffiliated.

In *monopolism,* one member participates by producing an overwhelming amount of detail in describing her ideas, feelings, and experiences. This serves to give her control over her anxiety, the group process, and its content, and at the manifest level has positive consequences for her.[9] The other group members tolerate and sometimes even encourage such communication because it protects them from self-disclosure and personal involvement. At the latent level, however, it has negative consequences for all group members, and hence for the monopolist. It prevents the group from fulfilling its purpose and the members from successful task achievement.

Scapegoating in formed groups is similar to the process in families. The deviant status serves important functions for both the individual member and the group. At the group level, deviance helps clarify behavioral norms, sharpen group boundaries, and promote solidarity. For the individual members, the contrast between self and the deviant member may be reassuring and offers protection against the fear of similar behavior or attributes in the self. For the deviant member, his status provides satisfaction as well as pain. He often is at the center of attention and may also partake of secondary gains in the sense of martyrdom, helplessness, and enslavement in the service of others.[10]

Usually the scapegoat is the most vulnerable member of the group. A school group of black youngsters may scapegoat the lone

Puerto Rican member. Her responses to the members' provocations may lead to the institutionalization of the scapegoating process. An adolescent boys' group may be threatened by the behavior of an effeminate member, and their communications are replete with ridicule and hostility toward him. Reciprocally, his responses influence the scope and intensity of members' reactions, and determines the extent of his acceptance and integration by the group or his exclusion through scapegoating. In geriatric facilities, the least lucid member tends to evoke hostility among the other members. She represents a safe target for the displacement of the members' feelings of despair, impotence, confusion, and anger. While either the group or the scapegoated member may provoke the attack, the frail and disoriented member's inability to fight back only frightens or enrages the other members, and triggers further attack.

While scapegoating serves to control and suppress serious group issues at the manifest level thus seeming to maintain group stability, it has negative consequences at the latent level which entrap the group as well as the scapegoated member. To the extent that a group permits its members to exploit one member in order to maintain their own functioning, all members become vulnerable to stress from personal, group, or environmental processes. The scapegoated individual suffers from grave harm, internalizing the negative perceptions of others as self-contempt which leads to destructive behaviors. The group members develop maladaptive relationship and communication patterns that reflect their evasion, denial, guilt, and projections.

Frank is a mildly retarded member of a "truancy group." He exhibits poor self-control and occasional clowning behavior. In an early meeting, Stanley was describing how his teacher makes school impossible for him. The work is too hard, and the teacher calls on him when he doesn't know the answers. As all the boys began to laugh, Angel asked Frank, "What're you laughing about?" I asked if anyone had a similar experience. Frank replied, "Yeah, in dancing class, all the kids laugh at me." He demonstrated his dancing, and explained that the teacher made him stand in a corner because he made mistakes. Billy said, "Frank, you're so damn stupid anyway." Angel added, "You don't even know how to read, write, or the multiplication tables." All the boys laughed and began to join in the attack.

Frank performs a critical function for the group, permitting members to evade the necessary work on painful problems and to displace their frustrations and anger. The intolerable school situation and the youngsters' hostilities are managed by focusing attention on the most problematic member—the clown—who mediates conflict by providing the group with comic relief. For Frank, the positive consequence is the momentary glow of attention. The fact that both the deviant and the group benefit from his being scapegoated underscores the transactional nature of scapegoating. But in the long run, the process has negative consequences for the deviant and for the group. It further isolates the scapegoated member, increases his differentness, making him liable for further labeling processes, and undermines his sense of self-esteem, identity, competence, and relatedness. For the group, the displacement of their negative feelings about themselves and one another onto the scapegoated member means that the group is unable to fulfill its function, complete its tasks, and the members do not grow and develop to their full potential. Thus, the social worker must understand not only what processes in the group and in its environment make scapegoating necessary, but also what processes in the scapegoat lead to his inviting and accepting the maladaptive communications and relationships. One must assume that in a group manifesting such a pattern, the group's stability is already precarious.

Social Work Function, Roles, and Method

The Social Worker and Maladaptive Interpersonal Processes

With families and groups whose maladaptive interpersonal processes interfere with their efforts to deal with life transitions and environmental issues, the social worker's function is to help the members to communicate more openly and directly as they work on common concerns, and to develop greater mutuality and reciprocity in their relationships. The worker relies on the enabler, teacher, and facilitator roles described in previous chapters. The worker also calls on the mediator role to focus on the family's and formed group's maladaptive communication and relationship patterns and functions and structures which generate them. This is internal mediation as contrasted to the external mediation described in chapter 4.

In the family, the worker may select the appropriate modality, meeting with the family as a whole, or with any of its subsystems alone, or in combination. He considers the extent to which the maladaptive pattern has become entrenched, and the availability and comfort of each member. In forming a group, the social worker himself actually participates in the development of the social structure, the group's culture, and its communication processes. He therefore has a clear status and role in the group's emerging structure. This fact distinguishes his position in the group from his position in the family or in an already formed group. In the latter two instances, he is an outsider to the members, and having "parachuted" in, must try to land softly.

In the early stages of the newly formed group's life, any maladaptive communications or relationships that appear tend to be relatively fluid and amenable to change because they are not yet fixed into patterns. In later stages, however, any maladaptive interpersonal processes may have become entrenched, often because the worker may have not recognized their emergence or their pervasiveness. This lack of awareness can stem, quite easily, from the fact that the worker is himself a part of the process that is entrenched—he is, in fact, entrenched himself.[11] This also happens in work with the family as the worker enters the family structure. In those instances, however, he is more likely to have been drawn into already existing patterns, rather than having been a participant in the development of the pattern itself, as he is in the formed group.[12]

Practice Method

The worker seeks a multi-dimensional understanding of the family or formed group in which continuing data and impressions about its structural elements and interpersonal processes and those of its subunits are integrated with available knowledge and theory. All the members must be helped to participate in this assessment, so that together worker and members examine structural elements, norms, values and goals, as well as the maladaptive interpersonal patterns. This helps to locate the differential effects on the family or group, the subunits, and the individual members. When a maladaptive pattern has been recognized, the worker asks herself, "What is keeping this family or group structure frozen so that it can't move away from this way of communicating and relating?" "What positive and negative consequences—both manifest and latent—does the pattern have for the collective as well as for the individual members?" "What are the primary sources of this pattern?" "Am I in any way caught up and unwittingly contributing to the pattern?" The worker not only must consider the effects of her own interventions, but must also take into account the members' disparate views of the nature and source of the maladaptive pattern. The worker describes and defines the problematic pattern in transactional terms as being lodged in the collective or subunit structures rather than in an individual. The selection of particular roles and skills to be used at any given moment arises from this assessment, and because the worker has sought the participation of all members at the outset, she is freer to involve herself with all members together and separately as needed.[13]

> Recently, Mrs. Casey and her two children had moved to a two-family dwelling owned and occupied by Mrs. Casey's 55-year-old widowed mother and her employed son. Mrs. Casey complained that her mother was driving her crazy. "She has been giving me grief about going out for a drink with my friends after work. I don't stay longer than an hour or so, but as soon as I walk in the door all hell breaks loose. She just doesn't want me to have a good time." I asked what their original agreement about child care had been, and Mrs. Casey said her mother was willing to take care of the kids after school, adding it's always been that way in her family. "My grandmother did the same for my mother. Besides, she doesn't have anything else to do. Since my father died, she doesn't work or anything." I asked if she and her mother had talked this out, and Mrs. Casey said they never talk. "We just yell or ignore each other. We're both stubborn and steam inside. By the time we're going to talk, we're too mad and just yell." Could she consider sitting down with her mother and talking over the arrangements? Mrs. Casey

> said, "No, it would just be one more yelling match." I wondered what she would think of all of us meeting together, since this seems to be a problem for the whole family, and may be part of the reason Robert is having problems at school. She thought that would be great, and said she'd ask her mother to participate.
>
> Mrs. Alexander called and said she'd love to talk about the baby-sitting arrangement. "That girl takes advantage of me. She thinks I'll always be there, sitting for the kids, even when she's gallivanting all over town. I'm sick of it. I have my own life to live. I want to go out and be with my friends, too. My husband was an alcoholic all his life. For years I worked, took care of the house, and watched out for him. Since his death, I'm free to do what I want. I have interests of my own. Don't get me wrong, I love the kids, but I feel I'm really being taken by Alice." I asked if Alice realizes how she feels about this. Mrs. Alexander said, "Of course she does, how could she not know it? Does she think I want to sit around all day in the house?" I said that it's pretty hard to know what she thinks without asking her. Mrs. Alexander responded that they don't talk about anything, they yell a lot, but don't ever seem to get anywhere.

Thus the decision was made to bring the grandmother into the session. This was a large step for a child guidance clinic that does no family work, and separates the child and mother by assigning two different workers.

The initial session was held at home. Not only does the home visit convey the worker's interest and availability, but in many instances it can reduce the anxiety and increase the comfort of the family members. It also permits the worker to see the family members in their natural environment. In visiting Mrs. Casey and her mother, the worker was struck by the lack of physical boundaries for the provision of privacy. Members of the two families customarily walked freely in and out of each other's living quarters, because the door separating the two units is kept open. Over the course of the joint sessions, both structural and spatial boundaries were strengthened.

Mother and daughter began to hear each other's needs, and negotiated a compromise solution with which each could live.

> At one point Alice said she guessed they were both losing out. "Even when I go out after work, I really don't enjoy it because I know I'll return and get hassled by mother. Even though I act like I don't care what she thinks, I do." Her mother said she couldn't believe her ears, "It seems like you never cared about my feelings or what happened to me." Alice said she had always thought her mother really wanted to stay home with the kids and only got mad just to hassle Alice. "I didn't know you wanted to go out with friends, who was to know you wanted to do that?"

The communication channels between mother and daughter were reopened. Both stubborn and strong-willed, they had engaged in a power struggle either by yelling at each other, or mutually withdrawing from each other. Both had realized this was problematic, but neither had been able to take the initiative to improve their communications. The worker's entry into the augmented family structure and her transactional view of the communication pattern led to the unfreezing of the structure so that firmer boundaries could be established. Both women were then freed to seek their new identities, expand their social networks, and develop greater reciprocity and mutual aid in their relationship with each other.

Transactions among the members provide the means by which the family and group can examine its communication and relationship patterns. The worker encourages each member's participation in the discussion of discrepant perceptions, disagreements, and conflicts. This requires establishing a secure atmosphere in which differences can be examined without threat or recrimination. Thus, the worker has to establish protective ground rules which facilitate open and direct communication. Explicit rules barring the use of physical abuse or threat, or of negative sanctions against the expression of feelings, opinions, or facts are set forth. These provide structural and normative supports for the weaker, lower-ranking members. The worker encourages the family or group to abide by the agreed-upon conditions. This minimizes the development of situations in which he has to protect or come to the rescue of the weaker member which can undermine his ability to mediate transactions. If the conditions of work are not explicit and kept before the family or group, maladaptive interpersonal patterns may become further entrenched.

Mrs. Grattan and her children (discussed in chapter 2) have not yet come to terms with the divorce, as a family or as individuals. Work has begun on their interaction and relationships with each other, mostly on the pattern of belittling. Gary belittles John, John belittles Eliot, and Eliot belittles the girls. The next older tries to establish authority or superiority by putting down the next younger. The pecking order and this way of relating have been pointed out to the children. John denies it. Gary, with strong feelings, says that he is the oldest and should be respected. The mother and the three boys each blame someone else.

> When Mrs. Grattan, Gary and John came to the fourth family interview, she sat between the two boys. The air bristled with the hostility between Gary and John. About midway in the interview, Gary threatened to beat up John when they left the office, because he felt John had sneered at him and belittled him. Gary felt John would never dare do such a thing if I weren't present to protect him, because John knows he can beat him up. Mrs. Grattan held herself stiffly, looked daggers at Gary, and said this was the sort of behavior which made Gary impossible to live with. Gary reiterated his threat. John said little, except to deny that he sneered or that Gary could beat him up.
>
> I referred to the competitiveness, the quick resort to threat or use of physical fighting. They had had fights before. What had they proven? When Gary repeated his threat, I reminded him of our agreed rule—no one was to be punished at home or outside the office for what was said during a session. Gary said he would not comply. I related to his anger, and said he was challenging me as he felt John had challenged him. When Gary turned to John and demanded to know why John always sneered, John said it was his way of defending himself. Gary rejected

> this as untrue. I tried to focus on the challenges family members throw out to each other, their pattern of showing strength, superiority by fights. The belittling, I said, has been a theme in several sessions. Gary became calmer, said he often says things he doesn't mean, and rather vividly described a civil war going on inside of himself.

The worker attempts to help the siblings relinquish their pattern of bitter competitiveness and rebuild a mutual support system. She invokes the "agreed upon rule" to protect the weaker member, and facilitates communications as the brothers struggle to deal more adaptively with the pain of the divorce. A stronger sibling subsystem and a firmer boundary between it and the single parent will help bolster Mrs. Grattan's shaky status and allow the children—especially Gary—to be children, and not substitutes for the missing father.

To examine structural elements and work on maladaptive patterns can be difficult. Family and group members require support, legitimization of their feelings and concerns, and validation of their strengths and adaptive behaviors. The worker must help members clarify their messages, examine inconsistencies, identify illogical or contradictory statements, recognize patterns and connect feelings to the content. The skills involved in these tasks are illustrated in three excerpts selected from a planned short-term service provided to a family in crisis. Mr. and Mrs. Clayton were beset by the convergence of numerous environmental and life transitional stresses (see chapter 1). They had withdrawn from each other and were contemplating divorce.

> Mr. C said he had also been giving some thought to a divorce, but implied this was not a definite decision. He thought the outcome depended a lot on his wife. She brought up his refusal to apologize for hitting her. He described what had happened as an accident, explaining it as an attempt to hold her arms when she got hysterical. He said he could easily apologize, but this would solve nothing. He thought his wife was refusing to accept the move from New York and refusing to make the necessary adaptations. They argued (he in a quiet, persistent voice, she in a loud voice, with tears in her eyes) about whether she was

refusing to do the necessary social entertaining to help him maintain and secure new contacts in his profession. What emerged was that Mr. C is feeling insecure in his new position, and is not certain he will want to renew his contract at the end of three years if he is offered a new contract. This is only the second position he has had since graduating from college. There are many more tensions in this firm, and he is more nervous at home than he used to be.

I commented that they were both unsure of themselves, both coping with new and difficult demands. Each was feeling deserted by the other at a time when they felt more need of each other. Mrs. C couldn't understand why her husband felt insecure, as she knew from the boss's wife that the firm was pleased with her husband. She felt Mr. C was spending a lot of time at the office to get away from her. He acknowledged she wasn't so pleasant to be with in the last few months, but the mountain of paper work required the extra time. Without disclaiming this, I asked if he could be handling his feelings of insecurity by putting in a lot of extra time. Often people do try to cope with these feelings in this way. He thought this might account for some of the extra time, but not all of it. As Mrs. C continued to be defensive and accusatory toward her husband and his diminished interest in her, I asked if this could be related to her fears. I said that her usual outlets were not available to her, not only because of the move but also because of her illness, which has made her more dependent. Both felt more vulnerable and resentful because neither has been as available to the other as each had hoped. This led to their discussion of how each one felt misunderstood and neglected by the other. I did not get involved in the content, but identified the feelings of need each was expressing for the other. I said that it was sad that at a time when they needed each other the most, they were pulling apart and considering divorce. Mr. and Mrs. C then let each other know they did not want a divorce, but neither could live without talking to each other and being better understood by the other.

The worker identified their underlying feelings of insecurity and their pattern of withdrawal from each other. She legitimized their feelings of vulnerability and resentment, and helped them recognize their common stake in improving the situation.

> The next interview centered on Mrs. C's anger at her own dependency, which she considers a weakness, and her feelings of uselessness. In response, Mr. C said he'd like her to do some library work for him. He needs to publish again and doesn't have time to do the library research. She has helped him before this way.
>
> Mr. C has come home a little earlier a couple of evenings, but they are still on edge with each other. Her loud, angry outbursts upset him. She reminded him that she has always been this way. He is different, being more nervous and tense. This has been difficult for her to get used to. She discussed her weight and her shame about being so heavy, relating this to her reluctance to dress up, go out, or entertain. They also discussed her reluctance to find a doctor in this area. I related to her feeling bereft in many ways. Mr. C was also struggling to cope with his feelings and new demands. I said they both find themselves feeling differently about themselves and toward each other. It was important for them to express the scared feelings, the anger, and their need for each other, as well as their feelings of disappointment.

Mr. and Mrs. Clayton are consistently encouraged to explore and confront their difficulties. The worker continues to lend her support, legitimize expression of their feelings and accept their differing perspectives on the interpersonal barrier. In the subsequent interview an important exchange takes place.

> Stemming from a discussion of her need to be useful and busy, Mrs. C brought out her brooding over the experience of her earlier brain tumor operation. Others were so upset over her loss of motor control before the operation, that she felt she had to reassure everyone and be brave. She was terrified just before going into surgery, but let no

> one know. When she attempted to express the terror and apprehension afterward, her husband said she shouldn't worry now—just be grateful she survived. Until now, she never had time to brood over the experience. Now that she is alone so much, she becomes upset and frightened as she relives this experience and feelings. Mr. C was very surprised—he had no idea his wife remembered so much. I was empathic with the terror, supported her need to talk about these feelings which were not only in the past—she was experiencing them in the present. It was not weakness, she had faced a life or death experience. To talk about these feelings instead of running from them could give her strength and reduce her anxiety. I related the feelings about the tumor surgery to her most recent illness. Also, I wondered if her anger at her husband for moving to this area was related to her being alone more and thus having to deal with these painful feelings. She thought this was very likely true. Mr. C wondered what he could do to help—why hadn't she told him before? Mrs. C said he'd only say why worry, it's all over. Mr. C said he didn't realize the depth of her feelings. I wondered if he could listen if Mrs. C talked about this experience and her feelings. He had no doubt of it. I asked if Mrs. C were willing to let her husband help her in this way. She said she would try.

The move and accompanying factors have produced high levels of anxiety in each partner. Each was too involved in handling his or her own anxiety, and feeling too rejected and disappointed, to empathize with the other, or to meet the other's needs. The more they needed each other, the more angry and disappointed they became. The social worker's help enabled them to recognize and express their anxieties and insecurities, in addition to their anger and criticism of each other. The latter feelings had to come first, and to be accepted by the worker. Discussion of the negative feelings, and recognition of their shared stress, enabled them to empathize with each other, and begin to regain a sense of intimacy and adaptive balance.

Anger and open conflict in the family or formed group can be particularly difficult for the beginning worker. He is apt to experience anxiety, a sense of powerlessness, and a fear of members' anger and of his own reactions. To cope with his own feelings, he may detach himself from the conflict and thus be unable to help the members deal with the interfering interpersonal processes.

> Mrs. Cohn signaled to me from her bed to come and talk to her. She had been on a seven-bed ward for three weeks. She had befriended three older and less mobile women, helped to feed them, and read to them. Recently, a younger woman had been admitted who displayed disruptive behaviors, such as spitting into the common waste basket and talking loudly. Mrs. Cohn found the behaviors difficult. As she talked to me, she began to cry, and complained about the new patient in a tone that was audible to everyone in the room. She depicted herself as being "victimized" by "that woman who just won't be a decent human being." I soothed Mrs. Cohn and also encouraged her to avoid contact with the woman by ignoring her. Mrs. Cohn seemed dissatisfied with my advice.

The worker missed an opportunity to help the natural group of ward members with their interpersonal difficulties. All members could have been involved in integrating the new member into the structure, and developing a new set of collective norms. Mrs. Cohn made sure that her complaints were public, but the worker's anxiety about a possible confrontation led her to avoid rather than exercise her mediating function.

When a worker experiences difficulty in dealing with his own feelings for a family or group member, he may withdraw, intervene preemptively, act-out, or vacillate among all these reactions. A student, for example, was assigned to a pre-discharge group in a mental hospital. After several meetings, a new member was added. She refused to accept the client role, and instead assumed the role of helper, which threatened the student.

> I said, "Mrs. Palmer is joining our group today, and I told her this morning what the group was about." She interrupted, "I'm quite aware of the purpose of a discharge group. I was in one last year and I contributed all I could.

> I finally resigned because I felt a less fortunate person should have a chance to be in it.'' I said, ''What about yourself, Mrs. Palmer, do you think you can also be helped by being in this group?'' She smiled and said, ''I do not think so, I don't have any problems, but I will be able to help other members.''

By attempting to get Mrs. Palmer to say that she could be helped in the group, the worker focused on the most frightening area for her—leaving the hospital. Mrs. Palmer might have been asked instead to describe her previous group experience. Other members could then have been asked to describe the current group. Together, they might have searched for connections in order to ease her entry. The worker's confrontation of Mrs. Palmer in subsequent sessions continued:

> There was a marked silence in the group. I said, ''It's so quiet today, why do you think that is?'' Mrs. Palmer said, ''Oh—is it more active other times?'' Mrs. Greenberg replied, ''Yes—we have been talking about some of the things that are scary about leaving here.'' Mrs. Palmer responded, ''I am sure you are afraid. You are always in a daze—you can't go anywhere.'' Mrs. Jackson turned to Mrs. Palmer and made a face. After a brief pause, Mrs. Greenberg said, ''I don't need a spokesman to talk for me,'' to which Mrs. Palmer retorted, ''Well, I think you do—you certainly don't say anything on your own!'' Mrs. Greenberg turned away and said, ''She knows everything, doesn't she?'' After this remark, there was another long period of silence. Mrs. Philips broke the silence by suggesting that Mrs. Palmer can be helpful to the group because she has been in a pre-discharge group before. She asked specifically about proprietary homes. Mrs. Palmer had many negative things to say about the homes. Confusion and sadness were registered on the members' faces. My anger was ready to burst through, and I said, ''Mrs. Palmer is making you all a little uncomfortable and sad.'' Mrs. Greenberg said, ''Well, there is a lot of truth in what she is saying.'' And Mrs. Burgio added, ''Yeah, I'd better

> get an apartment.'' I said, ''How else are you feeling about what Mrs. Palmer said?'' There was no response, and the meeting ended in silence.

The worker was immobilized by his anger and withdrew from the interaction. While he is probably struggling against retaliating, the group members feel abandoned. Finally, Mrs. Phillips searches for a connection between the new member and the group. Mrs. Palmer's comments needed to be partialized so that the group could examine specific content. But the worker's fear that he had lost control of the group inhibits his help. The group members sense that he wants them to take on Mrs. Palmer for him. They shy away from the struggle.

For the next two meetings, Mrs. Palmer dominated the meetings. Her anxiety about leaving the hospital trapped not only her, but the group and the worker. The worker felt he had ''lost'' the group. He became less active, and the group floundered. Attempts to reassert his leadership are evident in the subsequent meetings but the maladaptive communications and relationships between the worker, the individual member, and the group persisted.

> I said ''Lately, it has become difficult for all of you to talk in the group.'' Mrs. Palmer immediately said, ''It's not difficult, I have been talking.'' I interrupted her and said, ''For the last two weeks, you have taken us off the group focus and onto topics that have little to do with concerns about discharge.'' Mrs. Palmer retorted, ''Oh, no! You are so wrong. I think I have been right on the point.''

This particular meeting ended on a bitter note.

> I said, ''Mrs. Palmer, I think it must be hard for you as a new member in this group.'' She replied it wasn't hard for her at all. I continued, ''I think it is hard; every week you talk about anything but what we are supposed to be working on. How do you feel about being a new member in the group?'' She replied, ''I am not new. I know everyone, we live on the ward. You are new. And besides, I have been through this already in the other group.''

In Mrs. Palmer, the worker had met his match. He responded to the provocations as though he were a group member. He located the problem in the client and her psychological difficulties, and his vacillation between withdrawal and confrontation resulted in a web of maladaptive communications. Before work could begin on the group's structure and interpersonal processes, the worker had to recognize and accept his fears and vulnerability. By the next meeting, he had accomplished this task, at least in part. He acknowledged his mistakes, and succeeded in placing the interpersonal issue on the group's agenda:

> I said, "I have been thinking about something that Ms. Jackson said about taking a trip. I think it's a good idea, what do the rest of you think?" Mrs. Palmer responded, "I think it's a very good idea. I said so when she first mentioned it." I replied softly, "Mrs. Palmer, when Mrs. Jackson made the suggestion, I was so angry and hurt by you that I didn't even respond to it or to your support for the idea—I'm sorry." She smiled, but said nothing. Ms. Jackson quickly said, "I think trips would be fine. Like I said, it will give us some practice in leaving." As Ms. Greenberg began to speak, she was immediately cut off by Mrs. Palmer and withdrew. I waited for a moment and said, "Ms. Greenberg, you wanted to say something, but I think you got a little frightened by Mrs. Palmer. I can understand that—sometimes I also am a little scared of her—but I don't think she means to come on that strong." Ms. Bergio lifted herself out of her chair and said, "You, you are afraid, you are afraid of her, also—it's not because we are crazy?" I smiled and said, "Yes, I think we are all a little afraid of her—and I think she is a little afraid of us—we each handle being afraid differently." Mrs. Palmer returned my smile and said, "I am sorry. I didn't know I was having that effect on you. I am so frightened about leaving the hospital . . ."

The worker, by expressing his concerns and feelings instead of acting them out, lifted a heavy burden from the group. Their fears were legitimized, and their energies were released for work.

When anger is unexpressed, denied, or avoided, members and worker experience dammed up negative feelings which block communications.[14] Thus, it is essential for the worker to elicit these feelings and the associated content. By inviting the expression of feelings, he conveys care and respect for the clients and faith in their ability to communicate and to work on interpersonal obstacles. When family or group members act out their anger and frustrations, the worker must explore what underlies the interpersonal process, rather than negatively judging the behavior or protecting weaker members.

> I have observed rejection of certain men in my group at the nursing home. The more active members show an aversion to the less lucid men. Occasionally, a member will point to an individual who appears to be out of contact and say, "Look at that vegetable. You wonder why there's no action on this ward? Look at him—he doesn't even know where he is." The lack of response by the victim of these attacks increases the vehemence of the attacker and elicits open or silent approval of the attack by other members. Initially, I attempted to eliminate the hostility by defending the frailer member. But the behavior continued. The next time, I asked the attacking member what he saw when he looked at the other man. He responded, "The hospital staff think we are all like that. They think we have no feelings, nothing to say about anything. Like we are a bunch of cattle, a bunch of bums." As he said this, other members expressed their discomforts: "Yeah, bums . . . like we didn't work all our lives, like we lived off social security and welfare all our lives. We worked until we couldn't anymore." One member pointed at the disoriented man and said, "Even him, don't you think he worked hard? He can't help what happened to him."

The men's fear of being identified with the more impaired patients, their feelings of impotence, confusion, and anger would have remained latent, sustaining the maladaptive interpersonal patterns and interfering with the group's tasks had the worker continued to defend the symbolic scapegoats and herself. She moved beyond her initial preemptive interventions, and addressed the fears underlying the scapegoating. This helped the members move ahead on their tasks related to transitional and environmental issues.

In helping families and groups with maladaptive relationships and communication processes, the worker often assumes an active and directive role. He teaches members to use available collective resources to solve mutual problems: to recognize, identify, and partialize maladaptive patterns; to examine the consequences and tasks posed; to consider alternative changes and likely outcomes of each; to undertake necessary changes and evaluate the outcome. He provides pertinent information, offers advice and suggestions, models desired behavior and generally demonstrates through action the steps in problem solving. Often, he assumes a mediating role regarding communication, challenging impasses and maladaptive alliances, and encouraging nutritive exchanges and relationships. In families and groups characterized by inappropriate subsystem boundaries, he may be directive in suggesting changes in behavior. Centering the system in this way and restructuring it helps members change maladaptive relationships and communication processes.

The process is demonstrated in the Lapham family.

Mrs. Lapham and her 21-year-old son, John, had successfully maintained a close alliance that shut out his father. John had been born with a serious cleft palate and hare lip, which posed problems in physical care and feeding for mother and infant. Mother always felt father had rejected John at birth. Father denied this, but over the years he complained about the expense of repeated surgery, speech therapy, and prolonged treatment of John's severe eczema. At present, John is in a psychiatric hospital, as his doctor felt the emotional factor in the eczema was out of control. His mother, who herself had had four hospitalizations for depression, is barely tolerating the separation, but projects the difficulty onto father's financial complaints.

> Mrs. Lapham said John had told her his doctor had said the reason for his skin condition is his never having enough love and affection. While John was telling her this, his father walked back into the room and he stopped talking. I wondered what her reaction to this had been. She felt hurt, feeling the doctor was unjustly critical of her. I asked what made John stop talking when his father came into the room and what made him tell her something that, knowing the closeness of their relationship, he knew

> would upset her? She said John always told her things, then left it to her to tell her husband because Mr. Lapham always "blew his stack." I said it must be very hard on her always to be in the middle, and I wondered if it wouldn't be much easier on her to let them deal directly with each other rather than using her. She said she'd never thought of it that way. She thought maybe John was trying to get back at her for all he'd been through. He always comes to her. She even had to instruct him about sex because his father had refused.

Mrs. Lapham saw the social worker weekly, and John was able to stay in the hospital. For many weeks, Mrs. Lapham blocked the social worker's efforts to engage Mr. Lapham, but eventually he came and both parents were seen together until John's discharge.

From the family sessions it was clear that over the years Mrs. Lapham had gradually sealed off communication between father and son. Indeed, Mr. Lapham was excluded from all family roles but that of provider, while mother satisfied her emotional needs through John. Mr. Lapham's anger at this, and the lack of any support and acceptance, was reflected in his frequent outbursts related to the family's insatiable financial needs. The marital subsystem was virtually nonexistent, as both Mr. and Mrs. Lapham saw themselves only as parents. Nevertheless, the rigid structure began to change.

> Mr. Lapham can't understand how talking about their problems can help John's skin. I picked up on the fact that both of them had had heavy burdens over the years, and should really start enjoying things together. John was grown and should start assuming some responsibility for himself, rather than expecting them to continue taking care of him. Some positive feelings came through from Mrs. Lapham about her husband's steadiness at working, his concern for her, and his constant search for something to help their son. He needed some help—he was the only one who hadn't shown the strain, she said. I thought they both needed safety valves. Mrs. Lapham again brought up the doctor's negative comment, and I reassured her and

pointed out that John contributed his share to family interaction. . . .

Mrs. Lapham complained that John is not being taken care of by the staff. I agreed that hospitalization is hard, that in many ways John has to assert himself in a way he wouldn't at home. I wondered if she could encourage John to voice his needs to the nurses, as this could save wear and tear on her and take her out of the middle. She said she knows everyone here is competent, it's just that she knows what John likes because she's been doing it for so long. I said I thought this was a good reason for her and Mr. Lapham to start doing many of the things they had postponed for so long because of the problems with John. She says she has realized she needs outside interests, but all Mr. Lapham wants to do is sit around the house, and all he ever talks about are medical expenses, and John's skin. Mrs. Lapham went on to say she'd never realized how much she had depended on John's companionship, how much he'd stimulated her intellectually. I recognized with her that she is missing him. She said this had just occurred to her. She'd always known he'd grow up and leave, but this was so different from what she'd expected. Again, I recognized her suffering, interpreted it as a change rather than a separation, knew she could sustain this because John was going to benefit. She said when they visited last night, she couldn't get over the change. John's skin is clear and his disposition much better. He seems at peace with himself. . . .

Possible plans for John were discussed. This included his finding a job and a place to live within the vicinity of the hospital. Mr. Lapham was enthusiastic about this and went along with continued hospitalization if more immediate discharge would jeopardize John's gains. There was no evidence of his previous anger. He remarked how much more "human" John is, and was particularly pleased that John wants to go to work. I supported John's desire to be closer to his father, and his identification with Mr. Lapham

> in what he was saying to his father, and I pointed to Mr. Lapham's contribution to John's good qualities. I supported both parents' growing interest in shared activities. . . .
>
> Mrs. Lapham started the interview with how pleased she was with my advice about getting out, and her husband's changed attitude about going places. The past week they went to a dance for the first time in ages. I said I was glad they had had this good time together. She spoke of the new closeness between father and John, saying she had gotten tired of their using her as a go-between, and she noticed that things are going much more smoothly in their relationship since she told them not to bother her with their differences, but to go to each other.

In these excerpts, it is apparent that the boundary between mother and son was made clear and firm by helping mother set realistic limits on John's demands of her. Simultaneously, the marital subsystem was strengthened by encouraging the parents to seek pleasurable activities, and to seek them together. This permitted some easing of the triangulation that had isolated the father.[15] In addition, encouraging the mother to not allow herself to be used as a go-between, which she had not so subtly invited, relaxed the rigid boundary between father and son. Previous maladaptive patterns of communicating and relating to one another began to change through these structural changes. John and his parents were freed to work on their individual age-appropriate life tasks. John is now ready to move to independent living, and his parents are moving closer together.

Often, family and group members do not readily accept a worker's suggestions for change in relationships and communications. To give up entrenched patterns isn't easy. Resistance is an understandable reaction. In assuming the mediating role, the worker needs to keep the focus on maladaptive patterns. If members resist, the worker may purposely induce a crisis by challenging statements and perceptions or confronting role patterns. Such a crisis serves to unfreeze a rigid structure so that maladaptive interpersonal processes can be improved.[16]

In the natural friendship group, briefly described earlier in this chapter, the worker holds the focus on the stressful incident so they can work on maladaptive relationship patterns.

> Rita was ranting at Gladys and angrily repeating the incident as she had heard it. It was obvious from Gladys' expression that she didn't agree with all of what Rita said. I tried to get Rita's perception straight. I said, "Gladys, do you feel like everyone is attacking you?" Jean and Sue said they weren't attacking her—it was just between Gladys and Rita. I said both had been yelling at Gladys and they must have been mad at her for kissing Rita's boyfriend. Sue said she was just telling Gladys for her own good that she'd better leave other people's boyfriends alone. She said there had been an incident with Sue's boyfriend and Gladys which Sue had found out about, and it was lucky for Gladys that Sue hadn't said anything to her.
>
> There was a tense silence. Then, Rita was talking to everyone but Gladys who was sitting quietly. After a minute, I said, "I can't stand the atmosphere! Rita, you and Gladys are still very upset with each other. You're not talking to each other . . ." Rita said everything had been settled when she had hit Gladys. I said she was still sitting there fuming, and I was still upset about what had happened. This started a second and calmer round. I asked Gladys what she thought about what Rita was saying. She said she hadn't kissed Reggie twice, and Rita should tell Reggie not to mess with her again. I suggested she tell this to Rita. Rita said, looking at me, "All the boys play around like that." I suggested she tell this to Gladys, which she did. I asked Rita if she were saying she shouldn't say anything to Reggie about messing around with Gladys. Rita said no, she was going to talk to Reggie, but Gladys couldn't expect boys not to mess around. I said, "So when the boys play around, Gladys should . . . ?" Rita and Sue said, "She should say no! Leave me alone, etc." I asked Gladys, and she said, "I say, 'no, Reggie, now come on.' " (The no was soft.) I said to Rita

> and the others, "What would you think if you were the boy messing around with Gladys and she said that?" Sue said she'd push Gladys right into the bedroom. I said, "So Gladys doesn't say it like she meant it, doesn't say it firmly—right?" They agreed, adding that if Gladys continued to be weak like that, she would end up with a bad reputation. Gladys insisted that she does say no. Sue said she should get angry and yell, "No, you bastard!" I said it was hard to imagine Gladys getting angry. Gladys said, "Yeah, I get angry sometimes." There were more ideas about how Gladys should respond in other such situations, and she participated pretty well.
>
> Then there was discussion and criticism of Rita's slugging Gladys without either of them having said anything to the other. Rita said it was a spontaneous thing—she just walked in and let Gladys have it. The others criticized her for not saying anything to Gladys, and Rita said Gladys should have said something to her first. Gladys said she had been going to, but hadn't had a chance. I said the important thing was that, as mad as they were at each other, they had been able to talk about it. It had been hard to do, and they had done well.

With the worker's help, the group is able to work on an interpersonal conflict, and to experience success in dealing with it. She holds the members to the work, and does not allow them to avoid the painful encounter. Her firmness and persistence convey a strength and genuine concern, which in turn releases members' energies to confront the maladaptive process. She uses her own feelings to reflect the group's mood of anger, and she invites each member's perceptions of the situation. After pulling together the facts, she directs members to talk to one another rather than through her, and to examine the situation in a new way. She identifies and supports the common stake all members have in developing open and direct communication and mutually supporting relationships. Finally, she credits their ability to stay with and solve a difficult problem.

Family and group members need credit for their willingness to struggle and to risk themselves. There is, however, a subtle distinction between rewarding members' efforts to deal with difficult issues, and praising them for meeting the worker's values and expectations. The first is responsive to members' needs, the second reflects an imposition of the worker's own needs. Members need the worker's support, but not the burden of pleasing her.

When family or group members are unable to discuss their difficulties, the worker searches for other means to facilitate communication. She may structure experiences which provide members an opportunity to recreate problematic and painful episodes and to examine each member's role in contributing to the maladaptive patterns. By helping members to re-experience, rather than simply talk about the problem, the worker can broaden their awareness of the systematic nature of the pattern and stimulate changes in perception and cognition. To this end, various techniques are available.

Psycho- and sociodramatic techniques, such as role play, can be used to help members develop greater interpersonal empathy (role reversal), or to verbalize without interrupting one's pain (role soliloquy), or to dramatize a particular incident (role enactment).[17] The technique of "sculpting," through which members create physical–structural representation of their perceived relationship by the arrangement of bodies in space can be used to help members dramatically "contact" their relationship patterns.[18] A worker can also use techniques which provide family and group members with cognitive tools to examine their communication and relational patterns. In families particularly, genograms and ecomaps are useful tools.[19] Audio- and videotape allow members to hear and see themselves in action, and offer the worker the opportunity to stop the action and play back transactions.[20] Between sessions, behavioral assignments or tasks can be used, such as shared activities or monitoring behavior, to aid in the improvement of communication and relationship patterns.[21] Activities and program techniques provide another indirect means for changing maladaptive family and group processes.[22]

In a group of young adult retardates, one member was isolated and occasionally scapegoated. The group was unable to discuss the problem. The worker's creative use of an activity, dancing, was a helpful beginning step in integrating the member into the group's life.

While the others were dancing, I noted a spark in Barbara's eyes, especially when she watched Sheila dance with her boyfriend. I sat down next to Barbara, and asked if she knew how to dance. She was quiet. I asked if she enjoyed dancing, but still she didn't respond. I said maybe she felt that she couldn't dance as well as Sheila. She nodded and said, "And I don't feel like it." I commented that her eyes said she wanted to dance, and she smiled. After we watched together for a while, I took her hand to see if she would like to dance. She responded and joined the group briefly. She danced rather stiffly, by standing in place and moving her arms about. She seemed pleased, and after a while she sat down. I said, "You like to dance," and she nodded. . . .

In subsequent meetings, Barbara brought her own records, but she wouldn't leave her seat. I didn't pressure her, but let her know that I was available to dance with her whenever she would like. Sometimes, I sat with her when she was alone. . . .

In a later meeting, I noticed Barbara watched me dance with others. I danced her step, precisely as I could, and told the rest of the group that I was doing Barbara's step. She smiled in response. In a circle dance, I continued to dance her step and reached for her hand to join me. She did, saying that her step didn't fit this dance, so she couldn't do it right. I made an adaptation of her step and she said that she still couldn't do it. I held her hand and did it over and over again. She tried and got it. She joined the circle dance, smiling at me. I said enthusiastically, "You're doing great!" Together we taught "the Barbara" to the group, and she tried some of the steps the others were doing.

During the next meeting, she got up and danced spontaneously with Earl. After the meeting, I credited her progress. She laughed, obviously happy with herself. . . .

Barbara is on the way to being integrated into the group, and to participating in its activities and relationships. By differential use of various techniques—which require activity, engagement, involvement—the social worker can help family or group members to view a problem or a situation or a process in new ways and develop relationships and communications that support development and adaptive functioning.

Case Illustrations

The Ghiradelli Family

Bessie Ghiradelli, age 29, and her children, Lucia, age 13, Tony, age 3, and Bebe, age 1, are receiving AFDC. Homemaker service is also provided because Bebe is a seriously involved cardiac patient. The children's father lives with his legal wife and children, but continues to visit the Ghiradelli home. Ms. G asked for service because she felt overwhelmed, suicidal, and is convinced she is a "mess." She and the children were at loggerheads, and a contract was reached to improve communication within the family. This included clarification of structures, boundaries, and rules governing relationships and communications within the family and between the family and the outside world.

Ms. G keeps the two older children close, refusing to allow them to participate in outside activities, and she herself refuses to move outside the home to take in school and other events. Lucia is unhappy because of her mother's absence from her outside life in school, and because she is not permitted to join in the activities of her friends. Tony is hard hit by the encapsulation of the family by virtue of his being the only male member, so that being forced to stay home means he has no male companionship. He says he has to stay home because his mommy doesn't want to be left alone. Ms. G says she keeps the children and herself isolated because the outside world is evil and dangerous; she is the child of Italian immigrants, and says this is the way she was raised. When she was little, she was severely burned in an accident and has scar tissue over her face, neck and chest. She does not refer to her feelings about this as being related to her fear of social interaction. In addition, she feels stigmatized by her unwed status, her lack of education, and her dependence on welfare. She feels rejected by her parents, the children's father, and by life itself. It is clear, however, that she loves her children. Without them close she is empty and worthless. Boundary problems that affected communication and relationship processes were preventing the children from completing their developmental tasks, and the family from changing adaptively to a new stage in its own development. Environmental connections were weak and insufficient for the family's survival and continued development. All of the sessions, from which the following excerpts are taken, are with Ms. G, Lucia and Tony.

> I have begun to observe a pattern. Each time one of the children brings news home of an outside activity, in school or play, this is almost always met with derision, rejection, and always with the notion that it is completely unimportant compared to even the slightest happening in the home. Today, Ms. G told us that Lucia and she had a big fight about Lucia's joining the choir. She then turned to me and asked if she was too tough on the kids. I said it seemed as if she felt she was. She nodded, and then told me she is only trying to protect the kids. I suggested she turn to the children, tell them the same thing, and then ask them how they felt about it. After she did this, there was silence. Ms. G again asked how they felt about it. Lucia said, "You've got to leave us alone more, Ma." Tony said nothing, but hung his head. I asked him what he was thinking. He looked up and said, "I'm no baby." Ms. G looked to me and told me to tell them how tough the world is. I said to her that I shared her concern about the kids, but I also felt that exposing them to some things is important, too, and that joining the choir seems harmless. She began to sob and said that she didn't want to let the kids go from her and leave her alone. Lucia reached over and took her hand, and said, "We're not going, Ma—just trying to have some fun." I pointed up how hard it is for her as a parent to see her kids growing up, but this is a part of what all parents experience. She seemed comforted by that, and told Lucia she'd think about the choir.

The worker succeeded in having Ms. G communicate directly with the children instead of through him. This brought about more direct communication from the children to Ms. G. The worker empathized with Ms. G's feelings, but at the same time pointed up their inappropriateness with respect to the choir. Generalizing and legitimizing her feelings gave needed support to Ms. G in front of the children, a support overdue because her style of parenting had been the focus of attention for the past several sessions.

> I began the next session by saying that I had noticed that many of the arguments and tensions we'd been struggling with in the family seemed to be because the kids couldn't get involved with the world without Ms. G's approval, both for them and for herself. I wondered what thoughts the family had about this. Lucia said she wanted to do things other girls her age did, and it makes her angry when she can't. Ms. G said anything she does is for Lucia's own good. I said we know that, but I wondered if she could tell us what makes it so tough for her to give permission to expose the kids or herself to the world? Ms. G said a 13-year-old should be at home. Lucia said, "Because you were?" Ms. G got angry and said she was sick of Lucia's mouth. I pointed out that much of the tension seemed to come from the members' not really knowing what each could and could not do. Ms. G nodded. I asked if we could work on a compromise: Lucia could join the choir, and she must watch Bebe on Wednesdays to give Ms. G some time to do something outside the house. This suggestion was greeted by nervous laughter. Ms. G said she had never had the chance to be in a choir. Then she shrugged, and gave her permission. Lucia agreed to the deal.

By putting Ms. G's hidden fears of entering the world side-by-side with her expressed fears of its dangers for the children, the worker creates a small crisis, and the structure is momentarily unfrozen. The family-environment boundary, impermeable to nutritive input from the outside world for all the family, including Ms. G, is loosened by this intervention. While it would have taken longer, it would have been more helpful still had the worker stimulated the family to work out their own compromise solution.

> In the next session, Lucia said she was very upset that no one had gone to Open House at school the night before. She whispered this to me as I came in, and I suggested she bring it up at the session. As we sat down, Lucia did not take her usual place at the side of Ms. G, preferring instead to reflect her displeasure by sitting at the far end of the room. In tears, Lucia said, "I am very angry that no one came to the open house at school last night." I said, "You're mad because no one came?" and she nodded, "Everyone else's mother was there." I asked her to say it to her mother—which she did, with no response from Ms. G. All was quiet for a few minutes, and I waited to see if anyone would make a move. No one did. Then, I said, "How do you feel about what Lucia said, Ms. G?" She turned to me and said she was really sorry, but she just couldn't bring herself to go. I asked her to tell Lucia, and she did. Lucia then said, "There is to be a Christmas party at school that all of the parents are invited to." I asked the family, "How do you feel about your mother going to these events?" Lucia said, "Momma, will you come to the party?" Ms. G did not respond. Lucia then blurted out, "You better come or I'll never talk to you again!" Ms. G did not respond. I said, "Try saying it without the threat, Lucia." She began to cry and said, "Momma, I want you to come and act like all the other mothers." Mr. G finally said, "You know they are going to ask me where your father is, and want me to join the PTA, and embarrass me because I ain't got no husband or the money to join shit!" Lucia crossed the room, put her arm around her mother, and said, "We don't care, Ma. We just want you to be there."

All the work is beginning to pay off as Ms. G faces the fear of her own exposure, and the dread of being compared to the other mothers. Lucia, too, realizes that what has bothered her the most is the fact that her mother treats her so differently from the way her friends' mothers treat them. Many of those mothers are in a similar predicament to Ms. G's. It was Lucia's loving message of not caring what others think which provided the needed support for Ms. G to attend the party, which she did! Part of the movement in this session is due to the worker's insistence that the members talk to one another—a good idea, in general, but especially important in this family, because Ms. G has often tuned out what the children had to say. Communication channels are becoming unclogged, and boundaries more permeable.

> Ms. G began today's session by saying proudly that she had gone to the Christmas party at school and Lucia had made her proud. She said she'd been so "fucked up" about her own childhood she never knew that outside things could be so good. I commended her for going. And I said the more she allowed the children and herself to get out into the world, the more rich their lives will be, although there may be times when it won't be so pleasant. Lucia said that she joined the Brownies this week, and they asked if Ms. G could help run the troop. She's so excited because her mother agreed to do it. I said that knowing how good she is with kids, I know she will be a great leader. I asked if I could join, and we all laughed. I started to say something about what we had all learned from the experience, when Ms. G interrupted and said she could tell us the moral of the story: she has begun to learn that she can take it if going out means getting a hard time. I started to interject something, and she said, "Don't stop me now—I'm rolling." She continued that she had learned her kids are good kids, which makes her okay as a parent, and she isn't scared of being known as their parent. Lucia said that most of all Momma should know she and Tony love her no matter what, whereupon Tony crawled into her lap and said, "We love you, Mommy."

The structure is being refrozen, along with new patterns of communicating and relating to the outside world. This does not mean that the developmental issue, with which this all began, has been resolved. On the contrary, the struggle is only beginning. Opening the boundary between family and world will create problems for this family because of its particular experiences, its status, and the mother's deep-seated anxieties. Ultimately, it may be necessary to help Ms. G deal with her feelings about her facial disfigurement.

Mrs. G has flourished as the Brownie leader, but Lucia, who fought so hard to get her mother involved, is finding that having Momma around in her outside life can be a problem, too. As Lucia approaches adolescence, the struggle is likely to become pronounced. In a way, both mother and daughter are involved in an identity crisis, a setting ripe for conflict. Tony has not yet found a place for himself in the midst of this struggle, but he has become one of the most popular boys in his class. The absence of his father has created some problems, which manifest themselves in disruptiveness at school. To help him with this, the worker arranged for a Big Brother to provide the role model and confidante/friend he so desperately needs. The family committed itself to at least three outside encounters a week, and is keeping a weekly chart. The worker and family are discussing negative aspects of their exposure as these occur, in order to reinforce the fact that a failure does not have to lead to withdrawal. As the worker writes,

> When Tony crawled into his mother's lap after all the struggle and pain, and said, "We love you, Mommy," I knew right then that a family imbued with the gift of love can survive and flourish, amidst the most adverse conditions, as long as they can be helped to mobilize that love.

An Elderly Group's Racial Problems

An elderly female group comprised of seven women, ages ranging from 60 to 83, are meeting weekly to discuss common problems of welfare, housing, living alone, and relationships with family. Over time, Angela, the only black in the otherwise Puerto Rican group, began to withdraw from group interaction. She was distrustful and resentful, particularly toward Barbara, who occasionally expressed negative attitudes toward blacks. The worker's efforts to identify and discuss the emerging pattern was met with denial. The pattern was brought to the foreground in one meeting, however, when Angela publicly said she had a personal problem and asked to see the worker alone. The worker reported:

> I asked Angela if she might share her problem with the group. She replied that the problem cannot be worked

> on in the group, she will feel more comfortable talking to me alone. I asked what it was about the problem that made it difficult to share with the group. She said that some problems can be talked about in the group, but others cannot. Catherine raised another issue, and the other members joined her. I said, ''Hey, wait a second! Angela is upset—she has a problem which she is uncomfortable in sharing with the group.'' Catherine replied that if Angela wanted to see me privately, the group should respect her desire and let her do it her way. Barbara expressed some surprise at Angela's request, but supported Catherine's statement.
>
> I pointed out that concerns had always been shared in this group. They had been helpful to each other, and I felt Angela is having difficulty in getting close to group members and they to her. Juanita admitted she had been scared talking of her concerns the first time. She remembered Angela had been helpful to her and she would now like to be helpful in return. Catherine added she is willing to try to help, too. I noticed Barbara was frowning, and invited her response. She said, ''Maybe Angela doesn't trust us or lacks confidence in us. That's probably why she doesn't want to go into her problem with us.'' I asked for Angela's reactions and she assured the members that she likes and trusts them, but some problems are just too hard to talk about in the group. I asked, ''Are they problems that are painful to talk about or are they shameful to talk about?'' Angela said she is a little scared to bring the problem to the group. She doesn't know why, but she prefers to talk to me alone. Some members said, ''Well, if she doesn't want to talk, no one can force her.'' Angela appeared to feel vulnerable and said, ''I wish they would leave me alone.'' I abided by these sentiments.

When Angela suggested that ''some problems were just too hard to talk about in the group,'' the worker mistakenly focused on Angela's personal problem rather than inviting elaboration about the interpersonal issue that made it difficult to talk in the group. Angela probably felt she was being trapped into discussing her personal problem, and closed off discussion. Nevertheless, the worker did make a demand upon the group to work on the interpersonal issue, encouraged their participation, and thus laid a foundation for future work. In the individual session, Angela requested assistance with a relatively simple problem she was having with her welfare worker. The social worker focused on her difficulty in talking about this with the group.

> Angela said that she was ashamed to speak of this in the group because she really doesn't trust the members, particularly Barbara, who frequently disparages blacks and hurts her feelings. She believes Barbara would be uninterested in her problem, and might even laugh or spread gossip about her. When I said I could understand her hesitancy, Angela responded that she doesn't want to say anything because Barbara is a racist and cruel to anybody who is black. I wondered how she views the other members, and she said she likes them. I suggested that one member is keeping her from involvement in the group, and I would like to help her with this. She said she has been giving it much thought and realizes she should bring it up in the group. I asked what scared her the most and she said it is Barbara's cruelty and her fear of losing her own temper. We examined how this might go and role-played different ways she might handle responses.

The worker's support lends Angela the strength to engage the group's work on the maladaptive interpersonal process. Role play provided Angela with an opportunity to test out various approaches and responses, and helped her achieve mastery over her anxiety.

The next meeting began with Barbara stating that this group is like "three stones, one kettle, and a stirrer." After some laughter, members introduced issues for discussion, moving the focus away from Barbara's "joke." Angela remained quiet throughout this initial interchange.

> I asked Barbara what she meant. The group attempted to change the subject, but I asked who they thought was the kettle. Barbara looked at Angela, then around the room, and said anybody could be the kettle. I pressed her by asking if I could be the kettle. She replied, "Oh

no—you are the stirrer.'' I suggested that one of them must be the kettle. Barbara nodded. Angela said everyone knows she is the kettle. As members giggled, she added, ''It's obvious I'm the kettle. I'm black—the only black in the group.''

Immediately, members went to her rescue, pointing out that she really isn't black, but dark-skinned. They used Spanish words to suggest various shades, and said she couldn't be the kettle. I verbalized the members' discomfort and encouraged them to stay with the issue and not to feign ''color blindness.'' Angela picked this up, and said they are avoiding the issue because no matter what word they use, the fact remains that she is the darkest member in the group. They had made her very conscious of it. Barbara said, ''But being the darkest and being black are two different things''; to which Angela responded, ''Maybe, but as far as I am concerned, I know my color and see my color. I am black!'' Group members continued to refer to ''shades of brown.'' I suggested the group is a little scared of accepting Angela as a black, and I wondered what this was about. After a minute, Angela said their efforts to try to cover up her blackness make her feel terrible. Why do they act like there is something wrong in her being black? With much feeling she indicated how the group, but especially Barbara, hurt her with racial jokes and expressions of hatred for blacks.

After a long silence, Barbara told of her negative experiences with blacks, including muggings and robbery. Angela replied that all group members have had those experiences, but they didn't have Barbara's hatred and mistrust for all blacks, or didn't talk about them as if they were animals. She repeated how much this had hurt her, making her feel extremely uncomfortable in the group, so she just had to get this off her chest. Catherine attempted to redirect the discussion to generalized fear.

I encouraged the group to respond to what Angela had just said. Juanita said she feels badly about not saying anything sooner. She had also felt the tension in the group,

> and was glad Angela was able to get it off her chest. Carmen said she does find it difficult not to generalize her fear to all blacks, but in reality she was mugged by a Puerto Rican—"with those bastards, color of the skin makes no difference!" Barbara apologized to Angela for offending her in the past, and added she doesn't know why she talked like she did. I suggested that being afraid makes us do and say things that are hard to explain. Ann said this is something with which they can really try to help each other—"expressing and dealing with our fears, rather than hurting others and ourselves." I credited the group's work on this painful group issue. After this meeting, the group worked on helping one another with their common concerns about life transitions and environmental issues.

The worker helped the group members deal with the maladaptive relationship and communication pattern which had impeded their level of mutual aid. He provided support, energy, focus, and direction. He defined differences and commonalities, mediated transactions, and credited the group's efforts to change its structure. The group's natural developmental processes were congruent with the worker's determination: Angela desired greater involvement and participation; Barbara provided clues (such as her joke) that she wanted help with this area; the other members were uncomfortable with the tension, and genuinely liked Barbara. The worker's helping efforts and the group's readiness enabled them to overcome the problem in communication and relationship that was preventing their moving ahead on their common tasks.

Summary

In contemporary society, various family forms have evolved as variants of the nuclear ideal type: single-parent families, augmented families, and reconstituted families. There are also extended family and communal family structures. Each is vulnerable to stresses common to all family structures and to particular stresses related to the particular structure. The nuclear family of two legally married parents and their children is an undermanned, and therefore, weak organization for the complex functions it carries. It is particularly vulnerable to the loss of a parent because the entire system rests on the marital pair. Single-parent families often suffer from financial and structural pressures. Problems are posed in household management, child care, personal respite, and personal fulfillment.

The family comprises subunits, such as the marital, parent–child, and sibling subsystems demarcated by subsystem boundaries. When such boundaries are not clear and appropriately firm, they can be sources of maladaptive relationship and communication patterns that interfere with individual and family life transitions or with environmental issues. Similarly, the family as a whole must establish and maintain a clear, firm, yet permeable boundary between itself and the environment. If the boundary is too firm, there will be insufficient interchange with the environment. If the boundary is unclear or too loose, members will lack clarity about who and what belongs inside and outside the family, and hence will be unclear about role responsibilities and expectations. Over a period of time, the family evolves structurally related means for dealing with issues of authority, power, decision-making, and task allocation. These are lodged in the subunits of the family structure, helping to shape the patterns of relationship and communication, and are reciprocally influenced by them.

In formed groups, formational elements such as group size and composition may create problematic communication and relationship patterns. Groups can be too large or too small and thus provide inadequate opportunities or excessive demands for intimacy and task involvement. Groups that are overly homogeneous may lack vitality; while groups that are too heterogeneous may lack stability.

To fulfill its functions, the group evolves a social structure—a network of roles through which responsibilities are allocated and relationship and communication patterns established. Some group structures are too loose: while individual autonomy may be valued, members do not experience a sense of identity and support that comes from group solidarity. Other group structures may be too tight: while group solidarity may be valued, members are limited in their opportunities for nutritive interchange with the social environment.

Out of their individual beliefs, knowledge, and value orientations, the group members develop a set of group norms regarding rights and responsibilities, modes of work, and styles of relating and communicating. These norms are enforced by sanctions which unite group members and integrate the behaviors. Norms may be rigidly defined, ambiguous, and punitively or unevenly enforced, creating maladaptive interpersonal patterns.

Maladaptive interpersonal processes in formed groups are often reflected in such patterns as factionalism, monopolism, and scapegoating. While these processes are usually dysfunctional for most members, they serve a latent function of maintaining a group's equilibrium. In scapegoating, for example, deviance helps at the group level to clarify behavioral norms, sharpen group boundaries, and promote solidarity. At the individual level, the contrast between self and the deviant member may be reassuring and offer protection against the fear of similar behavior or attributes in the self. The deviant member acquires attention, with secondary gains in martyrdom, etc.

With families and groups whose maladaptive interpersonal processes interfere with their efforts to deal with life transitions and environmental issues, the social worker's function is to help members to communicate openly and directly as they work on common issues and concerns, and to develop greater mutuality and reciprocity in their relationships. The worker relies on the enabler, teacher, and facilitator roles described in earlier chapters. The worker also calls on the mediator role to focus on the family's and formed group's maladaptive communications and relationships and the functions and structures which generate them.

Factual, specific details of transactions provide the channel through which the worker can help family or group members to examine these processes. The worker encourages each member's participation in the discussion of discrepant perceptions, disagreements, and conflicts, and establishes protective "ground rules." She helps the members to clarify their messages and to examine inconsistencies. The worker identifies illogical or contradictory statements, points out patterns, and helps members to express the feelings connected to the message's content. She handles the sessions in a manner which provides the members an opportunity to recreate problematic episodes and to examine the contributions of each to the maladaptive pattern. By helping members to re-experience, instead of simply talking about the problem, the worker can broaden members' awareness of its systemic nature. Varied techniques have been developed to aid in this process, including role playing, sculpting, audio- and videotaping, genograms and ecomaps, activities, and behavioral tasks and assignments.

Throughout the work on maladaptive patterns, the worker must convey acceptance of members and support individual and collective strengths. She identifies and supports the common stake all members have in developing open and direct communication and mutually supportive relationships. Family or group members must receive credit for their willingness to struggle and to risk themselves in the difficult tasks of changing structures and processes.

Notes

1. See, for example, Salvador Minuchin, *Families and Family Therapy* (Cambridge: Harvard University Press, 1974).

2. A useful guide to the literature on new family structures can be found in Dorothy Fahs Beck, *Marriage and the Family Under Challenge,* with annotated bibliography by Emily Bradshaw, 2d ed. (New York: Family Service Association of America, 1976).

3. See, for example, Stephen Bank and Michael D. Kahn, "Sisterhood-Brotherhood is Powerful: Sibling Sub-Systems and Family Therapy," in Stella Chess and Alexander Thomas, eds., *Annual Progress in Child Psychiatry, 1977* (New York: Brunner Mazell, 1977), pp. 493–503. The authors state, "Siblings collude and align with each other, at times help each other resist the powerful vertical influences of parents. Other sibling systems serve to enmesh the youngsters even more with parents."

4. Minuchin, *Families,* pp. 51–60.

5. Ezra F. Vogel and Norman W. Bell, "The Emotionally Disturbed Child as the Family Scapegoat," *The Family* (Glencoe: Free Press, 1968), pp. 412–27.

6. George Simmel, "The Significance of Numbers for Social Life," Paul Hare, Edgar F. Borgatta, and Robert F. Bales, eds., *Small Groups* (New York: Knopf, 1965), pp. 9–10; Edwin Thomas and Clinton Fink, "Effects of Group Size," *Psychological Bulletin* (1963), 60:371–84.

7. Irving Miller and Renee Solomon, "The Development of Group Services for the Elderly," in Carel B. Germain, ed., *Social Work Practice: People and Environments* (New York: Columbia University Press, 1979).

8. Robert White and Ronald Lippitt, "Leader Behavior and Member Reactions in Three 'Social Climates'," in David Cartwright and Alvin Zander, eds., *Group Dynamics: Research and Theory* (New York: Row, Peterson, 1962), pp. 527–53.

9. Irving D. Yalom, *The Theory and Practice of Group Psychotherapy* (New York: Basic Books, 1970), pp. 283–88.

10. For analysis of these phenomena see Lawrence Shulman, "Scapegoats, Group Workers, and Pre-emptive Interventions," *Social Work* (April 1967), 12:37–43.

11. J. Leffer, "Counter-Transference and Family Therapy," *Journal of Hillside Hospital* (1966), 15:205–10; L. Loeser and J. Bry, "The Position of Group Therapist in Transference and Counter-Transference," *International Journal of Group Psychotherapy* (1953), 4:389–419.

12. Minuchin, *Families,* pp. 114, 139.

13. Harry J. Aponte, "Diagnosis in Family Therapy," in Carel B. Germain, *Social Work Practice: People and Environments* (New York: Columbia University Press, 1979), pp. 107–49.

14. Theodore I. Rubin, *The Angry Book* (New York: Macmillan, 1969).

15. Murray Bowen, "Theory in the Practice of Psychotherapy," in Philip J. Guerin, Jr., ed., *Family Therapy* (New York: Gardner Press, 1976), pp. 42–90. See especially, pp. 75–8.

16. Salvador Minuchin and Avner Barcai, "Therapeutically Induced Family Crisis," Jules Masserman, ed., *Science and Psychoanalysis, Vol. 14: Childhood and Adolescence* (New York: Grune & Stratton, 1969), pp. 199–205.

17. Raymond J. Corsini, *Role Playing in Psychotherapy: A Manual* (Chicago: Aldine, 1966); Jacob L. Moreno, *Psychodrama* (New York: Beacon House, 1946, 1959), vols. 1, 2.

18. Frederick Duhl, David Kantor, and Bunny Duhl, "Learning, Space, and Action in Family Therapy: A Primer of Sculpture," in Donald Bloch, ed., *Techniques of Family Psychotherapy* (New York: Grune & Stratton, 1973); Ann Hartman, "The Use of Family Sculpting in Teaching Systems Concepts," (paper presented at Annual Program Meeting, Council on Social Work Education, Chicago, 1975), mimeo; R. Simon, "Sculpting the Family," *Family Process* (1972), 11:49–58.

19. Ann Hartman, "The Extended Family as a Resource for Change," in Germain, *Social Work;* Philip J. Guerin, Jr., and Eileen G. Pendagast, "Evaluation of Family System and Genogram," in Guerin, *Family,* pp. 450–64.

20. A. David, "Using Audio Tape as an Adjunct to Family Therapy: Three Case Reports," *Psychotherapy* (1970), 7:400–17; S. Silk, "The Use of Video Tape in Brief Joint Family Therapy," *American Journal of Psychotherapy (1972), 26:417*–24.

21. Jay Haley, *Problem-Solving Therapy* (New York: Harper, 1976); Salvador Minuchin et al., *Families of the Slums: an Exploration of Their Structure and Treatment* (New York: Basic Books, 1967); Sheldon D. Rose, *Treating Children in Groups* (San Francisco: Jossey-Bass, 1972).

22. Ruth Middleman, *The Non-Verbal Method of Working With Groups* (New York: Association Press, 1968); Robert D. Vinter, "Program Activities: an Analysis of Their Effects on Participant Behavior," in Robert D. Vinter, ed., *Readings in Group Work Practice* (Ann Arbor, Mich.: Campus Publishers, 1967), pp. 95–110.

6

The Ending Phase: Termination

WE HAVE CONSIDERED the initial phase of social work practice and the tasks that face workers and clients as they begin their work together, and the ongoing phase, in which clients and workers engage in a range of tasks to reach their agreed-upon objectives. In the present chapter, we examine the final phase and its tasks, by which the work is brought to a close.

The decision to end their work together may be made jointly by the client(s) and worker. It may be imposed by the nature of the setting, as at the end of the school year, or at the end of a period of hospitalization. It may have been settled in advance as part of the mutual agreement, as in planned short-term service. Occasionally, the decision to end may come about through an unexpected event involving either the worker or the client, such as an illness, a move, or a job change. However the decision to end is made, the final phase poses specific tasks for both worker and client. The tasks include dealing with the feelings aroused by the ending; a review of what has been accomplished and what has yet to be achieved; planning for the future, including—where indicated—transfer to another worker or referral to another agency; and evaluation of the service that was provided. Like the initial and ongoing phases of helping, the ending phase requires sensitivity, knowledge, careful planning, and a range of skills on the part of the social worker. We examine these requirements within a framework of preparation, the stages in ending, and evaluation.

Preparation

Separations in life are painful experiences, particularly when they involve valued attachments. Even the termination of a brief relationship or one that was fraught with ambivalence can reawaken feelings connected to earlier losses, and thus may be distressing. The termination of a professional relationship can have a similar impact. If the experience of termination and its meaning to the particular client are ignored or mishandled, any gains which may have been achieved in the work together may be lost, and future involvement with social work services may be jeopardized. When the ending phase is handled well, however, termination can become a stage in growth and adaptation for both client and worker.

Ending is a mutual experience: the client needs to separate from the worker, and the worker needs to separate from the client. Both will have individualized reactions to the termination, depending upon organizational, temporal and modality factors, and relational factors. In preparing to help the client move through the termination phase, the worker must consider these aspects in advance, and anticipate their likely impact on the client(s) and on himself.

Organizational, Temporal, and Modality Factors

The agency itself influences the content and the process of ending, particularly with respect to temporal features. Organizations differ in how they structure and use time. A public school, for example, has a natural temporal structure that fits well both temporary separations or permanent endings. During holidays and vacation periods, temporary separations reflect natural pauses: the building is closed, family and friends may be more accessible, time is available for other activities. A temporary separation is less likely to stimulate feelings of abandonment and rejection than separation in other organizational contexts.[1] Similarly, completion of the academic year carries with it certain intimations of graduation. A permanent ending at this time meshes with the temporal structure, and may be readily connected to a sense of progress and achievement that minimizes the sense of loss.

Long-term treatment facilities for the chronically ill, the aged, and children provide a different temporal structure. Holidays and vacations for the worker represent painful times for clients who may already feel isolated and abandoned. The worker's absence may intensify the existing sense of desertion and feelings of depression. There is no natural point of "graduation" to coincide with the ending process. Client or worker may leave at any time. The client may be suddenly transferred or discharged, and the bed is empty. The worker may be transferred, or he may leave.[2] These aspects, which characterize even short-term institutional facilities, make endings difficult, and they require careful attention in preparing for termination.

The agency's definition of the status of social work student has consequences for termination. Where agencies present students to their clientele as regular staff and discourage students from disclosing their real status, unique problems in termination are generated. Beyond the ethical questions the student may have about this practice, he finds himself having to devise reasons for his departure. He fears being found out, and he experiences discomfort and self-consciousness in dealing with the ending phase. The client, in turn, senses the lack of authenticity, and may begin to question the student's credibility, and even his caring and commitment.

Where agencies are open and direct about their training function, and present their students as supervised learners, termination is less complicated by guilt and resentment. Clients expect the student's departure at the end of the academic year, and termination and transfer are more likely to be viewed as legitimate. Many clients, of course, are gratified by recognition that they have contributed to student learning in return for a valued service. In settlement programs, members often joke about "breaking in" another student. In university-affiliated hospitals, patients are keenly aware of the rotation of medical students, residents, nursing students, and social work students, and accept the arrangement as natural. This is not to say that termination may not be distressing in these settings, but only that honesty about the student status decreases unnecessary guilt on the part of the student and unnecessary resentment on the part of the client.

The temporal nature of the service itself also affects the ending phase. By definition, open-ended services do not carry a time limit or an ending date. The relationship intensifies over time, perhaps even carrying a freight of ambivalence and maladaptive dependency along with positive feelings of attachment.[3] When the worker introduces termination, for whatever reason, the client may experience shock and disbelief, and may perceive the ending as a personal rejection.[4] Planned short-term services, by definition, have a specified duration with a date for ending clearly stated at the outset. The dynamics of termination in planned short-term service are therefore very different from those of open-ended services. Clients are more likely to perceive the ending as an integral aspect of the service. Both client and worker mobilize their energies to accomplish specific objectives within the designated time period, and termination is an expected, and therefore neutral event.

The modality of service influences the ending phase in important ways. For the individual client, especially when there is personal investment in the relationship with the worker, termination can mean the loss of a valued attachment that has both realistic and unrealistic features. The client may experience anger, sadness, and perhaps a resurgence of helplessness. Such feelings are especially intense among those clients who are most dependent upon their environment because of age and physical factors affecting their competence and autonomy. This would include, in particular, children, the elderly, and the disabled or chronically ill.

In families and groups that remain intact, members will continue to some degree to have one another as a mutual aid or support system. There is less intensity in the relationship with the worker, particularly where the worker has been successful in opening channels of communication and strengthening relational linkages. Termination of the professional relationship may therefore be less stressful for a collectivity than for an individual. If, however, the family or group faces separation from one another, along with separation from the worker (as in divorce, a move away from the family, or the breaking up of a school or camp group), the combined loss may be even more painful and difficult to manage.[5]

Relational Factors

The intensity of feeling associated with a relationship and with its ending depends upon its duration and its qualities of mutual regard, respect, and reciprocity. It also depends upon earlier experiences with relationship and loss, and with the meaning attached to the particular relationship with the worker. The more sudden and unexpected the loss, the more difficult it is to manage the consequent realities and the feelings of sadness, abandonment, and anger. Without adequate opportunity to deal with the ending, the experience may be devastating. A depressed young adult describes her reaction to an unexpected termination with her previous worker: "Suddenly, she pulled the 'emotional trigger,' and I was again, and at once, a parentless child, a husbandless wife, a loverless lover, a mourning friend, a freezing entity in a deserted bus station—all that it has ever meant to be alone. And somewhere in that dense fog of isolation and loneliness, a whisper from reality said, 'You made it before. You can do it again.' But before the whisper could become a command, I had to get past, 'Do I want to?' "

The worker prepares for the ending phase by reviewing what is known about the client's previous experiences with loss and her means of coping with it. Through anticipatory empathy, the worker considers the potential impact of termination of this relationship on this client, and attempts to anticipate likely responses. With families and groups, she must consider the potential reactions of each member as well as the likely collective response.

> I had been working with a youth group in a group home, helping the members prepare for discharge and independent living. In trying to anticipate their possible reactions to my own departure, I immediately thought of the deprivations, losses, and separations in their lives. I felt that I would be one more in a series of females who had left or abandoned them. The experience may be more difficult because of status–role tasks involved in their also separating from the group home. I anticipated some regression and tried to imagine how each member might deal with my leaving. Bill might reject me; Tony will probably show how much he needs me; Sam will most likely withdraw. I thought the group itself might avoid the idea at first, and then become disruptive. This might be followed in later meetings by absences or lateness. I planned to deal with denial of my leaving by persistently presenting the reality,

> to deal with flight by "chasing" absent or withdrawn members, and to deal with depression and anger by inviting and partializing the intense feelings.

The worker, too, is subject to painful feelings and reactions.[6] A worker must therefore examine his own feelings about separating from a particular client and his own patterns of coping with loss, just as he does the client's. He must consider especially the potential for guilt about leaving and difficulty in letting the client go. Without such an examination, the worker might deny the experience himself. He might postpone announcing the ending date so there is no time left for being helpful. He might express his own ambivalence about the relationship through indirect communications, double messages, or repeated postponements of the ending date. The worker in the preceding example continues,

> I didn't have to go far within myself to touch my own feelings. I am aware that I don't cope with separations or endings easily. I know I tend to postpone the inevitable and to become detached. With these youngsters, I feel guilty about leaving them. I am abandoning them at a time when they are already confronting a major separation. I find myself wanting to avoid the issue, even to blame the agency, and to reassure the group. Nevertheless, now that I am aware of these possible errors, I am determined to invite the boys to express their feelings. I hope that if I do become defensive, I can still reverse myself and allow the youngsters to explore and express possible feelings of sadness, disappointment, and anger.

By being in touch with his general pattern of coping with loss, the worker is better prepared to deal with his own feelings, and he will therefore be freer to help the members deal with theirs.[7]

Stages in Separation

While people's responses to termination are unique, most of us seem to go through recognizable steps in dealing with the ending of a relationship. Whatever may be unique in each instance and however individual styles and pacing may vary, it is useful to consider four stages involved in dealing with the end of a relationship. The stages are analogous to those observed in dealing with the ultimate separation represented by death itself, though obviously they are not of the same quality or degree.[8] In general, the stages are: denial, negative feelings, sadness, and release. Each stage has its own tasks, but not every client will go through every stage. Some may not experience any stage except release! Organizational, personal, and interpersonal factors interact to determine the presence and sequence of stages for each client. Part of preparation involves considering these stages with respect to the particular client, and anticipating which tasks will require exploration and supportive effort by the worker.

The worker must be responsive to the tasks involved in termination by providing the time needed for their resolution. Time is a critical factor, for abrupt loss is difficult to manage. There is no time for the expression of feelings, the review of meaning, or planning ahead. Before the client is able to deal with the tasks involved, the reality of the ending must be presented. Even when the ending date has been agreed upon at the outset in planned short-term service, or mentioned at stated intervals in open-ended service, the actual presentation of the ending date is often met by denial as the first stage in the ending process.

Denial

The more satisfactory the relationship, the more likely it is that people will ward off the anxiety of separation by denying its reality. Initially, the client may forget its having been mentioned earlier, and he may attempt to avoid any discussion of it. The avoidance actually provides time to absorb the meaning of the imminent loss and to develop coping strategies for handling it. Thus, the denial is an adaptive maneuver; with the worker's help, the client can begin to relax the defense and to touch the feelings involved. Behaviorally, denial may be demonstrated by forgetting, as mentioned above, changing the subject, excessive activity, or regression.

A social worker in a mental hospital had been working with Mrs. Miller, a deaf patient in medical isolation with suspected tuberculosis. He was the first person with whom she had become engaged in a long while. She became dependent upon him for concrete assistance; now that he was leaving, she was unable to accept the reality of his departure. For a month she did not "hear" his statements about leaving or about his interest in helping her to become more self-reliant and to use other resources.

> Mrs. Miller greeted me with, "Where's my toothpaste?" I reminded her that we had agreed she would ask an aide for this. After pouting, she said she liked having me help her rather than anyone else. I said that because I'm leaving, it is very important for her to learn to use others, adding that I know how difficult this is, and I want to help her with it. She then placed a quarter on the table, and asked me to buy her a Sunday paper on Monday. She was holding on, struggling to keep our relationship intact. I suggested she ask the nurse to buy the paper, because I will soon be leaving, and she must get used to dealing with other staff members. She began to pout again. I wrote down that I like her, and this isn't easy for me, but I know she can do this for herself. She looked at me with a smile, and said she will ask the nurse. I wrote that maybe she can ask the nurse on Sunday night. She replied that she will ask her on Saturday so that she can have the paper on Sunday! I credited the idea, and suddenly she began to cry.

The worker's persistence and assurance of caring helped Mrs. Miller begin the task of facing the inevitableness of ending. His ability to do this rested on his awareness of his own difficulty in separating from her, with so many helping tasks still undone.

By contrast, another worker in a long-term, chronic-care facility was unable to help her group with the termination because of inability to handle her own feelings of guilt. She had successfully engaged a group of elderly, brain-damaged, socially isolated men with one another and with her. When she decided to leave the hospital, she could not tell her group.

> At this meeting I was going to begin about my leaving, and we got onto the subject of loss. It would have been natural for me to introduce termination, but I didn't—I

> couldn't. Mr. Jones was verbally rambling, and suddenly brought out his pipe, which was broken in two pieces, and sadly said, "Look at that . . . that's my only pleasure." It took a while to establish that what was upsetting him was that no one could help him get a new pipe, though he had asked several aides. He exclaimed, "It isn't much for a man to ask—to have a smoke—there's not much else." After we established that I would help him get a pipe after the meeting, I asked if Mr. Kley and Mr. Dobbs had similar feelings about something they had lost and were sad about? They didn't respond. I said that one thing that they all had in common was that they had lost part of their health. There was much nodding. Mr. Kley agreed, "Yeah—we all got sick." I said they also had in common that for them the hospital was their home. Mr. Jones said they were all together in this, like neighbors. I said I noticed the men hadn't known each other, even after many years—not even each others' names sometimes. Mr. Kley said, "Everyone has his own problems." Mr. Jones said the men couldn't remember, like himself. I asked why they thought we were getting together. Mr. Jones grinned and said, "The neighbors get together." We all laughed.

Literally and symbolically, the worker moved back to contracting, to the initial phase of helping—to the beginning instead of the ending. Immobilized by her own feelings, she avoided introducing and dealing with termination. She tried again the next week but, still unaware of her own feelings, she failed to anticipate likely individual and group responses to her announcement.

> I said that by the middle of next month I wouldn't be able to meet with the group anymore, as I am leaving the hospital. There were nods. Everyone was looking at me with a rather expressionless gaze. I said we had talked last week about having things we like broken or taken away. I asked if they remembered. No one responded. After several efforts, there still were no responses. I said this was hard to talk about, or at least I found it hard to talk about. There were more nods, but the men just looked at me. I asked if

> it were on their minds that I would be leaving. There was no response, and I asked Mr. Jones directly if it were on his mind. He smiled, and said, "That's nice." I was starting to get uptight. I asked if the men would like to continue meeting with another worker after I leave. They remained expressionless. I asked if they wanted to close the meeting, and they nodded affirmatively.

The worker's own denial of the meaning of the relationship induces a reciprocal denial in the group members. They withdraw not only from her, but from one another as well. To deal helpfully with denial requires awareness of one's own feelings about the particular relationship that is ending. This enables the worker to persist in presenting the reality of termination as the worker did with Mrs. Miller. Frequent reminders are often necessary, so that the painful reality remains on the agenda. With children, a calendar may be helpful, crossing out each completed session, and specifying the remaining number. But whatever the means used, the worker needs to focus on the issue, risk confrontation with pain, and elicit the expression of negative feelings.

Negative Feelings

As the initial denial is relaxed, and the reality of the ending is acknowledged, a period of intense reaction may follow. Some clients may turn the feelings inward, and experience the ending as a reflection of their unworthiness or the worker's disappointment with them. They may also develop physical symptoms or engage in self-destructive behaviors. Others may try to reintroduce needs or tasks which had been resolved or completed. They may regress, become excessively dependent, or in other ways attempt to demonstrate their need for continued service. Others may turn their feelings outward and experience the ending as a reflection of the worker's incompetence and lack of commitment. They may confront the worker directly with accusations of his lack of concern, or indirectly by silence, repeated tardiness, or absence. The intended message is, "I'll leave you before you leave me." The behavior attempts to lessen the pain of the perceived abandonment and, simultaneously, to provoke responses from the worker that will further justify the distancing.

> Walking back from the bus I noticed again what had been happening lately; the girls were very busy talking to themselves and teasing each other. Although it looked as if we were together, I was quite obviously apart. At one point, they actually walked in front of me, laughing over some joke, while I walked alone and behind them.
>
> Once again, I felt isolated from them. It made me sad, which must have been reflected in my face, for suddenly Judy noticed I was walking alone, and came and took my arm condescendingly. Tata's response was, "Shit on her." She and Judy, Carmen, and Kathy laughed hysterically. I said I thought they had seemed unhappy with me lately and asked if they wanted to talk about it. Kathy said they weren't unhappy about *anything*. I asked, "Even about my leaving in the summer?" Tata jumped up and shouted, "Nobody gives a shit about your leaving. Go ahead and leave now if you want to." There were tears in her eyes as she spoke.[9]

When such responses occur, the ending phase will be difficult for both worker and client. In order to help his clients use the experience for growth and consolidation, the worker must be both empathic and detached. That is, he must maintain sufficient identification with his client(s) to understand the feelings that have been aroused and their source. At the same time, he must move back from the experience sufficiently so that he is free to invite the expression of negative ideas and feelings about himself and the service. It is important that the feelings are accepted as real for the client. Premature reassurance by "sugar coating" the feelings should be avoided.

In the next example, the worker with a school-based group of sixth-grade boys responds to difficult behaviors with acceptance and understanding, thus legitimizing the members' resentment and disappointment.

> The boys put masking tape over their mouths. They hummed and moved around the room, gesturing and trying to communicate their thoughts to one another and me. Bill and Charles shook their fists at me. Their frustration and anger were clear. I said, "We have been a talking group

> all year and are very close, and I'm sad that you can't talk to me now.'' They took off the tape and ran around the room, shouting and wrestling. Finally, Bill yelled, ''Okay, cut it out. This isn't any fun.'' There was immediate silence. I suggested, ''You must be really mad to be acting like this.'' Charles said, ''Yeah, we're mad because you're leaving us alone.'' I said I knew it was hard because we are so close to one another. Charles asked whom he could turn to if he has trouble in school or at home. The other boys raised similar concerns. After a while, Ronald said, ''I think I know why we've been acting so bad today. You remember how we used to be bad all the time? It was because we had those problems and we couldn't talk about them. And today we've been bad just like in the beginning. I think it's because we have a big problem—you're leaving us.[10]

The worker avoided a power struggle over the boys' behavior. Instead, he suggested that their actions were connected to their feelings about his leaving. He made it possible for them to re-engage themselves with him and with one another.

In families and groups, individual perceptions and experiences often create disparate behaviors and responses to termination among the members. The worker must be sensitive to both the unique and shared responses evoked by her leaving. A session with a group of older adolescent residents of a group home illustrates the complexities involved.[11]

> I said it was hard to talk about my leaving. John said he was tired. He arranged three chairs together, and laid down across them. He talked about how close he felt toward his siblings, and said they are the most important people to him since his mother died. Nobody else matters. He described how hard growing up has been for him, and he emphasized his ability to make it by himself. Bill was watchful and restless, and I asked what he was feeling. He said nothing, but got up and left the room. Sam cursed at me, and followed Bill out. I went after them, and they returned. I said it's difficult for us to talk about my leaving,

> but we have worked too hard to run away from each other. Sam screamed that I had a nerve to "open us up"' and then leave. Bill yelled that he always knew I didn't care. "We are just a job." I'm just like all the other social workers they knew—"phony." I said I knew how much they're hurting, and I'm hurting, too, about leaving them.

In lying down, John expressed his fatigue and depression; in talking of important memories in his life, he attempted to negate the worker's importance. In contrast, Bill withdrew, and Sam acted-out. The worker stays with them, even pursuing Sam and Bill, and helped the members explore their shared feelings of resentment. In these ways, she demonstrated her caring about them and her faith in their ability to work together despite their negative reactions. Endings often call upon a worker to reestablish her credibility, skill, and commitment. A common error in this stage is the too early expression of her own sense of loss which may shut off the expression of the clients' negative reactions.

Sadness

As the reality of ending, and resentment about it are successfully confronted, both clients and worker are freed to experience their shared feelings of sadness at separating. The worker encourages and supports the client's expressions, and responds to them by sharing her own sense of intimacy and loss. She now can disclose the personal meaning of the experience, and invites the client to do the same. People have varying capacities for this kind of expression, and with some, the worker's recognition of their unexpressed feeling may be relief enough. Many clients, of course, will not feel anything as intense as sadness but only a mild regret, perhaps, that the relationship is ending. Hence, the worker must be surefooted in her empathy, guarding against the projection that results in overemphasis and overintensity. At the same time, she must be aware of her own and the client's attempts to cover up the feelings, and to avoid the embarrassment often associated with the expression of positive affect.

Both client and worker may attempt to escape into happy activities. Camp staffs, aware of the intensity of relationships that develop, structure end-of-the-season rites that help assuage the pain of separation—special campfires and other traditional ceremonies that serve to review achievements and to reaffirm the ties of comradeship. By contrast, an emphasis on farewell parties alone may interfere with the campers' experiencing the reality of separating. Alone on the bus, or back at home, the full measure of their grief spills out, to the dismay of parents.

The worker with the group of elderly men in the chronic-care facility helps the group experience together the sadness of leaving, instead of continuing to withdraw from one another and from her.

> As I reintroduced my leaving, Mr. Dobbs burst into tears. He looked at me, then down, and shook his head. I reached across the table and put my hand on his; he continued to weep. I said I knew this is rough. He wept harder, and Mr. Lawrence reached across the table and patted his arm. Mr. Andrews, immobile, watched with a blank expression. Mr. Jones' eyes filled, and he said, "There'll be nobody left for us. Men will watch tv." I asked if he is worried that there will be no more activities. He said, "Yes, ma'am, that's what I mean. You need to get up from sitting in front of that thing. You need to do things." Mr. Andrews and Mr. Kley nodded. As I mentioned the plans for another worker, Mr. Dobbs began to weep again, and couldn't talk. I said, "Mr. Dobbs, we got close this year, didn't we?" He nodded. I said I knew he and the others would miss me very much, just as I would miss them. They all nodded. I continued that sometimes when people have to say goodbye, like us, they feel very much alone. Mr. Dobbs said, "Yeah," and pointed to himself. I said I hoped they wouldn't shut each other out. They have learned to care for each other, and they still have that. They looked at each other and nodded. I looked at Mr. Dobbs and he responded clearly, "I understand, I'm with you."

The worker recognized with the members how difficult the subject of her leaving is. She responded to their feelings verbally and with the intimacy of physical contact, which is as important to the elderly as it is to children. Comfortably, she disclosed her own feelings of sadness. Together, members and worker feel the sadness and the closeness, and the members struggle to identify what the group experience has meant to them. The worker locates the strength in their situation: they have each other.

Moving past the negative feelings and experiencing the sad feelings requires time. In the same way, moving through the sadness to letting go of the relationship, to acceptance, also requires time. The worker with the group of preadolescent girls, described earlier, provided them with ample time to deal with the stages in separating. Without that time, it is doubtful they could have reached the degree of acceptance demonstrated in these excerpts:

> As soon as I mentioned my leaving, Nilda turned away and started looking at pictures on the bulletin board. She asked if it would be the same all summer, and I said she'd have to check with Joanne when she comes. She asked, "Who's Joanne?" I reminded her that Joanne is the social worker who will be taking my place. Nilda turned from the board, insisting, "We don't talk about her!"

For several weeks, the girls refused to refer to the new worker by name, and they avoided any discussion of her coming. But their curiosity and beginning acceptance finally generated some discussion.

> Lydia said she was wondering what will happen when I leave. I said Joanne is coming in to take my place. Lydia said, "But I may not like her." I nodded, and she went on to say that if she doesn't like her, she won't come back to the club. I said I thought most of the girls feel this way, but they will have time to see what they think of her. I reminded them they hadn't been too sure of me in the beginning, either; they didn't like to talk with me much and whispered together, instead. Lydia roared with laughter.

With acceptance growing, more open curiosity appeared the next week.

> Suddenly, Tata blurted out, "When is that other girl coming anyway?" I said she would arrive in the beginning of

> August. She shouted, "We are going to kick her ass!" I said that didn't surprise me. She added, "Well, you'd better tell her about us!" Nilda asked me if I had seen her and talked to her. I said I'd seen her a few times. Tata asked if I'd told her about them. Kathy said immediately, "Of course! What do you think they'd talk about?" I agreed, saying Joanne had asked me about them, and I'd said they might feel like kicking her ass at first but this didn't mean they wouldn't get to like her. Everyone laughed and I said I was serious, that this was just what I had told her. Judy asked me how tall Joanne is, and I said she was a little taller than I. Nilda exclaimed, "My God, another tall one," and asked if she is older than I. I said, "No, younger." Tata said she'd be too young to take care of them.[12]

Little by little, over time, the new worker became a real person, with a size, an age, and an interest in knowing the members. The process of gradual acceptance leads into the final step of release.

Release

Having faced and shared the pain of separating, worker and client may now feel that the tasks of termination are completed. Yet, the most important ones lie ahead, for it is the next set of tasks that provides the client with the opportunity to integrate the whole of his experience, and to find the meaning in it. There are three tasks in this final set: 1) recognition of gains and the specification of work yet to be done; 2) development of plans for the future, such as transfer, referral, or self-directed tasks; and 3) final goodbyes and disengagement.

The earlier stages of separation, if completed successfully, stimulate renewed energy for the steps in release. Where this is not so, however, the worker can provide energy by initiating and focusing the discussion. Joint consideration of where the agreed-upon goals and action now stand might be a starting point. "Let's examine together what has and has not been accomplished." Throughout the discussion, the worker emphasizes the client's strengths and the gains made, but also elicits discussion of any areas of remaining difficulty.

Plans for carrying on with the work, encouragement in the tasks, and the expression of confidence in the client's ability to deal with life tasks can all be combined with conveying the agency's availability for future services as needed.

In the following case, the worker had been meeting with the parents of a seriously disturbed teenaged son for two years during his long psychiatric hospitalization and after he returned home. She is leaving the hospital for a new job, and has worked through the early stages of separation with both Mr. and Mrs. Callen. In the next to the final interview, Mrs. Callen retells the story of the death and funeral seven years before of her beloved older sister. Then abruptly, she said,

> "I'm so mad at you. I keep saying that, and I didn't intend to. I don't know why I feel that way." I said it's natural and very understandable—we've shared a great deal together, and are going to miss each other. Mrs. Callen said, "That's it, I've been very close to you, and I never expected to be that way. I thought I would just come, and you would tell Tom (Mr. Callen) and me how Dick is doing." I said we need to talk about what she had found helpful and not helpful. She reviewed some of the struggles and the sad times. I pointed out the important part the parents had played in Dick's progress. Mrs. Callen accepted this, and then told about a cousin who had been mishandled by her parents, and about the way she and Mr. Callen had handled the same difficult moods in Dick.
>
> This helped us to go over the present situation at home with respect to Dick's relations with the other children, his attachment to his girl friend, and how he manages his earnings. I said many things are now going well, and added, "Perhaps the important remaining problem is the great disappointment you and Mr. Callen feel because Dick is not able to go to college?" Mrs. Callen acknowledged this, but said Dick's job is taking its place a little for them because of its technical nature. She then drifted into talking about a friend, and her shock and sadness at learning from him that he went home one night last week to

> find his wife, daughter, and furniture gone. There had been no provocation, advance notice, or anything. Mrs. Callen's own feelings of desertion and abandonment had clearly come to the fore again. I verbalized this, whereupon she returned to her feelings of anger and of being mistreated. Then she said it wasn't that she was mad at me—it was just maddening. She asked me more about my new job, where I would be, if it were a promotion or a change, and what my husband and children think about it. I answered these in simple factual terms, aware of Mrs. Callen's feelings that she somehow had proved unworthy of my continued involvement. Mrs. Callen then talked of the younger children. She added she doesn't know what she'll do when they grow up—but, perhaps by then she'll be glad. It was time to leave, and she said to me, "You should have another baby." I smiled, reached for her hand, and said, "I'm going to miss you very much—it is sad for both of us to say goodbye. And I'm glad we'll have next week together to talk more about your plans for managing things at home."

Mrs. Callen is beginning to recognize that she can make it on her own, even though she is still both angry and sad that a valued attachment is about to end. She is pleased with Dick's progress, and pleased with her own "growing-up," but at the same time she is yearning for a continuation of the protection that has been so similar to the protection her older sister had provided during a difficult childhood. With the worker's help, Mrs. Callen is moving toward release and a resolve to move ahead.

In work with children and the elderly, or where contracting has been more implicit than explicit, the worker may help clients find release by recalling together their shared experiences. This helps clarify where client and worker were when they started, where they are now, and even what new goals might be considered for the future. This work on release helps the client consolidate gains, complete any unfinished work, and make plans for the future. It is also the time when the client can be helped to see the strategies he has developed for dealing with his environment, for managing stresses in living, and for making decisions about the use of community resources and other important areas of his life. This helps make strength available for the potentially sad and intimate goodbye. In the case of the group of elderly men in the chronic-care facility, the worker writes:

> We began to discuss the things the group had done, re-living their activities together—bingo and horseshoes. I asked what they liked and hadn't liked about each activity. As they did this, I pointed to something positive each had accomplished in the group. "Mr. Jones, remember how hard horseshoes was in the beginning?" He nodded. "You got so good at it you made the highest points last time we played." He grinned. I remembered with Mr. Dobbs how he had struggled to stand up in his wheelchair to play horseshoes, and now he was really good at it. He and several others nodded excitedly. I remembered how Mr. Kley had given us the idea to make collages, how Mr. Caliagieri became so good at puzzles that he could help everyone else, and so on with each one. Each time there was pleased acknowledgment.

The worker helped the men to re-live their experiences, and she credited their strengths and achievements. The directive approach to elicit their shared memories is appropriate in the light of their mental disabilities.

In release, the worker also helps the client to consider various options, and which appears to be the wisest plan: transfer to another worker, referral to another agency, or termination. If the decision is to terminate service, the worker and client plan the phasing out of their work together. They may decrease the frequency and duration of sessions. They may arrange for a follow-up and review after a few months. Whatever the arrangement, the worker prepares the client to continue his work on any remaining tasks, and to deal with expected and unexpected events. Throughout, she credits his strengths and emphasizes the "graduation" aspect of termination.

In the following case, Mr. and Mrs. Rogers, in their forties, were being seen for twelve interviews, with the goal of improving communication between them. Their relationship had deteriorated, but both wished to preserve the marriage. They made good progress, and by the seventh interview the worker asked if they felt the need to continue.

> Mrs. Rogers turned to her husband. He thought they should have a period of weaning, and suggested a spacing of every two weeks. This was agreed upon.

During the eleventh and twelfth interview, Mr. and Mrs. Rogers agreed they were now communicating well, discussing their differences in an open way, and enjoying a social life together. Termination was a mutual agreement.

> Mrs. Rogers evaluated the experience as a very positive one. She expressed some apprehension as to what she would do if she should ever again get so angry with her husband. We reviewed what had occurred during the interviews, and how they could use some of this when problems came up in the future. If they did reach an impasse, they could reapply to the agency. Mr. Rogers did not make any evaluation of the experience or what its value would be for the future. He was satisfied, however, that they were again talking together and getting some pleasure from life.

Where transfer is accepted or mandated, the worker involves the client in planning the meeting with the new worker. Together they may decide that the new worker will observe one of their sessions followed by another session in which they summarize their work and specify future objectives. In the final transitional session, the new worker may assume primary responsibility. The gradual transition helps minimize the discouragment in having to begin all over again.[13]

Where referral to another agency is indicated and accepted or mandated, the worker has a linkage responsibility. This requires knowledge about community resources, obtained from resource manuals or the worker's informal professional network, or from direct visiting and investigation. After presenting the available alternatives, the worker helps the client plan for the initial contact with the selected service. If the client is to initiate the contact, the worker prepares him to deal with procedures and to anticipate complications. If the worker is to initiate the contact, she establishes client eligibility and assesses agency receptivity. When the referral is accepted by both client and agency, the worker prepares the new worker to receive the client. She helps the client to think about presenting his needs and priorities to the new worker. She may even participate in the first meeting, but in any case, it is imperative that she follow up to make sure the linkage is successfully joined.

When planning is complete, client and worker are ready for disengagement. Some clients may ask that the relationship continue on a personal basis; some may show appreciation through a gift to the worker; others may ask for the worker's telephone number or for a promise to correspond. These natural human interests need to be respected and handled with sensitivity to their meaning to the client. In our judgment, there are no hard and fast rules for handling them, although some agencies prohibit the acceptance of gifts or the continuation of contact. In actuality, most people have a need to give as well as to receive; most wish to continue a human relationship that has been rewarding; and most hope for some assurance they will not be forgotten. These pressures ought not to be regarded as part of the client's problem, but should be responded to out of understanding their human meaning for each client, and out of awareness that one's own human need for appreciation and continued involvement in the life of another should play no part in the worker's response. The following excerpt illustrates the pressures for continued involvement as a school social worker attempts to help a young girl achieve release and a readiness to move on to new relationships.

Sandy, age 17, had lost both parents the year before. Her mother died of cirrhosis of the liver and her father of spinal cancer. She now lives in the home of relatives, who are themselves heavy drinkers. During the contact, worker and client dealt with Sandy's anger, guilt, and grief over her losses, the conflicts with her relatives, the stormy relationship with her boyfriend and his subsequent rejection of her, and her own future plans. Sandy had known from the beginning the worker would leave at the end of the school year. Nevertheless, when the subject was introduced six weeks in advance, Sandy was devastated. Although unable to express her feelings about the ending, she did use the remaining time to work productively on other areas of her life. Worker and client decided upon a noon picnic for their last meeting.

Sandy got into my car, and I immediately sensed she was in an uncharacteristic "up" mood. She spoke animatedly of a recent humorous incident. We both laughed and then became suddenly quiet. Then we began to chat in a casual way. Finally, I said that it was pretty hard to talk, but not really talk about the fact that this is our last day together. Sandy said, "Yeah, but I really don't feel badly because I know I can see you again. I know you will be living in Center City, and you can become my friend. I don't care what you say, I can take a train there to visit you. I could also get your number and call you, so I don't really think of this as goodbye." I felt it would not be helpful to leave Sandy with these fantasies. I acknowledged that her wishes revealed her caring. And then, to help her face the reality of my departure, I continued, "You know, Sandy, this really is the end. We won't be able to meet every week like we did, things can't be the same." Understandably, Sandy countered with, "You talk like you don't want to see me or hear from me." Gently, I said, "I guessed it sounded as if I didn't care, but that isn't so—I do care for you very much. We have shared a great deal this year and have talked about so many important things. Now that it's time to say goodbye, it's especially hard." She quietly agreed.

It had been difficult for Sandy to express her anger and loss. So, I said, "Sandy, I think I would be pretty upset if people close to me were splitting." She gritted her teeth, "Yeah, everybody, and I don't have a darn thing to do with it. My mother, she had no excuse. She didn't have to drink. My father couldn't help it. It's not fair." I said softly, "It does seem very unfair, Sandy." She responded, "You're darn right, and now you. You know, you keep asking me if I'm upset with you and what do I think. I'm thinking that you really don't care. You just saw me each week because you had to, that's all. You don't care, because if you did, you would see me again." I told her, "You know it's easy to think that people—your parents, your boyfriend, your former social worker—come and go,

> and you have no control over it.'' She added quickly, ''Yes, you're right. What would you do if I telephoned you? Hang up?'' I said, ''No, I would feel torn also. I would be pleased and happy to hear from you, but I would also know that it was hard to say goodbye. That's what's hard to face, isn't it?'' She said it was. I said, ''So, even though deep inside we know we won't see a person again, we say, 'Oh, I'll see you.' It makes it easier for the moment.'' Sandy remarked that was true. I then reminded her how she felt when her former worker left. She hadn't wanted to meet with me at first. But then she made a choice, that in spite of her sorrow last year, she tried again. We talked about how much she accomplished this year and what starting with a new social worker will be like. Now that I am leaving, there isn't much either of us can do. I gently told her that even when people leave, like me, she might not see me. But what we had together and what she learned was something she would always have with her. That special feeling and the accomplishments, no one could take away.
>
> As we drove back to school, we both sat very still and quiet. Finally, I said, ''Sandy, I don't want you to leave until you have a chance to tell me what you are thinking. Try to say it now, rather than saying to yourself later, 'I should have told her.' '' Sandy turned to me and said, ''I'm going to miss you a lot. I just don't know what it will be like not seeing you every week. I really liked you a lot.'' She held back her tears. I said I felt the same way about her and added, ''I know it's hard for you. We'll both feel very sad later as you go back to school and I go back to my office, and we think about each other.'' Sandy said, ''I know,'' and we hugged each other. Then she left.

As Sandy attempts to avoid the permanence of ending, the worker helps her to confront the reality. She affirms Sandy's feelings of abandonment and anger, and responds undefensively and sensitively to questions about the genuiness of her caring. She helps Sandy to evaluate her accomplishments and to prepare for a new worker. Her final invitation, "Try to say it now . . . ," enables Sandy to express her affection, and to disengage with a sense of shared intimacy.

Evaluation

Endings can be particularly valuable to workers' efforts to build professional knowledge and to refine their skills. Careful assessment of outcomes with clients, identifying what was helpful and what was not helpful, and why, can gradually be generalized to the level of practice principles. In fact, much of what we consider intuition in the "gifted worker" actually represents the use of this kind of knowledge, too often not raised to an explicit, testable level. As one's experience grows, it is possible to observe patterns of responses across cases, to test out in practice one's hypotheses of what works with particular groups of people or particular needs, or particular situations. While practice theory rests on respect for individuality and emphasizes the need to individualize people, human beings also share many attributes, demographic characteristics, and common needs and life tasks. Their situations also have some qualities in common along with their uniqueness. The observation of such commonalities, in relation to those interventions that lead to positive or to negative outcomes, can increase the worker's knowledge and skill. Such observation also forms a base for the design of more structured research into practice. In their everyday practice, social workers have rich opportunities to note how people cope successfully with life stresses. These observations can be used in the design of procedures to help those who are having trouble in coping.[14]

The more one bases one's practice on mutual agreements with clients regarding problem definition, goals, planning, and action, the greater the ease in assessing outcomes with clients at the end. The problem-oriented record,[15] originating in health care settings and now spreading to other fields of social work practice, and goal attainment scaling procedures,[16] are formal structures that exemplify the evaluation process. But, whether worker and client assess outcomes formally or informally, knowledge increases and research questions emerge. Moreover, when evaluation is taken seriously by the worker and agency, practice becomes more effective, services more responsive to need, and accountability to the users of the service more assured.[17]

Most agencies require that workers complete statistical forms for agency use, regulatory bodies, or funding sources. The completion of such forms provides a measure of worker accountability to such bodies on the quantitative level. Accountability must also include professional responsibility to the client for quality of service. Such accountability begins with mutual agreements, and continues with ongoing joint consideration of progress in achieving agreed-upon objectives, and of how each participant—worker and client(s)—is carrying his or her role and associated tasks. Accountability is not complete, however, until the evaluation of outcomes during the ending phase. Creating the climate that will permit the client to be candid in his assessment of the service is a measure of worker skill.

Many workers and agencies, however, go beyond the ending phase in order to assure accountability. Hospital social service departments often are included in the hospital's questionnaire about total patient care. A social agency may use questionnaires after termination in order to tap client responses to the service. These are valuable, as they may reveal attitudes and responses that the client hesitated to share with the worker. Workers themselves may follow up at some time after termination to ascertain the client's present situation and to determine if gains continue in place. While some might suggest that this creates or prolongs dependency, we do not agree. We think that it demonstrates to the users of services the continuing interest and good will of the agency and its concern for the quality of its services.[18]

Case Illustrations

The Wayward Geniuses

A group of boys in a suburban high school was originally established to serve bright or creative but underachieving teenagers. The members, who felt "turned off by school," called themselves The Wayward Geniuses. After meeting for a year and a half, most were performing at higher academic levels and were more involved in pursuing their own interests. Slowly, the members each indicated waning interest in the group. Attendance became uneven and group discussions superficial and diffuse. The worker realized the group had achieved its purpose, the boys no longer needed to meet together to discuss their problems. He anticipated reluctance to terminate, however, since the boys had grown close and they counted on the worker's help whenever problems emerged. In the excerpt below, the worker takes initiative in helping them to address their readiness to terminate.

> The boys were talking informally as they waited for the arrival of the others. When most were present, I told the boys I wanted to say something I had been thinking about in the last few weeks. I said that I felt the group had been important to them, but that lately it seemed to have dried up a little. I knew they had used the group well over the past months, some more than others. Each had made some progress towards what he wanted for himself, and now we should discuss ending the group. There was a brief silence. Then Jack asked why I wanted to end the group. I responded that I thought the frequent absences and their not knowing what to talk about were ways of telling one another and me that it was time to end. Jack retorted, "You mean because we just bullshit every week?" I said, "I wasn't putting a judgment on bullshitting, it can be very valuable. Yet this group is held during school hours, and since you are excused from classes to attend, the group must be for the purpose of working on difficulties, not just to catch up on the latest news."
>
> Mike expressed disbelief, and said he didn't really believe the group should end. He asked if I was getting hassled by teachers, supervisors, or anyone to end the group. I said no. Mike said that I couldn't know what they were getting out of it, so how could I decide it should end? Jack answered, "It is sort of a place to come, but maybe it is no longer needed." Mike added, "Just because guys are doing better doesn't mean a problem won't come up." Different members then described how they now feel more in control of problems in school and with their families

now. Mike still held on and proposed, "Well, let's keep the group together just in case." I suggested that if a member had trouble and wanted help, I will still be in the school, and will be glad to meet with any one of them. Mike indicated that might work, but I was forgetting an important part of the group, what they had with each other. Ron agreed, and they offered examples of how they had helped each other with problems in the past.

Jack then asked me directly if I wanted to end the group because I was a student and didn't feel I was learning anything from working with them. I said, "It sounds a little like you're wondering if you let me down?" Jack said in a way that was true, but he was interrupted by Dick who said I was evading the question. I said it was not a matter of my learning, but rather that they no longer need my help. They again reminisced about the group: how rough things had been for each of them when they began, what happened over the year to each of them, how they had helped one another, and how I had helped them. Attention then turned to me. I said, "I can see it seems hard to let go, to break it up." Mike said, "Yes, it is." I smiled, and said he is showing it in the way he is trying to hold it together. I asked what made it hard for them to end the group. Eliot, who had been very quiet and seemed sad, started to speak. With some effort, he responded it was like an old marriage where the people don't really talk to each other and might be better off to let go, but can't. There was silence and some uncomfortable laughs.

I said, "Eliot was really on to something, endings aren't easy." I said they had worked hard to begin to work together and to get what they wanted out of the group and that makes it all the harder to end it. Several heads nodded. I then added that they seemed to be a little annoyed with me. Like, where did I come off telling them to end, or if I really cared for them, how could I leave them? Again there were nods, and Eliot said, "Yeah." They talked somewhat self-consciously about their anger with me. I encouraged their openness and affirmed the validity

> of their feelings. I added that I did care for them. I hoped that the decision about ending would be theirs and mine together. Ron asked when did I think they should end? I said there was work in ending, and I would like to help them with that during the next few sessions. He questioned, "And that will be it?" I said I guessed it would, and he said, "Wow!"
>
> Jack said he found it hard to think about ending. In a way, he could see that they probably should, but they have been together so long, it isn't going to be easy. Eliot said, it is sad, he did feel sentimental about the group. He began to fumble for words, and said he'd have to think about it more. Maybe he could talk about it at the next meeting. I said, "I hope so, for it sounded like others have similar feelings and need some time to put things into perspective." He nodded. Time was up, and I said the idea of terminating had taken them by surprise. I am really open to their reactions, and I think a lot may have been left unsaid. I told them I really want them to come back next week, so we can talk about it more.

In the following three sessions, the group continued to address themselves to the sense of nostalgia in ending the group, yet there was no real effort to continue the group. They shared mixed feelings of anger and loss, evaluated some of their experiences and progress, and made plans should any member need help in the future. Their final meeting was both sad and filled with a sense of accomplishment.

While the group will no longer exist, they will still have each other, since they are in the same grade. Spontaneously, as a final gesture, they drew an epitaph on the board, "Rest in Peace, signed, The Wayward Geniuses."

Mr. Frank

Mr. Frank had been hospitalized for severe, almost fatal neuropathy due to chronic alcoholism. After maximum physical rehabilitation had been achieved, the physiatrist referred Mr. Frank to the social worker in the outpatient department of physical medicine. He had now regained the use of his legs and feet and appeared not to be drinking, but was depressed, hostile, and occasionally expressed the regret that he had not died. He also refused to cooperate with the vocational rehabilitation counselor.

In the interviews with the social worker, Mr. Frank expressed loathing for himself, saying his drinking his life away had lost him his wife and friends. Despite his limited education, Mr. Frank was intelligent, well read, and had interests in philosophy, music, and art. These came to the fore in the interviews, as Mr. Frank began to feel better about himself. The weekly interviews continued for seven months, and Mr. Frank gained in self-esteem, and a sense of growing competence and autonomy. He never missed an appointment and, except for the vocational counselor, was on good terms with everyone in the clinic.

In the seventh month, Mr. Frank ended an interview by saying he was struggling with wanting to come and not wanting to come any more. He reported other patients were noticing he's the longest patient here and were teasing him about it. The worker agreed it was hard to keep coming, but added that she felt it was important for him to continue. At the end of the next interview, when the worker said, "Next week, same time?" in her usual fashion, Mr. Frank said no, he'd be in in two weeks. Before the worker could discuss it with him, he was gone. Two weeks later, Mr. Frank reported he had found a live-in institutional job as engineer in an old ladies' home. He was pleased with himself and with the job. They talked about this, and the worker writes:

> I wondered with him about continuing to come in. He said he wants to leave this with me. I referred to our missing last week at his request, and his feeling two ways about coming in. He took a deep breath and asked if I really want to know why. I nodded, and he continued, "I've enjoyed coming in. It's good to talk things over with someone. I think about it later. Certain things get clearer, but I've been afraid of getting too dependent on it—so much so I thought I should taper off. Now I don't know." I supported this idea of his achieving much, and that this is a time for us to consider plans for ending. I said I was being transferred to another area in two months, so we can begin

> to make these plans now. I told him that I think it is useful for us to continue until then, and I would like him to continue. What did he think? He agreed.

They did not touch on feelings about ending. Mr. F came in the next week, with little to say, even about his job.

> Presently, I commented that he seems lost in thought today. He said he was, and lapsed into silence again. After a bit, and with obvious effort, he asked if I remembered his saying last week that as much as he enjoys talking with me, he was afraid he is getting too dependent on it, and he thinks he shouldn't come anymore. I said I remembered, and wondered what his thinking about this is now. Mr. F said the real truth is that he cares too deeply about me to come in anymore. He is always very upset when he gets home, speaks to no one for several days, and is completely blue. It's not good, he won't come in anymore, he said. He referred to my always being a step ahead of him, of knowing exactly what he is thinking. I said that when two people have worked so closely together, it is very hard to say goodbye.
>
> This seemed to be the crux, for he went on with how in the past he has run from painful situations and run to drink, or he has provoked a parting by "cruel words," that he had considered calling me on the phone to say he wasn't coming anymore but he knew this was running away. For once in his life he was going to face up to a painful situation. I recognized with him how difficult this had been for him to face this with me, that it took courage, which I respected. He then ran off with the discussion and dealt with some fantasy material which I felt was better left alone.
>
> I brought him back to the decision facing us, reviewed his deciding to miss a session two weeks ago, his saying last time he feared dependence, and my telling him I was leaving. I suggested that now he has feelings around drawing his experience as a patient on this service to a close. These feelings are really related to his general feel-

> ings toward all of the people here, though he is funneling them onto one person, which is a kind of unreal perspective.
>
> He denied this, and described his positive feelings toward Dr. Lowe. He said they were quite different from the feelings he has toward me, and that he sees no point in coming back; he's in conflict about it. We talked about his feelings of loneliness and a good deal about his low opinion of himself, the two central themes of our work together. I stressed, and I think he heard, that this is his central problem, this is what we have worked on together, and he has made progress.
>
> He acknowledged the progress, but at one point slumped over, and said disconsolately that he continually asks himself, "What difference does it make?" I said he need not say goodbye to the clinic. He needs to say goodbye perhaps as a patient, but not as a friend. He can drop in here just as one would with friends. He is no longer viewed as a patient. He has accomplished his goal of physical restoration, and he has a good job. I said I thought he should continue coming in to see me, so we can talk about the feelings involved, instead of putting up with his present sleeplessness. He shrugged, and I mentioned that if he doesn't continue coming in to see me, he may not come to see his friends after I leave. He acknowledged this with feeling, and said he knows this is true of him—if he lets it go, he won't ever pick it up again.
>
> I also focused on the real change in him—his facing this, rather than running from it. "Yes," he said, "I don't think I'll drink." He talked of this in terms of coming and not coming in, and finally I commented he was finding it hard to leave this session. He acknowledged this, and said he would be in next week.

The excessive and unrealistic positive feelings threatened to undermine gains and inhibit Mr. Frank's continuing with the clinic. The worker chose to deal with the feelings by generalizing them to the service as a whole. It was essential that Mr. Frank continue his contact with the clinic for both psychological and physical health, and to do this he needed to move toward a more realistic perception of the relationship. Mr. Frank did come in regularly until the end. He was sad, often depressed, and he also became increasingly anxious in his job. He did not revert to drinking, however, and seemed able to use the worker's support and continued care and concern. He said he now preferred to come in every week instead of his original proposal of every other week, because he does not believe in tapering off with drinking or anything else—you either continue or you make a clean break. Because of his mounting anxiety, the social worker and the physiatrist decided he should be encouraged to continue with the new social worker who was to be assigned to the service, although he had been refusing all along to consider this possibility.

> Mr. F was describing his desperate feelings of being trapped with the old ladies. They are filed away at night, in tomb-like niches, and he is too. I wondered if the feelings he is describing are tied not just to the negative aspects of his job, but also to the fact that our sessions together are drawing to a close? He thinks they're due to a lot of things: his leaving the half-way house for the old ladies' home, his coming to the clinic, and now this separation. He thinks maybe he could have managed them one at a time, but not all at once like this—not when he has to also adjust to being sober, which is a different state altogether from being drunk. For twenty-five years he was really drunk all the time, and now he has to readjust to being sober. He described what he called panic, a feeling he is going to fly apart, he doesn't know if he can stand it. I said, "When you have those kinds of feelings, you really need professional help with them." He said, "You mean a psychiatrist? I won't go back to the state hospital." I said I thought the state hospital is inappropriate. Mr. F then said, "All I know is I've got a problem. I'm facing this fact now, and I realize it, I realize I need help. I'm tied in knots." I said I knew he hadn't wanted to start all over again with the new social worker, and I could understand what had prompted those feelings, but I really can't agree

> with him. I said the doctors and I feel this is really the reason why it is so important to keep coming here. Mr. Frank said, "I know this is what you meant, but I wanted to hear you say it again because I realize it now, I realize it's important for me to go on here. I don't have anyone else, no place to turn." I asked him if he would like me to make an appointment for him with the new social worker, Miss Dohr, and he said yes. I explained that she is coming on March 15, and we can arrange his appointments to continue on the same day as his day off, just as now. He nodded, and I told him that she will be a different person from me because she is younger than I am; but she is well-trained, has had experience, and will be very helpful. Mr. F said there are a lot of people in the world who think alcoholics are no good, that they deserve their fate. He told of two policemen he watched standing over the dead body of an alcoholic who had fallen, hit his head, and lay in a pool of blood. One policeman said he deserved what he got, and the other felt sorry. There are both kinds of people. I said he is wondering what Miss Dohr's attitude toward him will be, and I can tell him because I know her well, and she does not have those attitudes. He said he had a social worker at the hospital when he was so ill, who pressed him with questions while he was semi-comatose, until the doctor stopped her. She should have known better. I said he has a lot of questions about Miss Dohr, "You're wondering what she'll say and do, and if she'll understand you." I added that it's natural for him to worry about this, but I know her, and I know it's going to be all right. He said as long as I think that, he is ready to try.

The worker helped Mr. Frank to move away from the unrealistic feelings toward her, making it possible for him to continue the contacts, and finally to accept the needed transfer to the new worker. In the four sessions remaining, they worked on his depression, anxiety, and the symbolic nature of his responses to the job. They reexamined their original goals and assessed what had been accomplished. Mr. Frank acknowledged he felt better about himself, but said ruefully he had touched only the surface, there was much more he could have said. The worker handled this by saying that no one could ever fully know another, but perhaps some of this he would be able to talk over with Miss Dohr. The worker talked at length with Miss Dohr to prepare her for Mr. Frank's needs and style of working. She and Miss Dohr met with Mr. Frank together for a few minutes in the final session. Mr. Frank was sad, but he told the worker he would continue. In subsequent follow-ups, she learned that he did keep his weekly appointments and continued to abstain from drinking.

A Cottage Group

The group consists of five adolescent girls who live in the same cottage in a residential treatment center. They have been meeting with the worker for over a year, and she also sees them in individual and family sessions. The following excerpt is from the group meeting that took place three days after it had been announced in the cottage that the worker would be leaving the agency in several months.

> Three girls came in with each other and seemed in a happy mood. They said they'd had a good week in school. Beth arrived, singing "Everything is Beautiful." She took her seat and was laughing with everyone. I said, "Hey, it's great to see everybody in such a good mood and I hate to be a party pooper, but you know that I'm leaving and a lot of things between you and me will be drawing to an end." Margie said, "You have a hell of a nerve," and I said, "You mean about my leaving?" and she said, "Yeah, that and a whole lot of things." I said, "Okay, let's hear them. I'm sure that my leaving and the ending of the group has caused a lot of reactions in all of you."
>
> Nobody picked up on that, and Margie said, "Are we going to have a group next year?" A couple of the girls said, "Yeah, we want to have another group next year," and Beth said, "Let's have a party in honor of your leaving." She began talking about a party that they had been to, and all of a sudden Beth turned to me and said, "You're leaving, you Goddamned fink." Everybody stopped and looked at me. I said, "I'm leaving and that

makes me a fink.'' They all asked, ''Why are you leaving? Why do you have to leave us? Why can't you stay?'' A torrent of emotions poured out, and Jill said, ''Why are you leaving?'' I said, ''I don't know if it's the *reason* that really matters, it's more how you feel knowing that I'm leaving, for whatever the reason.'' They said, ''No, no, we want to hear the reasons, we don't understand.'' I said, ''Okay, let me try to explain. I'm leaving because I've been here for a number of years. Working here has meant a lot to me and you have all meant a lot to me. Yet a combination of things, the long traveling and working nights have become very hard for me, and I want to work nearer to where I live. That's pretty much the reason. If there's anything you don't understand, ask me and I'll try to explain more.''

Beth started to cry and said, ''You can't leave. We need you.'' I said, ''You mean you won't be able to make it without me?'' Margie said, ''You're the best social worker I ever had. I won't be able to talk to anybody else.'' I said, ''We have all been real close, and I guess the thought of starting over with somebody else is scary. What do you think it was about me that made it easier to talk to me?'' Beth said, ''It's because you cared about us. We knew that even when you were mad at us you were really sticking up for us, and you were really with us.'' Donna said, ''Yeah, but if you cared so much, you wouldn't be leaving.'' And I said, ''That's the thing, isn't it? How could I leave you if I really care for you?'' Gladys said, ''We know you care for us. We know you're leaving because you really feel that you have to.'' And then she just kind of shrugged; and I said, ''But the words don't help very much, huh? They don't take away the bad feeling.'' Beth said, ''That's right, what good does it do me to know that you care if you're not here?'' And Jill said, ''Yeah, you've been my social worker for a whole year. I don't want anybody else.'' There was a lot more talk about their not wanting anyone new. I said, ''You're upset with me, you have a right to be, but it's also hard for me to leave you.'' Beth said, ''If it's hard for you to leave us, then you wouldn't leave us.'' Margie said, ''No, Beth, that's just not the truth. It was hard for me to leave home. . . .''

Gladys put her head down and began to cry, and one of the kids hollered, ''Oh, cut it out. This hurts us as much as it hurts you.'' I said, ''Maybe it hurts each of you in a different way, and this is how Gladys is reacting.'' She picked up her head and said, ''Oh, leave me alone. None of you care about me,'' and Margie said, ''Yes we do, you don't want help. You just want to feel sorry for yourself.'' I said, ''You're all getting angry at Gladys, yet she's acting out how you feel. Is it that you hurt so much that you don't have room for anybody else's hurt?'' Jill said, ''She cries all the time. Who gives a damn about her?'' Donna said, ''I care about her, but I don't know what to do.'' Beth said to Gladys, who by this time had moved away from the table and was sitting alone on a chair, ''Gladys, why don't you come over here?'' Gladys just shrugged, and one of the other kids said, ''Aw, leave her alone.'' There was an uncomfortable quiet in the room, and I said, ''I don't think that you feel right leaving her alone,'' and Beth said, ''Well, what can we do?'' I said, ''What do you feel like doing?'' Beth got up and walked over to Gladys, put her arms around her, and said, ''You're scared, right?'' Gladys nodded and Donna said, ''We're all in that situation, too. Not only you.'' Beth said, ''But maybe it is different for Gladys.'' Gladys said, ''You have a mother and father. Every one of you has at least a mother or a father. Who do I have?'' Beth said, ''You have foster parents.'' Gladys said, ''Big deal. They don't want me.''

There was a hush in the room in the pain of those words. Beth said, ''I think I know how it feels. I think I know how bad it feels. And if you want to cry that's okay, but you gotta *live*. You got to pick yourself up. You gotta face it.'' Gladys shook her head, ''No,'' she said, ''I can't.'' Donna said, ''Even when you're alone you have to trust yourself.'' Margie said, ''That's pretty hard to do.'' Beth said, ''But you're not all alone, Gladys, you have us. We'll help you, and sometimes you'll help us.'' Margie said, ''You gotta have confidence in yourself.'' I said, ''How do you do that, Margie? Can you tell her?'' Margie said, ''You gotta think of the things that you do *right,* not only the bad things. Even when people leave you, you gotta think of what you did have with them, and all that was good. And then you got to believe that you're going to have somebody else, too.'' Beth said, ''You gotta learn to stand on your own feet. You gotta learn how to make friends.'' Jill said, ''You gotta take responsibility for what you do, even when it's hard.''

I said, ''It sounds like you feel that Gladys can do these things, even though now she doesn't think that she can.'' Beth said, ''That's right, and I mean it even coming from me. Lots of times I hate her, but other times I really like her and I remember when she was nice to me, and when she helped me, and I do believe in her, and I believe she can pick herself up.'' Beth took Gladys' hand and brought her back to the table. Then Gladys said, ''I feel real, real bad. Miss S's leaving hurts me more than anybody can know, but you've helped me and I want to thank you.''

There were tears in everyone's eyes, and I said, ''This is what it's about. This beautiful thing that you can do in helping each other, and you've got that now. You own that. And no matter who leaves, no matter how much it hurts, you can't lose that.'' Beth said, ''I hate you for leaving, but I know what you mean. I know you're right.'' Margie hung her head and I said, ''Go ahead, Margie, what do you want to say?'' She said, ''I know what Beth means also, and I want to feel that I can go on also, that we can even have a group without you; that we can keep helping each other just like we can in the group. I'm scared.'' And I said, ''Sure, it's a scary thing. Can you talk a little more about what you're scared about?'' Margie said, ''I'm scared that we won't be able to do it alone, that

> we need you to help us." Beth said, "Well, maybe we'll have somebody else who can help us." Donna said, "And maybe we'll have to help ourselves." Gladys said, "I know what you mean. I know that in the end I do have to help myself." I said to her, "But are you scared that you won't be able to do that?" She nodded her head yes, and once again she began to cry. Beth said, "We'll help you, too. Just like we did here this morning." And I had tears in my eyes, too, and I said, "Wow, you kids are fantastic." And they all kind of laughed and somebody said, "Maybe we'll become social workers, too," and that broke the tension.

The worker helped the members to express their feelings, and she accepted the legitimacy of their resentment. As members and worker experience their sadness together, energy is released to reach out to Gladys. The worker supports their sense of mutual aid and enables them to reaffirm their affection and need for each other. They can then contemplate the future without the worker but with one another. They express their appreciation and devotion by identifying with her, "maybe we'll become social workers, too."

Summary

In life, separations are painful experiences, particularly when they involve valued attachments. Both worker and client have individualized reactions to separation, but ending is also a mutual experience. The worker anticipates the client's and his own possible reactions by reviewing their respective experiences with previous losses and temporary separations, and their methods of coping with them. Based upon this preparatory understanding, he considers appropriate responses. Preparation is essential. If the experience of termination and its meanings is ignored or mishandled, achieved gains may be lost and future involvements jeopardized.

Organizational, temporal, and modality factors affect the termination experience. Organizations differ in how they structure and use time. Termination at the end of the year in a school setting, for example, meshes with the school's temporal structure and may be readily connected to students' sense of progress and achievement. Similarly, the temporal nature of the service itself affects the ending phase. In planned short-term services, for example, clients are likely to perceive the ending as an integral aspect of the service. In family and group services, members will continue to have one another after the worker leaves. Thus, termination may be less stressful for a collectivity than for an individual. If, however, the family or group has to confront simultaneous separation from the worker and from one another, the combined losses may be extremely painful and difficult to manage.

While each person's response to termination is unique, most people go through recognizable stages: denial, negative feelings, sadness, and release. Each stage has its own tasks, but not every person experiences every stage. Before the client is able to deal with the tasks involved, the reality of the ending must be presented in sufficient time to allow for full utilization of the termination experience.

The actual presentation of the ending date is often met by initial denial: people ward off the anxiety of separation by denying its reality. They gain time to absorb the meaning of the imminent loss and to develop adaptive strategies for handling it. The worker must persist, however, in presenting the reality of termination, so that it remains on the client–worker agenda.

As the initial denial is relaxed, the reality of ending is acknowledged, a period of negative feelings may follow. The worker invites and legitimizes these feelings, avoiding power struggles, premature reassurance, and expression of her own sense of loss. As the reality of ending and resentment about it are successfully confronted, then worker and client are freed to share their feelings of sadness. The worker encourages the client's expressions and communicates his own sense of intimacy and loss.

The successful completion of these stages of separation stimulates renewed energy for the tasks involved in release. These include mutual evaluation of the helping outcomes and processes, development of plans for the future, such as transfer, referral, or termination, and final goodbyes and disengagement.

Professional evaluation of interventions and outcomes with clients are essential to accountability and to elaboration of practice knowledge. As one's experience grows, it is possible to observe patterns of responses across cases and to test out one's practice hypotheses. The more the social worker bases her or his practice on mutual agreements with clients regarding problem definition, goals, planning, and action, the greater the ease in evaluating outcomes. When evaluation is taken seriously by the worker and agency, practice becomes more skillful and effective, and services more responsive and accountable to clients.

Notes

1. For discussion of worker vacation as a temporary separation, see Ann Hartman, "The Use of the Workers' Vacation in Casework Treatment," *Social Casework* (June 1960), 41(6):310–13.

2. Termination of employment has an emotional impact on the worker and the client. See Sidney L. Moss and Miriam S. Moss, "When a Caseworker Leaves an Agency: The Impact on Worker and Client," *Social Casework* (July 1967), 48(7):433–37.

3. In long-term treatment, much time and energy is invested in maintaining and sustaining the therapeutic relationship. Freud was reported to observe, ". . . for many patients the wish to be treated outweighs the wish to be cured," quoted in Irving D. Yalom, *The Theory and Practice of Group Psychotherapy* (New York: Basic Books, 1970), p. 278.

4. William J. Reid and Ann Shyne, *Brief and Extended Casework* (New York: Columbia University Press, 1969), p. 124.

5. For discussion of group termination, see James A. Garland, Hubert E. Jones, and Ralph Kolodny, "A Model for Stages of Development in Social Work Groups," in Saul Bernstein, ed., *Explorations in Group Work* (Boston: Milford House, 1973), pp. 17–71; Helen Northen, *Social Work with Groups* (New York: Columbia University Press, 1969), pp. 222–37; William Schwartz, "Between Client and System: Mediating Function," in Robert W. Roberts and Helen Northen, eds., *Theories of Social Work with Groups* (New York: Columbia University Press, 1976), pp. 171–76.

6. See, for example, Michael L. Glenn, "Separation Anxiety: When the Therapist Leaves the Patient," *American Journal of Psychotherapy* (July 1971), pp. 437–46.

7. Evelyn F. Fox, Marian A. Nelson, and William M. Bolman, "The Termination Process: A Neglected Dimension," *Social Work* (October 1969), 41(4):53–63.

8. Eric Lindeman, "Symptomatology and Management of Acute Grief," *American Journal of Psychiatry* (September 1944), 10:7–21; and Elizabeth Kubler-Ross, *Death: The Final Stages of Life* (Englewood, N.J.: Prentice-Hall 1975).

9. Adapted from a case record, *The Wanderers* (Pre-Teen Project: United Neighborhood Houses, New York City), mimeo.

10. Adapted from Alex Gitterman, "Group Work in the Public Schools," in William Schwartz and Serapio Zelba, eds., *The Practice of Group Work* (New York: Columbia University Press, 1971), pp. 69–70.

11. For discussion of termination with adolescents, see Jane Bolen, "Easing the Pain of Termination for Adolescents," *Social Casework* (November 1972), 53:519–627.

12. *The Wanderers*.

13. Beulah Roberts Compton and Burt Galaway, *Social Work Processes* (Homewood, Ill.: Dorsey Press, 1975), p. 427; and Maryonda Scher. "The Process of Changing Therapists," *American Journal of Psychotherapy* (April 1970), 24:278–86.

14. Bernard Bandler, M.D., "The Concept of Ego-Supportive Psychotherapy," in Howard J. Parad and Roger R. Miller, eds., *Ego-Oriented Casework* (New York: Family Service Association of America, 1963), pp. 37–44. See especially p. 33.

15. Rosalie Kane, "Look to the Record," *Social Work* (July 1974), 19(4):412–19.

16. Thomas J. Kiresuk and Geoffrey Garwick, "Basic Goal Attainment Scaling Procedures," *Social Work Processes*, pp. 388–400.

17. For further discussion on the evaluation process, see Howard Goldstein, *Social Work Practice: A Unitary Approach* (Columbia: University of South Carolina Press, 1973), pp. 263–75.

18. Anthony N. Maluccio, *Learning from Clients* (New York: Free Press, 1979).

7

Professional Influence: From Case to Cause

SO FAR OUR concern has been with the social worker's professional function in helping people deal with stress generated by life transitions, interpersonal processes, and environmental characteristics. We now broaden the conception of professional function to include responsibility for influencing the worker's own organization to improve its services, correct maladaptive processes, and increase its responsiveness to the needs of the population it seeks to serve or is expected to serve. This function transcends the particular needs of the worker's own clients vis-a-vis the agency, as discussed in chapter 4. Within this expanded function, the worker must take account of the employing organization's presence in the lives of all its actual and potential clients, seeking always to improve the goodness-of-fit between needs and services.[1]

We examine first the interplay of external and internal forces that create maladaptive features in the organization's provision of services. Second, we describe the practice role and methods involved in the five phases of influencing organizational structures and programs: preparation, initial organizational analysis, entry, engagement, and implementation and institutionalization.[2] The skills of the worker are illustrated and analyzed.

Organizational Problems and Social Work Response

Societal, Professional, and Bureaucratic Forces

Social needs and injustices are often brought to public attention through the vision and zeal of social reformers. As such persons and groups make the problem–need more visible, support is mobilized, public or private monies are made available to establish an administrative apparatus for fulfilling a societal function. In attempting to carry out its mission, the apparatus (department) confronts its own organizational imperatives, as well as various societal and professional forces affecting its practices.

Societal values and norms profoundly influence human service organizations. For example, society has made financial assistance and service available to the indigent. However, an ideological distinction between worthy and unworthy poor, the work ethic, and public reaction to the tax burden have led to the stigmatizing and stereotyping of recipients. Financial aid is provided in a punitive and demeaning manner, demonstrated by inadequate allowances, deteriorated, uncomfortable physical facilities, long waiting lines, and negative attitudes and behavior of some personnel in many urban welfare offices. These conditions attest to the impact on service delivery exerted by budget stringencies that are supported by societal and communal values and norms. In a similar way, the increased burden of educating immigrant and minority children has decreased public support for free compulsory education. Pressure has been intensified for the application of industrial mass production and management practices. Curricula have been standardized, pupil–teacher ratios increased, and support services decreased. Students' individualized learning needs have become secondary.[3]

Organizations depend upon public and private support and so are shaped by funding trends, and regulatory and accountability mechanisms. Funding becomes available and agencies respond with new programs that replace other programs. Some services receive as much or more than is required; others receive less than is required. A hospital patient in one department receives excellent care, while another patient in another department of the same hospital receives substandard care. The needs of rural areas receive less than proportionate attention than those of urban areas. From time to time, certain problems and needs receive national attention while others are overlooked. When one problem such as alcoholism increases in visibility and another, such as drug abuse, recedes in the public's attention, financing shifts. In response, an agency changes its direction and priorities. Some agencies, unable to initiate new programs, hold on desperately to familiar services and processes. Others, unable to define a clear function, change with each new trend in financing. All human service organizations are affected by these societal mandates and trends.

Professional interests do not always match client interests. Professionals are a critical interest group in organizational life. Their specific interests (e.g., in providing only daytime, weekday hours, and in servicing only those clients motivated for long-term treatment) often conflict with client needs. To achieve their interests, professionals and organizational administrators evolve certain trade-offs. Low salaries, for example, may be accepted in exchange for professional autonomy and limited accountability; or, undesirable work conditions and practice requirements may be accepted for high salaries or job security. These tacit agreements often lead to identification with the organization, its practices and procedures.[4] Socialization of the social work student within a tutorial pattern of master–apprentice field instruction, where power and authority is vested in one person, may encourage organizational docility and discourage risk taking. For full-time staff, primary identification with the agency is furthered and reinforced by organizational rewards of advancement, desirable office space, or congenial working hours dispensed for conformity and loyalty. As a consequence, client interests may be ignored.

Professional ideology also influences organizational practices and procedures. Since the realm of theory is characterized by logic and order, while life is a "buzzing, booming confusion," professionals understandably attempt to fit people into theories and categories so that they can be more easily "managed."[5] Some acquire and use a deterministic view of human behavior, in which either psychic or environmental forces are thought to be outside people's control. Clients are then perceived to be adrift in the sea of life: survival is dependent upon the velocity of the wind, the power of the waves, and the size of the ship.

Other social workers incorporate a phenomenological, existential view of human behavior, in which life forces are considered to be within people's control. Clients are then perceived to be steering a craft in the sea of life: survival is dependent upon their will, motivation and skill.

When an agency is characterized by extremely divergent professional orientations, clients may be held hostage to competitive interests, struggles, and discrepant practices. Yet, when an agency adheres to a single uniform orientation, clients are often expected to fit the prevalent approach. Creating and maintaining a responsiveness to client need is difficult to achieve, and requires steering a course between these extremes. Both stability and variability are necessary while change itself may be required to maintain stability.

Organizational Issues and Problems in Service Provision

Interdependent societal, professional, and bureaucratic forces can create practices which serve societal, professional, or organizational interests at the expense of client interests.[6] In general, organizational problems for users of services grow out of three interrelated areas: the agency's definition of its purposes and services; the structures and procedures used to coordinate and integrate organizational operations; and service arrangements.

How an agency defines its purpose and service may create problems for clients. As we have stated elsewhere, client needs tend to be defined by the services offered. If agencies define a client problem as located in the person, external forces are likely to receive insufficient attention.

> • At the Midchester Family Service, all applicants are channeled into open-ended individual psychotherapy. Planned short-term treatment, crisis intervention, or family treatment are rarely offered. There is also a high drop-out rate. Efforts to deal with the drop-out phenomenon will need to take into account the long standing psychoanalytic orientation of the clinic administrators; the staff's interest in long-term psychotherapy; the private practice model, in which each worker provides her own service; and any other features of the service which do not fit the needs and expectations of the clientele.

In such an agency, the definition of social work function reflects professional preferences, and results in service definitions and styles which are unresponsive to client needs. When agencies define their purpose and services rigidly, people may become lost in the service network, not eligible for service anywhere. When agencies' purposes and services are ambiguous, people may fall "between the cracks," because no agency appears to be responsive for their service needs.

To cope with community and bureaucratic pressures and forces, an agency evolves structures and procedures to coordinate and integrate the diverse activities of its participants. Such procedures may create unintended problems for clients. An authority structure, for example, may discourage staff differentiation and specialization. By its rigidity and constrictions, it stifles initiative and creative programing.

> • In the Ridgeway Settlement House, the director is unable or unwilling to delegate tasks and responsibilities to staff. The director, as the central organization figure, is involved in so many activities and projects that he cannot handle them all properly. At the same time, staff have inadequate information for performing their function, and require approval for every detail. Members are affected by the agency's general inertia and the staff's decreasing investment in the program.

In contrast, an authority structure may delegate too much decision-making, providing staff with limited leadership and accountability. Services remain uncoordinated, and each worker practices privately. In this pattern, professional role definitions and expectations are either specialized and narrow, encouraging isolation, or they are ambiguous and overlapping, encouraging competition. Similarly, agency policies and procedures may be overformalized or underformalized. Outdated rules may be imposed in new situations. Rules favorable to client needs may be systematically ignored.

Service arrangements may be inadequate, or inaccessible because of the agency's definition of its purpose and service and its related internal structures.

> • In the Eastend Community Mental Health Center, the adaptive tasks involved in the day patients' transition from 24-hour hospitalization to community reintegration are ignored. These clients fit into neither the inpatient nor outpatient departments. Thus, the catchment area requires a transitional service or a day hospital program for recently released hospital patients.

In other instances, services may be available, but their method and style of delivery discourage their use.

- The Longshore Community Services, a sectarian family agency, limits its intake to self-referrals. The agency does not attempt to make itself visible or accessible to the community. Since the agency offers no reach-out services, many clients who would make use of the agency's services do not know of its existence.

When organizational processes and structural arrangements place additional stress on users of services, the social work function broadens to include tasks of influencing.

Social Work Function

In response to strains among disparate interests of organizations, professionals, and clients, the social worker has a critical function.[7] She must maintain a vigilant stance towards organizational processes that bear on client services. When such processes become problematic, the worker must seek modification of the maladaptive practices, procedures, and programs. The professional function, as it pertains to the interrelated areas of problematic practices within the employing organizations is represented in figure 7.1.

We are now ready to examine skills needed by the social worker in influencing the employing organization to be more responsive to the needs of the population it serves or is expected to serve.

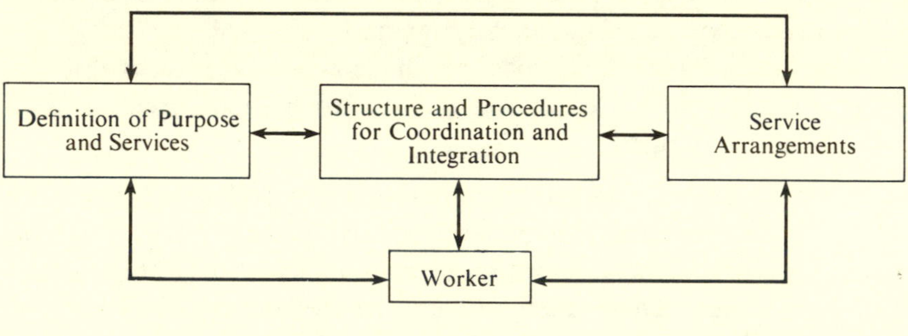

Figure 7.1 Organizational Problems and Social Work Function

The Processes of Influencing Employing Organizations

Preparation Phase

Preparation for influencing an organization begins with the identification of a problem. Users of service comprise the primary point of reference for this task. The worker obtains data about problematic organizational arrangements and practices through careful attention to clients' direct and indirect expressions, and review of records and other data. She is open to potential organizational issues reflected in a particular client's trouble.

Colleagues serve as another resource for problem identification. By attentive listening in staff meetings, in-service training programs, group supervision, and in informal conversations, the worker learns of problematic patterns. Specification and documentation of where and how the problem manifests itself are achieved through systematic observation, formal data collection, and informal conversations. In this manner, the worker begins to assess the problem's salience and relevance in client service. Once she has identified and documented the problem, the worker considers possible alternative solutions or objectives and the specific means through which each might be achieved. The advantages, potential consequences, and feasibility of each solution must be carefully examined. Based upon the initial impressionistic appraisal, a tentative change objective and specific means for achieving it are identified. The following examples illustrate the preparation process.

1. *Medical Hospital–Surgical Floor*

Problem: Definition of Social Work Function: The role of social work is limited to discharge planning. All other patients, regardless of their need for social work services, are overlooked.

Documentation: One woman, distraught about a planned amputation, was not referred because the family could take her home after surgery. Another woman in the terminal stages of cancer and severely depressed was not referred because her sons were making discharge arrangements.

Desired Outcome: The objective is to expand the social work function from case referral to case finding.

Means for Implementation: My initial, tentative plan is to use the team meeting, and try to broaden its content to include psychosocial needs of patients. I will use the discussions to broaden social work function, indicating to the team how I can be helpful to the patient being discussed, or providing an interpretation of his needs, his family situation, etc.

The team structure provides the worker with the means to demonstrate a broader function. In most problems related to definition of professional function, any effort to directly attack the ideology of others is a frustrating and fruitless task. Using existing structures avoids mobilizing an organization's ideological defenses, and increases the probability of success.

2. *Half-Way House*

Problem: Coordination and Integration Structures and Procedures: There is insufficient coordination among staff.

Documentation: The residents constantly complain about the lateness, poor service and quality of meals, inequities in house assignments, inadequate protection from other residents who steal or are physically abusive, and hostile and demeaning behavior by staff. Personnel are united in their complaints against residents and administration. They bitterly resent the residents' failure to cooperate, and the administration's insensitivity to staff needs and its ineffectiveness in coordinating services. They complain that house rules and regulations are not enforced by administration. The director locates the problem in the lack of staff initiative, creativity, and assertiveness in carrying out programs and policies.

Desired Outcome: The objective is to improve the house's internal operations and communications among the three groups.

Means for Implementation: My initial tentative plan is to obtain commitment to and sanction for creating an advisory staff group to the director. Once the advisory group is institutionalized, I will try to have residents added, and redefine the group as a house council.

The implementing means in this instance is a structural innovation which is feasible and can lead to permanent change. The worker defined the problem as lack of structure and procedures for coordination, and devised a means for integrating the various parts of the house system. If he had accepted the director's problem definition of staff inadequacies, he might then have sought improved staff functioning and skill through in-service training. When problems generated by missing structures and procedures, however, are defined as staff problems calling for in-service training, the dysfunctional organizational structures and procedures escape attention. They continue to affect service adversely.

3. *Psychiatric Inpatient Hospital*

Problem: Coordination and Integration Structures and Procedures: The interdisciplinary team is ineffective. Morning rounds, the team's major formal structure for integration, were designed for sharing and gathering information about patients. Yet, communication among the disciplines is minimal.

Documentation: I have observed that formal decisions about patient care are made primarily by residents, who lack relevant data. Decisions are made outside of rounds, so that staff is informed after the fact. Confusion among staff and patients results because everyone operates under a different set of impressions and decisions.

Desired Outcome: All staff fill out a different section of a form presently required within a week of a patient's admission.

Means for Implementation: My initial plan is to have the form completed at team meetings as a structure for the exchange of ideas and information.

Since the suggested procedure will save time, and so will be in the staff's interests, the plan seems feasible. If implemented and institutionalized, the procedure has the potential for long-term impact on the integration of new residents and staff. In contrast, defining the problem in interpersonal terms might lead to confrontation, sensitivity exercises, or single "rap" sessions. Such methods can mobilize defense systems of team members and lead to further deterioration. Any gains from them are usually short-lived.

4. *Union Setting*

Problem: Services Arrangements: The social program for retired members is poorly planned and carried out.

Documentation: Members have complained that programs are cancelled, guest speakers do not arrive for announced lectures, and most activities are dull. I have made the same observations. The program is not attracting new members, and is losing old ones.

Desired Outcome: The objective is to improve the quality of the social program.

Means for Implementation: I plan to obtain approval for and organize a steering committee of retirees, union program personnel, and myself to plan programs.

In this setting, a steering committee represents an acceptable way of doing business, so the proposed means is congruent with organizational norms. It will not appear to be a radical innovation, and it invites a broad representation of participants, particularly the lower ranking retirees. As union members, the retirees are entitled to services: when they become involved, their potential power will assure accountability to their interests. The new arrangement is likely to have permanent impact.

5. *Community Social Services*

Problem: Services Provided: The agency's intake practices discourage many applicants from using services.

Documentation: Telephone calls to a small random sample of persons who had failed to show up for their appointments or refused to make an appointment after intake provided initial data. People complained about the lack of evening hours; the lapse of several weeks between intake and assignment to a social worker; the demand to fill out numerous research forms; and adolescents' discomfort with detailed sexual questions asked by the psychiatrist.

Desired Outcome: The objective is to make intake service more responsive and relevant to client needs.

Means for Implementation: I plan to seek approval for an ad hoc committee to conduct a study into the high drop-out rate.

An ad hoc committee is an important structure for revising agency practices and programs. A direct assault on the agency's intake services may generate resistance. The agency prides itself on its scientific approach and has a full-time researcher, so the proposed research study group is consistent with formal and informal norms. The composition of the ad hoc committee will be important if change is to occur. Committee members will have to have sufficient flexibility to entertain proposed changes in intake arrangements, and sufficient respect to influence their colleagues.

Initial Organizational Analysis

Having tentatively identified and documented an organizational problem, selected an objective and means for achieving it, the worker now undertakes a formal organizational analysis. He assesses which environmental, organizational, and interpersonal forces are apt to support the proposed change, and which are apt to restrain it. An organizational analysis [8] is made to determine whether the objective and means are feasible. The analysis will reveal if more data are required, the problem needs to be redefined, or means for implementing the desired outcome need to be altered. If he is satisfied with feasibility, the worker then selects the appropriate entry points for the change effort.[9]

Environmental Forces. Social and physical environments affect all organizational processes.[10] The worker must evaluate features in the environment that may support and those that may oppose the change effort. Societal trends may be supportive of some changes and antagonistic toward others. Available funding encourages one innovation while lack of funds discourages another. Even fiscal constraints can induce and promote creative organizational change. A financially troubled agency, for example, may be receptive to changes in intake policies and procedures that reduce costs or expand the fee base, even though such changes are contrary to ideological orientations.

The extent to which the agency is held accountable for its services and practices to community groups is also important. Such groups include the board and its expectations and political pressures, and other organizations on which the agency depends for referrals and evaluation. Even the agency's physical location, condition, and size affect its relations with its neighborhood, and thus affect the effort toward change. Data about environmental forces can be collected through examination of written materials, informal conversations, and focused observations. From the data, the worker develops preliminary indices about environmental forces which are likely to promote or inhibit the proposed change.

Organizational Forces. Internal organizational characteristics also affect change processes. Complex organizations with a large number of professional disciplines and staff with advanced training are thought to have a higher rate of innovation. These agencies are characterized by diversity, openness to new methods and technologies, and competing interest groups, offering the lower-rank practitioner maneuverability. Organizations that are highly centralized with power located in a few elites, or highly formalized with a large number of codified rules are thought to demonstrate lower rates of innovation. These agencies are characterized by conformity, and standardized practices and procedures, offering the lower-rank practitioner less maneuverability. Knowledge about such organizational properties can be used as gross predictors for determining a feasible objective and means for achieving it.[11] Figure 7.2 shows the combined impact of organizational complexity and formalization upon receptivity to change.

In agencies characterized by a high degree of formalization and a low degree of complexity (C), the worker has to formulate extremely modest objectives, often limiting his desired outcomes to procedural changes, such as the enforcement of existing rules favorable to clients, or suggestions of new procedures to replace outdated ones. The modification of organizational purpose or basic programs is quite unlikely in a department of welfare or social security office. In contrast, a worker employed by a highly complex and informal agency (B) may aspire to greater functional, structural, or programmatic changes. In community mental health centers, the worker can often undertake more ambitious influence efforts. While a particular organization itself may have overall features of high complexity and low formalization, a department within it may not share those characteristics. For this reason, the organizational analysis must include the subsystem and its relation to the larger system.

		Complexity: Low	Complexity: High
Formalization	Low	+ − A	+ + B
	High	− − C	− + D

Figure 7.2 Impact of Organizational Complexity and Formalization Upon Change [(+) = Property increasing feasibility; (−) = Property decreasing feasibility].

Finally, less definitive statements can be made about agencies characterized by low formalization and low complexity (A) or by high formalization and high complexity (D). In a relatively undifferentiated community agency, for example, services may suffer from a lack of staff diversity and narrow ideological commitments. While the worker may be unable directly to influence the purpose and program of an organization that is low on complexity, he may have sufficient support and resources for indirect influence. A family or group consultant, for example, might be used to expose staff to new knowledge and technology.

Determining whether sufficient organizational supports and resources are available for the change effort requires an assessment of the status–role system of the staff's norms and interests.

Interpersonal Forces. In evaluating the status–role system, the worker tries to identify key participants who will affect and be affected by the proposed change. He seeks to estimate each participant's likely response to the influence effort and to evaluate its probable impact on individual job performance and satisfaction. If the desired outcome and means support a participant's self-interests by increasing prestige, self-esteem, autonomy, influence or authority, his or her support can be anticipated. Conversely, if the desired outcome and means threaten the participant's self interests by decreasing prestige, self-esteem, autonomy, influence and authority, then resistance to it may be anticipated.[12] Sometimes, these areas of support or resistance are easily identified; other times, they are complex, and it is difficult to predict their impact. A hospital social services director, for example, ordinarily represents a major force in support of any proposed change that increases staff size. But because of primary commitment to outside interests and involvements in writing and teaching, he may be threatened by the anticipated increased job demands, and resist the change. He may have competing commitments that create ambivalence or induce unpredictable responses. Thus, he may or may not conform to staff pressures and clients' interests. Or, on the basis of professional or personal values, he may do "the right thing" regardless of his own self-interests. While people usually act in their own self-interests, so their responses are fairly predictable, the complexities, subtleties, and idiosyncracies of human behavior require careful attention and preparation for the unexpected. Such attention includes observation of previous and present behaviors during formal and informal contacts with key participants. The worker notes each person's interactional patterns (e.g., risk takers, conformists, "closet" advocates), norms (e.g., work group pressures, individual and collective values) and activities (job responsibilities, outside interests), and what constitutes satisfaction and stress for each.

Worker Influence. The worker next evaluates his position in the organization and his structural and personal resources for influence. His structural location may or may not provide opportunities for interacting with key participants and obtaining essential data. Doctoral students, for example, quickly learn the importance of developing a relationship with the department secretary. She controls access to a critical person. To most students, she represents a source of influence to be cultivated. Similarly, while a baccalaureate or master's social work student may have a relatively limited structural position in her agency, she may have access to influential persons and opportunities to experiment, simply because of her student status.

A staff social worker will also need to examine the special features of her structural position for possible sources of influence. She must assess her personal position in the organization. Her professional competence, interpersonal contacts, commitments, and alliances are sources of influence. This assessment requires organizational self-awareness and the ability to see oneself as others do, rather than how one would like to be seen. Finally, she must consider her time and energy for the tasks involved in seeking change. For low-ranking participants, time and energy are essential.

Through the analysis of organizational forces, the worker can evaluate feasibility—that is, the potential for success. Where supports are strong and opposition is weak, feasibility is high. It represents a "green light" to engage in the change effort. Where support is weak and opposition is strong, feasibility is low. It represents a "red light," and objectives and means have to be reevaluated. Often, a change in the means for implementing the desired outcome creates feasibility without compromising the objective. In the earlier example of the union's inadequate retiree program, the worker had initially intended to have a professional hired. The analysis, however, revealed powerful constraints which mobilized a defensive stance by the department. The less threatening strategy of a steering committee diminished resistance and heightened feasibility.

Where supports and opposition are both weak, an open situation exists. It provides a "yellow light," suggesting that supportive elements have to be mobilized. And finally, strong support and strong opposition indicate potential conflict. It represents a "blinking red/yellow light." The outcome is unpredictable and a low-keyed approach is indicated. Chart 7.1 presents an organizational analysis. The overall pattern and direction reflects strong supports and moderate to weak opposition. This suggests feasibility and points to entry strategies to mobilize supports and decrease resistance. In the illustration, the outreach program can be readily connected to, or "piggybacked" onto agency financial pressures and threat of job loss.

Entry Phase

After determining feasibility, the worker has to develop an organizational climate receptive to the influence effort. He undertakes scout-

Chart 7.1

Organizational Analysis

Agency: Branch office, sectarian family agency.

Problem: Intake limited to self-referral, excluding many potential clients from service.

Desired Outcome: To reach more clients in community.

Means for Implementation: Community outreach demonstration.

Supports	*Intensity*	*Intensity*	Opposition
Environmental Forces			
Coordinating agency's threat of fund loss.	High	Low	Coordinating agency's loss of some control over accountability.
Threat to staff's job security.	High	Low	Undeveloped community relationships.
Interest and availability of religiously affiliated community agencies for collaboration.	High	Mod.	Present collaboration arrangements (e.g., co-leadership, fee splitting).
Organizational Forces			
Complexity: employs variety of professionals, historically has been somewhat unorthodox.	High	High	Decentralization and formalization: staff given wide latitude, with limited accountability.
Decentralized: in competition with other branches.	High		
Formalization: modest number of rules, but not rigidly enforced, often left ambiguous (e.g., job descriptions not defined, leaving opportunity for community work).	High		
Interpersonal Forces			
Administrator is experiencing environmental pressures, is liberal in views, and active.	High	Low	Administrator sometimes doesn't follow up.

Professional Influence

Supports			Opposition
Psychologist is service-minded, concerned about decline in number of clients served.	Mod.	Mod.	Psychologist is inactive in decision-making processes.
The social workers are quite liberal and client-oriented.	High	Mod.	The social workers have relatively low status and limited influence.
Psychiatrist is relatively uninvolved, follows administrator.	Mod.	Low	Psychiatrist may be threatened by outreach.
Educational consultant is invested only in school collaboration and will not restrain my efforts.	Low	Low	Educational consultant may be threatened. However, he has the lowest organizational status.
Total work group: high identification with branch, and perception of themselves as innovative, creative, and committed to serving their population.	High	High	Total work group: outreach could potentially mean more work, travel, uncertainties, and contact with less motivated clients.
	Worker Influence		
	Intensity	*Intensity*	
Supervised by administrator, which provides easy accessibility to critical participant.	High	Low	New-worker status limits right to undertake a new project.
Recent-graduate status provides legitimacy to experiment.	Mod.	Low	Motivation might be suspect.
Personal positioning includes excellent informal relationships; he is perceived as a highly motivated and competent worker. On several occasions, he has demonstrated competence in community contacts.	High		
He is highly motivated and has time and energy to undertake this influence effort.	High		

ing and positioning tasks to prepare himself and to influence the organizational structure (primarily the informal system) to respond favorably. The worker in the above illustration reported:

> I was aware of staff concerns about declining intakes and their fears of cutbacks in funding and staff cutbacks. During my informal discussions with staff members, I encouraged conversation on the decline in intakes and its effect upon the agency. I "felt them out" to ascertain their attitudes and thinking on the subject and their potential reactions to alternative solutions. When appropriate, I dropped hints about possible outreach to the community. I mentioned a suggestion made by a respected administrator at a central office meeting to offer premarital counseling groups. I invited their thinking about active case finding and collaborative projects to increase the agency's visibility in the community.

The worker begins informal discussion with organizational "friends," testing out possible reactions and inviting their ideas in mutual problem solving.

By contrast, an attempt by a social worker on a psychiatric inpatient service to have psychiatric in-patients decide on their own passes failed at the outset. Without informal scouting or positioning in advance, she raised the issue at a general staff meeting.

> At the conclusion of the discussion, I brought up the issue of patients' passes. The nurses immediately voiced their disagreement. The floor doctor identified the multidisciplinary conference structure as the appropriate mechanism. The meeting ended without any support for my idea.

The worker initiated action in the formal system prematurely. She mobilized defenses and precipitated immediate rejection. Support for proposed innovation or change must be developed and cultivated before "going public."

Brager and Holloway suggest three methods of preparing a system: personal positioning, structural positioning, and management of stress.[13] Personal positioning is essential for the lower-ranking participant. Since his ascribed authority is quite limited, he has to achieve a position of informal prestige and respect. Professional competence is a major means of gaining organizational influence. Where the practitioner's reputation for competence isn't visible or established with critical participants, this represents his first positioning task.

> I had been doing weekly intakes for several months, promptly and attentively. I involved Mr. Phillips, the director of intake, whenever I had a question about procedure. I had recently completed an intake on behalf of the husband of a client in treatment with an experienced worker. I consulted with the worker to get a better understanding and assessment of the case. She complimented my work and apparently discussed it with the director of intake and the agency director.

Being competent is not enough in itself; competence must be visible. Knowledge and expertise are critical resources for gaining professional influence. One's position in the agency's interpersonal network is another resource. The worker who is an insider, attentive to colleagues' interests and values, and who possesses interpersonal skills is effective and influential. An isolated practitioner who deviates from informal norms has limited resources for influencing organizational practices. Interpersonal friendships provide mutual support and foundations for change-oriented alliances.[14]

In positioning himself, the worker also examines such structures as ad hoc or standing committees and staff meetings as the base for the change effort. In evaluating group composition, he considers the driving and restraining forces represented by people, jurisdictional factors, and decision-making patterns. After selecting the appropriate structure, he considers which formal and informal processes may facilitate or retard movement. He then settles on the most effective person to introduce the idea, being quite prepared to give up any claims to ownership of the change idea.

Involvement of service users represents an important positioning consideration. Their evaluative feedback and anecdotal material are vital data for both personal and structural positioning. Segments of the actual or potential clientele may welcome opportunities to become involved in the change efforts. Their opinions about the proposal may be secured through questionnaires. A social worker in a child guidance clinic that professed to serve youth was interested in working with adolescents. She soon discovered, however, that few adolescents or their parents sought services, perhaps because of the agency's name, lack of publicity and outreach, and the reluctance of staff to get involved with "difficult teenagers." Her first step in influencing her agency to live up to its objective was to interest the director in forging links to the local junior high school as a way of increasing agency income. With his permission, she approached the principal and guidance counselor with an offer of group services to interested students. With them, she designed a questionnaire which was distributed to the students in their social science class. Response was almost totally positive. Armed with this data, the worker and the clinic director planned their strategies with respect to staff involvement, collaboration with social personnel, parental permission, etc. Their objective was to provide group services in the school, and eventually add individual services in the agency.

Hospital social service departments often seek an evaluation of their service from patients and families. These data can be important sources of support for change efforts. In addition, the process communicates to clients that their opinions are valued and utilized. In some instances, clients may be involved in later steps in a change process. A developmental disability clinic was threatened with closing when a new director changed the hospital's fiscal and service priorities. The clinic had been providing group services to parents of disabled children, and each of the groups was eager to contribute to staff efforts to sustain the clinic. They mobilized a telephone and mail campaign among their friends and neighbors, and they interested a local radio station and a neighborhood newspaper in their plight. Staff drew up proposals for funding. The administrator agreed to withdraw his plan to dismantle the clinic. Services to this needy group of children and their parents were safeguarded. In addition, the parents' self-esteem, competence, and sense of identity and autonomy were enhanced by their having taken action on their own behalf in a matter of deep concern to them.

In a family agency where evening hours were not provided, a worker concerned about the problem this posed to some clients secured the director's permission to invite several interested clients to a staff meeting, and later, to a board meeting. In such instances, the clients' own presentation of their needs can be more forceful in influencing staff and policymakers than the worker's presentation. Similarly, a child welfare agency that was reluctant to offer group meetings to foster parents was influenced to do so by a worker's carefully thought out proposal of content for the meetings, and her mobilization of the eager support of a large number of foster parents who called and wrote to the director about their interest.

In all such instances, it is essential that users of the service be fully informed of all that is at stake in their active participation, or even in their passive support of a change effort. The positives inherent in successful change may be easy to identify and share. Potentially negative consequences for clients must nevertheless be considered and shared with them, so they may make informed decisions about participation.

Like individuals, organizations can evolve elaborate defense structures through which the problem is rationalized, minimized, avoided, or denied. Before there can be motivation to examine and modify dysfunctional practices and procedures, some stress has to be experienced by organizational participants.[15] An important positioning task is to bring the problem and its consequences to the participants' consciousness by increasing its visibility and consequences. A worker in a union setting recorded:

> I made sure the director knew about the problems all staff were having with the scheduling of psychiatric consultations. I dramatized a recent experience I had with a member who waited two hours and wasn't seen. The director was disturbed by this incident.
>
> I also exchanged experiences with other staff members, and this created and maintained anxiety about the issue. Before long, several workers asked that the issue be placed on the agenda for a staff meeting.

In informal contacts, the worker listens to others' dissatisfactions, encouraging conversations about the problem. A heightened degree of stress often serves as an impetus for action by decreasing the defensive stance.

Where there is excessive stress, however, an agency's or department's staff may be overwhelmed by conflict or feelings of hopelessness. In such instances, the stress itself is a restraining force. In these situations, the worker can partialize the problems and help staff mobilize itself. A hospital team, for example, was locked in battle, and the hostility immobilized them from work on common goals. The worker attempted to reduce stress by suggesting the source of the problem was organizational rather than personality clashes. She began with non-medical staff, the most despairing group, validating their value to the team and strengthening their respective professional and organizational roles. Three excerpts from the worker's log are presented.

> We were sitting around shooting the breeze when Phyllis asked me what I thought of the new batch of residents. I stated that they weren't so new any more but that like everyone else, I missed the old ones. Jean agreed wholeheartedly and added that the new ones ". . . don't seem to care what anyone else has to say. Half the time they don't know what's going on with their patients." I asked if that's why she's stopped coming to rounds. Phyllis replied that there's no point going—she sits there like a bump on a log. Jean added that no one wants to hear what they have to say. I responded that it was a sad state of affairs when staff didn't communicate with one another because, "how else would I have known that Mrs. S was thinking about signing out because she was worried about her kids and needed help, if you hadn't told me? You know more about the patients in some ways than we do because you spend the most time with them." Jean responded, "*You* know that, but *they* (residents) don't." I stated that not coming to rounds wasn't the answer because then no one would talk to each other and the patients would suffer. Phyllis stated that that was the pity of it all. . . .
>
> Alice seemed quite despondent. In relating her need, she shared with us her impression that no one was interested in occupational therapy, questioning the value of her program to patients. I stated that her feelings seemed to have changed dramatically in the last three months. She

> described how the residents ignored her and devalued her program. I praised her program and skills, offering specific examples of impact she had had. I also pointed out that she wasn't the only one feeling this way, that it seemed that all the disciplines were questioning their value in rounds—citing social work as a case in point. Alice thought about this and stated that there did seem to be a general problem; no one talked except the residents. . . .
>
> Jackie suggested that people's anger with one another had developed into personality clashes, which were better left alone. I responded that while this was the result, it seemed to me the problem was basically one of communication among the team members. Jackie asked me to spell it out further. . . . Finally, I said that things were not going to get better unless we talked about it—that I could "understand staff's not wanting to discuss personality conflicts, which would get us no place. Perhaps there was another way to approach it, through improving communication in rounds—that really is the problem." Jackie thought about this for a few minutes, and then said that this approach certainly might defuse the problem, and it was worth a try. . . .

As staff depersonalized the struggle, they began to function with greater energy and resourcefulness. The positioning task was to reduce the stress so that the overwhelming problem could be confronted. In the process of redefining the problem, the social worker gained important allies for her objective of influencing the organization.[16]

Engagement Phase

These processes for achieving personal and structural positioning and management of stress help create a receptive organizational climate for the formal introduction of the identified problem and the proposed solution. Before going public, however, the worker must decide upon a general engagement strategy from among demonstration, collaboration, persuasion, and conflict.[17] In demonstration, the problem and proposed change is not explicitly discussed; the desired outcome is explained through action. In collaboration, the problem is identified and key participants are involved in exploring and developing solutions. In persuasion, a process of argumentation and bargaining seeks to achieve desired outcomes. In conflict, more extreme forms of pressure are applied. The strategy used depends upon the type of problem, the degree of goal consensus between worker and critical participants, and the worker's resources for influence.

Demonstration is a particularly effective strategy for problems associated with professional function and programmatic gaps. A desire to broaden the conception of an agency's or department's social work function, or to introduce a new modality, for example, may be best achieved by demonstration. By persistently and skillfully showing through action the value of group services, for example, a worker with limited organizational resources (rank), but sufficient personal resources (competence and energy), may neutralize, rather than mobilize organizational resistance. Action may therefore speak louder and more clearly than collaboration, persuasion, or conflict.

A new worker in a psychiatric hospital found herself without a professional function on the unit and in the interdisciplinary team. She sought to establish an identity, a professional "beachhead" for herself as a professional social worker. The problem was never directly shared with the interdisciplinary staff, the assumption being that "they couldn't care less" about helping social work to establish its identity. In fact, they might see such discussion as a threat to their own professional self-interests. The worker decided to move in gradually, demonstrate professional function and role, and increase the visibility of social service activity.

> As new patients were admitted, I became more active in planning for them. I made suggestions for in-patient care indicating need for family treatment, individual or family follow-up as an out-patient, etc. Much energy was expended, and at the beginning there was little receptivity. I was very willing to work on concrete problems, and the other staff did not have interest or skill in this area. So I began to develop an area of expertise—a bit of distinction from the rest of the staff. I made sure my activity was visi-

> ble by sharing my efforts with the staff during morning meetings and entering them in chart notes.
>
> I noticed that little attention was given to the patients' families. I began to contact families early, obtaining patient information for the treatment plan. These contacts represented another area of uniqueness, and soon became recognized as falling within the social worker's domain.

In recognizing her low-ranking position, limited resources, and competition for professional "turf," the worker demonstrated the distinct contribution of social services, rather than attempting to convince others how she should be used. The desired outcome was achieved without needing to explicate the problem, clarify respective functions, explain what social workers are supposed to do, or propose the idea of change.

Collaboration is an effective strategy in relatively open organizations where goal consensus exists, and there is either equity in resource distribution or the presence of close interpersonal relationships.[18] The worker can engage key participants in collaborative problem-solving through a shared search for data, possible solutions, and resources. He limits his activity to providing relevant information and mild persuasion, and does not attempt to convince or to change another's position.

A worker in a children's residential treatment center was concerned about poor handling of the children's bedtime. Most children currently were ordered to bed by child care staff, and some children were often assigned early bedtimes as punishment for misdeeds. At the same time, the worker had a genuine appreciation for the staff's problems: the management issues, their sense of being underpaid, overworked, and unappreciated. Bedtime was therefore equally problematic for the children and the staff. Based on her good relationships with the staff and her similar organizational status, she selected a collaborative problem-solving strategy.

> In my conversations with child care staff and their supervisor, I presented the dual nature of the bedtime problem, i.e., the therapeutic value of a different type of bedtime, and the child management issues. I have been

raising consciousness of the problem with various participants.

1) Psychiatrist: During a recent treatment conference I encouraged a parent to discuss her daughter's complaint about being put to bed early and missing her favorite T.V. shows. The psychiatrist agreed to look into the matter. At a subsequent clinical meeting, I presented my observations and concerns, and received a commitment to place the issue on a staff meeting agenda.

2) Child Care Supervisor: I shared my concerns and engaged him in thinking of ways to resolve the problem. He discussed different aspects of the problem and he welcomed knowledge about the uses and effects of punishment. Since children were punished by receiving early bedtime for infractions that occurred in the morning or previous days, I brought in behavioral studies on the lack of effectiveness of delayed responses to misbehavior. I did not make any suggestions about this material.

3) Child Care Staff: In my informal conversations with child care staff, I defined bedtime as a troubling time for them to manage, since many of the children were particularly difficult during this period, and I sought to engage them in a mutual search for solutions to the problem.

As a result of my collaborative efforts, the child care supervisor raised the concern in the child care staff meeting. A respected staff member, with whom I had developed a close relationship, stated that whenever she had time to tuck some of the children into bed, management was easier. A second staff member stated that telling stories was sometimes calming. They all complained that the lack of staff limited their time for doing this. The supervisor suggested that they use him as resource for unmanageable children, bringing the children to him so that group contagion would not take place. Staff was pleased with this structural change, and in turn, agreed to tuck the children in.

> At the next meeting of the clinical and child care staff, my supervisor inquired about a particular child. A child care staff member reported that she had been sent twice to the supervisor at bedtime, and this had calmed her as well as the other children. I suggested we spend a few minutes on additional suggestions for easing the problem further. One child care worker suggested that the recreation department could be useful in story telling or singing before bed. The child care supervisors and other staff agreed, and a meeting was arranged with the head of the recreation department. A program for this was successfully developed.
>
> At this same meeting, the psychiatrist referred to the use of early bedtimes as punishment and the research I had provided him. The staff was asked to consider alternatives for discussion next week, and I agreed to inquire into how other institutions handle punishment.

Here the worker fulfilled facilitating and educational functions. The definition of the problem emphasized and reached for goal consensus, as she engaged key participants in mutual evaluation and problem solving.

Persuasion is an effective strategy in situations characterized by goal dissent and disparity in power. Because the status quo represents an established and comfortable way of operating, it is presumed to be appropriate and effective. The existence of a problem must be brought home to key participants who then must be persuaded that solving the problem is necessary and feasible. To influence the opinions and ideas of others, the worker requires specific skills in developing and presenting the case for change, and participating in debate about it.

In presenting the case for organizational change, the burden of proof is upon the worker as proponent for change. Problem definition is the important first task. How a problem and proposed solution are defined determines, to a large extent, the grounds upon which arguments will be based. The worker has to develop arguments which demonstrate the existence of the problem, its seriousness, and the effectiveness of her plan to deal with it.

The problem must be defined clearly and recognizably, and supported by facts, and illustrative material, and if possible, by testimony of colleagues and clients. If a problem remains unrecognized, key participants will easily defeat or simply ignore the argument. A worker in a union setting, for example, attempted to persuade an administrator of a local to change procedures because retirees were inadequately informed about the termination of their medical insurance. She reflected upon her mistakes:

> First, I assumed Mr. Johnson knew what I was talking about when I referred to "Senior Care," and I did not take the time to review briefly the terms of this insurance coverage, and to connect it to the union's responsibility for informing members of changed coverage.
>
> Second, I did not discuss clients' situations adequately. I did not take advantage of the administrator's commitment to the service ethic by presenting large medical bills, describing complications in applying for medicaid, and relatives' threats to sue the Local.
>
> Third, I did not provide convincing statistics: e.g., the number of members with Senior Care as opposed to the number of eligible members, and the negligible cost of my proposal.
>
> At the end of my presentation, Mr. Johnson said, "Although this seems like a worthwhile proposal it may be a luxury, and we really can't be responsible for the members' not reading their newsletter." As I began to object, he thanked me for my interest, and we were dismissed. What I tried to do was to present my plan to get insurance information to the members. What I didn't do was the first step in the persuasion process—establish the need for the change.

Forces committed to the status quo attack the identification of a problem, either by denying its existence or by minimizing its seriousness. The worker has to acquire the necessary supporting data to establish need.

When the problem is effectively documented, argued and established, opposition forces may turn their attention to the proposed solution, challenging its desirability and feasibility, and identifying potential negative consequences. The worker must be prepared to "manage" these attacks, stressing the evidence for feasibility and positive outcome. If resistance is anticipated, the two-sided argument (one's own and the potential counter position) disarms the opposition, and to some extent dissipates it.[19] Humor and role play are effective in deflecting expected resistance or rebuttal.

If a positive response is expected, however, a one-sided argument is more effective, as reference to counter-perspectives may create doubts and resistances.[20] The one-sided argument should appeal to the self-interests and value systems of key participants. If anxiety needs to be aroused about the consequences of failure to act, it is done out of concern, loyalty, and identification with the organization, not out of dissent.[21] An extreme solution may be proposed to make it possible to compromise or fall back to a position which was desired in the first place. Various alternative proposals may be suggested, involving staff in the process, and increasing their investment in it and in its implementation.

Throughout the persuasion process, the worker assesses reactions, determining which positions are fixed and which positions are flexible. He makes changes in problem definition, proposed solutions, or the content and method of presentation, as suggested by his continuing appraisal. He may, for example, broaden the proposed solution to encompass the interests of neutral participants. Conversely, he may narrow the proposal in order to eliminate the objections of a powerful participant. Implicit in effective persuasion is skillful negotiation and bargaining.[22]

Conflict is a strategy rarely used by low-ranking participants in dealing with intraorganizational problems. The low-ranking practitioner is vulnerable to reprisals, and caution is necessary. At the same time, certain organizational conditions, such as violation of clients' rights, do require more adversarial actions, especially in the face of marked dissent over goals and methods. Before engaging in organizational conflict, however, the practitioner evaluates potential responses as well as her own resources. If her job or personal credibility are at stake, only severe injustices and unethical practices should require such risks and sacrifices. It is in neither the clients' nor worker's interests to achieve professional omnipotence through "death." The ultimate threat and risk need to be reserved for major issues. If there is ambiguity about organizational response or about the worker's resources, accommodation may only be achieved through a test of respective strengths.[23]

In undertaking an individual adversarial action, the worker takes a stance of organizational loyalty rather than one of moral indignation. Polite, respectful disobedience can be highly effective. A family agency, for example, as part of a purchase of service agreement, required workers to submit confidential data to the department of social services. After several unsuccessful efforts by a practitioner to effect a change in the policy, her supervisor demanded the confidential data. She politely refused the request, identifying the core issue of client confidentiality. She also expressed concern about the negative impact on the agency and its reputation, "should the practice become public." The agency retreated, and renegotiated the arrangement with the department of social services. Had the worker escalated the issue, an unnecessary crisis would have been precipitated. Calling attention to negative consequences was successful because it provided the leverage for testing relative power.

Group action can diminish the risk of reprisal. Collective positions, manifestos, petitions, or demonstrations are effective methods in dealing with powerful organizational participants and harmful practices.[24] The alliance or coalition must be firmly unified and committed. If members are intimidated and become mutually exploitative, a long period of powerlessness and despair will result. In undertaking collective action, the worker must first be sure each member is publicly committed to the cause in order to avoid finding himself with a group of "closet advocates" whose "barks" are ferocious, but whose "bites" are relatively benign.

Implementation and Institutionalization

After a desired outcome has been adopted, it needs to be put into action. Initial acceptance does not insure implementation. For the practitioner, much work and frustration may still lie ahead. An adopted change may be negated by a delay in its execution. It may be distorted, undermined or scaled down by executive participants, organizational processes, or by personnel responsible for the change tasks.[25]

Executive staff uncommitted or opposed to the adopted change may interfere with its implementation. They may simply become preoccupied with other issues, pay insufficient attention to necessary follow up, postpone implementation, or provide inadequate manpower and financial resources. After a worker influenced a local union local to adopt a steering committee for the purpose of improving programs to retirees, the director of the local changed the meeting time to discourage attendance. His ambivalence was quickly demonstrated:

> The day before the committee was to meet we learned the time had been changed to an hour earlier, and no notice had been sent out. We notified all members of the change and they managed to arrive on time. Their criticisms of the program created stress for the director and he cut the meeting short.

In this phase, an important strategy is to use informal and formal structures to reduce stress associated with the change. To maintain administrators' cooperation, the innovation has to be experienced as being in their self-interests. The worker in the above illustration came to this realization.

> I realized our failure to take the interests of the director into account. To repair the damage, I invited him to go out for lunch, and I discovered that he had long been interested in holding a reunion of the local's membership. I asked him to bring his idea to the steering committee, and I guaranteed my support.
>
> At the next meeting, I backed his suggestion for a reunion. My strategy was to join the adoption of the steering committee structure with his interest in planning a reunion. The Committee agreed to do the work, collect the necessary data, send out invitations, etc. He was pleased, participated throughout the meeting, and agreed to distribute our minutes to the membership.

The steering committee as an innovative structure was responsive to the director's interests. His stress was decreased and his involvement and commitment were increased. By identifying the influence effort with the director's plan, the viability and value of the steering committee was demonstrated. Acquiring and maintaining the commitment of key participants is essential. Their support provides the context and sets the tone for other participants' cooperation.

Organizational machinery may also create problems for implementation, moving too slowly to sustain previous agreements and maintain interests. People develop new interests and priorities; alliances and coalitions disintegrate over time. The worker seeks to keep the adopted change in people's minds and on the organizational agenda by having participants assigned specific tasks. If possible, he builds into the initial proposal a feedback system, such as regular progress reports to the staff to provide monitoring and accountability.[26] He identifies potential delay points in the decision-making structures, using all the strategies and skills discussed in the preparation, entry, and engagement phases to hasten the process.

Some organizational structures may be incompatible with particular innovations.[27] In changing from a traditional to an open classroom approach, for example, a school maintained its rigid temporal schedules and grading system. These structures undermined the desired change.[28] While some structures may be too rigid, others may be too flexible to support and integrate the innovation. Therefore, even before an adopted change is implemented, the worker attempts to make needed modifications in existing structures to increase the chances of success.

> As a new format for team meetings was adopted, I became aware that the time structure could cause frustration. At the first meeting under our new plan, I expressed my concern that there wouldn't be sufficient time to discuss patients scheduled for presentation at the end of the meeting. Staff agreed to extend rounds another fifteen minutes.
>
> The staff found this additional time beneficial. It eliminated the potential for stress arising from many designated tasks competing for time. Now each would receive sufficient attention.

The staff assigned responsibility for carrying out the innovation represent still another potential obstacle to implementation. Expectations may be unclear, or the staff may unwittingly distort the change objective. Those designated for the implementation tasks may lack the knowledge and skills for performing them. Others may lack sufficient motivation to commit themselves to the new way of doing things. Still others may be overwhelmed by the additional demands and suffer from competing time pressures. These situations arouse stress and may lead to poor performance. As a result, conflict and resistance are generated. Thus, from the outset, the worker concerns herself with the organizational participants who will be assigned responsibility for implementation. She is sensitive to and empathic with the anxiety aroused by changes in role expectations. She provides a clear conception of role requirements, and attempts to build into her implementation strategies the in-service training, consultation, and ongoing support necessary to assure interest, motivation, and skilled task performance. When knowledge, skills, and role clarity are present, the prognosis for successful implementation is markedly improved.

> The retirees are motivated to participate in the steering committee. Among them are some who are discontented with the present state of affairs. One retiree has already helped draft a proposal for several activity clubs. They are knowledgeable, skillful, and resourceful. They also have the time for work and follow up. These attributes were major factors in our successfully implementing the proposed steering committee.

Throughout the implementation phase, the worker must pay careful attention to task performers, needs for approval, and recognition. After a period of time, she evaluates the implementation process to determine whether the desired objective is being achieved and whether there are any unexpected negative consequences. She then initiates needed modifications before the innovation becomes standardized and formalized.[29]

When the change in an organization's purpose, structure, and procedures or services arrangements is no longer perceived as change, but as an integral part of its ongoing activities, the innovation has been *institutionalized*. It is ''frozen'' into the system.[30] Proof that an innovation has been integrated into the organization's structure is its remaining essentially the same even though some of the initial participants are no longer involved. To assure continuity, the worker lodges the innovation with a staff member of stable status, a person with "staying power."[31]

> Every six months the composition of the team changes when there is rotation of residents. In addition, the change of the resident-in-charge means that a new personality and work style is introduced. The head nurse is the key staff person in maintaining stability, so the structural change has been lodged with her. She orients new team members to the workings of the floor—the routines, procedures, etc—and will see that the change is carried over.

Other linking devices may be developed to ensure stability, such as inviting new staff to observe existing processes and procedures, or preparing a manual to formalize staff responsibilities. Whatever the method, the worker concerns herself with the institutionalization of the innovation.

Case Illustration

Hospital Inpatient Psychiatric Services

In this example, a social worker newly assigned to the inpatient psychiatric service of a large private voluntary hospital became increasingly aware of an organizational problem adversely affecting all patients. There was no structure for individualized planning for discharge. Patients were preoccupied with unrealistic plans. The medical leadership was disinterested in environmental resources beyond outpatient treatment. Family involvement was limited. Discharge decisions were made by the chief resident. Staff was alienated and appeared apathetic.

> As I began work on the ward, I gradually sensed the apathy, poor morale, and general inertia among the staff. In systems terms, there had been an increase in entropy following the loss of a beloved unit chief. The psychiatric unit became an "unattended system" and was proceeding

> toward disorder and disorganization, rather than order and organization. The staff (nurses, psychologist, residents, social worker) carried on in a mechanical fashion and had limited motivation to innovate because the present unit chief did not provide leadership. The attending psychiatrists, most of whom rely on drug therapy or electro-shock therapy, were responsible for many of the patients. They were poorly informed about institutional environmental resources and uninterested in considering them. The second social worker was interested in becoming a private therapist and was uninterested in family and environmental work. The patient population was uninformed about discharge. Their general passivity seemed to reflect the lack of activities that might have developed coping skills and a sense of competence.

After the problem had been identified, its existence and relevance documented, the worker specified two solutions or objectives: improving the quality of discharge planning, and involving patients in the discharge process. She selected two mechanisms to achieve those objectives. She planned to use team meetings to incorporate appropriate discharge planning into original treatment goals. This would involve other disciplines in ongoing discussion of discharge planning. Also, she envisioned a discharge-planning group that would provide a forum for patient-initiated involvement and planning. She planned to use a task oriented approach, involving patients in step-by-step activities. She assumed that successful task completion and a sense of mastery and competence could lead to successful discharge planning.

Next, the worker undertook an organizational analysis (chart 7.2). The force field analysis suggests moderate feasibility. It also points to strategies for mobilizing support for the change effort and neutralizing opposition to the change.

The worker was regarded as a motivated and competent social worker. She also had established numerous collegial friendships naturally and not as planned organizational strategies. Nevertheless, these interpersonal assets were opportune for organizational positioning.

> I made a conscious effort to be in the nurses' station more frequently, so that I could listen to and support many

Chart 7.2

Organizational Analysis

Agency: Inpatient psychiatric service

Problem: Inadequate discharge planning

Desired Outcome: Better discharge planning.

Means for Implementation: Incorporation of discharge planning into initial treatment plans; emphasis on discharge planning at unit conferences; a discharge planning group.

Supports	*Intensity*	*Intensity*	Opposition
	Environmental Forces		
The increasing hospital costs; demands for shorter hospital stays; and consequent need for alternative outpatient strategies and discharge planning.	High	High	Dearth of alternative rehabilitative facilities.
Limits on hospital stays set by Medicaid.	High	High	Medicaid's revocation of all passes from the hospital, delaying patient's readjustment into the community.
	Organizational Properties		
	Intensity	*Intensity*	
The setting's complexity (interdisciplinary diversity, staff turnover and competing interest groups).	High	High	The power is centralized in a few high status participants.
Limited formalized procedures, policies, etc.	High		
	Key Organizational Participants		
	Intensity	*Intensity*	
Unit chief's failure to provide leadership creates a vacuum and the opportunity for lower rank participant to innovate.	High	Low	Unit chief's failure to assume a leadership role leaves the staff with no motivation to innovate.
Respected occupational therapist supports need for discharge planning.	High	High	Dominance of "disease model" with emphasis on pathology and cure rather than on interaction between patient and situation.

Professional Influence			
Supports	Intensity	Intensity	Opposition
Staff's lack of knowledge about environmental and family work provides a void in which competence can be demonstrated.	High	Mod.	Low morale and assertiveness of other staff.
Staff's previous experience with a dynamic, innovative leader.	High	Mod.	Attending physician's lack of interest in environmental and family resources.
Potential for client involvement.	Mod.	Low	Other social worker's disdain for family and environmental work.
		Low	Passivity of patient population.
Worker's Position			
	Intensity	*Intensity*	
Worker's commitment to and competence in the ecological perspective: intraorganizational involvement; development and use of environmental resources; skilled in work with individuals, families, and groups.	High	Low	As the newest staff member, the worker lacks a historical perspective on the problem.
Relative automony provides leeway.	High		
Worker has developed informal, close relationships with staff, and is well regarded.	High		

> of their dissatisfactions with patient care (which often included their concerns about discharge plans).

Throughout the positioning process, she attempted to establish professional credibility and to assure its visibility.

> One case of which the unit chief particularly took notice, was that of a forty-five-year-old man admitted for a psychotic depression by a private physician. The pa-

> tient was to be given electro-shock therapy and then discharged to his eighty-year-old mother. Based on my interviews with family members, I pointed to vital factors which were being ignored in this plan. The unit chief was pleased with my assessment of strengths in the patient's family system, and my suggestions for situational experiences for the patient to generate a sense of mastery. He began to actively support my involvement with the attending physician.

These positioning behaviors (managing stress, demonstrating competence) led also to an informal alliance with two staff members, which became a force in team meetings.

> Since I had become friendly with the occupational therapist (a well-respected, influential member of the team), I often spoke to her about the problematic discharge process. We began to talk to an influential nurse, exchanging our dissatisfactions and suggestions. At team meetings, we supported and reinforced each other's efforts at discharge planning. As our alliance strengthened, we became more forceful in our statements regarding patients' strengths, family resources, and the need for systematic discharge planning. In time, the unit chief took sharper notice of this new vocal minority and began to support our views. The focus of team meetings became more attuned to "looking" at the patient, his family and community for strengths and resources which might be mobilized. Pressure from Medicaid also helped stimulate the consideration of alternatives to lengthy hospitalization. The unit chief and chief resident became almost miraculously, "resource" people, offering names of facilities with which they had had previous contact.

Before long each new patient's discharge plans were reviewed during the admission process. Team meetings focused on patients' social functioning within as well as outside the setting. Hence, discharge planning became an integral part of the service.

Having gathered the support of staff for more effective discharge planning, the worker undertook the second objective of establishing a predischarge group. She felt that formal sanction for a group service was needed, and she had to decide on who should present the proposal and where it should be made.

> While discharge planning was receiving more attention during team meetings, I had yet to present the idea of a discharge planning group. The other social worker was indifferent to discharge planning, and no one else seemed sufficiently enthusiastic about initiating programs that would entail more work. I, therefore, decided to present the idea myself.
>
> Several options were available concerning where the proposal should be made. I chose the team meeting, where at least one member of each discipline, and the unit chief and chief resident are present. My presentation could be more subtle there, in keeping with the informal tone of the team meeting. A formal presentation at a staff meeting, with more people present, might mobilize resistance to the idea.

The worker selected a joint problem-solving and educative approach. This would be less threatening than an adversarial approach. It would be conducive to discussion and probably successful in challenging the apathy and inertia which had maintained the primacy of the medical model. She decided to present the discharge-planning group as a means of strengthening present group services (the occupational therapist's creative activity groups and the residents' "insight" therapy groups) and as being responsive to staff concerns about patient passivity.

> The perfect moment arose at a team meeting, during which the unit chief and residents were discussing the positive effects of having patients take turns assuming chairperson roles at the community meetings. Knowing that establishing agreement with an audience on one topic promotes acceptance of a speaker's other positions, I added that the chairmanship provided experience for mastery that reinforces natural coping skills. The staff nodded

> in agreement, but then the issue submerged as they aired their mounting frustrations about patient passivity and unrealistic plans for discharge. I suggested there must be a way to help them plan for discharge by tapping the same coping skills and desire for mastery which the patients revealed as chairpersons. The team members were interested in this, and I raised the possibility of a "discharge planning group" on the floor. This might help the patients manage the tasks related to discharge, in the same reality-oriented fashion that they handle their presiding roles in the community meetings.The unit chief, residents, occupational therapists, and nurses were enthusiastic, and the discussion took a problem-solving turn. The usual apathy lessened, and several ideas were advanced. The unit chief suggested that one of the nurses, the occupational therapist, and I get together to plan the details.

The worker was skillful in connecting her plan to staff concerns about patient passivity and to their experience with patients' leadership capacities. Her idea of a discharge planning group appeared to emerge naturally in the discussion, and was not seen as an unwanted innovation. Her timing was on the mark.

In the later subcommittee meeting, the time, place, and format for the discharge planning group were determined. At the subsequent team meeting, the plan was approved. In order to institutionalize the service, two workers, one assuming the primary leadership role and the other a secondary one, staffed the discharge group. In the next group, the secondary leader would assume primary responsibility and would "break in" the next assigned worker. Through rotation, each worker would be responsible in providing the service with a colleague. In this way, the group would be institutionalized; the staff would learn from each other, and would hold each other accountable for the important service.

Summary

The interplay of societal, professional, and bureaucratic forces often creates practices which serve vested interests at the expense of client interests. Generally, clients' problems with organizations fall into three areas: the agency's definition of its purpose and services; the structures and procedures used to coordinate and integrate organizational operations; and service provision.

How an agency defines its purpose and service may create problems for clients. When agencies define their boundaries rigidly, people become lost in the service network, not eligible for services anywhere. In contrast, when agencies' boundaries are ambiguous, people fall "between the cracks," because no agency is responsible for their service needs. Agency structures and procedures may create unintended problems for clients. A rigid authority structure stifles staff initiative and creativity in responding to need. In contrast, an authority structure may delegate too much decision-making, so that the staff confronts limited leadership and accountability. Agency policies may also be too formal or not formal enough. Finally, service provision may be inadequate, or inaccessible—or available, but its methods and styles discourage its use.

When organizational processes become problematic, the social worker has a critical function: to seek modification of the unresponsive practices, procedures and programs. Influencing the employing organization involves the phases of preparation, initial organizational analysis, implementation, and institutionalization.

Preparation for influencing the organization begins with the identification of a problem. Specification and documentation of where and how the problem manifests itself is achieved through systematic observation, formal data collection, and informal conversations. The worker considers alternative solutions and the specific means through which each might be achieved. Having tentatively identified and documented an organizational problem, selected an objective and various means for achieving it, the worker undertakes a formal organizational analysis to determine feasibility. Key environmental, organizational, and interpersonal forces are identified, and their likely impact on the proposed change is evaluated. The worker also evaluates his own position in the organization and his personal and structural resources for influence. Through analysis of organizational forces, the worker determines whether the objective and means are feasible. More data may be required, the problem may need to be redefined, or the means for implementing the change effort may need to be altered to enhance feasibility. The worker next develops an organizational climate receptive to the change effort. He undertakes entry or positioning tasks to prepare the system. He may need to increase his informal prestige and respect based on professional competence and involvement in the interpersonal network. He may need to bring the problem to the participants' consciousness by increasing its visibility and consequences. Some stress has to be experienced by organizational participants before there can be motivation to examine and modify dysfunctional practices and procedures.

Before formal introduction of the identified problem and/or proposed solution, the worker must select a general engagement strategy from among demonstration, collaboration, persuasion, and conflict management. In demonstration, the problem and proposed change is not explicitly discussed; the desired outcome is displayed through action. This is a particularly effective strategy for problems associated with professional functioning and programmatic gaps. In collaboration, the problem is identified and key participants are involved in exploring and developing solutions. This is an effective strategy in relatively open organizations where goal consensus exists and there is either equity in resources distribution, or the presence of close interpersonal relationships. In persuasion, successive levels of persistence, argument, and bargaining are used. This is most appropriate in situations where there is a lack of consensus and disparity in power. In conflict management, more extreme forms of pressure are applied. It is rarely used by low ranking participants because of potential reprisals. At the same time, serious organizational problems do require professional commitment to adversarial action in the face of marked interference with client's rights and needs.

After a proposal for change has been accepted, it still needs to be put into action. Initial acceptance does not insure implementation. An adopted change may be delayed, distorted, undermined, or scaled down by executive participants, organizational processes, or by staff responsible for the change tasks. Acquiring and maintaining the commitment of executive participants is essential. The worker needs to connect the change effort with their self-interests. Similarly, he attempts to make necessary modifications in existing organizational structures to increase the innovation's chance of success. From the outset, he also concerns himself with the primary task performers, being sensitive to and empathic with the anxiety aroused by new role demands and expectations. He attempts to provide essential supports to assure adequate role clarity and skills.

When the change in an organization's purposes, structures, procedures or service arrangements is no longer perceived as change, the innovation has been institutionalized. To assure continuity, the worker lodges the innovation with a "stable" status, and develops linking devices for support, such as a manual of procedures.

Notes

1. In recognition of the importance of this broadened function, the Columbia University School of Social Work devotes its required fourth semester practice course to this subject. Course teachers met during 1975–76 to develop content and teaching materials. Our own ideas have been influenced and shaped by these discussions, and we acknowledge the contributions to our thinking made by our colleagues, Professors George Brager, Rosalyn Chernesky, Mary Goldson, Agnes Louard, Carol Meyer, and Irving Miller.

2. We recognize, in particular, the contribution of Professor George Brager. He helped us with relevant literature, and generously shared his ideas.

3. For elaboration, see Raymond F. Callahan, *Education and the Cult of Efficiency* (Chicago: University of Chicago Press, 1962).

4. See Andrew Billingsley, "Bureaucratic and Professional Orientation Patterns in Social Casework," *Social Service Review* (December 1964), 38(4):400–7; Irwin Epstein, "Professional Role Orientations and Conflict Strategies," *Social Work* (October 1970), 5(5):87–92; Henry Wasserman, "The Professional Social Worker in a Bureaucracy," *Social Work* (January 1971), 16(1):89–96.

5. While bureaucratic requirements often conflict with professional requirements, professional interests such as diagnostic classification and management are quite congenial with bureaucratic interests. For discussion of the differences and similarities between professions and bureaucracies, see Peter N. Blau and W. Richard Scott, *Formal Organizations* (San Francisco: Charles, 1962), pp. 60–74; Eugene Litwak, "Models of Bureaucracy which Permit Conflict," *American Journal of Sociology* (September 1961), 67:177–84.

6. For discussions of issues and problems in service provision, see Carel Germain, "An Ecological Perspective on Social Work Practice in Health care," *Social Work in Health Care* (Fall 1977), 3(4):67–76; Alvin Gouldner, "The Secrets of Organizations," *Social Welfare Forum* (New York: Columbia University Press, 1963), pp. 161–67; Shirley Kaufman, "Sex Discrimination in Family Agencies," *Social Work* (November 1977), 22(6):461–65; Robert Scott, "The Selection of Clients by Social Welfare Agencies," in Yeheskel Hasenfeld and Richard English, eds., *Human Service Organizations* (Ann Arbor: University of Michigan Press, 1974), pp. 485–98; Robert D. Vinter, "The Social Structure of Service", in Alfred J. Kahn,

ed., *Issues in American Social Work* (New York: Columbia University Press, 1959), pp. 242–67.

7. McGowan identifies various sanctions for this broader conception of professional function: legal, ethical codes, and client pressures. Brenda G. McGowan, "Strategies in Bureaucracies," in Judith Mearing, ed., *Working for Children: Ethical Issues Beyond Professional Guidelines* (San Francisco: Jossey-Bass, 1978), pp. 155–80.

8. Lewin characterized the status quo in any social system as the balanced result of countervailing forces driving toward and against change. A "force-field analysis" helps the practitioner to identify and visualize the specific forces promoting and resisting change. Kurt Lewin, "Group Decisions and Social Change," Eleanor E. Maccoby, Theodore R. Newcomb, and Eugene L. Hartley, eds., *Readings in Social Psychology* (New York: Holt, Rinehart & Winston, 1952), pp. 207–11.

9. Abels applies "force-field analysis" to group supervision. Paul Abels, "Group Supervision of Students and Staff," in Florence Whitman Kaslow, ed., *Supervision, Consultation, and Staff Training in the Helping Professions* (San Francisco: Jossey-Bass, 1977), pp. 195–98; Brager and Holloway apply "force-field analysis" to organizational change. George Brager and Stephen Holloway, *Changing Human Service Organizations: Politics and Practice* (San Francisco: Free Press, 1978), pp. 107–8; Jenkins uses it to assess a school setting. David Jenkins, "Force Field Analysis Applied to a School Situation," in W. Bennis, K. Benne, and R. Chinn, eds., *The Planning of Change* (New York: Holt, Rinehart & Winston, 1962), pp. 238–44.

10. Blau and Scott, *Formal Organizations*, pp. 59–86.

11. Jerald Hage and Michael Aikens, *Social Change in Complex Organizations*. (New York: Random House, 1970), pp. 37–40.

12. For elaboration, see Brager and Holloway, *Changing Human Service Organizations*, pp. 80–103.

13. *Ibid.*, pp. 157–76.

14. John Wax, "Power Theory and Institutional Change," *Social Service Review* (September 1971), p. 45:277–80.

15. Dalton identifies "tension or a felt need for change" as one of the most important conditions for successful innovation. Gene Dalton, "Influence and Organizational Change," in G. Dalton, P. Lawrence, and L. Greiner, eds., *Organizational Change and Development* (Homewood, Ill.: Richard D. Irwin and Dorsey Press, 1970), p. 234.

16. For an insightful presentation of hypothesis and strategies in positioning oneself in an organization, see David Mechanic, "Sources of Power of Lower Participants in Complex Organizations," in W. Cooper, H. Leavitt and M. Shelly II, eds., *New Perspectives in Organizational Research* (New York: Wiley, 1964), pp. 136–49.

17. Brager and Holloway specify three broad "tactics": collaboration, campaign, and contest: Brager and Holloway, *Changing Human Service Organizations*, pp. 129–53. Morris and Binstock conceptualize six "pathways of influence"—obligation, friendship, rational persuasion, selling, coercion, and inducement: Robert

Morris and Robert Binstock, *Feasible Planning for Social Change* (New York: Columbia University Press, 1966), pp. 116–27. Patti and Resnick describe two central strategies—collaborative and adversarial: Rino J. Patti and Herman Resnick, "Changing the Agency from Within," *Social Work* (July 1972), 17(7):48–57.

18. Brager and Holloway, *Changing Human Service Organizations,* pp. 131–32.

19. Marvin Karlins and Herbert I. Abelson, *Persuasion: How Opinions and Attitudes Are Changed* (New York: Springer, 1970), pp. 24–6.

20. *Ibid.,* p. 22.

21. The worker's organizational credibility is essential to effective persuasion. Carl I. Houland and Walter Weiss, "The Influence of Source Credibility or Communication Effectiveness," *Public Opinion Quarterly,* (Winter 1951–52), 15:635–50.

22. For further discussion of persuasion and bargaining, see George Brager and Harry Specht, *Community Organizing* (New York: Columbia University Press, 1973), pp. 300–34.

23. Lewis Coser, *The Functions of Social Conflict* (New York: Free Press, 1956), pp. 133–34; Kenneth Boulding, *Conflict and Defense* (New York: Harper & Row, 1963), pp. 145–88.

24. For further discussion of conflict tactics, see Saul D. Alinsky, *Rules for Radicals* (New York: Random House, 1971); Jay Haley, *The Power Tactics of Jesus Christ* (New York: Grossman, 1969).

25. For a discussion of barriers to implementation and acceptance of an innovation, see Neal Gross, J. Giacquinta, and M. Bernstein, *Implementing Organizational Innovations* (New York: Basic Books, 1971), pp. 122–48.

26. Gerald Zaltman, Robert Duncan, Jonny Holbeck, *Innovations and Organizations* (New York: Wiley, 1973), pp. 70–78.

27. Some organizational features that promote acceptance of innovation may hinder its implementation. Organizations with low formalization, for example, tend to encourage innovation, but also tend to hinder routinization.

28. Gross, *Implementing.*

29. For more thorough discussion of implementation, see Jeffrey Pressman and Aaron Wildavsky, *Implementation* (Berkeley: University of California Press, 1973), pp. 87–124.

30. Kurt Lewin, *Field Theory in Social Science* (New York: Harper & Row, 1951).

31. Robert Pruger, "The Good Bureaucrat," *Social Work* (July 1973), 18:76–83.

8

Social Work Practice and Its Historical Traditions

THE INTEGRATIVE METHOD of the life model of practice is both an outcome of historical trends and a response to current pressures within the profession. New or emerging forms of practice need to be understood in the light of professional traditions that have spurred their development. They need to be understood also in the light of demands placed upon the profession by external forces in its environment and by internal forces within the profession. Both past and present shape the characteristics of practice. In this chapter, we trace themes and trends in the historical development in the United States of social work's practice purposes and methods. We pay particular attention to the historical dialectics of cause–function (social action–clinical treatment) and generalist–specialist practice. These historical dialectics help to explain the existence and nature of contemporary practice issues and efforts to integrate divergent traditions.

Early Societal and Professional Themes

Occupational Forerunners

The process of divergence began in the United States when two streams of thought appeared in the nineteenth-century arena of social welfare, then called "charities and corrections." One was more interested in theory and the other in methods of help. Both streams arose out of the social events, requirements, and ideologies of the times. Profound transformation in the social order had taken place in the years after the Civil War. Change was everywhere: in the westward push by wagon and later by rail; in the migration from farms to the towns and cities; in the movement of vast tides of immigrants away from old world oppressions and famines to new world freedoms and opportunities; in the expansions of knowledge, science, and technology; in the development of graduate education and increasing specialization and professionalization in the occupational structure. Greatest of all, perhaps, were the changes in values and norms as the nation shifted from an agrarian to an industrialized, urbanized society. To most citizens, these movements, changes, and expansions seemed to offer unlimited opportunities for all who wished to respond to them. In actuality, the twin forces of industrialization and urbanization, with which these movements and expansions were interdependent, were accompanied by severe social disorganization. Industrialization (as well as rationalization and bureaucratization of production) led to the concentration of wealth and power and the growing alienation of labor. Persistent poverty was aggravated by cyclical depressions. Crowded urban slums and poor rural areas were characterized by wretched housing, inadequate schools, and oppressive work arrangements. The Government itself favored and was, in fact, in thrall to the nation's business interests. The principle of laissez-faire was for the poor; the principle of free enterprise advanced the interests of the rich and the powerful; and the Supreme Court upheld property rights at the expense of human rights.

After the Civil War, more and more of society's "dependent classes"—its paupers, insane, and criminal groups—came under the aegis of state administration. Increasingly, their public care and control moved from a single locus of responsibility in the village overseer and the local almshouse to state boards of charities, state insane asylums, and prisons. Child-saving agencies and voluntary associations for relieving the plight of the poor appeared in the private arena. A number of persons who were engaged in such public or private work joined with a group of New England intellectuals, interested in the new social science movement in England, to organize the American Social Science Association (ASSA) in 1865. Soon after the initial meetings, however, conflicting concerns overshadowed their mutual interests.

The interest of the ASSA intellectuals lay in developing knowledge about the operations of the social order so that social conditions could be changed. By contrast, the interest of those directly engaged in the care and control of society's "misfits" lay in developing the best methods for such control, care, and containment. The latter practical group considered their pressing and present concerns were overlooked by the emphasis of the intellectuals on theory development geared to achieving an uncertain gain in an unknown future. In 1874, the practice people withdrew from the ASSA and established the Conference of Charities (CC) which, in 1879, became the National Conference of Charities and Corrections (NCCC), and which is now known as the National Conference on Social Welfare (NCSW).[1] Temporarily, at least during the 1880's, the tension between theory of social causation and methodological concerns receded; exchanging experiences in the use of different methods received primary attention. Until journals and other organizations developed, the NCCC was the principal forum for this kind of exchange.

Ideologically, the dialectical development in social work practice was more complex. Several currents of conflicting ideas appeared, and even within each current there was little unanimity of opinion. One stream of ideas was associated with the Poor Law philosophy of the colonial and antebellum periods. It included, for example, the principle of less-eligibility and the settlement laws, which themselves had earlier roots in England and Europe. This stream was often accompanied by a concern that charity might lead the needy into pauperism by weakening their moral fiber. The Puritan Ethic, which viewed dependency as the consequence of sin, and the Calvinistic emphases on work and on individualism fortified by the frontier spirit, were congruent with a repressive stance. It was an ambivalent stance, however, since there were strong threads of piety involved, especially in attitudes toward the poor. One such thread was the humane concern for the suffering of others, as in the parable of the Good Samaritan. Another and perhaps stronger thread was the promise of salvation through the giving of alms. In this view, the poor existed so the rich might give to them, receive grace, and enter the kingdom of heaven.

Another ideological current was a growing interest in science and its promise of unlimited progress through knowledge and technology. Indeed, it was this interest coupled with idealistic reformism that had led to the establishment of the ASSA. If physical laws governed the universe with such magnificent precision as Newton and others had shown, the argument ran, then laws governing society and the interaction of human beings might also be discovered. It seemed to ASSA intellectuals, and later to some groups within the NCCC, that such laws could then be used to create a better society. Many who held this conviction appeared also to believe that environmental causes were more salient than personal waywardness in most forms of human distress. Thus, the conflict between theoretical and practical interests was also related to tensions around the nature of causality which developed in the 1880's and continued in the decades that followed. In general, the theoreticians believed causality lay in the environment, while the methodologists believed causality was to be found in the wickedness, shiftlessness, and weakness of individuals.

Connected to the interest in science, yet ultimately nonscientific in outlook, was the rise of Social Darwinism that applied Darwin's ideas about the survival of the fittest to societal processes. Social Darwinism provided a rationalization for the exploitation of the powerless by the powerful. Political thought, interacting with capitalistic developments, became increasingly dominated by conservatism and its emphasis on economic freedom and the sanctity of private property. Political, philosophical, religious, and pseudo-scientific ideas thus combined to help create a point of view in society that opposed environmental reform.

Within this matrix of social ideas and events, the newly formed occupational group, exemplified by the NCCC, was joined in the late 1880s by two more groups. These were the charity organization societies that began in the United States in 1887 (Buffalo), and the neighborhood settlements that began in 1886 (Neighborhood Guild of New York City). Both appeared almost simultaneously, and each was imbued with ideas and structures that originated in Victorian England. Both spread rapidly around the country and, although the two movements took somewhat different ideological positions and different practice outlooks, they possessed important similarities. Both appealed to young, upper- and middle-class, well-educated idealists of the day, and most especially to young women. Higher education for women had only just begun on any recognizable scale and a new group of young women students and graduates were eager to be of service. Both they and the young men at the new graduate schools, who also joined both movements, sought to have an impact on the social problems increasingly visible in the 1880s and 1890s. The young women were also looking for ways to become financially independent.

Both movements had a strong religious cast, influenced by the ministry of the social gospel. Many charity organization society (COS) secretaries, especially in the early years, and several settlement head-residents were ministers. Most were Protestants, but later there were also Catholic and Jewish settlements, as well as sectarian charitable associations. Deeply committed to serving others, both the COS and the settlement groups believed they had found the structure that would solve the grave social problems of their era. Despite their similarities, however, the differences between the two movements were to have a profound effect on the dialectical development of social work practice.

The Settlement Movement

To the founders of the settlements, the sources of most urban misery lay in the environment. To live among the poor, sharing their joys and sorrows, their struggles and toil, was to be a good neighbor. The "settlers," as they called themselves, asserted that their work was not charity but good neighboring, and so they worked to provide such amenities as clubs for boys and girls, classes for adults, and summer experiences in the country for children and adults. For the settlers, conflict between the classes stemmed from a lack of understanding each other, and thus, they needed to relate to each other. Such interaction between the poor and the settlers would improve the former, and through the "gentle attrition of interaction," people would begin to understand each other and resolve their conflicts.

The settlers' devotion to democratic values and a liberal social philosophy went hand-in-hand with an abhorrence of anything that smacked of charity and what the settlers saw as charity workers' parsimoniousness in the face of need. In times of economic depression, neighboring included creating work projects for workmen who had lost their jobs and had no way to provide for their families. The required investigation and verification of need, however, was a repugnant function to the settlers, and they considered it appropriate only in times of great emergency.

The settlers soon concluded that their well-intentioned efforts to improve the quality of life for their working-class neighbors were minimally effective in reducing the hardships imposed by the nature of the physical and social environments. They became intensely aware of tenement conditions, lack of sanitation, poor schools, inadequate play space, long working hours in factories and sweated industries, child labor, and the many obstacles faced by immigrant populations in their attempts to adapt to their new environment. The interests of the settlers broadened to include the painstaking collection of data and careful social research to support their legislative activities on behalf of environmental reforms. Increasingly, settlement residents aligned themselves with the Women's Trade Union League. They supported the strikes of organized labor. They were instrumental in forming the consumer movement that worked to improve working conditions through the use of the boycott. They played a significant role in the early woman movement. They worked for sanitation, tenement reform, the playground movement, and child labor legislation.[2] They were in the vanguard of social reform all during the Progressive Era until its end in World War I. Many worked for the unpopular peace movement of the time, and Jane Addams of Hull House, severely criticized during the war, received the Nobel Peace Prize many years later in 1931 for those very efforts.

From the beginning, the settlers were affiliated with colleges and universities, and sometimes were based in them. Graham Taylor of the Chicago Commons, with the help of Jane Addams and others from Hull House, established the Chicago School of Civics and Philanthropy which, in 1920, became the University of Chicago's School of Social Service Administration. Settlement connections to the social scientists of the day were strong. John Dewey and his friend and colleague, James Tufts,[3] were frequent visitors at Hull House, and Jane Addams often referred to their influence. It appears to have been a reciprocal influence since Dewey, upon joining the Columbia University faculty, continued his settlement affiliation at the University Settlement in New York City. Dewey's philosophy of pragmatism, his interest in the experimentalism of science and the instrumentalism of ideas, reintroduced humanistic values into the materialism of the times and profoundly influenced the settlement leaders. Other social scientists lived and worked in the settlements around the country to gain experience and to collect social data concerning comn the disease sense, but was rather to be a service offered in terms of agency function.[6] They based many of their ideas on the psychoanalytic concepts of Otto Rank who himself had broken away from Freud. They added the concept of agency function as the limiting aspect against which clients tested their ability to ask for and to use help. The term "functional" came to be applied to the new school of asework thought to distinguish it from the traditional or "diagnostic" school of casework thought. Throughout the 1940s the conflict aged between the two schools, and began to subside only in the late 950s. Despite the uneasy strains that persisted over the two decades, nany practitioners today acknowledge the incorporation of important deas from the functional school into the mainstream of practice. These include ideas about relationship, uses of time and fees, and the nfluence of the agency setting on social work practice. Others assert hat both schools of thought were guilty of overemphasizing method ithin a psychological orientation that led caseworkers away from ocial concerns. The controversy was supplanted by the pressing ocial issues of the 1960s and 1970s, including civil rights, the Vietam War, and the war on poverty, all of which threatened the role of asework in the profession and in society.

A significant feature of the casework method was its having een cast in a medical metaphor.[7] As early as the 1880s, charity orkers, speaking in the medical idiom, referred to dependency as a social disease" to be cured by "social physicians" prescribing emedies on the basis of a "diagnosis" of individual need. The gradl institutionalization of the metaphor that occurred in the 1920s, 30s, and 1940s reinforced a preoccupation with internal processes that diagnosis and treatment tended to focus on the person while vironmental forces—seemingly fixed and intractable—receded fur-r into the background. Even when Hamilton introduced a more listic view of the person-in-situation,[8] most caseworkers and case-rk agencies found it difficult to move beyond a vague and global nception of environmental manipulation limited to foster care, rk with collaterals, and concrete services. As important and essen- as social provision was, it did not lead to a critical examination of tures in the environment that were associated with the problems eworkers "treated."

In their long effort to perfect the method, caseworkers succeeded

munity and neighborhood problems. Still others came as guests to conduct classes for the residents and for the neighbors.

Through their participation in the NCSW (Jane Addams, in 1910, became the first woman to be president in the organization's 36-year history), the settlers exerted influence on the occupational group that was beginning to think of its calling as social work. Their interest in the environment as a causal factor in human distress, their alliance with social science as the means for understanding environmental relations, and their commitment to social reform were important aspects of the discussions and debates in the forum of NCSW through the 1890s and until World War I. With the end of the Progressive Era, the settlement movement lost its momentum. Although some reforms were achieved after the war, the settlers were never again as powerful in the occupational circle; they remained outside the mainstream of practice and theory developments.

The Charity Organization Movement

The charity organization societies, whose philosophy was characterized by the watchword "scientific philanthropy," aimed for the rational, efficient distribution of alms, modeled after the division of labor and other methods of the new capitalistic bureaucracies. This objective was to be achieved by organizing the various charitable organizations within a community in order to eliminate duplication and fraud. Methods were designed to separate the unworthy from the worthy poor, and included investigation and verification of need, registration, classification, conferencing, and written records. The unworthy poor were deemed to be the responsibility of public indoor (institutional) relief, while the worthy poor (victims of circumstance, such as widows with children) were considered deserving of outdoor aid (in their own homes) provided by privately sponsored charitable agencies.[4]

Because there was constant apprehension that alms might destroy the individual's drive toward independence, an important additional component of the COS method was the "friendly visitor." Where possible, help was to be "not alms but a friend," or when alms were needed, such help would be given in conjunction with the services of the friendly visitor. Possessing middle- and upper-class virtues, the visitor would be able to bring to the poor an example toward which they could aspire. Like the settlement residents, the friendly visitors were volunteers, and their work was directed by a paid agent or secretary. Some university faculty were affiliated with COS's, seeing them as laboratories for the development of sociological knowledge, and some college and university students served as friendly visitors. The emphasis within the COS movement, however, was on developing the most effective methods of rehabilitating the poor one-by-one, while relatively little attention was given to uncovering environmental causes of poverty. Nevertheless, some COS leaders were deeply concerned about environmental issues, just as some settlers cooperated with the charitable societies and even served as friendly visitors.

When the need for advanced training was recognized by charity workers as a way to increase the effectiveness of their method and to gain professional status, the New York City COS created the first school of philanthropy in 1898, which later became the New York School of Social Work, and later still, the Columbia University School of Social Work. In contrast to the schools established by settlements, many COS-sponsored schools resisted university affiliation. During the early years, the East Coast schools furnished an apprentice-type training in agencies, provided by agency personnel and supplemented by class work, rather than a university-based education drawing upon social philosophy and social science, as in the schools founded by settlement leaders. The resistance to becoming involved in university education stemmed, in part, from the fear that an emphasis on theory would blunt the visitors' natural warmth and helpfulness. Eventually, however, the apprenticeship model was incorporated by all schools as the field work component in graduate education. Similarly, all schools eventually became affiliated with universities, since this offered the surest avenue to professional status. Theory and practice then became blended in the graduate school, although greater emphasis tended to remain on method and less on theory and social philosophy.

Professionalization

The Casework Method

By 1895 the principles of scientific philanthropy had become organized into what was called the casework method, and were further

codified by Mary Richmond's *Social Diagnosis,* publish
During the first two decades of the twentieth century,
spread from the COS's (soon to be known as family agen
pital social service departments, child-placing agencies
social work field, court clinics, and state mental hospital
friendly visitors had been superseded by paid worker
eager to achieve professional status. COS staffs were j
aspiration by the caseworkers in psychiatric and gene
who were themselves achieving some measure of status
laboration with physicians. During World War I, the
the casework method for work with soldiers' families
strated that it could be applied above the poverty line
problems in family life. In 1915, the NCCC was shock
by Abraham Flexner, in an invitational address, that so
not a profession, since its liaison function between i
other professions was not a professional function.[5] Th
is particularly ironic in the light of the increasing impor
to social work's mediating function in the dehumaniz
sonalized organizational world of the 1970's.

Flexner also asserted that social work did not h
transmissible method which would qualify it as a prof
next fifty years, the casework segment of the prof
energy and thought to developing such a method, an
importance of its unique mediating function. The qu
was aided by knowledge gained in experience in the
and child guidance movements of the 1920s. It was
Virginia Robinson's *A Changing Psychology in So*
published in 1930, and was further advanced by the
tributions from psychoanalysis. During the Great
former COS's, now becoming known as family agen
a change in function by which relief-giving was tr
new public programs. The private agencies were thu
the opportunity to experiment with the new ps
oriented procedures. This freedom also supported t
method, especially a method focused on individual c

Beginning in the mid-thirties, a new controvers
the casework segment, one that also supported the pr
method. Faculty at the University of Pennsylvania
Work constructed a view of casework which was nc

in developing an individualizing service that subscribed to the canons of logical thought and drew upon knowledge and values as a base for the method. They struggled to maintain an openness to new ideas in order to develop greater effectiveness. What appeared to be missing for the casework method, however, was a conceptualization of the environment that would take into account its complexity, and from which interventive measures could be derived. This fact, together with the infusion of psychoanalytic theory, a tendency to model the style and trappings of practice on the psychoanalytic-psychotherapist practitioner, and the prestige associated with psychiatric casework, assured the continuation of the medical metaphor of diagnosis and treatment.[9]

The transition from an earlier psychoanalytic emphasis on drives and defenses to an emphasis in the 1950s on the adaptive functions of the ego helped to encourage greater interest in environmental interactions. Similarly, additions to the knowledge base from the social sciences in the 1950s and from general systems theory in the 1960s expanded the caseworker's diagnostic understanding to include the dynamic environment. These additions did little, however, to change the focus of treatment, because diagnosis continued to locate problems mainly within the person.[10] Important exceptions to this obfuscation of the environment included the developments of milieu therapy, crisis intervention, and family work in the 1960s and 1970s. Each of these approaches, to differing degrees, located problems in interactional and external factors.

The Group Work Method

During the 1920s, social group work emerged from the settlement, recreation, and progressive education movements. From the settlements, the group work method derived its institutional base. Some early group work leaders had been settlement residents and were influenced by the settlers' devotion to the base of democratic groups for the development of responsible citizenship, mutual aid, and collective action. They were experienced and skillful in leading groups for children and for adults.

From the recreational movement, social group work gained its interest in the value of play and activities. Many early group workers had been associated with youth-serving organizations, the camping movement, and community centers. Group workers were influenced by organized recreation as a means for building character. They believed that participation in leisure-time group activities leads to personal development and to the acquisition of desired social attitudes and values.

From the progressive education movement, group work acquired a philosophic base. Dewey had stressed that democratic citizenship was best assured through democratically oriented classrooms, in which the group experience was used to help pupils learn and discover together. To live democracy represented the most effective means for learning democracy.[11] Creative group life in the schools could lead to responsible citizenship on which the future of democracy depends.[12]

The first group work curriculum in a school of social work was introduced at Western Reserve University in 1927, although a group work course had been offered there since 1923. By the 1930s, the recreational and educational components of group work practice had been clearly identified, and practitioners from various fields were invited into the American Association for the Study of Group Work (AASGW), founded in 1936. Over the next two decades, until the mid-fifties, group workers maintained their commitments to the reciprocity between individual satisfaction and the social good, and to the positive impact of group experience upon both the individual and society.[13] Coming as they did from the settlements, recreation settings, and the progressive education movement, they conceived group work functions as including: the development of personality to its greatest capacity; the fostering of creative self-expression; the building of character; and the improvement of interpersonal skills. For them, group work functions also included the development of cultural and ethnic contributions; the teaching of democratic values; the support of active and mature participation in community life; the mobilizing of neighborhoods for social reform; and the preservation of ethical and middle-class values. This conception of group work functions has been termed the "social goals" model of group work.[14]

The need for clarity of purpose and for the development of systematic knowledge led to the establishment of the American Association of Group Workers (AAGW) in 1946. Although group workers had initially resisted identification with any one discipline, they now began to move closer to the social work profession. In 1956, AAGW was incorporated into the National Association of Social Workers. In the process, group work gained greater professional acceptance and legitimacy.

The practice committee of the group work section of the NASW assumed responsibility in 1959 for developing new working definitions of social group work practice. The search for a unifying statement of professional function may have been, in part, a response to McCarthyism and the hostile political environment. The prevalence of a repressive philosophy and mood undermined group work's assumptions and aspirations. An emerging view of groups as conspiratorial and subversive, rather than as microcosms of democratic society, stripped away the social goals ideology. Because method was still undeveloped, social group workers were now left without a theoretical and philosophical base. They turned inward to self-evaluation and professionalization, and they turned away from the social action and social reform traditions.

Unable to agree on a common, precise definition of social group work's purpose and function, the practice committee invited several group workers to offer their frames of reference. In his remedial model, Robert Vinter moved toward the more developed case work paradigm of social study, diagnosis and treatment.[15] Through similar processes, individual group members having problems in social functioning were to be treated within the group context. The group itself possessed no collective function, and especially not one of social action. As casework agencies and casework departments became increasingly interested in group approaches, the model's conception of group work function found increased support. In its move away from group work's historic commitment to developmental services and to social causes, however, this model placed the burden of change upon the individual. The environment received little or no attention.

William Schwartz shared Vinter's commitment to the development of a professional methodology. Rather than moving toward casework's medical metaphor, however, he proposed a systemic and generic conception of social work function.[16] While maintaining the vision and, at times, the romanticism of the social goals model, Schwartz developed an interactionist, reciprocal conception of group work in which the worker maintains a dual focus on the individual and the social system (the group, the agency).

Both the social goals and reciprocal models viewed the group as having the potential for mutual aid. In the reciprocal model's formulation the worker is to have no preconceived goals or "hidden agenda," but is expected to "mediate" between agency services and client needs. The relationship between the individual and society is viewed as symbiotic, even though the mutual need may, at times, be unrecognized or ambivalent. The worker's function is to mediate between the individual and the group, between the group and the agency. The symbiotic conception, however, tends to becloud the power inequities in social structures, and thus gives insufficient attention to methods of influencing organizations.

In spite of the limitations noted above, both models made important contributions to the development of the group work method and to the increased use of group workers in various settings. In the late 1960s and 1970s, spin-offs and accretions to both models appeared. Theorists associated with the remedial model incorporated behavioral therapy into their practice.[17] Emanuel Tropp, whose ideas resemble the interactionist–reciprocal model, developed a humanistic, developmental perspective on group work practice. His approach presents a clear alignment with life transitions and their associated tasks.[18]

The realities of practice have pushed group work to synthesize and integrate its major models. Distinguishing among them has become increasingly difficult both in practice and in school curricula.[19]

The Community Organization Method

While casework as a method originated in the COS, and group work as a method originated in the settlements, community organization as a social work practice method derived some of its characteristics from both the COS and the settlements. The last of the three practice methods to be recognized, community organization took some of its tasks from the COS interest in pioneering new services to meet needs, coordinating existing services, and establishing central informational and statistical services for all agencies. This inheritance was a primary emphasis in the decades between 1910 and 1930, when community organization sought an institutional base in the developing community chests and councils.

The characteristic settlement emphasis on neighborhood services also persisted in the community organizers' interest in developing, expanding, and coordinating services. The settlement interest in social action and social reform, however, was missing in the early development of community organization, perhaps because of the reactionary climate after World War I and the dominant emphasis on rugged individualism within the culture. Instead of challenging institutions, the community organizer coordinated agencies and won the support of business interests in the community. Any effort to encourage citizens to band together in attacking social problems was experienced by the local political structure as threatening, and was quickly defeated.[20]

Although the period of the 1930s through the 1950s was characterized by the chaos of depression, World War II , and post-war recovery, community organization remained largely unchanged. The social action and social protest movements of the 1930s took place outside of community organization, which maintained its involvement in chests and councils and in the newly developing United Funds. The period did see, however, the beginnings of theoretical development. Even here, the emphases were chiefly on the adjustment between social resources and social welfare needs,[21] intergroup processes within the councils themselves,[22] and such generic social work features in community organization as problem-solving and various helping roles utilized in working with committees and council groups.[23] The lack of a social change perspective and a focus on process instead of on goals meant that issues of power and controversy were not addressed or recognized.[24]

Modern community organization practice emerged in the 1960s and 1970s. The impact of massive poverty existing side-by-side with affluence, the persistence of social pathologies despite the advances in knowledge, and the civil rights movements influenced community organization beyond anything experienced by casework or group work. Community organization shifted from its role and function of coordinating services to a concern with social problems as the targets of its intervention. The earlier preoccupation with process gave way to an emphasis on goals related to social change.[25] As this occurred, community organization began to resemble the concern with social goals that characterized the earliest group work practice as it emanated from the settlements. Like the social goals model of group work, community organization lacked a professional knowledge base and a practice method to implement its aspirations for social change.

By the early 1970s, however, new social science theories supported the shift from cooperation and coordination to intervention into various societal, bureaucratically organized systems on behalf of the disadvantaged segment of the community. Brager and Specht published the first formulation of the theory and practice of community organization in its modern form.[26]

The central concepts on which modern community organization is based are power, social change, and conflict. Emphasis is placed on power within a social system: its location, sources, and the levels where it appears. The degree of accessibility to power and the potential for organizing countervailing power are assessed in order to plan the strategies and tactics for achieving social change on behalf of the powerless. Social change can create conflict, and conflict can lead to social change. The community organizer is therefore concerned with issues of conflict management in the attempted resolution of social problems. At first there was an occasional tendency to view agencies in an undiscriminating way, and to use adversarial strategies nondifferentially, as though the agency were the enemy in every instance. More recently, the development of tools for organizational assessment and the formulation of interventive procedures have provided a differentiated view of agencies based on an increasingly sophisticated understanding of their complexities.[27]

External events and internal professional processes have moved community organization to examine broader societal problems, and to develop new curricular emphases upon administration, social policy, and social planning.[28]

Latent Consequences of Historical Trends

Methodological Divisions

One consequence of social work's historical development has been the tendency to define people's needs or problems on the basis of the method of service. Because of the separate development of practice methods, agencies and workers defined themselves as casework agencies and caseworkers, or as group work agencies and group workers, or more recently as grass roots organizations and community organizers. While an occasional host setting, such as a hospital, might have both caseworkers and group workers and even community organizers on its staff, most practice maintained sharp methodological distinctions. In recent years, this tendency diminished as more group workers recognized the need for contact with individual members of the group, and more caseworkers experimented with group and family approaches.

Such methodological divisions in social work education and practice prevented an examination of the commonalities across methods, and thus inhibited the development of a distinctive social work method of practice directed to the social functioning of individuals, groups, and families. The divisions led to past and present struggles to establish the generic or core knowledge base for all social workers, and to many dysfunctional curriculum accommodations, such as courses in basic concepts, first-year generic and second-year specific courses, and the current dissension over generalists and specialists. The casework method itself had been concerned in the 1920s about the diversity of casework practice in many different settings, the difficulties in communicating across settings, and the modifications of method imposed by the nature of the setting. The Milford Conference of leading casework practitioners and educators concluded in 1929 that all caseworkers required a generic core of knowledge, on which specific knowledge according to setting could be built. The method itself, however, was thought to be recognizable across settings.[29] The profession continues in the 1970s to struggle with the generic or core knowledge issue, now made more complex by the differential levels of professional education, the place of in-service training after such education, and the question of where generic and specific knowledge can best be located educationally.

Today's environments impose an array of adaptive tasks on people, whether they are functioning as individuals or in families and groups. It therefore is unreasonable to define needs in terms of a particular practice method and the restrictive self-definitions of worker and agency. For us, it is the nature of the need itself, and the associated life tasks involved in meeting the need or solving the problem, that determines where to draw the boundaries that "encase" the individual, the family, or the group. We have attempted to show in the preceding chapters that a unified or integrative method of social work practice serves people, no matter where that boundary is drawn.

The method emerges from the social purpose and rests upon an integrative theoretical base. The social purpose refers to the value placed on the kinds of transactions social work prefers for people: those that release the potential for growth and adaptation of people and at the same time increase the growth-inducing capacities of the environment. The life model seeks to respond to the social purpose by developing an integrated method that rests on social work values and an integrating theoretical base.

Cause and Function

Earlier in the chapter, we described the tension between those who supported environmental reform and social action ("cause"), and those who favored a focus on individual change and the development of a transmissable method by which to achieve such change ("function"). In general, the first group included members of ASSA, settlement workers, and, much later, most of the group work segment of practice. They were interested in social science theory as a basis for environmental reform, and maintained an alliance with the social sciences, at times even seeing themselves as applied social scientists. They were also humanistic in their concern for human rights and equality between themselves and those they served, and in their later emphasis on democratic values and social participation (social goals). They lacked, however, a well developed methodology for carrying out their sense of mission.

The second group, in general, was comprised of state board members, charity workers of the 1880s and 1890s, and, much later, the casework segment of practice, joined later still by the segment of group workers practicing on the remedial model. This second group began as anti-theoretical and practical, and later developed rational, efficient methods in order to generate a scientific philanthropy. As the casework method of diagnosis and treatment developed, it sought to become increasingly scientific through constructing a base of psychological, biological, social, cultural, and practice theory, and through observing the principles of evidence, logical thinking, and evaluation of outcomes for a scientific orientation and a systematic approach to practice. The second group believed itself also to be humanistic in its espousal of self-determination, respect for client difference, and support of client dignity and worth. Yet in recent years, the second group suffered criticism for a latent anti-humanist, social control bias in its problem definitions, service procedures, and role definitions for clients.

The casework segment of practice had assumed the dominant position in the early occupational group largely because it possessed an organized method, and was represented by many more practitioners. It was the caseworker's preoccupation with method that led in 1929 to the first explicit formulation of the cause–function issue. Porter Lee, in his 1929 presidential address to the NCSW, traced a changing conception of social work as a movement concerned with a cause, to its assuming the character of a function.[30] In Lee's view, both cause and function are valuable and essential for social welfare: a cause won depends upon organization, method, and techniques for its implementation. A tendency to become overly preoccupied with method and process, however, can lead to a blunting of commitment. Goals associated with client need then become displaced by goals associated with organizational maintenance. Lee envisioned a synthesis in which social work would develop its service as a function of well organized community life, without sacrificing its capacity to inspire enthusiasm for a cause. In the succeeding years, practitioners and social work educators took opposing positions, some supporting cause and others supporting function, thus effectively polarizing the profession.[31] This polarity tended to interfere with the development of a practice that takes both positions into account as two complementary features of a profession concerned with human distress and fostering of human growth in diverse life situations.

In the preceeding chapters, we provided practice concepts and principles designed to reduce, in part, the polarity between cause and function, social action and treatment, and to address the issue of social purpose. We use the term "in part," since social action can be addressed at many levels of the social environment, from the neighborhood to the society. Our concern in chapter 7 was with that part of the environment represented by the organizations and institutions that employ us, the social workers. These organizations represent a salient presence in the lives of our clients; indeed, many clients depend on certain organizations for their survival. The organization is also a salient presence in our professional practice, shaping its direction, and perhaps constraining its goals and means. When the organization is unresponsive to the needs of those who use or could use its services, the organization itself becomes an object of change. Organizational change is a significant element in social change: helping to change a school procedure, a hospital policy, or an agency practice that creates stress or fails to meet need, is an important social work function that implements the social work cause or purpose of improving environments. Helping our own agencies and institutions work better for those who use our services brings cause and function into a more complementary relation.[32]

Summary

Historical dialectics of cause–function and generalist–specialist practice help to explain the presence and nature of contemporary practice issues and efforts to integrate divergent traditions. The process of divergence began when two streams of thought appeared in the nineteenth-century arena of social welfare, then called "charities and corrections." Industrialization and urbanization were accompanied by severe social disorganization. After the Civil War, state administration became responsible for the poor, the insane, and criminals. In the private arena, child-serving agencies and voluntary associations responded to the plight of the poor. A number of persons who were engaged in such practice joined with a group of New England intellectuals to organize the American Social Science Association in 1865. Soon after the initial meetings, however, conflicting concerns overshadowed their mutual interests. The former was more interested in methods of help, and the latter in theory. In 1874, the practice people withdrew from ASSA and established the Conference of Charities which, in 1879, became the National Conference of Charities and Corrections (which is presently the National Conference on Social Welfare).

The newly formed occupational group was joined in the late 1880s by the neighborhood settlements and the charity organization societies. Both appeared almost simultaneously, spread rapidly around the country, and appealed to young, upper- and middle-class, well educated, primarily female, idealists. Despite these similarities, however, the differences between these two movements were to have a profound effect on the dialectic development of social work practice. To the founders of the settlements, the sources of most urban misery lay in the environment. They became involved with tenement conditions, lack of sanitation, poor schools, inadequate play space, long working hours in factories, child labor, and the many obstacles faced by immigrant populations. They worked to provide clubs for children, classes for adults, and camp experiences. They provided good neighboring, not charity. To the charity organization societies, the watchword "scientific philanthropy" meant the rational, efficient distribution of alms. Duplication and fraud had to be eliminated, unworthy poor separated from worthy poor. The friendly visitor provided an example of middle- and upper-class virtues to be emulated by the poor client.

By 1895, the principles of scientific philanthropy had become organized into what was called the casework method, and were further codified by Mary Richmond's *Social Diagnosis,* published in 1917. Volunteer friendly visitors had been superseded by paid workers who were eager to achieve professional status. During the great depression the former COSs, now becoming known as family agencies, underwent a change in function by which relief giving was transferred to the new public programs. The private agencies were thus provided with the opportunity to experiment with the new psychoanalytically oriented procedures, and to search for a method focused on individual personality change. The gradual institutionalization of the medical metaphor that occurred in the 1920s, 1930s and 1940s reinforced preoccupation with internal processes so that diagnosis and treatment tended to focus on the person, while environmental forces—seemingly fixed and intractable—receded into the background. Thus, while caseworkers succeeded in developing a method for individualizing service that subscribed to the canons of logical thought and drew upon knowledge and values as a base for the method, what appeared to be missing was a conceptualization of environment that would take into account its complexity, and from which interventive measures could be derived.

During the 1920s social group work emerged from the settlement, recreation, and progressive education movements. From the settlements, the group work method derived its institutional base. From the recreational movement, social group work gained its interest in the value of play and activities. From the progressive education movement, group work acquired a philosophical base. Over the next several decades, until the mid-fifties, group workers maintained their commitment to the reciprocity between individual satisfaction and the social good, and to the positive impact of group experience upon both the individual and society. While group workers espoused their objectives and aspirations, their "social goals" method remained basically undeveloped. Unable to agree on a common, precise definition of social group work's purpose and function, the practice committee of the group work section of the NASW invited several group work theoreticians to offer their frames of reference. Two major divergent streams were elaborated and pursued. The remedial frame of reference moved toward the more developed casework paradigm of social study, diagnosis, and treatment. The reciprocal frame of reference proposed a systemic and generic conception of social work function, in which the worker maintains a dual focus on the individual and social system. Both perspectives made a major contribution to the development of a professional group work methodology.

The last of the three practice methods to be recognized, community organization, derived some of its characteristics from both COS and the settlements. In the decades between 1910 and 1930, community organization sought an institutional base in the developing community chests and councils. It took some of its tasks from COS interests in pioneering new services to meet needs, coordinating existing services, and establishing central informational and statistical services for all agencies. Its theoretical development in the 1940s and 1950s emphasized the adjustment between social resources and social welfare needs, intergroup processes within the councils themselves, and problem-solving and various helping roles utilized in working with committees and council groups. Social action and social reform emphases were by and large missing in the early development of community organization. In the 1960s, community organization shifted from its role and function of coordinating services to a concern with social problems as the target of its intervention. Like the social goals model of group work, community organization lacked a practice method to implement its aspirations for social change. By the early 1970s, however, central concepts of power, social change and conflict, and related operational methods were explicated. More recently, community organization has developed new curricular emphases upon administration, social policy, and social planning.

One consequence of social work's historical development has been the tendency to define people's needs or problems on the basis of the method of agency service or the worker's specialization. The methodological divisions in social work practice and education prevented an examination of commonalities across methods, and thus inhibited the development of a distinctive, integrated social work method of practice. The life model seeks to respond to the need for an integrated method.

A second consequence of social work's historical development has been the tendency to dichotomize people's need for environmental reform and social action (cause) and for individualized method and skills (function). Through the years, social work practitioners and educators took positions in support of either cause or function, effectively polarizing the profession. Opposing positions tended to interfere with the development of a practice that takes both into account as complementary features of a profession concerned with fostering human growth in diverse life situations. Both cause and function are essential for social welfare: work with a cause depends upon organization, method, and techniques for its implementation; a function depends upon a professional commitment and vision about social injustices. The life model seeks to respond to the need for an integration of cause–function emphases.

Notes

1. See, for example, *Journal of Social Science* (1869–1874) vols. 1–6; *Proceedings*, Conference of Charities (1874–1888); and *Proceedings*, National Conference of Charities and Corrections (1889–1916).

2. The best known original sources for understanding the philosophy and activities of the settlement movement are Jane Addams, *Twenty Years at Hull House* (New York: Macmillan, 1910); and Lillian Wald, *The House on Henry Street* (New York: Holt, 1951).

3. James Tufts later wrote an influential book, *Education and Training for Social Work* (New York: Russell Sage Foundation, 1923).

4. For discussion of the early COS, see Roy Lubove, *The Professional Altruist* (Cambridge: Harvard University Press), 1965.

5. Abraham Flexner, "Is Social Work a Profession?" *Proceedings,* National Conference of Charities and Corrections (1915), pp. 576–90.

6. See, for example, Jessie Taft, "The Relation of Function to Process in Social Case Work," *Journal of Social Work Process* (1937), 1(1):1–18.

7. For further discussion of the uses of metaphor, see Carel B. Germain, "Social Casework," in Harleigh B. Trecker, ed., *Goals for Social Welfare, 1973–1993* (New York: Association Press, 1973).

8. Gordon Hamilton, *Theory and Practice of Social Casework,* rev. ed. (New York: Columbia University Press, 1951).

9. Carel B. Germain, "Casework and Science: A Historical Encounter," in Robert W. Roberts and Robert H. Nee, eds., *Theories of Social Casework* (Chicago: University of Chicago Press, 1970), pp. 3–32.

10. See Helen H. Perlman, "The Problem-Solving Model in Social Casework," and Florence Hollis, "The Psychosocial Approach to the Practice of Casework," *ibid.*

11. John Dewey, *Democracy and Education* (New York: Macmillan, 1930); William Kilpatrick, *Group Education for Democracy* (New York: Association Press, 1940).

12. See, for example, Mary Follett, *Creative Group Experience* (New York: Longmans, Green, 1950); Edward Lindeman, "The Roots of Democratic Culture," in Harleigh B. Trecker, ed., *Group Work: Foundation and Frontiers* (New York: Whiteside & Barrows, 1955).

13. Grace Coyle, *Group Work With American Youth* (New York: Harper, 1948); Alan Klein, *Society, Democracy, and the Group* (New York: Women's Press, 1953); Gertrude Wilson and Gladys Ryland, *Social Group Work Practice* (New York: Houghton-Mifflin, 1949).

14. Catherine P. Pappel and Beulah Rothman, "Social Group Work Models: Possession and Heritage," *Journal of Education for Social Work* (July 1966), 2(2):66–78.

15. Robert D. Vinter, "Group Work's Perspectives and Prospects," *Social Work With Groups* (New York: NASW, 1959).

16. William Schwartz, "Group Work and the Social Scene," in Alfred J. Kahn, ed., *Issues in American Social Work* (New York: Columbia University Press, 1959).

17. Rosemary C. Sarri, "Behavioral Theory and Group Work," in Paul Glasser, Rosemary Sarri, Robert Vinter, eds., *Individual Change Through Small Groups* (New York: Free Press, 1974).

18. Emanuel Tropp, "Social Group Work: The Developmental Approach," *Encyclopedia of Social Work* (New York: NASW, 1971), pp. 1246–52.

19. Norma C. Lang, "A Broad-Range Model of Practice in Social Work Group," *Social Service Review* (March 1972), 46(1):76–89; Robert W. Roberts and Helen Northen, eds., *Theories of Social Work With Groups* (New York: Columbia University Press, 1976).

20. An example is the Cincinnati Social Unit founded by Wilbur Phillips. See Courtnay Dinwiddie, *Community Responsibility: A Review of the Cincinnati Social Unit Experiment* (New York: The New York School of Social Work 1921).

21. See, for example, Robert P. Lane, "The Field of Community Organization," *Proceedings*, NCSW, 1939.

22. See, for example, Wilbur I. Newstetter, "The Social Inter-Group Work Process," *Proceedings*, NCSW (1947), pp. 205–17.

23. Mildred C. Berry, "Current Concepts in Community Organization," *Group Work and Community Organization*, NCSW (1956); Genevieve W. Carter, "Practice Theory in Community Organization," *Social Work* (April 1958), 2(2):49–57.

24. Murray G. Ross, *Community Organization: Theory and Principles* (New York: Harper and Brothers, 1955); Ernest B. Harper and Arthur Dunham, eds., *Community Organization in Action* (New York: Association Press, 1959).

25. Charles Grosser, "Community Development Programs Serving Urban Poor," *Social Work* (July 1965), 10(3):15–21.

26. George Brager and Harry Specht, *Community Organizing* (New York: Columbia University Press, 1973). See also, Charles Grosser, *New Directions in Community Organization* (New York: Praeger, 1973).

27. See, for example, Rino Patti and Herman Resnick, "Changing The Agency From Within," *Social Work* (July 1972) 17(4):48–57; and John Wax, "Developing Social Work Power in a Medical Setting," *Social Work*, (October 1968) 13(5):62–71.

28. Unfortunately, community organization and group work receive insufficient attention in some schools' re-organized curricula.

29. *The Milford Conference Report: Social Casework, Generic and Specific* (New York: American Association of Social Workers, 1929).

30. Porter Lee, "Social Work: Cause and Function," *Proceedings*, NCSW (1929), pp. 3–20.

31. Some professionals have attempted to bridge this polarity. See, for example, Bertha Reynolds, "The Social Casework of an Uncharted Journey," *Social Work*, (October 1964), 9(4):13–17; William Schwartz, "Private Troubles and Public Issues: One Social Work Job or Two?" *The Social Welfare Forum, 1969* (New York: Columbia University Press, 1969), pp. 22–43.

32. We recognize that social workers especially educated as planners, policy analysts, and researchers may, in their daily practice, address the economic, political, and social issues in social problems. Some work at federal levels and others at state and local levels. Some social workers, educated as practitioners with individuals and groups, may join their "macro" colleagues in these efforts. Certainly all social workers can seek to influence legislative bodies through their professional association and affiliations with other politically active groups. As individual citizens, practitioners can join health system agencies, parent groups seeking to influence school systems, and can support such consumer groups as Welfare Mothers. They can make use of the media to educate the public in areas where social workers have special expertise: the needs of children, the elderly, and families, and issues regard-

ing full employment, mental health, etc. All such efforts at social change represent the professional concern for "cause." In our own effort to set forth the theory base of the life model from which practice principles and skills can be derived, we have been concerned with the social change efforts of the practitioner with individuals and groups. Hence we focus on the organizational environment: on behalf of a specific client seeking entitlements and resources (chapter 4), and, in chapter 7, on behalf of the population of service users or potential service users in the employing agency.

Index

Index

Index